HARVARD STUDIES IN URBAN HISTORY

SERIES EDITORS   Stephan Thernstrom
Charles Tilly

Ħ

HARVARD STUDIES IN URBAN HISTORY

FORTUNES AND FAILURES

WHITE-COLLAR MOBILITY IN NINETEENTH-CENTURY SAN FRANCISCO

PETER R. DECKER

HARVARD UNIVERSITY PRESS
CAMBRIDGE, MASSACHUSETTS
AND LONDON, ENGLAND   1978

Library of Congress Cataloging in Publication Data
Decker, Peter R   1934-
  Fortunes and failures.

  (Harvard studies in urban history)
  Includes bibliographical references and index.
    1. Merchants—California—San Francisco—
History.   2. Social mobility—California—San
Francisco—History.   3. White collar workers—
California—San Francisco—History.   4. Occupa-
tional mobility—California—San Francisco—History.
I. Title.   II. Series.
HF3163.S4D42   301.32   77-12557
ISBN 0-674-31118-3

TO THE MEMORY OF ROBERT J. MARONY

PREFACE

The American dream of equal opportunity, an ideal that reflected the Jeffersonian belief in meritocracy, permeated our society throughout most of the nineteenth century. The gospel of the self-made man, in the words of Irwin Wyllie, "glorified material progress and inspired men to believe that they could enjoy salvation in this life as well as in the next. It encouraged the lowly to defy inherited orders of caste and custom, and to rise as far as their talents would allow. In keeping with the democratic faith it honored activity above repose, and judged merit on the basis of achievement."

Despite the common acceptance of the Jeffersonian ideal, the social system as it actually operated in the nineteenth century often failed to match the expectations nurtured by the ideology. Recent social mobility studies have demonstrated that only a small number of laborers in Boston, Poughkeepsie, Philadelphia, and other eastern cities managed to discard their blue-collar rags for white-collar riches. These findings have tarnished considerably the American image of the self-made man in an egalitarian society.

If eastern cities in the nineteenth century suffered from a hardening of the social arteries, what about the rest of the nation, specifically west of the Mississippi? Did the fledgling cities of this region, before the closing of the frontier, offer opportunities superior to those in the older, more class-ridden cities of the East? Or did those individuals, rugged or otherwise, who migrated to the West in the belief that superior opportunities did exist on the frontier, fail to discover the occupational and financial success that the American dream promised? Could it be that the advertised riches of the land of milk, honey, and gold were a myth and that the western city, even in its infancy, possessed the same imposing barriers to social mobility as the eastern urban centers?

San Francisco seemed an appropriate city to investigate to answer these questions. In the brief span of thirty-three years, it grew from a sleepy Spanish village of approximately 500 residents in 1847 to the leading metropolitan center on the West Coast and, with a population of 233,000 in 1880, became the ninth largest city in the nation. From the dank adobe huts in Yerba Buena Cove housing a few Spanish missionaries in the 1840s to the palatial mansions of American capitalists atop Nob Hill in the 1870s was but a short distance in terms of time and space. But it was a quantum leap in terms of the transformation of a minor Spanish mission to a major American metropolis.

Within the context of the city the focus must be on the merchants. Their capital and leadership were initially responsible for the economic vitality of the city. San Francisco was a trading center and its merchants for two decades monopolized a network that extended the length of the West Coast and east to the Rocky Mountains. Moreover, recent social mobility studies have, in their primary emphasis on the blue-collar laborer, generally neglected the white-collar worker. We have learned that the experiences of the blue-collar workers in eastern cities generally disprove the rags-to-riches ideology, but we know relatively little about the other 40 percent of these urban populations— the white-collar workers. In the second half of the nineteenth century the common laborer and the skilled mechanic may not have advanced into the white-collar world with the regularity they expected, or in such large numbers as once posited by historians. Yet there may well have been a high degree of social mobility within the white-collar world.

Who then were these pioneer merchants who traveled thousands of miles in search of new opportunities? What were their social origins, and did they discover in this "instant city" career opportunities superior to those experienced by white-collar workers in other American cities during the same period? What gains accrued to those who made a geographic move of considerable distance to improve their economic and social position? And if San Francisco did offer relief to those who sought an escape from the economic and social constrictions of their former communities, were the advantages of this urban frontier city equally shared by native-born and foreign-born, blue-collar and white-collar? These questions are discussed for the first generation of merchants—those who arrived in San Francisco prior to 1852—in the first four chapters.

The pioneer merchants, besides providing the business leadership for the city, also organized, directed, and eventually controlled the first voluntary associations of San Francisco. The manner by which the merchants transferred and maintained their occupational and financial status within the social fabric of the city is investigated in Chapter 5.

The preeminent position held by the merchants in the 1850s began to decline significantly in the following two decades. The transcontinental railroad and new manufacturing transformed the city from a regional and isolated mercantile center to a national industrial metropolis. The response of the merchants and the effect of this transformation upon their individual careers and status in the community is the subject of Chapter 6. After the Civil War a new, predominantly foreign-born group of merchants replaced the pioneer merchants. The origins and career experiences of this post-industrial generation are traced in Chapter 7. By 1880 the city had attained maturity. Industrialization, besides altering San Francisco's basic economic structure, had caused an expansion and rearrangement of the city's social geography. The degree to which San Francisco's internal social divisions were transferred upon the urban landscape is investigated in Chapter 8. A discussion of the new elite, those who came to replace the once-preeminent merchants, is reserved for Chapter 9 and the concluding chapter.

One group of important merchants—the Chinese—is excluded from this study. Although they performed generally the same financial and political leadership roles as their occidental counterparts, they did so within the confines of the Chinese community—a distinct culture within San Francisco. The majority of the population opposed the intrusion of the Chinese, including their merchants, into the wider economic, political, and geographic spheres of the city. To have included the Chinese in this nineteenth-century study would have been to mix and thereby confuse two very separate cultures.

Source materials for San Francisco have survived the earthquake of 1906 and the more recent destructive practices of city and state officials who, for lack of storage space, have discarded valuable tax and voting records. The federal census for San Francisco (1860-1880) has been an invaluable source, but unfortunately the 1850 census for the city was lost somewhere at sea while in transit between the West and East Coast. California replaced it with its own state census in 1852, a poor substitute considering its present physical deterioration, but nevertheless useful. City directories exist, but there are few tax, voting, marriage, death, or real estate records. One very useful source has been the R. G. Dun Company (now Dun and Bradstreet) credit ledgers, which included individual credit reports on approximately 3 million Americans in the second half of the nineteenth century. The collection (indexed by state, county, and individual) was extremely useful for obtaining property data about individual merchants. Other sources included voluntary association membership lists, "elite" directories, newspapers, and those "mug" book biographies which most cities propagated to advertise (often falsely) their wondrous civic leaders.

Biographical data were collected on approximately 7,000 individuals who resided in San Francisco between 1850 and 1880. After coding, the information was transferred to tape and calculated on a computer. With one exception (the geographic data on residential patterns) all data were programmed through the SPSS (Statistical Package for the Social Sciences). I have brought most of the tables forward into the text. One may be found in Appendix A, along with Methodological Notes to explain sampling techniques, sources, and statistical calculations. Scholars seeking tables and bibliographical suggestions beyond those included in the notes are referred to the author's doctoral dissertation, which is available on loan from Columbia University.

The study is, to a degree, quantitative. The computer, however, provided no substitute for human judgment. For while I proceeded throughout the project remembering Joseph A. Schumpeter's advice ("We need statistics not only for explaining things, but in order to know what there is to be explained"), I was constantly aware of the ease with which the computer compounded human error. As Karl Kapp, participant at a recent international conference on the quality of life, so aptly put it: "Had there been a computer in 1872 it would probably have predicted that by now there would be so many horse-drawn vehicles it would be impossible to clear up all the manure." In the belief that history is and must remain a humanistic art and not a numbers game, I have attempted to support quantitative findings with the more traditional qualitative historical documents (diaries, newspapers, and letters); these sources are always more revealing, and certainly more human, than the numerical tabulations derived from a computer printout.

Finally, to measure the degree of social mobility for the city merchants, I have utilized the determinants of occupation, property, and place of residence. Where and when appropriate, I have compared the merchants' careers with the experience of the general employed population of the city, and, where possible, with the experience of workers in other American cities during the same period. The scale for occupational mobility—the single most important variable for this study—is generally the same as that utilized by other contemporary historians who have investigated the phenomenon of social mobility in nineteenth-century American cities. A degree of commonality in the methodology, of course, allows for valid and very necessary intercity and interregional comparisons.

So many people assisted me in the trek through San Francisco's social history, that in many ways this book is their cooperative creation. First I wish to thank Robert Lovett at Baker Library, Harvard Business School; Peter Hanff and Irene Moran at Bancroft Library, Berkeley; and the reference staff of Butler Library at Columbia University. Archivists at other libraries also provided assistance. The California Historical Society, the California State Library, The Huntington Library, the Magnus Library at the Center for the Study of Western Jewish History, the Mystic Seaport Marine Historical Association, the New York Historical Society, the New York Public Library, and the Society of California Pioneers deserve special recognition.

Those who assisted me at various stages of research include Stuart Bruchey, William Chafe, Sigmund Diamond, John Hammond, Theodore Hershberg, Jonathan Kelley, Herbert Klein, Albro Martin, Walter Metzger, Rodman Paul, Donald Treiman, Dennis Van Essendelft, David Ward, and Sam B. Warner, Jr. My several drafts were significantly improved by the careful reading and helpful suggestions of C. William Domhoff, Aida Donald, Herbert Gans, Kenneth Jackson, Sydney Nathans, Moses Rischin, David Rothman, Anita Safran, and Peter H. Wood. For assistance with the photographs I am grateful to Larry Dinnean and Mrs. Compton at the Bancroft Library, Deborah

Ginberg at the Society of California Pioneers, Warren Howell of John Howell Books, Gary Kurutz of the California Historical Society, and to Arthur Mejía, Jr., for allowing me access to his family albums. Peggy Nelson and Suhasini Sankaran assisted with data collection, and Janice Blinder, Donna Hines, and Sue Ramm patiently and professionally typed the final manuscript.

Three institutions deserve special recognition: the National Institute of Mental Health, whose social history fellowship granted me the opportunity to begin the research; the history department at Columbia University, which encouraged it; and the Institute of Policy Sciences at Duke University, which allowed me the time and resources to finish it.

Finally, I owe a special acknowledgment to Clyde Griffen and Stephan Thernstrom. From the beginning they always asked the questions to which this book attempts to respond. Their help, encouragement, and friendship guided me through some very dense verbal and statistical thickets.

My wife, Deedee, and children, Karen and Chris, sustained it all, not only without complaint, but with joy and laughter and love.

CONTENTS

ILLUSTRATIONS AND MAPS

TABLES

PART ONE
THE PIONEER MERCHANTS

1

THE WESTWARD MIGRATION

Stories of riches lured Spanish, French, English, and Russian explorers to the coast of California in the sixteenth and seventeenth centuries. Sebastian Urzcaino, a Spanish naval officer, claimed the land in the name of the Spanish crown in 1602, but not until the mid-eighteenth century did Spain, under Charles III, move to take permanent possession of California. To colonize in Alta California, as elsewhere in its New World possessions, Spain devised a system of missions to convert heathen Indians to the ways of western civilization, with presidios (military posts) to protect these Christian outposts from domestic or foreign attack. In 1776 two Spanish natives, Francisco Palou and Benito Cambon, established a small mission and somewhat larger presidio on the present site of San Francisco. They named the settlement Yerba Buena after the herb found in abundance on the surrounding hills.

Yerba Buena Village

The Spaniards at Yerba Buena specialized more in Christian baptisms than in commerce or agriculture. They were generally unsuccessful there and elsewhere in California in attaining a surplus-producing agricultural economy despite fertile land and temperate weather. The large cattle herds did, however, provide an item for trade. In 1822 Mexico, in an attempt to ease her own financial burden in the first year of independence from Spain, opened the California ports to commerce with the United States. Boston hide traders immediately monopolized the California trade. These "hide droughers," known also by the Mexican Californians as the Boston Men, scoured the California coast for hides to supply the boot and shoe factories of Lynn, Woburn, Brockton, and Natick, Massachusetts. In return the Boston trading houses dispatched to their West Coast agents "assorted cargoes of plain cottons, prints, handkerchiefs, shoes, hats, coarse woolens, hardware, fancy goods, and, in short, specimens of all the cheapest fabrics."[1] This initial monopoly of the coast trade later gave to Boston and a few of her merchants a preeminent position in the first years of the commerical life of San Francisco.

The hide trade lasted only two decades. By the early 1840s New England developed sources for leather closer to its factories. Yet the legacy of commercial contacts remained. Richard Dana's *Two Years before the Mast* described not only the natural beauty of the California coast but also the potential importance of the Bay of San Francisco. When California "becomes a prosperous country," wrote Dana, the Bay Area "will be the center of prosperity . . . its facilities for navigation, affording the best anchoring grounds in the whole western coast of North America, all fit it for a place of great importance."[2]

Other besides the Boston Men reported on the anticipated riches of California. Since the 1820s American diplomats in Mexico had written to their superiors in Washington predicting the future economic and geographic importance of California. Colonel Anthony Butler, chargé d'affaires in Mexico, wrote President Andrew Jackson that California was "an empire in itself, a paradise in climate . . . rich in minerals, and affording a water route to the Pacific through the Arkansas and Colorado rivers." Though his geography lacked precision, Butler appealed to the imaginative impulses of those who sought a passage to India and the riches of the Far East. Later, in 1842, Waddy Thompson, United States Minister, advised Secretary of State Daniel Webster that the United States should acquire California since the harbor of San Francisco was "spacious enough to receive the navies of the world."[3] Another American, destined to play a leading role in the United States' acquisition of California in 1846, Thomas Larkin, confirmed these accounts. Writing in 1845, Larkin, consul at Monterey, envisioned 2,000 American fishermen off the coast of California by 1848, and described the massive dimensions of the harbor, "capable of great defences," which "will hold perhaps all the vessels in the world."[4] And two months before the declaration of the short-lived California Republic, Larkin appealed to the ideology of manifest destiny and exclaimed: "From the Port of San Francisco . . . the Anglo-Saxon race would soon send their exports over the whole Pacific Ocean. It must and will be the medium place from New Orleans and

New York to the China ports now open to the whole commercial world.''⁵ Thus by the end of the Mexican War, the accounts of early explorers, Yankee traders, and government officials all pointed to the prospective strategic and commerical importance of the territory of California.

Yet a first-hand inspection of the village of Yerba Buena in 1846 would not have inspired confidence in its future. Approximately 200 people lived and worked in some fifty structures, all canvas, frame, or adobe, scattered haphazardly in the few level areas near the water. A handful of merchants, who remained in Yerba Buena after the hide trade declined, supplied the multinational village with goods shipped in from New England, Mexico (Mazatlán), and the Sandwich Islands. Small cattle and grain ranches and a few poorly maintained vineyards surrounded the village toward the interior of the peninsula.

The annexation of California by the United States in 1846 failed to alter immediately Yerba Buena's insignificance as a minor port along the West Coast. By 1847 there were only 459 people living in Yerba Buena, 375 of whom were whites, the rest Indians (34), Sandwich Islanders (40), and Negroes (10). By far the largest number of whites were native-born Americans, the rest natives of Mexico, Chile, California, and northern Europe. The first survey of the occupational distribution of the town listed the majority of Yerba Buena's residents as working in skilled crafts (51 percent); another 13 percent in unskilled blue-collar positions; and approximately an equal number employed as farmers (7 percent), clerks (8 percent), professionals (9 percent), and merchants (10 percent). On the eve of the Gold Rush in January 1848 the town population reached a little over 800. Commerce was limited to the simple needs of the community and to providing the increasing number of New England vessels with shelter, repairs, and provisions before crossing the Pacific to the Sandwich Islands or China. Visiting sailors off whalers, navy frigates, or cargo ships searched the shores of Bird Island (Alcatraz) for fresh pelican eggs, collected firewood on Goat Island (Yerba Buena), filled water barrels from the fresh water springs in Sausalito, and inevitably frequented the one crowded saloon near the town wharf.⁶

One event occurred in the early history of Yerba Buena that radically altered its destiny. Ships consigned from foreign or domestic ports to California often showed on their manifest ''San Francisco,'' a designation indicating San Francisco Bay but not a specific port within the bay. A group of merchant entrepreneurs in Benicia, across the bay from Yerba Buena, were already at work directing ocean vessels into their newly established port. The town fathers of Yerba Buena countered by ensuring that the name of their town coincided with the maritime map designation of the bay, San Francisco. William T. Sherman, the Civil War general and one of San Francisco's early bankers, reflecting upon the name change in his "Memoirs," commented that even though Benicia possessed the "best natural site for a commercial city," ships that now cleared for San Francisco "came pouring in with their contents, and were anchored in front of Yerba Buena." Thus San Francisco survived the attempt of Benicia to establish a port of entry, and by a simple name change ensured itself a monopoly on trade in the Bay Area.[7]

In many ways it was the perfect setting for a port city that would soon monopolize trade along the West Coast. Situated just inside a mile-wide passage from the ocean, the town was protected from its gales and currents, and the surrounding waters were deep enough to allow ocean vessels to anchor close off shore. Vessels entering San Francisco had but a short sail through the mouth of the harbor at the Golden Gate around the tip of the peninsula clear of the ocean fogs, and into the protected waters off Clark's Point. Benicia, too, possessed the advantages of a deep-water, fog-free haven, but at a greater distance from the entrance to the Golden Gate. What the Benicians neglected to advertise and what the San Francisco boosters would never admit was that, compared with Benicia, the weather in San Francisco (the City of Flowers) was abominable. Rain and dank heavy fog hung over the town for months, whereas across the bay sunshine and warmth engulfed a forgotten community. While mariners and merchants damned the cold dampness of San Francisco, President Polk questioned the wisdom of the nation's forefathers to locate the national capital in a swamp—another town site not selected for its salubrious climate.

President Polk, in fact, did as much to advertise San Francisco and California as any West Coast resident. News of the January 1848 gold strike at Sutters Fort had already filtered back East, but in one of his last presidential messages before leaving office Polk publicized and gave executive credence to the often conflicting reports emanating from San Francisco and the mining districts to the north. He observed that the California mines "were more extensive and valuable than was anticipated," and that the amounts of gold were of an "extraordinary character," as authenticated by United States military authorities in California. Further, Polk predicted, San Francisco would be to the West Coast what New Orleans was to the Mississippi Valley and the Gulf of Mexico. San Francisco, he claimed, was "destined to rival in importance New Orleans itself."[8]

The Lure of Gold, Profits, and Opportunities

In late 1848 bold headlines in weekly and daily newspapers across the nation announced in detail the rich gold deposits in California. Factory workers in Hartford, Connecticut, dirt farmers in New York's Mohawk Valley, Maryland fishermen, and merchants along the Eastern Seaboard read the accounts of the immense riches dug from the golden earth of the United States' newest acquired territory, California. For some, visions of gold meant the immediate release from the dreary patterns of tilling, planting, and harvesting; for others an escape from an oppressive factory, an intolerant boss, a nagging wife, an authoritarian father, or a collection of bad debts. But to all, California conjured up visions of the adventurous life where, with a little muscular effort and some assistance from the Almighty, a quick fortune could be collected and parlayed into a prosperous life at home. California gold meant instant gratification to a nineteenth-century society unaccustomed to such opportunities.

It is not difficult to imagine how in 1849 a reader of the nation's most prestigious paper, the *New York Tribune*, would be impressed with the reports of gold mounds ready to be plucked by the hearty adventurer. Atop the lead editorial expressing Horace Greeley's own endorsement of the exaggerated accounts of the gold discovery, the headline printed in bold type read, "Great Quantities of Gold." There followed a letter detailing the richness of the mines. "I can only say that the most exaggerated accounts may be believed. A few days ago a gentleman came down [to San Francisco] from the mines bringing with him $12,000 in gold dust, which he dug out in the space of six days. I have it from persons, eyewitnesses, whose veracity cannot be doubted."[9]

Letters from the mines filled the pages of other newspapers with reports of Eldorado's riches. New Yorkers received reports from ex-members of its resident army regiment who had filtered into California from Texas and Mexico after the Mexican War. One letter from a former officer in Colonel Stevenson's First New York Volunteer Regiment assured his readers they should "have no fears of the accounts of these [gold] discoveries . . . being exaggerated; it is almost impossible to exaggerate. The deeper they [the miners] descend into the earth, the richer seems the reward." A letter in the *Missouri Statesman* guaranteed a fortune to those who came to California and "used industry and economy." The readers of the *Independence Exposition* (Missouri) were informed that one of their local carpenters "has dug out more gold in the last six months than a mule can pack."[10]

In addition, the newspapers ran descriptions of the best land and sea routes to the West Coast, the possible dangers that might be encountered (particularly on the overland route), the type of provisions required, and the estimated cost of passage to San Francisco. They described the weather as temperate and good enough for digging the year round and supported the notion that fortunes could be accumulated in six months for those hearty and adventurous enough to reach the gold fields.

Some read of the high wages being paid in San Francisco because most of the residents of the town had departed for the mines with the first reports of gold in the summer of 1848. Laborers in New York could not fail to be impressed with the ten to sixteen dollars a day for unloading foods along the waterfront. But the primary attraction was gold, and the promise of quick fortunes appealed to all classes.

Horace Greeley had urged "the fortunate and comfortable" to hold back and "give the first chance at the Gold Region to those who have as yet no chance elsewhere." A considerable number of the "well-employed," however, did not share Greeley's sense of fair play. His own paper reported in the early weeks of 1849 that along with the many mechanics of the city who were leaving for the mines, "many gentlemen well known to the public . . . have left comfortable and lucrative situations here . . . in the hope of more speedy enrichment." Members of some of New York's prominent families (Livingston, Le-Roy, Schermerhorn, Beekman, Ray, and Jones) departed for the mines in the same month as did fifteen workers from the Hartford,

Connecticut, Colt pistol factory, a few Vermont farmers, and a Baltimore stevedore. All shared the zeal and the expectation that with a little pick and shovel work a fortune would be secured.[11]

The merchants who emigrated to California went not to extract riches from the mines (though a few did travel to the "diggings") but to extract profits from the miners. With reports filtering back to the Eastern Seaboard of the multitudes arriving in San Francisco bound for the mines, it took less business experience than imagination to realize that these new arrivals would need food, clothing, and provisions in the mining towns springing up near Sacramento and Stockton. San Francisco with its harbor was the natural supply point to the northern and southern mines via the navigable Sacramento and American Rivers. And as ships began unloading at the town's single wharf in late 1848, Boston, New York, and Baltimore merchants could not but be impressed with the reports of high prices and large profits realized from the initial sales of boots, hardware, lumber, and foodstuffs.

The Boston merchants, because of their earlier California contacts through the hide trade in the 1820s and 1830s, were the first to learn of the bullish prices at the San Francisco port. A few of Boston's native sons advised their friends at home in late 1848 and early 1849 of the profits to be made through shipment of goods to San Francisco.

William D. M. Howard, San Francisco's leading merchant in 1848 and a former Bostonian, knew the Bay Area market as well as anyone. Born in Boston in 1819, the son of a merchant and banker, Howard went to sea as a cabin boy rather than to Harvard following graduation from high school. Later he joined the hide trade, clerked for a short time for a merchant in Los Angeles, returned to Boston in 1840, and then came back to California as an agent for the family's merchant firm. In 1845 he bought out the Hudson Bay Company's store in Yerba Buena and in partnership with another Bostonian, Henry Mellus, formed the first major trading and commission merchant establishment in the Bay Area.

Boston merchants were aware of Howard's knowledge of San Francisco and sought his advice as shiploads of miners began arriving in the summer of 1848. Responding to a letter of inquiry about the San Francisco market, Howard wrote to Benjamin T. Reed, a prominent Boston merchant, that the gold supply was of major proportions and

Portrait of five pioneer civic leaders of San Francisco. First row (left to right): Jacob Leese, Thomas Larkin, William D. M. Howard; second row: Samuel Hensley, Sam Brannan.

that with the great influx of miners, provisions were in short supply. "People here are perfectly crazy," Howard reported in June 1848, and "this town has almost deserted" for the mines except a few of the merchants who (like Howard himself) were "doing a very excellent business." Because of the shortage of supplies in San Francisco and the anticipated emigration in the fall, Howard recommended that his friend send "out an expedition immediately for this port." "My brother has often written me about coming out and I have always discouraged it," Howard continued, "but I now write to [advise] him to invest what funds he has in your vessel and to come out in her." Howard's bullish prophecy for the immediate future of San Francisco was exhibited when, in the same letter, he concluded:

I should wish to have all I have invested with you in this voyage and have as few [others] concerned in it as possible . . . If you do this Sir, it must be done immediately before others hear of this and have a chance to fit out, and I would advise keeping all this a secret until the vessel has sailed . . . there will undoubtedly be a number sent immediately for this coast, and ours must be the first to arrive . . . 'Tis in my opinion a grand speculation and I feel sure will turn out well . . . I should like to invest as much as $8,000 if possible. I enclose you a list for such a cargo as I think would be wanted here.[12]

Many younger sons of eastern merchant families, after serving for years their apprenticeship as clerks only to see their older brother or cousin move into positions of authority and importance, believed that opportunities were far more advantageous on the West Coast than in the counting rooms of Boston, Salem, New Bedford, or New York. Sons of some of Boston's leading merchant families (Otis, Macondray, Hubbard) were soon on their way to San Francisco. S. Griffith Morgan, son of a famous New Bedford merchant family, departed for San Francisco because he was "sick of poverty" working in the family merchant business, "for at home the prospect for me is blank"; and in a letter to a friend insisted that "California offers more inducements than New Bedford." Morgan, who left his wife and child at home, expected to make a quick profit in California so that, upon his return, he might then attain more easily the high status of his father and uncle, both merchants. In another letter, Morgan urged a friend from Philadelphia to join him in San Francisco in a "country full of enterprising men," filled with "large resources," and "destined to be eventually the great mart of the Pacific." A former New York City resident, in a letter to his brother at home, wrote "that capitalists at home cannot appreciate the opportunities the country offers for making money . . . many of you will be awakened as it were from a sound sleep, when you find, . . . that San Francisco is the greatest city on the American continent." Further, he observed, doing business in San Francisco "is but one-third the risk of doing business in New York since all business transactions are in cash."[13]

Reports of California's wealth spread throughout the Eastern Seaboard and the South. Baltimore residents read of a local merchant "who sent to California a year ago [1848] on a venture $5,000 worth of old store goods, has received the bill of lading from San Francisco for $35,000 in gold dust." Two peddlers from Selma, Alabama, Jesse and Leopold Seligman, who later left for San Francisco to set up a general merchandise store and eventually founded a leading international banking house, were advised by their oldest brother, Joseph, of the fantastic prices charged for dry goods in San Francisco. At a family conference in New York, Joseph urged them to depart immediately for San Francisco, but candidly advised, "if you go, it is to be a merchant, and not as a gambler hoping to make a strike." Levi Strauss, another recent Jewish immigrant from Germany, set out for the new commercial opportunities on the western shores of California with some dry goods and tent canvas. A Down East lumber merchant envisioned a 200 percent profit on a shipment of cut pine upon reading the "prices current" listing in the Bangor newspaper. A Connecticut ship chandler, with no desire to hunt for gold, intended to go to San Francisco, "get through with my business," and with his profit "go back east" as soon as possible.[14]

The foreigners who went to San Francisco to pursue merchant occupations were attracted to the West Coast for many of the same reasons that attracted the native-born. But the deciding factors were somewhat different, and unlike the native-born, many of them decided before their departure for San Francisco to make California their permanent residence.

In Germany, for example, a wave of anti-Semitism, particularly in Bohemia, Posen, Bavaria, Baden, and Upper Silesia, sent many German Jews to the United States, including California. In some German principalities Jews were forced to pay special taxes and were subject to harsh regulations governing citizenship. In the small towns and rural districts of Bavaria, a young Jewish man could hardly have hoped to become a permanent resident or to marry in his native place if he could not obtain the right to citizenship. The number of Jewish inhabitants in each district was restricted: "youth growing up into manhood had to wait for the death of one of the older inhabitants to free a 'place' or else leave the district." With the blighting of all hopes for full emancipation, particularly in Bavaria, many German Jews departed with their savings for the United States.[15]

Those German Jews who arrived on the Eastern Seaboard were not, for the most part, of the merchant class. The overwhelming proportion arrived without capital; indeed most of them were impoverished. The United States represented for the Germans an opportunity for economic advancement, be it the labor market of New York or the mines of the High Sierras which, beginning in 1849, were reported in German newspapers.[16]

In fact, throughout Europe newspapers carried news of the recently discovered placer mines. Merchandise speculators in Paris advertised for investors to buy into joint-stock companies which anticipated profits of 1,400 percent annually![17] Traders in Latin America, particularly Mexico, Chile, and Brazil, who had commercial ties with the coast of California throughout the first half of the nineteenth century received glowing reports about the commercial opportunities in San Francisco. News of the golden placers filtered across the Pacific to the Hawaiian Islands, Australia, and China, where future miners and a few merchants made ready for the transoceanic voyage to San Francisco.

Financing the Voyage and the Venture

It was one thing to be attracted and enticed by the glowing reports, frequently inaccurate and exaggerated, but another matter to locate transportation and finance the trip. The cost of sea transportation from the East Coast to California ($150 to $500 depending upon the ship, route and comforts desired) did not totally exclude skilled workers from obtaining passage. The most common arrangement for financing the trip to California, be it over land or by sea, was the joint-stock company.

It seemed that every American community had its joint-stock California Trading Company, though by far the greatest number were from the vicinity of the seaboard states. In Massachusetts alone at least 150 of these companies were formed in the year 1849-50, draining Nantucket of one-quarter of its voting population and New Bedford of 800 men. Sag Harbor, New York, lost so many young men to the California gold fever that the town's whaling fleet lay unmanned in the Long Island port for nearly two years for lack of a crew. While residents of the larger cities such as New York, Boston, Richmond, Baltimore, Hartford, and Philadelphia formed large joint-stock companies, smaller, less well-financed companies came to life in rural Oswego, New York, Defiance, Ohio, and Vergennes, Vermont. Five joint-stock companies were registered in London and others formed in some of the major cities of France, Germany, Mexico, Peru, Chile, China, and the Philippines.[18]

The joint-stock company was a joint partnership arrangement in which a member purchased a minimum number of shares at a price often designed not to exclude the poor, and it served as the primary financial and legal device to transport more than half of those who departed the states for California. One could buy into a joint-stock company for as little at $200, though the average was no doubt closer to $500. When approximately $10,000 had been raised, the elected company directors purchased a ship, hired a captain and crew, stocked the vessel with the necessary provisions for the three- to four-month voyage around the Horn and shipped off for California. If the company was composed primarily of miners, they usually carried with them equipment "designed and manufactured especially for the California mines." Some joint-stock companies, and particularly those composed of traders and merchants, carried goods with which to speculate in the San Francisco market. Upon arrival in San Francisco, the company sold the ship and cargo at a profit, divided the profits among the stockholders per their shares, and disbanded the partnership.[19]

The working class did invest in these schemes, though the itinerant poor could not afford even the smallest investment. The average shareholders were the artisans who invested their life savings to purchase the minimum number of shares which would guarantee their passage to California. Most shareholders undertook the journey, but a few, "mostly sons of prominent men," preferred to make the initial investment and remain at home and await the return of dividends from California. Of those who had no savings, some mortgaged their property, others borrowed from friends and family, and a few went so far as to advertise their skills and diligence in the local newspaper hoping to find a taker who would finance their dreams.[20] A New York City tinsmith placed the following notice in the *Tribune*:

A young man, now engaged in the sheet-iron and copper business, who possesses a practical knowledge of the trade, a good education, and general business qualifications, is desirous of emigrating to California for the purpose of establishing himself in it there, but lacks the requisite capital. He would prefer to obtain a partner with from $800 to $1,000 or more, cash capital to go out with him for that purpose. Or, he would like to make some arrangement with someone about to commence the hardware business there, which . . . would be a profitable operation to both parties. Or any other arrangement by which the advertiser's object can be attained will be acceptable.[21]

Some eastern merchants and clerks traveled to San Francisco as "supercargoes," or agents. By this arrangement, an East Coast businessman purchased and assembled an export cargo with which to experiment in the San Francisco market. He then shipped the goods off to San Francisco with a supercargo, who upon arrival sold it to the best advantage of the owner. Sometimes the agent charged the owner a commission on the sale plus the cost of his own passage. The more common practice appears to have been the arrangement of a limited partnership in which the supercargo owned a minority interest in the cargo, agreed to charge no commission, but instead took his prorated share of the profits (or loss) upon sale in San Francisco. He then remitted the profits, either in bills of exchange, produce, or specie, back East to the majority owners.[22] Young eastern merchants and counting-house clerks discovered that a supercargo arrangement with a respected merchant firm allowed them to profit from the initial sale of goods upon arrival at San Francisco. These young men, many of whom were sons or close relatives of the eastern merchant elite, could then become the West Coast agents for a New York or Boston merchant house or, preferably, establish their own independent business.

Few of the original San Francisco merchants, however, possessed enough capital of their own to participate in a supercargo arrangement. Of a sample of seventy San Francisco merchants in 1852 known to have resided in New York City in 1847-48, only 15 percent were found to own any personal or real property in their own name—the average amount for the property holders being $7,000, or approximately $14,000 adjusting for undervaluation of assessments. Another 5 percent had property listed for their father, mother, or brother. The credit reports of R. G. Dun and Company, whose business it was to investigate the financial resources of individuals, confirmed the impression that those who departed for a merchant career in San Francisco had little capital of their own.[23] The Seligman brothers went with money borrowed from their oldest brother. A New York City merchant, Morris Spreyer, inherited a few thousand dollars and then departed for San Francisco. A few left with the earnings and training of a merchant clerk and what money they could borrow, hoping to parlay their counting-house experience into the fortunes of a commission merchant in San Francisco. Then there were the merchants— probably no more than 20 percent of the first generation—who sought relief in San Francisco from "some debts left unsettled" back East.

One New York merchant in debt to eastern creditors complained in a letter to a friend that despite his best efforts to hide his past financial embarrassments by conducting business under an assumed name, San Francisco's business community knew the amount of his indebtedness and the identity of his creditors. "My career," he lamented, "is part of the history of the place." But, as the New York merchant was quick to point out, there were others like him who carried heavy debts to San Francisco. "Some of the best men here come to San Francisco embarrassed like myself and are doing business under other's names in the same way, until they can adjust their own affairs."[24]

Over half, R. G. Dun reported, left with money borrowed from business partners, as did James and Edward Flint, founders of one of San Francisco's most eminent commission merchant houses, having little or no money of their own. Others, like H. F. Cutter and W. J. Reynolds, both young men of wealthy Boston families, financed their first business venture with money borrowed from their relatives. Gerson Rosenstock of Baltimore sent his son Samuel to San Francisco to investigate the market before ordering goods for future shipment and speculation.

Less than 10 percent of the individual credit accounts investigated included capital resources in excess of $5,000 prior to departure for San Francisco. Of equal significance, only about 5 percent of the merchants were reported by R. G. Dun to own large profitable enterprises. Most were small operators, generating limited profits with no capital reserves of their own. The more successful and wealthy merchants remained at home, and if interested at all in the California trade placed limited amounts of venture capital in individual speculative shipments. The few wealthy merchants who did go to San Francisco with their own capital or unlimited credit lines to the East, gained a significant initial advantage in San Francisco.[25]

Those with merchant ambitions, but without the necessary capital of their own, sought lines of credit before their departure. Many of the early San Francisco merchants had family ties with their eastern creditors and suppliers in the same manner that the early New England merchants held similar bonds with their English creditors in the seventeenth century. Where there were no blood relationships, creditors were careful to grant funds only to those who were known to possess sound character and some business experience: a faithful clerk who wished to leave the ledger books in the New York or Boston office for the commercial hustling of San Francisco; an experienced partner sent to investigate the possibilities of establishing a branch office on the West Coast; or a younger son whose spirit of adventure might be parlayed into a family profit. A common device for extending credit was to give the departing voyager a power of attorney to act on the behalf of the creditor, who took as security the bill of lading for the cargo shipped. Some would take loans, with relatives or business partners guaranteeing the loan note.[26]

Letters of credit from eastern merchant houses were carried to the West Coast and upon arrival presented to a San Francisco bank or merchant house for working cash. The eastern commercial network of business friends and acquaintances was extended to the West Coast also through letters of introduction. These letters from an eastern merchant to a friend or business associate already established in San Francisco assisted the bearer to locate new business opportunities and were often used for purposes of credit. One New York merchant writing to a San Francisco businessman in 1848 about the son of a friend (a New York City alderman) requested, "I shall deem it a personal favor if you would give him all the information and advice he may need, and introduce him to such persons as he may desire to know . . . P.S. I would add that W. Libby takes out quite a lot of our medicines for sale. Any help you may render him in this business will be gratefully acknowledged."[27]

While some eastern merchants viewed the San Francisco market as pregnant with profits, few of the affluent merchants were willing to gamble a large portion of their working capital on a California experiment. Some merchant houses granted loans in the form of venture capital as a means of cautiously testing the turbulent market.[28] Collections from the sale of goods in San Francisco frequently took from six months to a year from the time of the initial loan or direct investment until such time as the proceeds of the sale returned East. To tie up large amounts of capital in such speculative ventures was not the habit of the established merchant houses of Boston or New York which, with the exception of the East India traders, were accustomed to commercial transactions that were normally completed in no more than two or three months.

Eastern banks, at least at the outset of the California trade, appear to have played a small role in financing the first merchant enterprises. Again, considering the investment opportunities in the East, bankers believed the risks involved in the California trade outweighed the opportunities. The banks no doubt agreed with the R. G. Dun and Company investigator who, upon noting the business activities of a Baltimore merchant, reported he "speculates in Calif., and that is regarded unsf. [unsafe]." A merchant with an established reputation for prompt payment of debts was more likely to obtain credit from another merchant, a relative, or friends than he was from an eastern bank.

Those with no credit lines open to them other than family sources—and this included most of the Jewish merchants—relied upon small savings or liquidated any assets that could be transferred quickly into cash. One German immigrant who originally worked in Philadelphia as a gardener moved to New York City in the late 1840s, leased a lot, and grew flowers in upper Manhattan. Eventually he accumulated $6,000 from his flower business and opened a butter store on Fulton Street. Here, R. G. Dun reports, "he continued doing a fair business until he caught the Cal. fever in '49 when he converted his ppty. [property] into money and butter, and went to San Francisco, and opened an establish. [ment] and there was v. [ery] successful."[29]

With capital, however accumulated, the early merchants then put together a cargo to carry with them to San Francisco. Advertisements filled the eastern newspapers with goods "suitable for the California market." C. T. Longstreet, a New York clothing merchant at 64 Nassau Street, advertised in the *New York Tribune*: "There is no item which will pay so good a profit in California as clothing, and I have a large stock on hand well adapted to that market which I will sell very low for cash." Merchants bought up items reported to be in short supply in San Francisco or in oversupply in New York or Boston. They searched the markets of New York, Baltimore, Boston and New Orleans: "The sending out [to San Francisco] of a cargo was a matter of an experiment. We had [on board] cigars, dry goods, hardware, boots, and shoes, clothing, etc. The cigars were rather a feature of our cargo. There were about a million of them, costing about $3.00 a thousand. They had been made in Connecticut, and were . . . consigned . . . to a New York house, which had failed to sell them, and they were shipped off to California as an experiment."[30]

Items reported in short supply in San Francisco commanded the attention of those preparing to depart from eastern ports. In the winter of 1849 California-bound merchants scoured New York for guns, hardware items, oil cloth, and clothing of all descriptions. The *New York Tribune* reported that in the midst of the rush to California, the clothing establishments of the city were thronged, some of them unable "to meet the extensive demands made upon them." Many of the emigrants took "at least a dozen full suits with them for their own use, and many more are taken out for sale." Goods of every description including "articles which have been long unsalable, are packed up and sent away by the merchants, to try their fortune in the Pacific Market." Manhattan's business center bustled with the activity of merchants preparing their cargoes for the awaiting vessels. "Boxes, bundles, and bales crowd the sidewalks," reported the *Tribune*, "and hundreds of drays convey to the wharfs the freight now being stored away in seventy vessels bound for the Gold Region."[31]

At the docks, ships and passengers made ready for the California voyage. Packing crates filled the holds of the ship, prefabricated wooden houses crowded topside, and captains furiously searched the swelling ranks of volunteers for the most experienced seamen to crew on the white water voyage. Shipowners, if the ship was not owned by the passengers, instructed their captains where to seek return cargoes for their vessels. Family and friends crowded the docks to bid their farewells and to be reassured by the departing merchants that, after a brief but profitable sojourn in San Francisco, they would be home within a year. With a favorable wind, the laden vessels departed for Eldorado.

The Journey West, by Sea and by Land

The vast majority of the merchants came by water to San Francisco. The overland trip, across the Great Plains and the Rocky Mountains, posed severe problems for men unaccustomed to map reading, Indians, or mountain blizzards. Besides, goods could be shipped in large quantities more cheaply from New York to San Francisco by ship than from Saint Louis to Sacramento by wagon.

The Pacific Mail Steamship Company, headed by William E. Howland and William H. Aspinwall of New York, captured much of the early passenger and freight trade. It had received a government mail subsidy of $199,000 in 1846 to run a monthly service from the Pacific side of the Isthmus of Panama to San Diego, San Francisco, and Astoria, Oregon. By 1849 the New York company put on additional ships to transport the increasing trade from the Isthmus to San Francisco. Commodore Vanderbilt's ships carried much of the tonnage of the first leg of its trip from the eastern ports to the Isthmus.

The Panama passage, however, though shorter in distance than the Horn circuit, was not the preferred route until the completion of the trans-Isthmus railroad in 1855. To traverse the Isthmus by raft and mule, with baggage and freight, exposed to the dangers of "Panama (Yellow) Fever," smallpox, cholera, and heavy rains, held little appeal. While some travelers may have chosen the Isthmus route because it cut a month off the longer trip around the Horn, its perils also included murderous muleteers, hijackings, and alligator-infested waters. If fortunate enough to survive this ordeal, it was not uncommon for a passenger to arrive in Panama City only to discover that the Pacific Mail Steamship Company had oversold tickets on one of its creaking packets for San Francisco. No doubt many merchants believed they would rather be late in San Francisco than dead in Panama. Thus, according to the Report of the Custom House in San Francisco, 15,597 voyagers reached San Francisco via Cape Horn in 1849, while only 6,489 came by way of the Isthmus. By the mid-1850s the Panama passage became increasingly popular with the introduction of more reliable guides and trans-Isthmus transportation facilities.[32]

The voyage by sea around the Horn, though deemed safer than the Panama route, possessed its own dangers. One ship, the *South Carolina,* took thirty-five days to circumvent the Horn. Headwinds, heavy seas, snow, and hail cascaded the vessel in her fight to gain headway through the Straits of Magellan. The California gold fever in 1849 placed a heavy demand on the shipping fleets of the eastern and gulf ports. In the first years of the migration, old packet ships, long past the twenty years which was the normal life of a ship, were sold at auction and pressed into service for the dangerous voyage around the Horn. There was a feverish demand for anything that would float, and as one maritime historian noted, "San Francisco caught the dregs of the merchant marine." Some ships never reached the tip of South

America. The older packets frequently sprang leaks or lost their fragile rigging off the eastern coast of Brazil and limped into Rio for extensive repairs and fresh provisions. On one March day in 1849 there were reported to be 1,200 Americans in Rio from fifteen California-bound ships replacing spoiled food, broken spars, rotten beams, and ripped sails. In the ships that were able to continue, the passengers experienced cold weather, sea sickness, scurvy, cholera, smallpox, diarrhea, and the monotony of molasses, mush, and bean soup.[33]

The accommodations of the *South Carolina* were typical. Sixty passengers occupied cabins and 110 people lived below deck where, according to one account, "there are no windows, and lamps are kept burning through the day and evening to give the passengers light enough to see, to eat and walk about." Berths were erected along the sides of the bulkhead, two persons to each berth. Passengers furnished their own dishes and bedding, stored in trunks beneath their bunks. The food was prepared forward in the galley and brought aft in kettles and eaten on pewter plates while crouched on one's bunk. Saturday was ration day: 1/4 pound butter, 1/4 pound cheese, and 14 ounces of sugar. Breakfast consisted of coffee and hard bread—usually dipped in the coffee to soften it. Pork and beans, boiled rice, corned beef, and duff (flour with raisins boiled in bags) was served for the middday dinner, and mush always appeared at supper. If an epidemic broke out, such as smallpox, those stricken were removed from below decks, their bedding and clothes thrown overboard, and the victims placed unattended in a separate tent on the cold, wet forward deck. Captains were generally unsympathetic to the complaints of their passengers, particularly in times of epidemics, and the surly crews had little to do with their human cargo except to break into their freight in search of liquor.[34]

Those merchants who attempted a transcontinental journey generally experienced similar discomforts and dangers. One group of pioneer merchants who hoped to speculate in San Francisco with a wagon load of gunpowder, machinery, and a circular saw purchased at Fort Independence, Missouri, quickly realized that their oxen could not pull the overloaded wagon across the Nebraska plains, much less the Wyoming mountains. Accordingly, they buried their gunpowder in the hope of recovering it on a future trip. The merchant traveler noted, sadly, that they "buried in this way a large stock of drugs and medicines, everything necessary to start a complete drug store." When they reached the desert, the dead oxen and cattle of former parties marked the trail to California. Thirsty from a critical shortage of water and concerned only with surviving the murderous heat, the gun-powder speculator recollected years later that "some of our party were glad to be able to suck blood from some of the dead animals to quench their thirst." Optimistic hopes of large profits in San Francisco had long passed, "all our brilliant expectations of making our fortunes out of goods with which we originally started had long since vanished."[35]

Another pioneer merchant together with his brother and a friend traveled from Lawrence, Massachusetts, to Pittsburgh by train, hence to Saint Louis and on to Independence, Missouri, by river boat. Thirty-one of his fellow boat passengers (mostly Mormons on their way to Salt Lake City) died of cholera in a period of forty-eight hours. In Independence the survivors purchased a wagon, four mules and some steers, joined a sixteen-wagon company, and set off across the plains. At night, guards were posted to defend the party against Sioux Indians. Exchanging food for the guide services of a band of friendly Sioux, they crossed the North Platte to Fort Laramie. At Laramie the company disbanded. The merchant brothers sold their wagon and goods, and with the small proceeds headed off on horseback with three pack mules to Salt Lake City. There on July 20, 1849, the Mor-mons invited them to join in the festivities celebrating their second an-niversary in Salt Lake. A week later, at the head of the Humboldt River, the friend departed for an unknown destination and the two brothers decided to temporarily forgo a merchant life for the more im-mediate riches of the mines. After 102 days of travel from the Missouri frontier, they crossed the High Sierras and arrived in Pleas-ant Valley. Finally, having mined for six months, clearing twenty dol-lars a day, they arrived in San Francisco to commence their merchant careers.[36] This circuitous land route from Lawrence, Massachusetts, to San Francisco was actually followed by others, either out of igno-rance about the expense and dangers of a transcontinental journey, their impatience to reach California, or the inaccessibility of their home to a major seaport.

The relative expense and difficulty of the transcontinental route to the West Coast compared to transportation by sea determined, to a large extent, who would migrate to California. It was far easier and considerably cheaper for an individual on the Eastern Seaboard to arrange transportation to California than for a resident of the interior Midwest or South to purchase wagons, horses, supplies, and hire a guide for the overland journey. Because certain eastern cities already possessed or had the capacity to build a shipping fleet to transport both passengers and cargo, there would be a disproportionate migration from New England and the mid-Atlantic states.

The two major embarking ports for San Francisco were New York and Boston. Of the 775 vessels that left eastern ports for California in 1849, 214 were from New York and 151 from Boston; no other port sent more than 42. With the introduction of the faster clipper ships in late 1849 and early 1850s, New York, which built approximately one-half and owned two-thirds of these sleek vessels, and Boston continued to dominate the sea lanes between the East and West Coast. The 16,000-mile route from the East Coast to California was barred to foreign vessels because it was construed as "coasting trade." The New York and Boston merchants who owned clipper ships for the China trade, quickly rerouted their Orient-bound ships via San Francisco with passengers and freight rather than send them ballast-laden around the Cape of Good Hope.[37]

Migration Patterns

The migration of San Francisco's first generation of residents, including the merchants, was a selective process that reflected a distinct East Coast to West Coast pattern. Whereas almost three-quarters of the nation's twenty million people in 1850 resided in either the mid-Atlantic states (33 percent), the Old Northwest (22 percent) or the South (19 percent), eight of every ten San Francisco residents in 1852 who migrated from a former residence *within* the United States, had formerly lived in either New England or the mid-Atlantic region. Approximately half had come from the mid-Atlantic (52 percent) and over one-quarter (28 percent) from New England. The latter represented twice the number that might have been expected to emigrate from this region, considering that only 14 percent of the nation's population resided there at midcentury. The merchant migration conformed to these patterns except that an even higher percent had formerly lived in the mid-Atlantic or New England states. New York and

Massachusetts together accounted for over half (54 percent) of the former merchant residences.[38]

Clearly, the nation's merchants did not migrate to San Francisco in the early 1850s in proportion to their general distribution throughout the national population. Less than 5 percent, for example, of the first San Francisco merchant generation formerly resided in the South, which accounted for almost a fifth of the national population and about the same percentage of the nation's merchants. Only 2 percent of the merchants had migrated from the states of the Old Northwest, where approximately another fifth of the nation resided. Among the total employed male population of San Francisco a similar pattern emerged. No doubt the shipping lanes which originated in the Northeast and mid-Atlantic regions partially accounted for this disproportionate migration. Also, it was along the East Coast where the nation's major trade and commercial centers, capital resources, and developed trade networks were centered. This was reflected in the fact that probably half of the San Francisco merchants from these two regions formerly resided in Boston, New York, Philadelphia, and Baltimore. The proportion of former urban residents would no doubt have been higher had it been possible to include in the calculations cities of 10,000 or larger. The migration from within the United States, therefore, was interurban, from Eastern Seaboard cities to San Francisco.[39]

San Francisco also attracted a surprisingly large number of foreign-born, considering that they composed only 10 percent of the entire United States population in 1850. Within the employed male population of the city, the foreign-born actually outnumbered the native-born, 53 percent to 47 percent, a unique situation for an American city in the mid-nineteenth century. Within the merchant ranks, however, the native-born outnumbered the foreign-born better than three to two. But if the native-born were overrepresented in the merchant occupations, so too were the Germans, who accounted for only 7 percent of the city's male population but occupied a disproportionately high 14 percent of the merchant positions. The Irish and French, and to a lesser extent the English-Scots, were underrepresented in the merchant community as compared with their respective distributions in the San Francisco male population.[40]

Finally there were some interesting migration patterns among the foreign-born merchants. Only about three out of every five migrated directly from overseas, about the same number as emigrated from the mid-Atlantic states. About a third of the foreign-born merchants in San Francisco emigrated from New York, the vast majority of whom had resided in the nation's merchant capital, New York City. This was particularly true among the German-born merchants. Few foreign-born merchants migrated from the South, New England, or the Old Northwest, though some 14 percent departed the New West, primarily from New Orleans.

But why had so many foreigners, merchant and nonmerchants alike, and generally the least affluent, migrated to San Francisco? Certainly residence in eastern cities (where the foreign-born clustered), with their transportation networks to San Francisco, was an important factor. Also significant was the fact that the opportunities for the foreign-born in eastern cities did not match those available to the native-born. Studies of social mobility in Boston, Philadelphia, and Poughkeepsie, New York, have demonstrated that the native-born fared better than the foreign-born, and that patterns of "blocked mobility" existed for the foreign-born.[41] The foreign-born probably perceived the West, in particular San Francisco, to hold opportunities for them superior to those available in Boston, New York, Baltimore, New Orleans, or in their own native countries, and thought them worth pursuing. That the transportation was readily available at their back door only heightened their anticipation of "making it" in the American West.

The Instant City of 1850

As the ships arrived and the transcontinental adventurers filtered in from the High Sierras, San Francisco added approximately 15,000 to its population in the first six months of 1849. In the last half of the year, approximately 4,000 immigrants a month poured into the city for a total of 39,000 arrivals in 1849. Many departed for the mines, but by the end of 1849 the city's population was estimated to be between 20,000 and 25,000. Considering that there were only about 2,000 or 3,000 residing there at the beginning of 1849, San Francisco experienced massive demographic changes in that one hectic year.[42]

The town itself covered an area of about half a square mile, the boundaries being Powell, California, and Vallejo Streets and the water line which extended nearly a quarter of a mile south of Jackson Street, near Montgomery. At the beginning of the year there were no wharfs into deep water with the exception of a landing place at Clark's Point located near the intersection of Broadway and Battery. Here lighters shuttled between the shore and the vessels anchored in the harbor transferring passengers, their personal possessions, and cargo. One recent arrival, accustomed to being waited upon back home, offered a dollar to a "shabby looking fellow" to take his trunk from the dock at Clark's Point up to the main street in town. The fellow "put his hand into his pocket, pulled out a handful of gold and said, 'I will give you three to take it up yourself.' " Tents and makeshift shacks straddled the barren sand hills or were scattered amidst the few permanent structures along the town's muddy streets.[43]

Almost immediately distinct residential and commercial districts emerged in San Francisco. Along Montgomery Street, near the water's edge, were located the largest and most influential importer and auction houses that sold to the local merchants and those of the interior mining towns. The sand hills behind Yerba Buena Cove were quickly knocked down by a steam excavator and the earth pushed into the cove to provide additional working space in a town where level land near the water's edge was at a premium. Wharfs constructed at the foot of Clay, California, Sacramento, Washington, Jackson, Pacific, and Broadway reached out over the mud flats into deep water to allow vessels to unload directly onto them. The streets above Montgomery became the center for specialized trades. The dry goods houses were on Clay, the stores and booths of peddlers lined Commercial Street, and furthest north from the water stood the warehouses. The retail trade centered on Kearney Street; to the south on this street were situated the hotels and to the north, at the base of Telegraph Hill and along Broadway, the saloons, houses of prostitution, and Sydney Town—a tent village of Latin Americans and Australians.

An elected town government existed but performed, at least initially, only the minumum duties expected by a population which did not come to Eldorado to be governed but to exploit. The state government was nowhere to be found, but the federal government was somewhat more visible through the operation of the custom house and post office. Churches were built but seldom filled. The gambling halls,

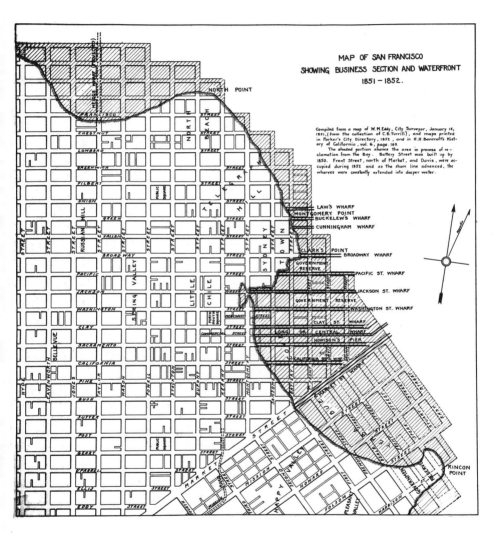

MAP OF SAN FRANCISCO
SHOWING BUSINESS SECTION AND WATERFRONT
1851 – 1852.

markets, wharfs, and burgeoning stores commanded the attention of the city's population.

By 1852 the state census taker counted some 35,000 people in the city. When gold seekers left for the mines they were replaced by those returning from the Sierras, or others migrating to San Francisco from abroad or the eastern states. The city was a portal through which many passed and few remained. In the geographically mobile nineteenth century, the glitter of gold was enough to attract a transcontinental and transoceanic migration that produced an instant city in less than two years; a city which would be no ghost town but a metropolis commanding, for the remainder of the nineteenth century, the commercial life of the American West Coast.

Even as the second half of the nineteenth century began, San Francisco as a city possessed certain characteristics and performed certain functions that placed it in the upper hierarchy of American cities. First and foremost it was a port city, surrounded by deep navigable waters, and unlike some other port cities, close to ocean shipping lanes. A vessel need only clear the Golden Gate to be at the city wharfs without the long upriver voyage necessary at the ports of Baltimore, Philadelphia,

The waterfront in 1852, with a river steamer in the foreground. Lacking return cargoes to the East, the abandoned ships (at right) were often used for storage because there were not enough warehouses on land.

A forest of ships' masts crowds the main harbor in the early 1850s.

Shops and the Bella Union tavern surround the city's first public square, the Portsmouth Plaza, laid out in the mid-1850s at the corner of Kearny and Washington streets.

and New Orleans. In addition, San Francisco was ice-free, protected from ocean winds, and convenient to two major navigable rivers. Boats could navigate the Sacramento in high water 395 miles to Red Bluff and 400 miles up the San Joaquin to Sycamore in Fresno County. Also, depending on the size of the vessel, limited navigation was available on the Feather, American, Stanislaus, and Tuolumne Rivers.

Second, like Boston and New Orleans, San Francisco was a regional entrepôt or "central place" city that performed comprehensive services for the surrounding territory. The city imported goods not only for its own population but for the hinterland towns of the mining areas and later for the surrounding agricultural districts. By 1852 San Francisco ranked second in the United States behind New York City in terms of tonnage entering the port. The interior of the state depended totally upon the supply lines which emanated from San Francisco. California in 1850, with a population of 91,000—one third residing in San Francisco—did not yet have an agricultural economy capable of supplying its population. She ranked last of all the states in 1850 in average cash value per acre with only 12,000 acres of improved land, and last in value of home manufacturers.[44]

San Francisco's wharfs, however, received virtually all of the goods demanded in the mining areas, and in a very few years these same wharfs would load export cargoes for domestic and foreign ports. Acting as transfer and coordinating agents, San Francisco merchants assembled cargoes and shipped them on inland barges and river boats owned by the city merchants to the inland towns of Stockton and Sacramento. No cargo was too small or too cheap; in one way or another it all passed through the hands of the merchants or the facilities of the port. The city's monopoly of the trade in California and the Rocky Mountain territories was secure, at least until the completion of the transcontinental railroad in 1869, and no other West Coast seaport would begin to rival San Francisco's outstanding position until late in the nineteenth century.

San Francisco was a city where trading, rather than producing, generated the local economy. Consequently, trader-merchants prevailed in a higher ratio (14 percent) than in any other American city. Wholesale houses received orders for everything from carpet tacks to rockcrushing machinery. Ships delivered leather boots from Boston, woolen clothing from New York, flour from Valparaiso, and lumber from Astoria. As one urban geographer noted: "From 1848 to 1869, from the discovery of gold to the completion of the transcontinental railroad, the Bay of San Francisco was the warehouse for the economic life of California. Into that structure poured the mass of goods necessary to support a far from self-sufficient population . . . the men who came . . . were entrepreneurs, not farmers, so their economic existence depended upon the presence of a warehouse kept filled by full-time merchants."[45]

This was no frontier community developed in stages by trappers, homesteaders, farmers, and eventually merchants. San Francisco never really existed as a village but immediately adopted a metropolitan economy with specialized full-time merchants who extended their trading network from San Francisco to the multivillages of the mining districts and the interior Rocky Mountain territory. San Francisco served as the vital link between the hinterland trade and the extended trade of New York, Boston, and the foreign ports of Europe.[46]

Here, in a city generated by commerce, some 3,100 merchants— native-born Americans, Germans, French, Irish, Peruvians, and Italians—would make their mark. Youthful and energetic, they sought their "manifest destiny *million*."[47] The miners came to dig and the merchants came to trade, but they all carried the optimistic spirit of the adventurous gambler. None envisioned failure, only success—the joy of a new-found fortune and the expectation that one's destiny could be transformed by one's energy.

2

THE 1850s

When the second half of the nineteenth century opened, San Francisco as a city was barely a year old. Its flimsy structures of wood and canvas, the mud of its streets, and the hawkers who, in a multitude of foreign languages, peddled their wares on Long Wharf gave the impression to the newcomers that they had arrived not in a new and permanent community but at a traveling carnival that would disappear when the festivities were over. At the heart of the celebration was gold, and those who swarmed into the city came to dig nuggets from the Sierras or profits from the diggers.

A Decade of Growth

The spirit of the gambler attracted over 450,000 to the port of San Francisco between 1849 and 1860.[1] Most of the migrants to the city left immediately for the mines and satellite towns, but by 1850 some 30,000 decided to settle in San Francisco, and by 1860 the number rose to 56,000. The 87 percent increase is not as high when compared with Buffalo, 92 percent, Saint Louis, 106 percent, Brooklyn, 175 percent, or Chicago, 265 percent, during the same decade. Still San Francisco ranked as the fifteenth largest city in the nation by 1860, larger than Charleston, Providence, Pittsburgh, or Rochester in population. During these first ten years the city transformed itself into a relatively stable community of artisans, merchants, and capitalists. San Francisco by 1860 had become a mercantile metropolis whose economic and cultural hinterland encompassed the entire region west of the Rocky Mountains.

By 1860, with its infant foundries, mills, manufacturing firms, merchant houses, and capital, and no longer totally dependent upon foreign suppliers, San Francisco had gained a measure of economic independence. Already in the early 1850s the value of San Francisco's $8 million export trade exceeded that of the more established ports of Savannah, Georgia, Portland, Maine, and the combined exports of Richmond, Norfolk, and Philadelphia. And by 1860 only New York, Boston, New Orleans, Philadelphia, and Baltimore exceeded San Francisco in total tonnage entered at the port. With the development of California agriculture (wheat, wool, hides, flour) and San Francisco manufacturers, the volume of the city's exports ranked ahead of Richmond, Portland, Baltimore, and Philadelphia, but behind New York, Boston, New Orleans, Charleston, and Mobile. Trade with the Far East had expanded to the point in 1860 where San Francisco monopolized the trade with Hawaii and the Philippines, carried on a small Japanese trade, and split the China trade with New York City.[2]

San Francisco was a predominantly mercantile city where the wharf, the warehouse, and the counting house were the foci of the economic activity. Those who initially accumulated the most capital were the middlemen—shipping merchants and importers, agents, brokers, auctioneers, commission merchants, and factors. They were the men who with their capital resources would direct the economic, political, and cultural affairs of the city in its first decade of growth.[3]

The city's 3,100 merchants composed 14 percent of the 1852 working male population of San Francisco and were similar in many ways to the general population of the city. They were young—81 percent of the merchants were between the ages of twenty and forty, averaging twenty-eight years of age.[4] The rigors of the trip to California had filtered out the elderly and infirm and generally discouraged women and children from the migration. Initially only 15 percent of the merchants and 16 percent of the general population brought their wives with them to the West Coast and even fewer (10 percent) transported their children. Males outnumbered females seven to one. Few could find, much less afford, the luxury of a single family dwelling. Most lived with others—a friend, relative, or business associate—in a multiroom dwelling, boarding house, or hotel and paid exorbitant prices at the myriad of local restaurants or ate at home. A few merchants (3 percent) had live-in servants, usually Irish, while the other merchants tended as best they could to their own domestic needs. Frequently the place of business and residence were the same, the merchant and his clerk sleeping upstairs in the store.

The period 1849 to 1860 was critical for both the city and its merchants, for the events of this decade would determine the future direction and economic skeleton of the city. They were years of severe economic dislocations and hardship. Goods flooded the market, fires devastated property, and business recessions struck the city at random as residents, and particularly the merchants, attempted to insert a measure of order into the chaotic marketplace. Fortunes made in good times were destroyed as quickly as they had been accumulated. The early optimism of 1849 gave way by 1860 to caution, and in many cases, despair. A few men gained great wealth, the promise of which had attracted them to San Francisco in the first place. But among the first generation merchants almost half had departed the city by 1860— disillusioned and disheartened.

Years of Boom and Bust

The early merchant found it difficult to survive and adjust to the city's economic environment in the 1850s. He traded in a market of which he had little knowledge and even less control. In the 1850 decade the economy of the city cycled through periods of boom and bust in much the same unpredictable fashion as the roulette wheel selected its winners and losers. By 1858 San Francisco had experienced four major business cycles, all quite independent of the national economy: June 1848-January 1850—boom; February 1850-April 1852—recession; May 1852-December 1853—boom; January 1854-January 1858 —depression.

The early boom period, which lasted approximately eighteen months, advertised to the world the immense profits available in San Francisco. A merchant who purchased bread in New York for six cents a loaf and carried it with him to San Francisco in 1849 discovered eager buyers at fifty cents a loaf. Another enterprising merchant brought with him aboard ship four framed houses, fourteen by twenty-eight feet. Purchased for $147 each in New York, they fetched $1,000 in gold upon arrival in San Francisco.[5]

During the initial economic boom the cost of living in San Francisco was certainly one of the highest in the nation. Where gold dust was the primary medium of exchange, common laborers demanded and received an ounce a day (sixteen dollars), and mechanics earned as much as twenty-five dollars a day. But residents also realized that the amount earned in New York in a week could easily vanish in San Francisco in a day. Merchant one-story establishments with a twenty-foot front on the street rented for $40,000 a year, small rooms for commercial enterprises of twenty square feet rented for $200 to $400 a week, and boarding houses charged thirty dollars without board. One resident observed that it was actually cheaper to have his clothes sent to the Sandwich Islands for washing than to have them laundered in San Francisco.[6] Another account of San Francisco prices in 1850 reported, "Eggs sold at one, two and three dollars apiece; inferior sugar, tea, and coffee, at four dollars a pound in small quantities, or, three hundred dollars a barrel; medicines . . . a dollar a drop . . . and ten dollars a pill or purge, without advice; or with it, from thirty, up . . . to one hundred dollars. Spirits . . . from ten to forty dollars a quart; . . . picks and shovels ranged from five to fifteen dollars each; and common wooden tin bowls about half as much."[7]

By the early spring of 1850 prices began to plummet as eastern merchants, hoping for a quick profit, flooded the San Francisco market with goods. Bales of expensive supplies were not worth their storage, and the auction houses began to rattle off shiploads of merchandise at nominal prices. By August 1850 Boston banks were refusing credits to California shippers; and beef and pork which fetched anywhere from sixteen dollars to thirty-five dollars a barrel in May 1850 could expect no more than ten dollars in the summer of 1851. In the same period the price of flour dropped 15 percent, coffee 30 percent, and sugar 60 percent. The recession seriously affected wages and was the occasion for considerable unemployment.[8]

A local trader reported in late 1850 to a relative back in Philadelphia that there were enough goods in San Francisco for the next year and a half, and with the drop in prices, "You can't sell any thing in wholesale at present not much no How. A little store will cost me about $250 a Month, and to Retail I have not got assortment enough and to Peddle in the City is not much[;] there are too many running."[9] Another resident of San Francisco advised his father, an upholsterer, against coming to San Francisco and observed that the best opportunities existed for jewelers, female cooks, and chambermaids. Even the world's oldest profession was overcrowded—"the market is overstocked with prostitutes." In another letter to his father, this same resident complained,

Business is very dull here + a great many are idle *entirely unable to get a days work* and I know many that have not had a day's work for 6

or 8 weeks and some longer than that[;] I have mad[e] every exertion
to get work, I have been here now 15 working days and have only
worked 5 out of that time; I earned only thirty-two dollars for the five
days, wages are a getting down as they only pay from 5 to 7 dollars per
day . . . and the[re] is so much competition now it is almost out of the
question for me to try to undertake work myself, + besides a man has
got to be pretty well acquainted before he can get any job . . . how
sadly disappointed people are when they arrive here; they all form a
verry wrong idea of this place, about making a fortune in a hurry.[10]

By mid-1852 the San Francisco economy had begun to recover.
Prices rose, relative scarcity followed glut, and those merchants who
withstood the temporary depression and held their goods without having to sell out at low prices took advantage of the higher prices in the
second half of the year. The quick fortunes of the 1848-49 period,
however, were more difficult to come by. The boom lasted at most but
a year and a half. The summer of 1853 saw the decline of gold production from the mines and a similar decrease in the number of immigrants to California. Whereas some 64,640 people were reported to
have arrived by sea in San Francisco in 1852, only 35,396 came in
1853. Approximately 30,000 shipped out of the city in the same year.
Once again goods were a glut on the market; the newspapers parroted
the usual complaint of the merchants that they and the city were
"struggling along under the unhappy effects of this wild speculation
of Eastern shippers, and will in all probability feel its influence for
many [months] yet to come." Wages declined to the point where the
laborer and skilled mechanics earned in a day half of what they commanded in 1849.[11]

Then in early 1854 a major depression hit San Francisco. The gold
seekers in the Sierras discovered that the original gold which some
were fortunate enough to collect through a simple panning procedure
had long disappeared. Now large and expensive quartz crushing
equipment was needed to unearth treasures. Miners too poor to purchase more technologically advanced equipment departed in droves
for San Francisco and their eastern homes. And as the demand for
goods from the mines decreased, San Francisco merchants and bankers called in their credit. The building boom collapsed, volume at the
port shrank by half, real estate values dropped 30 to 40 percent, and
business failures more than doubled. In February 1855 the leading

banking house in San Francisco (and California), Page, Bacon, and Company, closed its doors, forcing a number of smaller institutions and individual merchants into bankruptcy. Soon thereafter Adams and Company, the express and banking house with branches throughout California, also failed. In the next three years there were 471 major business failures in the city, totaling approximately $14.5 million in liabilities. Business conditions revived temporarily in the fall of 1856, but the city was almost immediately hit by the Panic of 1857 which, though not as severe on the West Coast as in the East, did hurt the economy. San Francisco only recovered a measure of economic stability in late 1858.[12]

Cyclical Oversupply

The oversupply of goods in the San Francisco market was the single most important factor that fueled the excessive business cycles in the 1850 decade. The merchants attempted as best they could to inform themselves of the supply and demand of their own marketplace. But the communication networks both within the city and with other commercial centers with which San Francisco traded were primitive even by nineteenth-century standards.

Despite the efforts of the local newspapers to report the cargoes of ships unloading at the wharfs, a merchant found it difficult to learn the quantity of items already in the city. It was even more difficult to determine what goods were on their way to San Francisco from eastern ports. Even if one could obtain a two-month-old New York or Boston paper, they contained little in the way of commercial intelligence. Eastern shippers faced the same problem. Not knowing the current state of the market in San Francisco except from San Francisco newspapers (equally outdated) or letters from individual merchants, they shipped goods reported to be in demand and found instead a flooded market. No clearing house or central marketing device other than the gravity of supply and demand existed, to inform either San Francisco merchants or their colleagues at eastern ports as to the state of the local marketplace.

Lacking a rational system of communication, the merchants attempted to devise their own. Local newspapers began to report more thorough commercial intelligence, but even they could not forecast either the volume or type of goods in transit to San Francisco. The early clearing houses for commercial information were the city's bars and saloons. Here, merchants exchanged commercial intelligence, attempting as best they could to determine who was importing what from where, when it would arrive, and its effect on the San Francisco market price. All the while, orders continued to arrive from the interior mining region and the Oregon and Arizona Territories. Additional news was gathered from ships' captains recently arrived from eastern and foreign ports. The merchant then judged what would be needed two or three months hence and ordered the items from the East. But as would be expected, the system failed miserably.[13]

First, informal gatherings in saloons were no substitute for a rational communication system encompassing all merchants. While a group of four or five in one bar plotted a commercial venture in woolen shirts, a similar scheme was devised in another saloon down the street. Too often what passed for commercial intelligence across the bar room table turned out to be rumor. The *Alta California,* the paper read by the English-speaking merchants, complained that San Francisco was a "city of rumors, a great whispering gallery, where any report, however absurd, is repeated again and again, with a thousand additions, so that a glut and a scarcity occur on the same day."[14]

In fact few merchants in San Francisco knew what to expect in their own marketplace. The demand for goods from the mines was never constant but continually subject to the unpredictable luck of the miners. Also, lack of rain in the mining regions dried up the streams and rivers needed to wash gold; or floods obstructed roads and halted mining operations altogether. More critical, the city merchants were unable to predict the volume of supplies in San Francisco because eastern shippers failed to solicit the advice of the San Francisco merchants as to the needs of the local and regional market. Too often New York or Boston merchant adventurers consigned "blind" cargoes to a local San Francisco merchant with instructions to dispose of the cargo "at best advantage" to the eastern shipper. A San Francisco paper complained that "the blame . . . for the disastrous results of adventurers here belongs chiefly, if not wholely, to the shippers at home. The recklessness . . . under which they have crowded and hurried off ship load after ship load of all sorts of trash unsaleable in their own market [is] a perfect nuisance here."[15] A former resident of New Bedford wrote home: "It is the people at home that are running the trade of this country—not the people here."[16] A merchant in San Francisco who acted as agent for a New York merchant reported in a letter in late 1850:

This place is literally smothered with an over supply of everything, and it will not mend until the system of adventure shipment shall cease, and goods sent only to order. Now everybody all over the world ships everything, and if only a small amount is sent by each shipper, it swells into an immense aggregate at this point; when you reflect that we have at this time a fleet of six hundred in port—and to supply what? Why an entire population of less than the city of New York—how can they [San Francisco] consume the commerce sufficient for at least ten million of people.[17]

Items which once sold profitably in the boom period of 1849-50 were by June 1850 declared in surplus or "a drug on the market." Canisters of gunpowder found no purchasers and were left outside exposed to the weather. Boxes of chewing tobacco were used to support the sills of houses. Crates of crockery, barrels of ship bread, hams, and broken boxes of pipe were deposited about the beach front, buried in the sand, or used to fill mud holes in the street. Even liquors in a city constantly thristing for alcohol were unsaleable in an over-supplied market. One merchant reported that he passed "every day on my way to work at least fifty cases of brandy half buried in the sand on the beach, which have probably been there for six months." On the west side of Montgomery street, the main commercial thoroughfare in the city, 100-pound bags of Chilean flour, cooking stoves, and a damaged piano bridged a gully which exited onto a double row of boxes filled with shoes. One French journalist estimated that there was enough excess tobacco in San Francisco to supply each inhabitant for sixty-five years and enough boots and shoes to outfit each pair of feet in the city with one hundred shoes.[18]

In an attempt to stem the tide of unwanted cargoes into the city and thereby control their own markets, local merchants took pains to report back to their eastern shippers the specific needs of their city. "I know," wrote a San Francisco importer to his supplier in New York, "there is an immense quantity of merchandise on the way, which will have to be forced onto the market at a great sacrifice." But, he added, merchants were "aware of this fact, will not purchase now unless at moderate prices." Therefore New York should not "ship for the present any article but of building material and even then you must govern yourselves by shipments that have been made by others."[19]

San Francisco merchants complained that even when advised of market conditions on the West Coast, eastern shippers disregarded their advice. The *New York Herald* printed a letter from a San Francisco merchant who wrote, somewhat in spoof but nevertheless in anger, of New York's greed to exact a profit in San Francisco through the shipment of unsolicited goods. He complained that New York had been advised of market conditions in San Francisco, yet the Empire City stubbornly refused the advice and sent out several hundred shiploads of goods; most of the articles sold at half their cost and the remainder burned in a fire. The letter continued,

Some two hundred of your vessels have cleared for China and the East Indies; the balance, say five hundred remain in port from our inability to negotiate further drafts on you. Most of them are less liable to sink, as they now lie on the sand flats, than they would be if sent to sea, and we would advise their remaining . . . some forty or fifty years. We would advise the immediate shipment of some five hundred assorted cargoes, as the supply in the market is not more than sufficient for fifteen months. Any articles quoted at high prices, the consumption of which is limited, should be shipped in large quantities, in order to compete with the host of other shippers. In shipping durable goods, you need never provide for the payment of the duties, as we are at all times prepared to advance the amount of ten percent per month interest, or, if you prefer, have the goods stored in the celebrated U.S. fireproof bonded warehouses, at the trifling expense of seven dollars per ton the first month, and three dollars each succeeding month. An anniversary fire is confidently expected on the 14th inst[ance], when we hope to close out most of our consignments.[20]

By the mid-1850s, in the midst of a depression, with wharfs and warehouses filled with unsaleable goods, San Francisco merchants implored the East to "export from a knowledge of our wants, supply and resources." But in the end, like the luck of the roulette wheel, chance, it seemed, was the only discernible system at work in the San Francisco marketplace. A San Francisco merchant despaired at the irrationality of the market system: "The merchants of New York need no information in regard to the fluctuations in the San Francisco markets. They know too well that no calculation can be relied on in that direction. So great is our distance from sources of supply, so unequal the passage of different vessels, and so difficult it is to know, even approximately, the amount of shipments, and especially orders on foreign ports, that the most careful estimate is no more to be relied on than the most arbitrary 'guess.' Chance . . . may favor the merchant sometimes just as it does the gambler."[21]

All the while San Francisco blamed New York and Boston for the problems associated with the oversupply of goods, the merchants continued to gear their trade to the optimistic expectations of an expanding economy. The immense profits made in the first six months of 1849 served as a measuring stick against which all San Francisco merchants in the early 1850s compared their success. "No man will do business here for less profit than 50 percent and mostly the retail price is just double the wholesale," reported one merchant. And in an economic environment geared by a growth mentality which refused to accept self-control, San Francisco merchants flooded the markets with goods and at the same time expected profit margins to equal the golden days of early 1849.[22]

Local boosterism continued to foist on the nation the impression that San Francisco's growth potential was unlimited and that she was "already the commercial emporium of the Pacific . . . destined to become, next to New York, the storehouse for the products of the world." In fact, as San Franciscans viewed their provincial world, the eternal blessings of the city were the work of God. "Men cannot make seaports," the *Alta California* editorialized; "Heaven has done this, and our beautiful bay cannot by all the combinations on earth be despoiled of her position and destiny." Speaking for the merchants, the *Alta* continued, "We have the population. The Americanized Saxon blood will do it. We are the direct line between Europe and the Pacific. We must be the only receiver of its commerce and riches . . . it is coming when San Francisco will be the first commercial city of the world. We are willing that this shall be our epitaph and will stake our future fame upon the prediction." Other American cities believe God to be in their employ but few could point to such high profit margins of His making. In the end, San Francisco had only herself to blame for the gap between brilliant visions and hard times.[23]

The Montgomery Block, one of the city's first major commercial buildings, financed by the merchants in the mid-1850s for their offices. Telegraph Hill is to the left.

The merchant who found himself with excess goods on hand and no immediate buyer, had a number of options open to him. He could, if a vessel could be chartered and a crew located at a reasonable price, ship the goods back East or overseas in search of a more profitable market. Or the goods might be stored in a local warehouse in anticipation of higher prices in six months' time. But given the high storage costs, due primarily to the shortage of lumber and suitable structures for storage, few merchants were willing to outlay thousands of dollars on the gamble that items which were in oversupply in June would be in demand in December. Creditors in the East demanded the immediate return of their advances, local bills had to be paid, and valuable liquid capital, always in short supply, could not be tied up in unsaleable goods. Eastern shippers advised their San Francisco merchant-agents to sell the cargo as quickly as possible, "not to hold on for higher prices," and if not sold within two or three months, "put up at auction and sell to the highest bidder." Better to admit a failure and dispose of the cargo with the crack of the auctioneer's hammer than sit idly by while others put their capital to work in more profitable items.[24]

The particular consequence of the excessive supply of goods in the post-1849 market was "the sudden and extraordinary increase in the auctioneering business." Many merchants began their careers in the aution house. Arriving in San Francisco without merchandise but with some capital, a considerable number of fledgling merchants attended auction sales, purchased an order of merchandise, wheeled their new purchase to a tent, hung out a sign, and opened for business —all in one day. Inland merchants from Sacramento or Stockton also turned up at the auctions in search of bargains. Auctions were a speculative game in which all participated, directly or indirectly. Bargains, though, were more common for the buyer than the seller. Besides the purchase of large inventories of hardware, dry goods, or provisions one popular game was to purchase "blind" chests left in storage by miners, who failed to pay storage costs and lost their personal chests to the auction block.[25] An early practitioner of the art of blind auction purchases described his luck at the game. "After I had earned a few hundred dollars by laboring at grading streets . . . I commenced to attend auctions, and was generally fortunate in my purchases. On one occasion I bought six large cases of goods which were sold 'blind' to pay storage, paying $160 for them. They proved to contain a fine lot of hardware of every kind, which I sold next day to a merchant for $500." The man soon gave up the game of auction purchases when upon one blind purchase he discovered himself to be the proud owner of a human skeleton![26] After a while, the auction house owners began to take out the valuables before the sale and "fill the trunks with old clothing and brick-bats before putting them up at auction," and as one unfortunate speculator reported, "a great many got stuck that way."[27] Yet despite the best efforts of the auction houses, and the bargain prices they offered, the demand for goods in no way matched the oversupply in the San Francisco marketplace. There were periods of equilibrium prior to the late 1850s when business stabilized, but they were the exception rather than the rule.

Recurring Fires

The fires of the early 1850s (eight in all) added yet another unknown to the commercial difficulties of the city. The property damage in these fires totaled over $25 million, most of it suffered by the city merchants. No insurance companies operated in San Francisco at the time, and the few business establishments covered by eastern companies were only partially reimbursed. The fires were particularly destructive to the city's central business district where virtually all the commercial establishments were located. It was a rare merchant who did not suffer fire damage to either his store or warehouse.[28]

The fires destroyed the life savings of many small merchants. One shopkeeper wrote after the May 1851 fire: "Many of our friends lost every dollar they had in the v.orld. Some had written home for insurance, but no companies were found to take the risks, and when their letters from home informed them of the fact, they felt they were beggars."[29] Another merchant, after another fire the next month, reported to a relative in Philadelphia:

I shall stay here now and try to make up my losses. My wish is only to bring back again what I brought Here[;] there fore it is impossible for me to tell when I go back again. You may Really Believe me[.] Since I left Philadelphia I look ten years Older. In all my Days alife I have not been so down Hearted as I have been for the Last 6 weeks . . . Lazard + Goldman have lossed Heavy also. there fore look out for Straus + Goldman if you have sold them any thing. Potsdamer + Rosenboum lossed $14,000 . . . A man got one misfortune [the May 4, 1850 fire] then comes one after the other [the June 14, 1850 fire] . . . Simon Shloss is Selling off fast and intents to go Home Soon[;] a great many will go back again by next fall. Stein lossed some by the last fire too. In the Last fire were Tow [two] Jehuden [Jews] Burned to deaths[;] again they stood in their Store to save their goods.[30]

Men with assets of $50,000 on one day were penniless the next—a not uncommon occurrence. One merchant who suffered losses in the

December 1848 fire estimated at $70,000 but who recovered to make $100,000 six months later, lost everything in the May 1851 fire "and owed ten thousand dollars besides."[31] If enough had been salvaged, most merchants attempted to recoup and begin again; but a few left permanently for their homes back East, their hopes and savings wiped out in a city which, in its haste to accumulate property, failed in the basic precautions against property's greatest adversary—fire.

Some survived by clever design or luck. Those with shops located near the water could load their inventory on lighters and float it safely to the middle of the harbor. A handful of merchants, such as Macondray and Co., had the foresight to store their goods in one of the two fireproof warehouses. The affluent merchants could also afford the hundred dollars per cartload demanded by scurrying draymen more than eager to transfer merchandise to safety for a tidy profit. And the few stores which luckily survived the fires, profited immediately from the shortage of goods in the market. The Seligman brothers sold out their total inventory of dry goods within a week in a market where prices rose between 15 and 25 percent.[32]

Yet supplies lost in the fires were almost immediately replaced by new shipments. A letter from Macondray and Co. of San Francisco to W. F. Parrott, a Boston merchant, described temporary dislocations and future apprehension.

Our merchants and traders are a good deal crippled and have at present no place to do business, and the demand is consequently only for the supply of immediate wants. A great many goods were however stored afloat, and . . . we are inclined to think that with imports yet to arrive . . . no great difficulty exists. We would therefore caution our friends against being hurried into renewed shipments until more accurate information can be obtained. At present, prices are entirely irregular . . . We cannot give any better guide for the state of our market than the statement that goods generally have advanced 15 to 25 percent.[33]

The city rebuilt quickly after every fire but still it took eight fires to convince the residents that not only did they desperately need more adequate fire protection but also bricks and mortar would have to replace wood and canvas if the city wanted to exchange conflagration for commerce.[34]

Shortage of Money and Capital

Of immediate concern to the merchant was the supply of money, both as a medium of exchange and as an investment resource. Coins, particularly those of denominations over twenty-five cents used in retail transactions, were in short supply in the early 1850s. Coins of less than twenty-five cents were almost totally absent given the inflated prices of the San Francisco market. To compensate for the lack of coins of all denominations, gold dust served as a substitute until the establishment of a branch mint in San Francisco in 1854. The issuance of paper currency had been prohibited by the state legislature and with no federal mint west of the Mississippi, merchants had to conduct business transactions either by the simple barter of commercial items or through the more common exchange of gold dust. By 1851-52 a shortage of gold occurred when the San Francisco banks, through their agents in the mining areas, purchased all available dust. The city merchants desperately needed the gold both as a medium of exchange within the city and for remittances to eastern creditors. The merchants brought dust where and when they could, often without assaying its value, with the result that eastern creditors frequently complained about the odd mixture of gold, sand, and quartz particles.[35]

A major annoyance to the merchants was the federal regulation that prohibited the payment of import duties in ingots or dust. The United States Treasury required gold coins, which meant the added expense to the merchants of having to import coins from the East to pay duties at the San Francisco Custom House. When the United States Assayer in San Francisco, responding to merchant complaints, contracted with a local bank to coin fifty-dollar slugs, Congress prohibited their acceptance in payment of custom duties. Though this prohibition was not enforced, the supply of coins remained a critical problem for the city until the late 1850s when the newly minted coins made their appearance.

The coin shortage only reflected the more severe lack of capital in San Francisco. In the early boom years of 1848-1850 almost all sales were in the form of cash. Merchants, with limited amounts of capital of their own, demanded cash in a healthy economic environment where gold was plentiful. But after 1850 they began extending credit to customers, particularly to the upcountry merchants in the mining areas. Credit was usually extended until Steamer Day at which time the merchant demanded his money so that he could remit funds to eastern creditors, send cash advances for new goods, or deposit funds in an eastern bank. A number of merchants maintained separate accounts in eastern banks. "It was part of the prudence in the California merchant having obligations to meet in the Atlantic states," said one San Francisco import merchant, "to keep there a reserve fund, as large as possible, to draw upon in case of an emergency."[36]

Bank loans were available to the merchants on a selective basis. As early as 1850 San Francisco banks offered short-term bank loans at approximately 10 percent interest rate a month. Rates dropped off in 1853 to between 2 and 2½ percent for long term loans. Unsecured loans could be had at between 2 and 3 percent a month. The merchant-shopkeepers experienced the most difficulty in obtaining loans. They did not appear to have credit lines to the local banks, and what additional money they needed came generally from noninstitutional sources—friends or family. The larger merchants could more easily obtain credit from local banks and foreign sources than from eastern financial institutions or those San Francisco banks which served as branch offices for eastern banks. Easterners continued to look upon the California trade as a speculative risk. However, the local bankers, many of whom were originally merchants in San Francisco or the East, or who combined a merchant occupation with a banking function, provided the necessary capital to rebuild after the fires and recessions. Capital was also available from foreign sources. William Sherman, a local San Francisco banker, dismayed that California gold left the state for eastern banks as fast as it came down from the mountains, observed that foreign money in the San Francisco market loaned at high rates of interest did not compensate for the capital loss.[37]

The capital resources for San Francisco's economic growth were thus supplied, if only indirectly, from the East and Europe. Either in the form of a personal loan, as from a father in Boston to his son in San Francisco, or an institutional loan from a New York or London bank to its San Francisco branch office and hence to the merchant, an adequate though uneven supply of capital existed in the 1850s. Through the international and eastern money market, however, San Francisco was tied to the fortunes and fluctuations of the national economy. Such ties would cause economic dislocations additional to the already severe problems of the local economy.

Efforts to Order the Economy: The Chamber of Commerce

To operate and survive in the San Francisco market, which cycled through periods of temporary booms, recessions, and depressions, the first generation of merchants were forced either to rationalize the economic environment of their city or face financial ruin, close shop, and move on. In the 1850s their efforts, both collective and individual, were generally unsuccessful, for they schemed against each other to a degree which all but destroyed the spirit and limited accomplishments of their collective action.

The formation of the San Francisco Chamber of Commerce was the first major collective effort by the city's merchants to insert a measure of order into the chaotic marketplace. Founded in late 1849 by the leading merchants of the city, the Chamber of Commerce sought to order its own internal commercial ranks and, by requesting assistance from governments at all levels, to promote the general commerce of the city. Its constitution and by-laws, and hence its functions, were modeled after the Chamber of Commerce in New York. In local matters affecting almost all members, it set standard commission rates and established a board of arbitration to hear disputes arising out of mercantile transactions. The committee of arbitration afforded the merchant community "a tribunal . . . in which disputes arising out of mercantile transactions might be arranged on equitable bases," thus avoiding the expenses and delays of litigation. The committee's service was used extensively by the merchants, particularly in matters related to damage claims. The chamber also set the valuation standard for foreign coins used in the San Francisco market, and established uniform pilot, freight, cartage, and wharfage rates in an attempt to standardize charges and make San Francisco competitive with other ports.[38]

Aware of their dependence for economic livelihood upon forces outside of San Francisco, the city's merchants, through the Chamber of Commerce, petitioned Congress for assistance to halt the practice of eastern merchants who shipped unwanted cargoes of "unspecified merchandise." The petitioners complained that they could not forecast the supply or description of goods to San Francisco and hence were unable to control prices in their market. In order to rationalize the trade, the San Francisco Chamber of Commerce in 1856 memorialized Congress to pass a law "providing, that all goods, wares and merchandise shipped from the Atlantic to the Pacific ports of the United States shall be entered and described on the manifest of [the] vessels . . . the amount and kind of property shipped." In an attempt to improve communications with other commercial centers and attract more business to the city, the merchants, through the Chamber of Commerce, also requested Washington to provide faster and more frequent mail service from the nation's eastern and southern ports. Another request called for government assistance to improve the competitive position of their harbor, with projects to dredge deepwater shipping channels, and build lighthouses, bonded warehouses, a federal mint, a coastal navy, a trans-Isthmus railroad, and a transcontinental telegraph and railroad. In addition they petitioned Congress to remove inequitable custom duties, tariffs, and state bankruptcy laws.[39]

Individually the merchants sought to order in a more efficient manner their own business procedures. The lack of procedure and information available to the merchants of 1849-50 left too much to chance. And as one visitor on the scene in the early 1850s observed, the merchants exhibited "less method and system in their transactions than any class of traders I ever saw." "Whatever they do," he complained, "is done in a helter-skelter, topsy-turvey sort of way. They never take time to do a thing well, but are always going and coming, or bustling about in such a manner, that one would suppose they are making preparations for some calamitous emergency, rather than attending to the every day routine of an established occupation."[40]

Improved Communication with the East

One very important individual routine which the merchants attempted to improve was that of more frequent communication with commercial establishments in the East. For at a time when the East exerted considerable influence in the San Francisco marketplace, it behooved the San Francisco merchant to cultivate these valuable eastern contacts. Also, the western merchant stood to profit handsomely from any new business directed to him. The son of a New Bedford whaling merchant, S. Griffiths Morgan, who through his father and uncle held valuable commercial contacts with merchant houses in Boston, New York (Grinnell, Minturn and Co.), and Cranton (Nye, Perkins and Co.), kept the companies abreast of the market conditions in San Francisco. In return, Morgan received valuable information about business conditions on the American East Coast and in China. Another merchant who brought with him to San Francisco business contacts from New York, Boston, Philadelphia, and Brooklyn, and hence a large volume of commission business, constantly cultivated, and when necessary placated, his eastern suppliers. As a result, his reputation was such that when a merchant requested from New York's leading shipping company, Howland and Aspinwall, the name of a reputable San Francisco merchant contact, Alfred Robinson received the trade and the commissions.[41]

San Francisco merchants also called upon their merchant relatives in the East to report business conditions, make purchases, or provide necessary credit. A San Francisco surveyor turned commission merchant arranged for the shipment of bedding, stationery, and gunpowder through his father and brother in Philadelphia. The Seligman family in New York kept the brothers supplied in San Francisco. A Philadelphia merchant purchased dry goods for his nephew in San Francisco, and extended to him credit while awaiting repayment in gold dust. And all the time commercial information passed back and forth between East Coast and West.[42]

The San Francisco merchant continually performed important services for his eastern associates. The importer who worked on commission located a market for the goods and remitted the proceeds (either in gold or by bank draft) to the eastern owner. For ships chartered by an eastern company, the San Francisco merchant arranged for repairs, located cargoes, and directed the vessels to their next destination. Or if goods were destined for the inland towns, he arranged for their transshipment by river boat, obtained the necessary insurance, and paid all local bills. When ships could not find return cargoes or goods could not be sold at a profit, the San Francisco merchant, with the power of attorney from an eastern associate, disposed of the ship and cargo at best advantage to the owner. Or if he anticipated a bullish market, the local agent stored the goods, informed the eastern owner, and waited

The Merchants' Exchange on Battery Street, the center for transacting business among the merchants in the 1850s. The old Customs House is to the left.

impatiently for the rise in prices. Finally, the San Francisco merchant constantly informed his eastern suppliers as to quantities and prices of goods in the local market.[43]

The San Francisco merchants also performed some personal services for their eastern associates. They reported on the welfare of mutual friends and relatives, passed on messages, and searched out investment opportunities. In addition they purchased real estate and mining stocks and even collected debts from those who, by moving to San Francisco, attempted to escape their eastern creditors. A New York merchant learned from his brother of efforts to collect the debts from two New York City merchant-exiles who sought refuge in San Francisco.

I [have] taken pains since my arrival here to ascertain if anything could be collected from Misters Baxter and Howes on account of a Note I brought from you against them . . . I hear that he [Howes] has refused to pay any of his old debts. I called on Baxter, who told me, that as soon as he was in a situation for it (which he thought would be before very long) he should make a proposition for settlement with his creditors[;] he has to my knowledge been unfortunate here, having been burned out twice + losing heavily each time[;] I have not thought it advisable to take any legal steps to secure the demand, as it would cost from $50 to $100 + would result in nothing, as all such suits do in this place.[44]

These quasi-merchant services not only assisted eastern merchants to gauge the business climate of San Francisco but, more importantly, served to maintain the valuable personal contacts in the East which the San Francisco merchants desperately needed in order to survive the ever increasing business competition in their city.

Occupational Specialization

A further measure undertaken by the city merchants to insure their economic survival in the San Francisco marketplace was their gradual shift in the 1850 decade from merchant generalist to merchant specialist. The early 1849-50 merchants dealt in a multitude of goods and services. The house of Little and Pope sold on commission bricks, molasses, flour, tobacco, candles, clothing articles, cigars, spices, cement, barley, meats (pork, beef, and ham), apples, whale oil, lumber, and coal. A merchant with a hardware store saw the opportunity for a high profit in butter, purchased 80 kegs, and profited handsomely from his brief venture into the commodity market. Many of the larger establishments such as the commission house of Godefrey and Sillem and Co. in their first two years in San Francisco, besides trading a multitude of goods, also served as bankers, credit managers, debt collectors, and purchasing agents. The merchant-bankers who had capital reserves of their own also bought and sold gold, and traded drafts and bills of exchange through business connections in eastern cities for their San Francisco customers. They guarded their customers' gold in locked safes and were called upon "to pay out certain amounts for the owner upon written or oral request." Sometimes the merchant mixed the funds of his client with his own, "making use of them as needed in his business, but expecting . . . to meet any orders drawn on him or to return the funds to their owner when demanded. Sometimes the depositor would be allowed a small rate of interest. Other times nothing would be paid."[45]

Merchants in the early 1850s also ventured into real estate speculation. In fact, it seemed that just about everyone—merchant-banker, carpenter, ship's captain, jeweler—speculated in real estate. In the early 1850s land in and around San Francisco "was a commodity to be traded for profit fully as much as it was a site for a metropolis." The merchants owned the majority of the commercial buildings of the city, including for a while the United States Custom House, and most of the private residences, wharfs, and undeveloped but valuable beach lots. They also speculated early in property south of San Francisco— San Mateo, Santa Barbara, Los Angeles, San Diego—to where the more successful would retire.[46]

In addition to the full-time merchants, nonmerchants—those who defined themselves as employed in other occupations—often crossed occupational lines seeking quick and profitable bargains in the marketplace. Add to those the constant migration of eastern and foreign merchants to San Francisco in the early 1850s, and the result was an overcrowded occupation. The city merchants composed almost 15 percent of the working male population of the city in 1852, and with over 3,000 merchants in the marketplace, the individual merchant had either to meet the competition or face financial disaster.

The result of the pressure was an emerging specialization among the merchants which in turn helped to improve the distribution of goods throughout the city's mercantile network. The new division of labor also sorted out from the marketplace those part-time, profit-seeking nonmerchants. Lawyers and doctors, while continuing to speculate in real estate, left merchandising to the merchant and devoted their talents to clients and patients. The merchants devoted their attention to the supply and demand requirements of the commodities they knew best and, by so doing, attempted to cut their financial losses. Commission merchants began to specialize in specific services or commodities. An early commission merchant noted the new trend: "Bankers and merchants no more; commission houses are ceasing to be jobbers; furniture houses no longer sell anchors and chairs; silks and ribbons are no longer found forgotten under piles of overcoats."[47]

The wholesale trade, for example, passed more and more to the larger specialized merchant houses. The *Merchants Magazine and Commercial Review* reported in late 1851, that

Early in the year the attention of all classes and callings was directed
to this new field [San Francisco trade] for commercial enterprise, and
it was deemed merely necessary to make shipments there to realize a
golden harvest. As might have been expected, the anticipation of
many were doomed to disappointment . . . The trade, of late, has
passed into fewer hands, and is now confined principally to experienced mercantile houses, who are cautious in their shipments, and
generally send out assorted cargoes, selected with a regard to the
wants of that merchant, and which, so far, have yielded satisfactory
returns.[48]

And a San Francisco commission merchant warned a friend in New
York not to move for there were already too many merchants in San
Francisco. He wrote: "Do not advise anyone who is . . . situated in
New York to come here, for the competition will be greater than there
and here there is no stability." The merchants' newspaper complained, "We have too many merchants—too many mechanics—too
many traders, doctors, lawyers—in proportion to our interior population." "We need," the paper concluded, "the equalization of our
country to our city population." Under intense competition, the merchants were forced to specialize in order to survive.[49]

About the time San Francisco called for more miners and farmers to
settle in the interior and hence serve as consumers for the merchant
warehouses, California agriculture had developed to a point where
surpluses in certain commodities were common. By the mid-1850s
merchants who once imported grain and foodstuffs from the East
Coast and South America, had to redirect their trading network and
specialize in specific commodities. California wheat production,
which increased from 17,000 barrels in 1850 to 6 million barrels in
1860, opened up new merchant positions. But it also demanded the
expertise of the specialist rather than the services of the older and outdated merchant generalist. By 1860 the only merchant generalists in
the city were the retail shopkeepers.

Attempts to Improve Local Business Ethics

Whereas the merchants, through their individual and collective
efforts, worked to order their own commercial marketplace and occupational ranks in a rational manner, there appeared to be no similar

effort to improve the business ethics which governed individual behavior and destiny. The early regulations governing business operations failed to detail as illegal certain practices considered unethical by eastern commercial standards. And even where laws attempted to set mercantile standards and procedures, lax enforcement of these laws encouraged, in the merchant's hasty pursuit of profits, flagrant violations.

Custom duties, for example, were frequently avoided by merchants who failed to enter all cargo items on a ship's manifest, purposely mislabeled goods, or falsely valued imports. The United States Customs Collector complained to Washington that too many San Francisco merchants avoided duties altogether by transferring their cargoes from ocean ships to coastal boats in small coves near the city. Importers frequently avoided the posting of bonds on American-made goods, which, because these items were placed on ships that stopped at foreign ports on their journey from the East Coast to San Francisco, were considered by customs authorities to be foreign goods subject to duties. Simply by altering the ship's log, more and more vessels made "nonstop voyages" between the East and West Coast until the mid-1850s, when Washington altered the custom regulations.[50]

More common, however, where the perfectly legal schemes designed by cunning merchants to outmaneuver competitors. Those with valuable commercial intelligence from the East parlayed into a profit the knowledge that certain goods were on the way West. William T. Coleman, one of San Francisco's most eminent import merchants, described how he outwitted his competitors amid the fluctuations of the San Francisco market. When a flood of goods was known to be on the way to San Francisco, Coleman advised that to be successful

a merchant must quickly dispatch his stock to the interior, or else, on a falling market, go slower when prices were advancing. Commodore Martin was the marine reporter of the day and boarded ships at the Heads [Golden Gate], bringing in the news . . . Independent of regular subscription to Martin's enterprise, and [my] subscription to the Merchants' Exchange, I paid Martin fifty dollars a month to report to me privately before he did to anyone else . . . He would sometimes report to me a ship coming in with a cargo of goods that were high and prices sensitive. At noon, or before three o'clock, my entire stock of the article would be loaded for Sacramento, Marysville, Stockton . . . with instructions to correspondents to close them the next day at auction, . . . and before the vessel came to anchor everything would be gone. This required very prompt action and sharp work. The next day the report of these vessels would have its decided effect on the market in San Francisco, but the interior people learned of it later.[51]

Thus Captain Martin collected his fee from Coleman, and no doubt from others as well, while Sacramento merchants and consumers paid dearly for isolation and Coleman pocketed his profit.

Less cunning but no less ambitious merchants rushed out in small boats to meet incoming ships and bargained with the captain for a valuable cargo. The captains did not know the current market prices of their cargoes, and when offered 50 to 100 percent above the purchase price, they joyfully sold out for themselves or for the account of the cargo owner. One merchant observed that "the merchant who got to the vessel first was generally the luckiest fellow." Others anxious to receive market information from eastern cities eagerly sought letters at the post office on steamer day. Unwilling to wait hours in line which often stretched ten blocks from the single window inside the frame post office, merchants found willing takers within a hundred yards of the window eager to exchange their place in line for as much as twenty dollars.[52]

Monopolies accrued to certain merchants either by chance or design. A merchant finding himself with a shipment of consigned goods known to be in short supply had eager purchasers outside his office the next morning. The seller with buyers outside, one importer reported, "would naturally feel that in case the first did not accept his terms, the second one would, and consequently he might put up his prices to suit himself." In the early days, 100 percent markups were frequently demanded and received, and it was the "shrewder sort, and those having the best knowledge of their business" who profited from monopolistic situations.[53]

As common as the monopolies which occurred through chance or the fluctations of the market, were those engineered by design, particularly in "certain articles of daily use and absolute necessity."[54] One San Francisco merchant firm monopolized the importation of wheat before California began to produce for her own population. Claus Spreckels cornered the early sugar market and instructed his agents in the mining towns to do the same. Another merchant complained that the newspaper and periodical business in San Francisco "is monopolized by one man here because he has got an agent in New York who looks out for him."[55] Sometimes monopolistic greed led to large losses. A San Francisco merchant instructed his agent to buy up every wooden bucket and milk pail he could locate in Stockton. The same day the firm purchased buckets and pails in San Francisco and Sacramento. As instructed, the Stockton agent purchased all available buckets at an average price of three dollars per dozen. He later committed to his diary, "I was instructed not to sell till I got word from San Francisco. I was offered for those I held two hundred percent profit, but was not permitted to sell. Our San Francisco firm wanted twenty-five dollars per dozen. The result was those who wanted buckets had them made of tin, sheet iron, and anything they could use. The speculation was a miserable failure. The price was so high that it paid to bring them across the Isthmus from the east. Our loss was very large, as we held thousands of dozens. This mania . . . ran in every kind of merchandise that was wanted."[56]

Another profit-making scheme engaged in by a few unscrupulous San Francisco merchants was to receive goods on consignment from an East Coast merchant, sell the goods at a heavy profit, and report back to the original owner that because of the flooded market his shipment brought only a small profit. A variation was for a San Francisco merchant to purchase the cargo for his own account, allowing the original owner a small profit, and turn around and sell it at considerable profit to himself. Eastern merchants with limited knowledge of current prices in San Francisco in the early 1850s had no alternative but to trust the integrity of their San Francisco contacts. One Boston merchant who believed a San Francisco merchant had sold his cargo without returning the proper profits to Boston wrote to him angrily: "We know your markets as well as we do that of New Orleans and have been surprised and disappointed at your report of sales and shall write you more on the subject hereafter." The Boston merchant threatened his San Francisco agent with legal action and sternly reminded him that his good reputation in Boston would suffer if his unethical behavior continued.[57]

With improved communication to the East Coast and the increased reliance of San Francisco merchants upon eastern suppliers, such practices declined. Nevertheless, unethical behavior continued among the merchants well into the late nineteenth century. As members of a class which appeared decidedly more concerned with the ultimate end of accumulating material wealth than with the means by which their fortunes could be earned, the merchants exhibited at worst habitual greed and at best concern for the reputation of their marketplace and city.

"Luck Alone Ruled His Destiny"

Anyone visiting Yerba Buena Cove in the 1840s would barely recognize the location in 1850. Sleek clipper ships filled the harbor, people of all nationalities thronged the streets, fancy hotels, stores, theaters, and churches stood on what were once barren sand hills. Only the Mission and the Presidio seemed unchanged. Richard Dana revisited the port where, twenty-five years earlier, he had shipped out on a hide and tallow vessel. He noticed a pile of dry hides lying on a wharf beside a vessel. To him, the hides had "brought us out here, . . . and it was only by getting them that we would escape from the [west] coast . . . to home and civilized life." But by 1860 San Francisco was home and civilized life to over 50,000 people. They had built a city which in ten years had been transformed from a temporary collection of wooden shacks and canvas tents into a permanent metropolis.

The city had changed not only in appearance but in function. Dana inquired of a sailor on the San Francisco wharf in 1860 about the hide trade. He responded, "There is very little of it." Dana asked, "Then the old business of trading up and down the coast and curing hides for cargoes is over?" "Oh yes, sir," the sailor said, "those old times of the *Pilgrim,* and *Alert California,* that we read about, are gone by."[58] In their place were warehouses, manufacturing and merchant establishments, banks, and shipyards. The commercial center of the West Coast resided in San Francisco, and its trading network extended to Europe, Latin America, and the Far East. It was in fact the warehouse for the West Coast and the interior regions as far east as the Rocky Mountains.

Amidst increasing competition within the merchant occupations, and after repeated efforts to order their economic environment subject to booms, depressions, and fires, the earlier spirit of optimism had given way to anxiety. No discernible rational patterns for economic stability and survival were evident to San Francisco residents by 1860. The gambling spirit, born in the earlier days of the gold rush, still existed. "Men revelled in great projects and hazardous operations, preferring great risks to the game of plodding industry," reported California's first prominent historian, Hubert H. Bancroft. But even those merchants who engaged in "plodding industry," and put their best individual and collective efforts in the 1850s to the task of bringing order to their chaotic marketplace, discovered too often the difficulty of forecasting the future. Certain limited measures had improved their mercantile environment relative to 1849-1859. Yet little had changed in the first decade. One early resident observed that the city's merchants found "that luck alone ruled his destiny, the requisites to success elsewhere . . . had little to do with it." Accident and chance, the merchants believed, rather than rational human calculation continued to dictate their immediate individual and collective destiny.[59]

3

OCCUPATIONAL MOBILITY

The kind of work one does has been found to be the most reliable indicator of social stratification. As one historical sociologist has noted: "Observers of social life—from novelists to pollsters—have found that occupational class is one of the major factors which differentiate people's beliefs, values, norms, customs, and occasionally some of their emotional expressions."[1] Used as both index and indicator of class position, occupations can be used as an important determinant of a society's structure. And to trace the movement of a man or group of men from one occupation at one time to another at a later stage is to trace the path of vertical or horizontal movement within social space. "The sum of those movements determines the patterns and rate of social mobility, the degree of openness, within a society."[2]

The Occupational Scale

It is extremely difficult to set a hierarchy, or scale, of occupations so that individuals who are traced over time may reveal their career patterns. Yet the scale predetermines to a large extent the patterns and rates of social mobility that the historian will discover in any population under study: "The categories that are chosen form the parameters of social mobility and the intervals on the hierarchy of social rank. They determine which shifts between specific jobs can be considered instances of vertical mobility and which differences of occupation between people can be said to indicate differences of status or class."[3]

Since this study is concerned primarily with white-collar mobility, specifically occupational mobility within the merchant class, merchant occupations were rank-ordered to reflect the reality of the mid- to late-nineteenth-century occupational world of San Francisco. The aim of the measurement is to be specific enough to discover small but significant occupational changes, yet broad enough so that mobility rates are not generated artificially by excessive classification levels.

The classification scheme must also account for the diversity and functional differences within this occupational group. Therefore this study includes peddlers, traders, and corner grocers, as well as the more prestigious import and commission merchants and merchant-manufacturers, all of whom were directly involved in the process of distribution. The rationale for including peddlers, traders, and petty shopkeepers in a study which also focuses on higher status merchants is that it allows for the investigation of occupational mobility within the total spectrum of the mercantile sector. Excluded, however, are those who traded in real estate, stocks, or money (finance-related services), and those employed exclusively in the artisan crafts.

A merchant occupation carried with it a high level of prestige in mid-nineteenth-century America. The merchants generated the capital and directed the commerce in communities large and small across the country. In the larger cities of the East Coast, particularly in New York and Boston, they assembled a commercial network which returned immense profits and hence prestige. They built churches, libraries, schools, and museums, and acquired the material possessions expected of their life style. In San Francisco, too, the midcentury merchant commanded high status. Upon the death of one of the leading citizens, a San Francisco newspaper editorialized, "He was a merchant. There is no profession more honorable."[4]

But there were distinct gradations within the merchant occupation. At the top were the commission merchants, importers, wholesalers (including those who combined wholesaling and retailing), jobbers, and later the merchant-manufacturers. The commission merchant sold goods consigned to him by shipping merchants or wholesalers at another port. He seldom owned the goods but usually sold them for his client to retailers, or more commonly, to wholesalers. The wholesalers, sometimes known as jobbers, were the link between the producer of commodities and the retail customer. They provided the producers with a market and with some idea of its demands and scale, while assuring the consumer access to specific products of a determined type at a specified time. Additionally, they helped to finance retailers by selling them goods on credit of one to three months.[5] The merchant-manufacturers, those who produced goods such as stoves, rope, furniture, and other household items, and sold them either wholesale or retail, were relatively few in number until the 1870s.

Below this rank were the general retail merchants—those who owned their stores in partnership with others, or if in business alone, traded in items or commodities crafted or manufactured by someone other than themselves. In terms of items traded, the general retail merchants were those who sold clothing, dry goods, hardware, provisions, produce, and spices.

Lowest on the occupational scale were the petty merchants: the retail shopkeepers, dealers, traders, grocers, and peddlers who, although not listed as merchants in the city directories, nevertheless performed a merchant function. The grocers were the most numerous within this category. Dispersed throughout the city, the corner grocers sold a variety of family groceries "not necessarily much of any one thing, but a little of many kinds of family supplies, so as to meet the contingent wants of the residents of the surrounding blocks." The wife of the owner frequently assisted in the store. Almost all grocery shops had a bar in the rear, shielded from view by a board partition with a separate entrance from the outside, and a suggestive sign: "Sample Room."[6] Also included in the category of petty merchants were those who traded in items such as boots, hats, or cigars which they frequently handcrafted in their small shops.[7]

In order to measure occupational mobility of San Francisco's first generation of merchants, it is not enough to investigate simply the movement of individuals within the confines of the merchant occupational scale. Many people moved from nonmerchant white-collar jobs (clerk, saloon keeper, civil servant) and the blue-collar ranks (tinner, drayman) into the merchant occupations. Also a large number of merchants departed their commission houses and retail shops for eventual careers in banking, manufacturing, or saloons. Therefore, to measure the direction, distance, and frequency of these occupational changes, the three merchant occupational categories were placed within the general context of the city's total occupational hierarchy.

Finally, the occupational experience of the San Francisco merchants was compared with that of the general working populations of the city and, where data were available, with that of other cities in approximately the same period. In an attempt to make the study generally comparable with those mobility studies already completed, the nonmerchant occupations were ranked and grouped according to the social-economic groupings of occupations originally devised by the census statistician Alba Edwards in the 1930s and employed, with minor modifications, in most American mobility studies that have been carried out since then. The merchant groupings for this study (petty shopkeepers, general merchants, and the importers-wholesalers) were then inserted into the Edwards scale and placed within the occupational hierarchy relative to the nonmerchant groupings.[8] (For a methodological discussion of two samples, the merchants and the general employed male population of the city, see Appendix A, "Methodological Notes." The occupational scheme utilized for this study is listed in Appendix B.)

Occupational Scale

  I High White-Collar
  - (1) *Professionals*
  - (2) *Major Proprietors, Managers, and Officials* (to include importers, commission merchants, wholesalers and wholesaler-retailers, and merchant-manufacturers)
  - (3) *General Merchants* (retailers)

  II Low White-Collar
  - (4) *Clerks and Salesmen*
  - (5) *Petty Proprietors, Managers, and Officials* (to include peddlers, traders, and dealers)

  III Blue Collar
  - (6) *Skilled, Semiskilled, Service*
  - (7) *Low Manual*

Occupational Instability

One of the most apparent characteristics of San Francisco in the early 1850s was the high degree of occupational flux, indeed disorder, which existed in the city. Preachers without congregations served drinks in saloons, a physician pared potatoes and washed dishes in a local restaurant, and a number of unemployed lawyers were seen fishing around the wharfs for crabs. "Men were not in the least fastidious about their occupation," one visitor noted; and few, it seemed, were engaged in the trade or profession for which they had been trained. Another observer of the San Francisco scene reported that the "great recognized orders of society were tumbled topsy-turvey"; doctors and dentists performed as best they could as draymen, barbers, or shoeblacks; merchants tried laboring and some laborers entered merchant occupations. It appeared that every class in the city, "adventurers, merchants, lawyers, clerks, tradesmen, mechanics," rented, but usually owned, "lodging-houses, eating and drinking houses, billiard rooms and gambling saloons." Seeking quick profits in an expanding city, "they dabbled in beach and water lots . . . and new town allotments over the whole country; speculated in flour, beef, pork and potatoes; in lumber and other building materials; in dry goods and soft, hard goods and wet; bought and sold, wholesale and retail, and were ready to change their occupation and embark in some new nondescript undertaking after two minutes consideration."[9]

Much of the initial instability in San Francisco's occupational structure was directly related to the fortunes and misfortunes of the miners. Success in the mines resulted in a shortage of labor and a demand for merchandise. Similarly, slack times in the mines caused a decreased demand for goods while scores of unemployed miners sought alternate employment in San Francisco. Almost immediately after the initial influx of gold seekers passed through San Francisco on their way to the mines, the first group of discouraged miners returned to the Bay Area. To unearth gold demanded both physical labor and superb luck. Many disappointed men, more accustomed to clerking at a counter than digging into quartz, eventually departed the mine fields not only without gold, but also without their health. For a time miners averaged between eight and sixteen dollars a day, but even then daily living expenses, particularly for food, all too often equaled the daily diggings. Disillusioned in their expectation of an immediate fortune, the miners filtered back to San Francisco and, if they could afford transportation, to the East Coast. There were reports of quick fortunes in rich placers, but by 1850-51 a mood of discouragement prevailed in the mining towns of California. One miner reported to his father,

It is a wicked *shame* that *such glowing accounts* of the miners success should be pictured out in the *newspapers* + cause people to leave their happy homes + family + friends to be thus disappointed . . . when will people in the states learn to believe that there is thousands here that would be glad to get enough gold to get home with, + it is too true: there are only one or 2 out of an hundred that make much more than their living in the mines . . . it is the hardest work that a man ever tryed to do . . . I will go back to San Francisco + get work + provide for my family; had I known what I know now, I never would have left my home and family for California, but I may profit by it in some way, for if ever I live to get home, I shall have learned a lesson that will do me some good.[10]

With little to show for their efforts and lacking the capital to return home, many miners moved to San Francisco. Although they had failed in the mines, the gold seekers were enticed by the reports of merchant profits in the city. And for those not accustomed to the hardships of outdoor living, the comfort of urban life "was something more to their taste."[11] One San Francisco resident, looking back on his disappointing mining experience, probably expressed a common opinion when he recollected, "I had never been accustomed to any hard labor, and consequently was unfitted for mining, and though I was in a rich locality, it occured to me one day I was not getting rich very fast . . . I had made an average of about ten dollars a day. This proved so far short of my brilliant expectations, that I abandoned the business of mining in disgust and proceeded to San Francisco."[12]

In the city, the former miners entered a variety of occupations. A surprising number of clerks, "who had tried mining and found it beyond their powers of endurance," sought employment in their old line of work. A commission merchant in San Francisco wrote to friends back East about the flock of returning miners and reported, "we have applications almost every day by clerks for employment. The labor at the mines is too severe." A few had some savings to open a store of their own. Others were forced to work for someone else, save, and if attracted to merchandising, order an invoice of goods and hope to turn a profit on the initial sales. But most, it seemed, accepted any job so long as it paid well, and with a shortage of labor in San Francisco from 1849 to 1853, an ounce a day (sixteen dollars) attracted into the blue-collar ranks those who in former days, before they tried mining, had worked as lawyers, merchants, clerks, brokers, and ship captains.[13]

There was not so much a labor shortage in San Francisco as a shortage of blue-collar workers. The cost of the voyage from the East Coast to San Francisco and the mines had filtered out many in the labor pool who normally would have filled the blue-collar jobs in the city. Those blue-collar workers who came West did not migrate, at least initially, in such numbers as to satiate the demand for service and skilled or manual labor. In addition, the blue-collar workers who had migrated to California came primarily to work the mines; and while they were probably no less successful at it than the miners who had formerly occupied white-collar jobs in the eastern states, the latter had accumulated small savings with which to move to an urban center demanding their services. Wages therefore in the blue-collar occupations remained high, the highest of any city in the United States. Also, the white-collar job market, even given San Francisco's phenomenal growth in the early years, could not absorb the growing numbers of those migrating into the city with white-collar training. The inevitable result was that "men who lived in comfort and affluence at home were often glad to get the most menial occupation in San Francisco."[14]

Given the general level of occupational flux in San Francisco between 1849 and 1852 when the city grew from 3,000 to over 30,000, those who filled the merchants' houses came from diverse occupational backgrounds before arriving in San Francisco.

Occupational Origins and "Shipboard" Mobility

Of the first San Francisco merchant generation in 1852, six out of every ten had formerly occupied a merchant position before arriving in the city. The rest had either moved from clerical work (20 percent) or the blue-collar ranks (18 percent), and of the second group, three out of every four entered from a skilled or semiskilled trade. However, within the more prestigious ranks of commission merchant, importer, and wholesaler, only 10 percent moved from the blue-collar ranks. The entry rates from blue-collar to the other merchant categories—general merchants (20 percent) and petty-merchant shopkeepers (26 percent)—confirmed a distinct pattern. The higher the merchant rank, the larger the proportion transferring from prior merchant jobs and the fewer moving from blue-collar positions into merchant positions.[15]

The previous occupational experience of the native-born and foreign-born merchants was surprisingly similar in the early 1850s. Approximately six out of every ten in both categories engaged in a merchant occupation before their arrival in the city. There was also little difference in the recruiting pattern of the native-born and foreign-born merchants from among ihe blue-collar ranks. In fact, the recruit-ment rate from the working class about equaled the percent drawn from the clerical occupations, which were traditionally considered to be the major training ground for the merchant occupations. The first generation of merchants, both native-born and foreign-born, experi-enced high rates of occupational mobility in the process of their geo-graphical transfer to the city.[16]

A somewhat different perspective of shipboard mobility is obtained when we refine the direction of the occupational move. For example, a New York City retail grocer who sold fresh staples at the streetcorner stand and then moved to San Francisco where he imported shipments of merchandise and sold wholesale, made an occupational leap of considerable distance. Similarly, the mobility of a barber from New York to a position of county clerk in San Francisco was clearly an occupational advancement, especially as the job was worth about $100,000 a year.[17]

Utilizing Edwards' seven-level occupational scale with which to measure shipboard mobility rates, a more realistic view of the occupa-tional flux of San Francisco's first merchants emerged from the data. More than half (54 percent) of the first generation of merchants moved up at least one step on the occupational ladder between the time they departed their former residence and entered a merchant occupation in San Francisco. As a group they were far more likely to experience upward occupational mobility than the general employed population of the city. Of all employed males, only about a third advanced while more than half remained occupationally static in their move to the West Coast.[18]

As would be expected, the rates of occupational mobility increased with the status-prestige level. Of the petty merchants, grocers for the most part, almost half had experienced downward occupational mo-bility in their geographical transfer to San Francisco. Either they lacked the original capital to establish themselves at the same level as their previous job, or lost what capital they did possess in an unsuc-cessful speculative endeavor. The occupational success of the general merchants and importer-wholesalers resulted less from their mobility within the merchant occupations than by their occupational advance-ment from blue-collar and nonmerchant clerk positions. Whereas well

Table 3.1. Occupational mobility rates: prior occupation to merchant occupation, 1852 (in percent).

	Upward	Same	Downward	(N)
Petty merchants	26	26	48	(20)
General merchants	49	45	6	(68)
Wholesaler-importers	75	25	—	(40)
All merchants	54	36	10	(128)
Native-born merchants	55	35	10	(95)
Foreign-born merchants	52	39	9	(33)
General population	36	51	13	(55)

SOURCE: California State Census, 1852.

over half of the general merchants and importer-wholesalers had formerly worked in merchant occupations, only about a third of them experienced occupational advancement in their move to San Francisco. Of the former nonmerchants, however, four out of five had experienced an occupational advancement by attaining a general merchant or importer-wholesaler position after arriving in San Francisco.

A New Bedford, Massachusetts, commission merchant who moved to San Francisco in the early 1850s noted the degree of occupational mobility among the merchant class of the city when he complained to a friend in New York: "Many shippers to California are men of limited means . . . and most of the common merchants here . . . were brought up in a business very different from what they are now in." A provisions merchant from Boston departed for San Francisco in 1849 with a dozen barrels of apples. He sold his apples on the San Francisco wharf at a large profit and entered the hardware business. A newsboy in New York City, after selling 1,200 copies of the *New York Herald* upon arrival in San Francisco, opened a retail and wholesale book and stationery store. A man entered a specific merchant activity in San Francisco not because of his training, though that helped, but following his intuitive sense of what item or merchant service appeared in demand, and happenstance.[19]

There were, of course, those commercial exiles sent out to San Francisco by the merchant houses of New York, Boston and Baltimore

—partners or junior employees of the firm, sons or nephews of the owner—who, with ample lines of credit, moved up quickly after their transfer to the West Coast. They accounted probably for no more than 10 percent of the total merchant population, but their impressive eastern business connections gave them a decided advantage in the San Francisco marketplace.

The sons and relatives of New York's merchant houses were sent off to the counting houses and shipyards of San Francisco in the early 1850s in much the same way as New England sent its merchant offspring to New York in the 1830s. A maritime historian of New York who described the development of his port noted that many of the merchants migrated "on their own," but a "considerable part of the migration resulted from the common practice . . . of sending a partner, relative, or junior employee of a firm to handle the business at another port and thus keep all the profits and commissions under control." The practice was so common that "the more active the port, the more such 'commercial exiles' it sent out."[20]

While a few of the top merchant positions were filled by the transcontinental migration of the relatives and business associates of the eastern merchant elite, the ranks remained open and hence available to those seeking occupational opportunities in San Francisco between 1849 and 1852. Three-quarters of the prestigious commission merchants, wholesalers, and importers in 1852 had advanced from the following background: blue-collar occupations, 10 percent; nonmerchant white-collar jobs, 20 percent; the lower status merchant ranks, 45 percent. In fact more importer-wholesalers had merchant experience as petty shopkeepers than had served as importer-wholesalers in their previous occupation. And among the general merchants, where one-fifth formerly wore a blue collar and an additional one-quarter had moved directly from a clerkship, the recruitment pattern also suggested excellent occupational opportunities. Of those emigrating to San Francisco, 40 percent had never worked in a merchant occupation, yet more than half moved up, while only one in ten suffered a loss of occupational status. And as they compared their positions in San Francisco with their former occupations back home, most could find satisfaction in having moved to the West Coast. They had, indeed, experienced shipboard mobility.

Mobility within the City

The degree of shipboard mobility experienced by the first generation of San Franciscans tells us only about the occupational opportunities that initially existed in the city. The more important question is, what were the occupational career patterns of the merchants *after* they settled into their first job? Did they maintain or even advance their occupational status in this frontier city? Were the occupational opportunities in San Francisco—both for the merchants and the general male population—superior to those in the other American cities in the mid-nineteenth century?

The careers of the merchants, and indeed of all groups within the city, were determined in large measure by shifts in the economic structure of San Francisco over time. Between 1852 and 1880 the number of white-collar jobs, particularly of clerical and sales positions, increased. At the same time, as manufacturing establishments expanded in the decades following the Civil War, the merchant occupations declined relative to other white-collar positions.

Table 3.2. Occupational distributions rates, 1852 and 1880 (in percent).

Occupation	1852 (N = 669)	1880 (N = 731)	Percent change
Blue-collar			
Nonskilled	20	10	-10
Semi- and skilled	44	46	+2
All blue-collar	64	56	-8
White-collar			
Petty proprietors (nonmerchant)	6	6	0
Petty proprietors (merchant)	10	4	-6
Clerical, sales	7	15	+8
General merchants	3	3	0
Importer-wholesalers	1	1	0
Managers, large proprietors, manufacturers (nonmerchant)	3	6	+3
Professional	6	9	+3
All white collar	36	44	+8
All merchants	14	8	-6

SOURCE: California State Census, 1852, and Federal Census, 1880.

The most dramatic occupational shift occurred within the clerical-sales category. The number of these jobs relative to others in the city more than doubled in the span of three decades. Positions in the non-merchant managerial and manufacturing fields also doubled in the same period, and professional jobs increased significantly. The premium placed on skills by manufacturing establishments was reflected in the contraction of the nonskilled blue-collar jobs. Also there was a definite trend away from the small, one-man shops of the 1850s toward the larger mercantile establishments of the 1880s. As the city grew from 30,000 in 1852 to 233,000 in 1880, nonmerchant white-collar job opportunities were increasing while merchant positions were shrinking relative to all occupational opportunities in the city. Given this trend, it is important to determine whether the first-generation merchants maintained their occupational status or experienced downward mobility.

Compared with high white-collar workers in two eastern cities, the San Francisco high status merchants—the importer-wholesalers and general merchants—fared poorly. In Poughkeepsie and Boston, for example, 7 and 8 percent respectively of the high white-collar workers in these two cities slipped to a lower occupational level between their first job and last job; in San Francisco the slippage rate was 13 percent. However, among the low white-collar petty shopkeepers, the largest of the three merchant groups in absolute numbers, over half were upwardly mobile during the span of their careers in San Francisco—a rate twice as high as that for the low white-collar workers of either Boston or Poughkeepsie.

Finally, among the low manual workers in San Francisco, only 13 percent had moved into white-collar occupations in their last job, half the climbing rate of Boston and somewhat lower than the experience of the low manual workers in Poughkeepsie. Almost half, however, managed to move into the new skilled blue-collar jobs created by San Francisco's manufacturers in the 1860s. The skilled workers in San Francisco discovered no occupational opportunities that exceeded the experience of their counterparts in either Boston or Poughkeepsie.[21]

It can be concluded from table 3.3 that the white-collar sector of San Francisco had a higher level of occupational flux, both up and down, than either Boston or Poughkeepsie. In the blue-collar sector, San Franciscans found fewer opportunities to move into white-collar

Table 3.3. Comparative occupational mobility rates: first to last job, 1850-1880 (in percent).

First job, 1850	Last job, 1880				
	High white collar	Low white collar	Skilled	Low manual	(N)
High white collar					
Boston	92	8	0	0	(26)
Poughkeepsie	93	5	1	1	(96)
San Francisco	87	11	2	0	(270)
Low white collar					
Boston	25	61	9	6	(109)
Poughkeepsie	25	61	6	8	(389)
San Francisco	57	40	3	0	(63)
Skilled					
Boston	4	22	60	15	(82)
Poughkeepsie	8	23	60	10	(830)
San Francisco	8	15	66	12	(61)
Low manual					
Boston	4	24	13	59	(93)
Poughkeepsie	2	13	17	68	(685)
San Francisco	3	10	47	40	(30)

SOURCE: Boston and Poughkeepsie data from Stephan Thernstrom, *The Other Bostonians* (Cambridge, Mass., 1973).

occupations than did workers in the two eastern cities. On the other hand, because of the very general four-tiered occupational scale, the figures tend to blur, if not hide, some very important career movements within the occupational structure of San Francisco. The experience of the merchants, and hence the explanation for their success or failure, is best viewed from the perspective of an occupational scale that accounts for white-collar levels more sophisticated than "high" and "low."

Because of the economic disruptions at work in the San Francisco marketplace in the 1850s, there was every reason to expect high rates of downward mobility within the merchant occupations in that decade. There were, however, some very significant differences between the experiences of the three merchant groups.

The high status merchants, those who owned the commission houses, wholesale outlets, and import firms, found it difficult in the 1850s to maintain their occupational status. Given the high level at which the importer-wholesalers commenced their careers in San Francisco, the possibilities for advancement were limited to the professions—an unlikely occupational route. In fact, less than half even managed to maintain their occupational status in the 1850s. That half of them had slipped to the level of general merchants, or a lower status, only served to demonstrate the severity of the economic disruptions at work within the prestigious merchant occupations of the city. High occupational status, once attained, held no guarantee of long-term security.

Importer-wholesalers were among those who, in their geographical move to San Francisco, had experienced the highest rate of upward mobility. Yet in less than ten years after their arrival, many of these occupational gains had been eliminated. Lack of experience in merchant endeavors did not explain their lack of success in the 1850 decade, since 70 percent had worked in a merchant occupation before moving to the city. Rather, it was that they competed in an unsettled commercial environment. The unknowns in the San Francisco marketplace—fires, recessions, and the lack of experience among those with whom they dealt in business—affected not only their financial assets but also their occupational status. Also the trend towards occupational specialization placed increasing pressures upon the larger importer-wholesalers and commission merchants. Those among them who could not adjust to economic and demographic pressures that dictated occupational specialization, failed; and the economic loss was accompanied by downward occupational slippage. In the eight years before 1860, an equal number of importer-wholesalers slipped in occupational status as maintained their rank.

The opportunities for the general merchants were far superior to those of the importer-wholesalers. Almost nine out of every ten either advanced or maintained their occupational position; and of the 20 percent who moved up, two-thirds became importer-wholesalers in the 1850 decade, and the rest entered banking, real estate, brokerage, manufacturing, or professional occupations.

Only the small shopkeepers exceeded the upward occupational mobility rate (26 percent) of the city's overall male population. Almost all of the shopkeepers' upward movement was a vertical one into higher merchant occupations. A little more than half of the first-generation petty shopkeepers who remained in San Francisco through the

1850 decade had attained general merchant status by 1860, and another 20 percent captured even higher positions. Retail grocers emerged in 1860 as wholesale provisioners, and cigar-stand owners opened larger retail outlets or transferred into wholesaling. However, those who so prospered were fewer than these figures would suggest. Since mobility rates were calculated only for the ones who *remained* in the city throughout the 1850 decade, the percentages failed to account for the large number of petty shopkeepers who had departed by 1860. And while it may be said that seven out of every ten shopkeepers who resided in San Francisco throughout the 1850 decade experienced upward occupational mobility, less than half of all shopkeepers in 1852 chose to remain in the city for eight years.[22]

When mobility rates were adjusted for the variable of out-migration (1852-1860), a somewhat different pattern emerged. Among the petty shopkeepers, far more departed the city than either maintained or improved their occupational status. And although it was impossible to determine the geographical destinations and hence the subsequent careers of the out-migrants, it must be assumed that the opportunities in San Francisco for the petty merchants were considerably less favorable than their rate of upward mobility, unadjusted for out-migration, would suggest. Otherwise, over half the first generation of shopkeepers would not have departed the city. One major reason for their departure related to their limited financial assets and their incapacity to withstand the economic chaos of the city, a discussion reserved for a subsequent chapter. Leaving the out-migrants aside, however, all ranks of merchants, with the exception of the importer-wholesalers, either maintained or improved their occupational positions in the 1850 decade at a rate significantly higher than that experienced by the overall employed male population of the city, the majority of whom were blue-collar workers.

If the merchant persistence rates for 1852-1860 appeared low, they far surpassed the overall rate for the general population of the city. Three out of every four employed males in San Francisco in 1852 had departed the city before 1860. The high rate of out-migration from San Francisco was in fact part of a nineteenth century "American way of life." Less than 40 percent of the populations of Boston and Philadelphia in 1850 remained within their respective city limits through the end of the decade. San Francisco, though a city of 56,000, conformed

Table 3.4. Occupational mobility rates, 1852-1860 (in percent).[a]

Sample group	Upward	Same	Downward	Departees	Persisters	(N)
Petty merchants	32	10	2	56	44	(126)
General merchants	11	36	7	46	54	(366)
Importer-wholesalers	1	30	31	38	62	(151)
General population	6	16	2	76	24	(643)

SOURCE: California State Census, 1852; San Francisco *City Directories,* 1852-1860.
a. Adjusted for out-migration.

more to the experience of some small Midwest **rural** communities than it did to the bigger cities of the East.[23] San Francisco's unique position at midcentury as the major port of entry not only for the California goldfields but for the entire West Coast, certainly accounted for much of the migration into and through this frontier city. The majority of those who disembarked at San Francisco had traveled well in excess of 5,000 miles by sea to arrive in a city which lacked, in the early 1850s, even the most primitive housing and had hardly any social institutions that might serve to anchor a migratory population. What does seem striking was that after all the physical hardships and sacrifices associated with the initial migration to the West Coast, three-quarters of the first generation of San Francisco residents chose to leave the city within eight years of their arrival. By comparison, the eastern cities were also filled with large numbers of immigrants, who clung somewhat more securely to their new surroundings than the thousands who filtered through San Francisco monthly on their way to the "diggings."

In order to isolate the phenomenon of out-migration from the investigation of occupational mobility and to provide a better measurement of the *distance* of occupational moves rather than just the direction ("up," "same," or "down"), an incremental occupational prestige scale was utilized. Use of a prestige scale displayed an occupational mobility pattern somewhat different from the direction scale.[24]

The petty merchants clearly outperformed the other more prestigious merchant occupations. The general merchants and importer-wholesalers were far less upwardly mobile than the general popula-

Table 3.5. Mean occupational prestige scores, 1852-1880.

Sample group	1852	1860	Last job	Difference 1852-last job	(N)
Petty merchants	38.6	44.3	46.9	+ 8.3	(63)
General merchants	45.0	46.5	48.5	+ 3.5	(168)
Importer-wholesalers	57.0	49.4	50.9	-6.1	(102)
Blue-collar	29.9	33.5	35.9	+ 6.0	(91)
General population	37.6	40.5	42.8	+ 5.2	(147)

SOURCE: California State Census, 1852.

tion. In fact, mobility among the blue-collar workers exceeded that of the two highest merchant categories in the period 1852-1860. Of particular significance was the comparatively large slippage distance experienced by the importer-wholesalers.

When the occupational careers of the first merchant generation were viewed from the perspective of thirty years (last job), the pattern was similar to the 1850-1860 decade except that the importer-wholesalers had regained in the 1860s and 1870s a small portion of the occupational ground lost in the 1850s; the general merchants had similarly advanced, and the small number of the shopkeepers who had remained in the city, more often than not, experienced further occupational advancement. The petty merchants moved up a far greater distance than did general merchants. On the other hand, those importer-wholesalers who were downwardly mobile had slipped to a point at their last job which was only slightly higher than the point to which the petty merchants had climbed. The occupational distance among the first generation of merchants had so narrowed by 1880 that, in terms of occupational prestige, there was no great difference between those who commenced their occupational careers as petty shopkeepers and those who started as high perstige importer-wholesalers.

The last-job destinations of the merchants further illustrated the fluidity within the occupational structure of San Francisco. The small shopkeepers moved exceptionally well in the occupational structure. For example, the 18 percent climbing up to the highest merchant occupations (importer-wholesaler), plus the 22 percent who transferred to managerial occupations (banking, money and stock brokers, manufacturing), far exceeded the 16 percent moving upward into the general merchant occupations. In other words, four out of every ten petty merchants had leapfrogged the general merchant level for either the high-status merchant and managerial occupations or the professions by the time of their last job. The Seligman brothers, who commenced as small shopkeepers in the early 1850s, were bankers (the Anglo-California Bank) in the 1870s. George Eggers, a small retail grocer in 1849, owned one of the largest wholesale grocery businesses on the West Coast by 1870. A frequent customer of the Bella Union (probably San Francisco's fanciest gambling saloon in 1850) recollected that the peddlers who plied their goods in the gambling houses in the early 1850s were, by the late 1870s, among the most important merchants in the city. "Often I have purchased a few cigars of a man in the saloon, who is now [1878] one of the largest merchants in California. From among the lowest class of traders of that day some of our present richest merchants have sprung."[25]

The occupational mobility of the general merchants and importer-wholesalers was more orderly and less spectacular since the occupational distance they could climb was more limited. However, of the general merchants who proceeded up the occupational ladder, 11 percent entered the importing or wholesaling business and 22 percent transferred out of merchant occupations into high-status managerial positions or the professions. Of the original importer-wholesalers, almost 30 percent had dropped back into general merchant occupations by the time of their last job, and an additional 10 percent had slipped even further to clerical and sales jobs, or became small shopkeepers. Over half, however, had, by the time of their last job, maintained their occupational status either by remaining within their high-status merchant positions, or transferring to nonmerchant high-status managerial occupations. A number of commission merchants in the mid-1850s, for example, liquidated the assets of their commission houses to invest in real estate, a horizontal rather than vertical move.

This discussion, based on a snapshot of the merchants' occupational level in the early 1850s and another glimpse of their last occupation, unfortunately hides the high degree of occupational flux within the white-collar ranks of the city. The career of Louis Bonestell is illustrative of the frequency with which merchants and nonmerchants changed employment and moved back and forth through the occupational scale.

Bonestell had worked as a farmer in the Catskill Mountains of New York before departing for the California gold fields in 1849. His career as miner, however, lasted less than a year, for by 1850 he worked as a carpenter in San Francisco. With his savings Bonestell purchased the newspaper route of *Alta California* for $600, hired two assistants, and after eight months sold the route for double the purchase price. He then entered the stationery and printing business (the newspaper *Wide West*), but lost all his money in the venture. Bonestell then borrowed $1,000 to try his luck in the grain business, but that too failed. He then bought a small storehouse, unfortunately located next to the headquarters of the Vigilance Committee, which everyone believed was susceptible to fire, and failed once again. All this happened in less than seven years. Bonestell wrote about his occupational career after 1856:

After recovering [from the storage business loss] I took a position in a book and stationery store at a hundred dollars a month—opened the doors at seven A.M., swept out and got things ready for business and stayed on the job till I closed up at ten at night. After a few months I went to work for Mr. J. J. LeCount [a book and stationery merchant] remaining with him until he went out of business [in the late 1870s] . . . Rather tired of business I left the city in 1878 to farm a ranch I had acquired near Bakersfield . . . and after eight months a complete failure, we returned to San Francisco to the field I knew. I became the representative of the A. D. Remington Co. paper manufacturers of Watertown, New York . . . A year later [1880] I bought out their western interests and founded the firm of Bonestell and Company [printers, publishers, and paper manufacturers].[26]

Bonestell over the span of three decades changed jobs eleven times in a wide range of occupations. Like others, his career dipped and climbed in both merchant and nonmerchant endeavors. But he did return to the job he knew best—printing and selling books—and in the process experienced a net occupational gain in the three decades.

Among the first generation of the city's residents, the one nonmerchant occupational group which experienced extraordinarily high rates of upward mobility were the clerks; well over half of them had progressed up the occupational ladder into merchant, managerial, and professional occupations. Many of the second generation San Francisco merchants (post-Civil War) had received their merchant training in the 1850s and 1860s not on the quarterdeck, the common New England experience, but in the counting house. A clerk's duties included delivering goods, maintaining accurate financial records if there was no bookkeeper, and copying letters and billing. One San Francisco general merchant expected his clerks in the store by 8:00 A.M. at which time they were to "dust and clean their departments." The clerks were instructed, according to a handbook, that when serving their customers they were to make "no distinction as to class or dress . . . the same patience must be exercised with all." The clerks were allowed one evening off every two weeks except during the holiday season. With time and more training went increased responsibility. Once they gained confidence and respect of their employer then, under the proper circumstances, the faithful clerk might be offered admission to partnership in the merchant firm.[27]

Whereas the first generation of white-collar workers experienced a relatively high level of occupational mobility, at least among those starting in the lower ranges of the white-collar occupational scale, the blue-collar workers discovered few opportunities in this frontier city. Only 13 percent of the low manual workers in San Francisco had moved into white-collar occupations by the time of their last job, half of the climbing rate of Boston and somewhat lower than the experience of the low manual workers in Poughkeepsie. And although the low manual entry rate into the skilled trades in San Francisco exceeded that of Boston and Poughkeepsie, the skilled workers of San Francisco discovered no better opportunities in the white-collar class than did skilled craftsmen in the two cities of the East. The overcrowding and intense competition within the white-collar occupations, from those already residing in the city and the thousands arriving from the East each year, probably accounted for the small number of skilled workers who moved out of the blue-collar ranks.

The occupational barriers faced by the blue-collar workers in San Francisco were reflected in their extraordinarily high out-migration between 1852 and 1880. Only one out of every ten blue-collar workers in 1852 remained in San Francisco for three decades. Recent studies of other nineteenth century cities have similarly confirmed that "persons of the lower rungs of the class ladder were far more likely to move than those of high ranks."[28]

But even in the white-collar ranks persistence was low. The bulk of the out-migration, as we have seen, occurred in the 1850s when the petty merchants were far more likely than either the general merchants or the importer-wholesalers to leave the city. In the 1860s and 1870s, however, the departure rates among the different merchant groups were approximately equal. Still, by 1880 the importer-wholesalers were twice as likely to have remained in the city as the first generation of shopkeepers or the general employed population of the city, over 60 percent of whom were blue-collar workers. The only major exception to this trend, where the thirty-year persistence rates did not correlate with occupational status, was among the first generation of clerks and salesmen. Here, in the occupational category which expanded most in terms of available jobs between 1850 and 1880, one in four of the clerical and sales force in 1852 remained in San Francisco until 1880 or later—a persistence rate somewhat higher than any of the merchant groups.

Occupational Mobility, Persistence, and Ethnicity

The relationship between persistence and occupational mobility still must be explained. If, as suggested by some scholars, the upwardly mobile are more likely to persist in a community than the downwardly mobile, why would the importer-wholesalers who, in their three-decade occupational career pattern were the least mobile as a group, be those most likely to remain in San Francisco? And why would petty shopkeepers—those most upwardly mobile—be the first to leave?[29]

Age did not explain the phenomenon since there was no significant difference in the mean age of the three merchant groups. Nor was there any major difference in the age distribution between the merchant groups when divided into age cohorts. Death rates, therefore, did not explain the differences in out-migration.

There were, nevertheless, some ethnic differences in the persistence and occupational mobility rates among the foreign-born which partially explained the relationship between these two variables. The native-born were more heavily represented in the merchant occupations than the foreign-born, despite the fact that over half the general population of the city was foreign-born. Also the higher the occupational level, the higher the percent of native-born occupying the merchant positions.

Table 3.6. Representation in merchant occupations by nativity, 1852 (in percent).

Sample group	Total native-born	Total foreign-born	English/ Scottish	Irish	German	Other
(N-643)[a]						
Petty merchants	57	43	8	6	18	11
General merchants	59	41	12	4	16	9
Importer-wholesalers	74	26	11	2	6	7
General population (N = 669)	47	53	14	12	7	20[b]

SOURCE: California State Census, 1852.
 a. The number includes all three merchant categories.
 b. The largest single group in the "other" category for the general population was the French, 9 percent.

There were also distinct ethnic patterns among the foreign-born in the merchant occupations. For example, the Germans were almost three times more numerous in the petty merchant occupations than they were in the general population. The Irish, on the other hand, were underrepresented in the merchant occupations, particularly in the more prestigious positions. Only the English and Germans, among the first generation of foreign-born merchants, occupied prestigious merchant positions in numbers comparable to their presence in the overall population of the city. The native-born, however, controlled almost three-quarters of all high-status merchant occupations, but numbered less than half of the general population.

Of the foreign-born in the petty and general merchant occupations, the Germans were the most numerous, well over half of them German Jews. Many had come from the villages in Germany to the cities of the Eastern Seaboard and New Orleans, and later migrated to California during the Gold Rush. In New York the Jews were closely associated with the clothing trade centered on Chatham Street, where, for the most part, they worked at the skilled trades (merchant-tailor, for example) or owned small retail stores. With the discovery of gold, some of the Jewish clothing merchants departed for California with money borrowed from their family. Once established in California, they would, like Levi Strauss and the Seligman brothers, order goods through their relatives back East. Some Jews went to the mining towns not so much as miners, but primarily as retail merchants of clothing, dry goods, tobacco, and general merchandise. In fact about half of the retail shops of the mountain towns were owned by Jews. When they had gained experience and accumulated some capital, many Jewish merchants left the interior towns of California to open retail stores in San Francisco. A recently arrived relative from Europe or the East Coast was then assigned to the branch store in the interior to learn the business and the language.[30]

From wherever they migrated, both first and second generation German Jews were well represented in the merchant occupations in San Francisco. They clustered in the cigar trade, dry goods, and particularly the clothing business. Also many of the early peddlers in the city were Jews. One observer estimated that by 1860, 9 percent of the population of San Francisco were German Jews "comparable in . . . density only to that of New York at the time."[31] The Jews, therefore, were well represented not only in the total foreign-born population of the city, but also in the merchant class, particularly among the petty shopkeepers.

In terms of the direction of occupational mobility for merchants and nonmerchants alike, the foreign-born were slightly less upwardly mobile than the native-born, but also (clustered as they were within the lower reaches of the white- and blue-collar ranks) less likely to experience slippage. Throughout all occupations, the foreign-born found it more difficult to move ahead. The advantage rested with the native-born at all occupational levels among the merchants and the general population.[32]

With one major exception, the use of mean prestige scores confirmed the same general pattern. Whereas among the petty shopkeepers the percentage rate of upward mobility for the native-born was higher, the actual occupational distance traveled by the foreign-born shopkeepers was greater. Most of this movement among the foreign-born was accounted for by the Germans. And, although it was not possible to determine with any precision the actual religion of an individual, an investigation of the surnames of the German petty merchants suggested that well over half were probably Jews. Their rise from peddler to merchant followed the general experience of the Jewish peddler in the East and Midwest.[33] The occupational career of August Helbing in San Francisco followed a path common to many

German Jews. Born in Munich in 1824, Helbing graduated from an industrial school and worked in a mercantile firm in Munich until 1849. The reports of gold in California and negative economic and political conditions in Germany encouraged Helbing and two friends, Moritz Meyer and August Wasserman, to leave for the United States. After a brief stay in New Orleans they migrated to San Francisco in October 1850. With Meyer, Helbing established a small dry goods firm and subsequently became a partner in the wholesale crockery business of Helbing, Strauss & Co. Quite aside from his occupational career, he helped establish the Eureka Benevolent Society which assisted the widows and orphans of Jewish immigrants and the sick and destitute. He also founded the Pacific Institute—the forerunner of the Mechanic's Institute and Mercantile Library. Helbing's career, like that of Levi Strauss, whose successful venture in canvas pants allowed him to move from a small store in Sacramento to a large manufacturing plant in San Francisco, was typical of the long occupational distances traveled by some German Jews who started in the petty merchant ranks.

Less spectacular in terms of occupational success but more typical were the scores of German peddlers and retail merchants in the 1850s who, by 1880, owned and operated retail clothing stores and wholesale outlets associated with manufacturing establishments. Joseph Meussdorfer began his career as a hat and cap peddler. By 1880 he owned stores in Sacramento and Portland, and manufactured a line of hats; others he purchased from Paris, New York, Boston, and Danbury and Norwalk, Connecticut. As a wholesaler he supplied orders from towns and cities throughout California; Victoria, British Columbia, Portland, Oregon, and Denver, Colorado.[34]

The high rates of upward occupational mobility within the petty merchant ranks, where the German Jews clustered, suggested that the Jews may have been largely responsible for the high mobility rates within this merchant group. Lack of more complete ethnic and religious data for the petty merchants prevented quantitative confirmation on this point. However, observers on the scene often commented on the occupational and financial success of Jews in San Francisco. "In commercial matters they [the Jews] are leaders. In any business pursuit involving traffic, they are, as a class, more successful than those who reject their faith . . . They are leaders in, and control . . .

the principal mercantile businesses. The clothing trade—here as elsewhere—is monopolized by them, and the principal dry goods houses, and crockery and jewelry establishments belong to the Jews. In the manufacturing industries they have control of the shoe and soap factories, and the woolen mills . . . They are also largely interested in the grain trade of the coast, and the Alaskan fur trade.''[35]

The higher rate of occupational mobility among the German shopkeepers did explain, in part, their relatively high rate of persistence in the city. But occupational experience could not account for even higher rates of persistence of this group among the general merchants and importer-wholesalers.[36]

The German general merchants who failed to match the occupational advances of their native- or foreign-born colleagues continued, nevertheless, to persist at a significantly higher rate. And, despite their occupational losses, the German importer-wholesalers were twice as likely to persist thirty years than the German shopkeepers who, as a group, were experiencing the most impressive occupational gains. In fact, the persistence of German merchants was higher than that of either the native-born or foreign-born merchant populations regard-

Table 3.7. Occupational mobility and persistence, first job/last job: San Francisco, 1852-1880.

	Prestige score			Percent in city, 1880	(N)
	First job	Last job	Difference		
Petty merchants					
Native-born	38.5	46.2	+ 7.7	8	(72)
Foreign-born	38.8	47.8	+ 9.0	15	(54)
German	39.0	48.9	+ 9.9	22	(23)
General merchants					
Native-born	45.0	49.1	+ 4.1	21	(215)
Foreign-born	45.0	47.8	+ 2.8	22	(149)
German	45.0	46.5	+ 1.5	32	(57)
Importer-wholesalers					
Native-born	57.1	50.4	-6.7	23	(112)
Foreign-born	57.0	52.4	-4.6	21	(39)
German	57.0	53.9	-3.1	50	(10)

SOURCE: California State Census, 1852.

less of occupational hierarchy. Of all ethnic merchant groups, the Germans were the most persistent in the city.[37]

Other factors, of course, influenced people to move away from the city that related not at all to the variables of occupation and ethnicity. The ties of family among all merchants, regardless of occupational level or prestige, were, no doubt, a compelling factor influencing an individual's decision whether or not to remain in San Francisco or return home. The city may have held out occupational opportunities for the ambitious but it certainly did not possess, in its frontier quality during the 1850s, the comforts associated with the more settled areas of the nation. Few among the residents of San Francisco in the 1850s thought of it as home. One merchant, in a letter to his family in New Bedford, Massachusetts, wrote: "I meet very few people in this city who have any idea of making this [San Francisco] a permanent residence; they make their pile or get discouraged and go home."[38] Frequently the attractions of home outweighed either the occupational or financial inducements of San Francisco. A successful clothing merchant, after two and a half years and $14,000 in his pocket, returned home to New York to marry his fiancee. Another New York native wrote in his diary, "I made up my mind to close up my business relations [in San Francisco] and return to New York. I could have drawn out at that time quite a fortune, but I had promised to return home within three years. I had now been absent two years and four months, and I was anxious to see 'the girl I left behind me.' "[39] At all occupational levels, merchants were attracted back to the towns and cities which they considered home. Letters from relatives and friends were a constant reminder that their presence was missed. Wives complained of loneliness and, in some cases, financial hardship. Others implored their husbands to return for the sake of their children. Parents wrote about illness or the need for a son to return home to oversee family affairs left unattended by his absence in San Francisco. These very human decisions, decisions which in no way lend themselves to measured quantification, affected all merchants regardless of occupational status.[40]

In the end the first generation of merchants in San Francisco did discover occupational opportunities, but they were limited to specific occupational levels, and within these levels to specific nativity groups. The importer-wholesalers, predominantly native-born, and others who had experienced the highest rate of shipboard mobility in the process of their geographical transfer to San Francisco, quickly discovered in the 1850s the dangers associated with lofty occupational position. (And those who rode down the occupational escalator most quickly would also be the ones, in later years, most likely to participate enthusiastically in a violent experiment to preserve and protect the social order.) Despite their moderate occupational advances in the 1860s and 1870s, the first generation of high white-collar merchants (importers, wholesalers, and general) ended their occupational careers at a level only slightly higher than where the petty merchants terminated their careers.

Within the general employed population of the city, only one in ten had persisted within the city for three decades; three-quarters had departed within eight years after first arriving in San Francisco. Of those who had persisted throughout the 1850s, only 10 percent of the blue-collar workers managed to cross the occupational barrier into the white-collar world, a rate considerably lower than that prevailing during the 1850s in Boston (18 percent) or Poughkeepsie (17 percent). One could advance within the blue-collar occupations, and about half managed to do so in the 1850s, but to rise from the blue-collar ranks into any of the white-collar occupations was an occupational leap few experienced.

Successful occupational mobility did not guarantee that a man would settle in San Francisco. But leaving mobility aside, even to persist and survive required energy, experience, and money; luck also helped. A leading merchant in the San Francisco community throughout the first three decades of the city, and one who barely managed to maintain his own high occupational status as an import merchant commented upon his own experience when he reflected in the early 1870s, "all is still a lottery." There were many among the first generation who would agree with his existential observation.[41]

4

PROPERTY, CREDIT, AND PERSISTENCE

Merchants measured their personal success not by their movement along an abstract occupational prestige scale but by the black ink in their account books. The opportunity to accumulate instant fortunes was, after all, the generator for the initial migration to the city. What follows, therefore, is an investigation of social mobility from the perspective of property to see if the occupational patterns were reflected in the financial resources of the city merchants in the 1850 decade.[1] (For a discussion of how property data were gathered for this chapter, see Appendix A, Methodological Notes.)

San Francisco's First Monied Men

The 1850 decade opened with every indication that fortunes could be amassed with relative ease and a degree of luck. Within six months of the gold discovery and the concurrent demand from the exploding population of miners, a small group of monied men had emerged in San Francisco. Merchants for the most part, they were those, one observer noted, "who by chance were on the spot" when gold was discovered or who arrived in San Francisco immediately after the discovery at Sutter's Fort. They arrived when goods, in short supply, commanded high prices and with financial resources, their own or borrowed, they banked away spectacular profits.[2]

Some men accumulated profits through a preconceived plan or scheme, others simply experienced luck. Anywhere from 100 to 500 percent profits on a single cargo and an initial investment of $5,000 were not uncommon. Purchasers at auctions stockpiled goods for which they anticipated a future demand. In addition to reinvesting in goods, those with money took advantage of usurious lending rates of 60 percent per annum and 10 percent per month. Or merchant profits could be invested in real estate where even more spectacular profits were registered. As an early account of San Francisco reported, "the richest men in San Francisco have made the best portion of their wealth by possession of real estate.'' Those fortunate enough to hold town lots ''from the times before the discovery of gold, or who shortly afterward managed to secure them, were suddenly enriched beyond their most sanguine hopes.'' One merchant received $10,500 a month from rentals of his real estate before the fires of 1851; from December 1848 to December 1849 his profits in merchandise ''outside of speculations in real estate, were $110,000,'' and he reported that ''other merchants with greater capital made much larger sums.''[3]

Those who had accumulated quick and impressive fortunes in San Francisco by 1851 were listed in a pamphlet entitled *A 'Pile' or a Glance at the Wealth of the Monied Men of San Francisco and Sacramento City*. From San Francisco, 570 individuals were named with the estimated worth of their personal estates. Based upon this wealth, the monied men, who represented approximately 2 percent of the 27,000 working males of San Francisco in 1851, owned between 75 and 80 percent of the personal and real property of the city.[4] That so few owned so much was not in itself surprising. San Francisco followed a pattern that existed in New York, Boston, Philadelphia, and Brooklyn. However the percent of total wealth owned by the rich of San Francisco exceeded that of the elites of these eastern cities in the same period. Also the average wealth of each member of San Francisco's first monied elite ($33,600) was, by any standard for the 1850s, a considerable sum.[5]

Almost without exception the rich held high-status occupations; over 60 percent were merchants and 25 percent held other high-status white-collar positions. The amount of money owned bore a direct relationship to occupation. Three-quarters of the wealthy merchants and one-third of the entire group were commission merchants and importers. Of those who owned $50,000 or more, four out of five were commission merchants, bankers, money, stock, or real estate brokers, or professionals—all high-status occupations. No clerk or petty merchant owned more than $50,000, and the few from the lower-status white-collar occupations (3 percent) who were included among the monied men owned considerably less.[6]

Of San Francisco's first monied class, four out of five were native-born whereas over half of the city's population were born abroad. This may have resulted from an initial advantage of the native-born, who had either ample capital of their own, or more commonly, excellent lines of credit with eastern merchant houses. A commission merchant best summed up the situation in a letter to his brother in New York when he observed that capital "is the great consideration here, without it nothing can be done, with plenty of it, any amount of money can be made." Another observer asked rhetorically who were these early monied men of San Francisco? "Stem-beer tavern keepers? Gamblers all? Ditch diggers? Scum? as was sometimes alleged with respect to San Francisco's social origins? Far from it, but . . . merchants, sea captains, importers, attorneys, real estate investors, many of them with the 'best of connections' back East, and back South."[7]

Lest we take too seriously the social snobbery of the foregoing observation, it should be noted that not all immediate financial success in the early 1850s accrued solely to the higher social classes nor was it necessarily limited to men. For it appears, as one observer noted, that "those who owned and operated the 'crooked' gambling tables and those who lived on the money of the public women," were equally successful. Indeed, the economic cycles of the 1850s did not seem to have affected adversely the business of "public women." A cursory inspection of the 1860 census for San Francisco indicated that there were well over 1,000 prostitutes in the city whose individual financial assets averaged in excess of $3,000. One practitioner of that ancient profession, known variously as the Countess of Campora and the Flower Queen, "whose beautiful efflorescence had been a joy and admiration of Chile for many years," moved to San Francisco at the height of the Gold Rush where she "commanded fabulous prices." An admirer of the Countess noted for posterity that he "never knew a woman who could procure such a large income by [so] abusing her sex."[8]

Those who bartered goods rather than flesh experienced far different pressures in the 1850s, a decade of economic loss rather than profit. Also the experience of the monied men, who gained their initial fortunes in 1848-1850, in no way represented the experience of the majority of San Francisco residents in the decade following the early boom period. Given the paucity of individual financial records, the precise quantitative degree of financial loss suffered by all ranks of the first generation of merchants in the 1850s is difficult to determine. Relative to the other city merchants, the petty shopkeepers ranked lowest in mean property and hence were least likely to demand, or eligible to receive, large-scale credit. Therefore, because R. G. Dun tended to exclude this group from its investigation, the personal assets for a significant number of petty merchants could not be determined for the early 1850s.[9] Other sources suggested, however, that the first generation of small shopkeepers were no more successful in their attempts to accumulate capital or to survive the recessions and depressions of the 1850 decade than were the more affluent general merchants and importer-wholesalers. In fact, given their lack of capital resources, they were probably the least likely to profit in a decade of economic loss.

However, from a systematic study of the R. G. Dun and Company credit reports, adequate financial data were derived for the general merchants and importer-wholesalers to allow generalizations regarding the magnitude of their losses. Their assets declined approximately 9 percent and 24 percent respectively over the span of the decade. An early observer on the scene noted: "There are but few persons who have spent years in [San Francisco] without meeting with reverses in business. In no part of the world are poverty and affluence so nearly mingled in the same cup. Nowhere is fortune so fickle; nowhere do so many, all in a day, go from wealth to want." "I know of two men and see them every day," the wife of a city merchant wrote in a letter home, "that have lost a fortune. One has twice lost Thirty Thousand Dollars, yet he seems quite happy now with the prospect of making another 'pile,' as anybody else I see." But more typical were the merchants who, unable to obtain credit or locate a new affluent business partner, failed to make "another pile" and considered themselves fortunate if, at a minimum, they managed to recoup their initial losses.[10]

The disastrous fires of 1851-52 and the economic recessions and depressions of the decade, particularly the Panic of 1857, destroyed a fair share of the merchant establishments of the city. Of the merchants who were in business in San Francisco before 1852, almost four of every ten were reported by R. G. Dun and Company to have experienced a net property loss by 1860; and of the losers, well over half had departed San Francisco by the close of the decade. These were, by and large, the more affluent and prestigious merchants who, with their substantial capital assets, were best equipped to turn an initial commercial adversity into a later profit. The petty shopkeepers, marginal operators whose total capital resources seldom exceeded a couple of thousand dollars, were even less likely to survive the economic dislocations of the decade.[11]

The high rate of business failure in the city in the 1850s reflected the unsettled economic conditions. The bank failures of 1854 hastened a commercial crisis in which hundreds of merchants failed, often carrying creditors with them. "Many failed as many as three times and started anew, others took subordinate positions or drank themselves to death," reported historian Hubert Bancroft. "Not one in ten of the San Francisco merchants of 1849," Bancroft concluded, "was doing business in 1855." Between 1855 and 1860, there were a reported 692 declared bankruptcy cases totaling in excess of 17.5 million dollars of debts. Of the business failures reported in 1855 alone, merchants, almost all of whom were either general merchants or importer-wholesalers, accounted for 58 percent of those filing insolvency cases.[12]

A number of failures may have been encouraged, to some extent, by lenient bankruptcy laws. William T. Sherman, a San Francisco banker at the time, reported that both the law and the courts sanctioned approval of a release from partial debts unless an individual involved himself in fraud. R. G. Dun reported instances of merchants and other San Francisco businessmen who "made money by failing." A man's home and personal property were not included in the accounting of individual assets available for the settlement of debts. And some merchants, realizing that they were about to fail, transferred assets to their wives who, in turn, opened up small stores and employed their husbands as bookkeepers or salesmen. Sherman noted that "merchants of the highest name, availed themselves of the extremely liberal bankrupt law to get discharged of old debts, without sacrificing much, if any, of their stocks of goods on hand, except a lawyer's fee." They realized the wisdom of the old adage that "'many a clever fellow had been ruined by paying his debts,' and they did not intend to be ruined by any such course."[13]

But if merchants escaped payment of their total liabilities through the courts, they remained accountable for at least a portion of their debts. The settlement figure was usually pegged to the liquid assets. At the completion of the bankruptcy proceedings, it was the exceptional merchant who, in fact, had "made money by failing." Most were left totally devoid of assets with which to commence a new business enterprise. The declaration of bankruptcy was an admission of failure—a public advertisement to the community that all future business transactions with that person, particularly the issuance of credit, would have to be conducted with extreme caution.

Rather than appear in court and attract public notice, most merchants who failed in business sought private settlements with their creditors who, wishing to avoid the delays and expense of the courts, usually accepted between 30 and 50 percent of their outstanding bills. If such private settlements were added to the public bankruptcy cases in San Francisco during the 1850 decade, the rate of failure was probably somewhere between half and two-thirds of all merchants. The R. G. Dun credit reports for San Franciscans are filled with instances of private settlements between debt-ridden merchants and their creditors—usually other merchants.

The city's chaotic economic environment dictated in large measure the merchant's profit or loss margins. Only a few businessmen with large capital reserves could afford to maintain large inventories and await higher prices; the majority were forced to sell at lower prices in order to recover a portion of their investment. "It was often the case," lamented one early merchant, "that losses on merchandise were so heavy that subsequent profits would not make up for them." Added to the problems associated with surplus inventories, the ravages of fire indiscriminately destroyed property. Approximately three-quarters of all merchants in San Francisco were burned out by fire at one time or another before 1852. R. G. Dun reported that two dry goods merchants made several fortunes in San Francisco "but lost them by fire and now [1852] are making nothing."[14]

The recession hit hardest at the import and commission merchants who, because of the dollar volume of their trade, extended and received credit more extensively than small shopkeepers or general retail merchants. When eastern creditors called in their notes, the San Francisco commission merchants frequently were unable to meet the demands. One such merchant, S. B. Throckmorton, had overextended himself in dry goods and real estate as the Panic of 1857 approached. New York wholesalers refused to extend his credit because of the outstanding debts of $12,000 to $15,000 he owed in New York before his departure for the West in 1850. Throckmorton pleaded for time, but to no avail. When the Panic of 1857 hit, he found it impossible to re-pay his eastern creditors. His San Francisco customers could not pay their bills, and when he was unable to sell a piece of beachfront prop-erty to the federal government, financial disaster finally struck. In a letter to a business associate in New York he rationalized his failure:

I thought, at one time, that I had at least brought myself to a condi-tion that insured comfort and competency to my family; but I see now I was mistaken. I made no bad bargains such as people make some-times, and ruin themselves. I engaged in no speculation [in fact he speculated heavily in real estate]. I committed no extravagances; I simply overstaid my tide, and the waters fell and left me aground. At one time my estate was considered the best and soundest in the country . . . My judgement *then* was extolled by everybody, and my credit (as far as I chose to use it) was without limit; my debt was small (comparatively) and my income large . . . but time changed. All who owed me failed. I paid all promptly, my income fell off, my debts in-creased and you know the rest.[15]

The losses of the more affluent merchants were sometimes covered by the combined assets of their partnership or, if a branch store, par-tially covered by the eastern home office. The Seligman brothers sur-vived because, as R. G. Dun reported, they had "good credit in New York City"—specifically from an affluent brother and a wealthy wholesale establishment. But too often partnerships broke apart in the midst of the recessions because one partner, whose personal invest-ment in a mining stock or waterfront lot had turned sour, withdrew his capital from the partnership to cover his personal debts. Or the main store in New York or Boston, where the Panic of 1857 hit hard-est, failed and carried with it the San Francisco branch.[16]

High business expenses in San Francisco added another burden to the economic problems of the merchant. The added expenses not only cut into profits, but, where the profits were small or nonexistent, served only to deepen the economic crisis. For example, insurance protection against losses at sea, water damage, and theft and fire cost almost twice as much as similar coverage along the East and Gulf Coasts, and even so was frequently unavailable. Depending upon the type of article shipped and the number of transshipments necessary to transport the cargo from the East Coast to San Francisco, freight rates ranged from 10 to 50 percent of the value of the cargo. When the cargo arrived in port, fees were exacted by pilots, the city health officer, the harbor master, owners of lighterage vessels, and wharfs. Importers and wholesalers had the additional expenses of transferring goods to warehouses, storage fees, and custom duties. Finally, no merchant could operate without a city license (renewable annually), with the fees, scaled according to monthly receipts, paid quarterly. The fees discriminated most severely against retail shops, pawnbrokers, and peddlers.[17]

To illustrate the fiscal hazards of merchant entrepreneurship in San Francisco, consider the case of a merchant partnership (two shipping merchants) with annual business expenses of about $18,000. These included interest charges, storage, rent ($7,200), salaries for a clerk ($2,400) and bookkeeper ($1,800), licenses and taxes ($2,700), and individual partner expenses ($1,800 each). The merchant partners complained they had to maintain a gross volume of $300,000 a year just to pay the business expenses of the partnership![18]

A commission merchant complained to his principals in New York that his $10,000 annual income barely supported him in the style to which he was accustomed. His cook demanded and received $200 a month; and as much as the merchant wanted a servant at an additional cost of $1,800 a year, he could not afford the luxury. In a letter to New York explaining his expenses, the merchant pleaded for higher commissions. "Please look at this! A captain of a vessel is offered from three to five hundred [dollars] per month—sailors are getting one hundred . . . and stevedores, six dollars a day. Carpenters are getting eight and ten per day. A room the size of your counting room would let for two hundred dollars pr. month. Clerks are offered two and three thousand dollars a year, and turn their noses up at that. Board at the Hotel six dollars pr. day. Thus you can make a small estimate of . . . my expenses pr. annum."[19]

Shopkeepers built additions on their stores so as to accommodate boarders. Merchants' wives replaced salesmen and clerks. One wholesale liquor dealer augmented his meager earnings by collecting, for a fee, the property and poll taxes for the city. Another merchant decided to forego his unprofitable business for the more profitable profession of politics. As a city supervisor, R. G. Dun reported, "he made a handsome thing of it . . . built a residence which with the lot cost $20,000 . . . and is estimated [to be] worth at least $90,000 to

$100,000.'' The usual number of merchants continued to frequent the gambling palaces but not, as formerly, for the purpose of entertainment and relaxation but rather to recoup at the roulette wheel what they had lost in the marketplace.[20]

The most spectacular attempt to recoup personal losses occurred at the height of the 1857 depression. Henry Meiggs, a lumber merchant, believed that the North Beach section of the city would become in time an area of commercial importance equal to that of the older downtown area. He built a saw and planing mill at North Beach for lumber shipped in from Mendocino County. Soon Meiggs owned a dozen mills in the North Beach area and a 2,000-foot wharf. He borrowed heavily in San Francisco to build his mills (which were producing planks for the city streets) and to invest in additional real estate purchases. To secure the loans, Meiggs gave as security city warrants which he forged with the signature of his friend, the mayor. As his bills mounted, the forgeries were discovered; Meiggs chartered a ship and fled to South America with $8,200 in cash and $20,000 of outstanding bills. Within 5 months, he had established himself as one of the leading businessmen in Valparaiso, Chile.[21]

The most exotic failure involved Joshua A. Norton, a native of England who arrived in San Francisco in 1849 with $40,000. By 1853 he had built up his real estate investments into assets reputed to be worth a quarter of a million dollars. With the profits he attempted as a grain dealer to corner the rice market, and lost his fortune. But in the process he gained a kingdom by proclaiming himself Emperor of these United States, and later, Protector of Mexico. He issued various decrees, one of which was to abolish the offices of the president and vice-president of the United States, and the speaker of the house. When, after the failure of his rice scheme, Emperor Norton needed cash, he simply issued notes of the Imperial Government of Norton I. Adored by the city for his eccentric style, Norton never lacked for credit in stores or restaurants, in part, no doubt, because he rarely requested credit in excess of a dollar.

Joshua A. Norton's ascent to an imaginary throne was atypical, but his descent on the occupational ladder was a common experience for the high-status merchants. Commission merchants and importers, who in the midst of the recessions lost thousands of dollars in personal assets, either commenced a new merchant business with more affluent partners (in their old line of work or as retail merchants), dropped out of merchandizing for a lower-status job, or left the city altogether. R. G. Dun cited hundreds of cases who lost both their property and occupational positions in the 1850s. One example, typical of many, were two wholesalers who "were doing a large business, failed . . . Cronin now a poor cobbler and Markley not here." A few descended into politics, a calling (at least in San Francisco) not considered a high-status occupation. R. G. Dun reported the case of a large liquor importer who in the midst of the Panic of 1857 "went into insolvency, now worthless, and a Politician."[22]

When failure hit the family grocers, whose profit margins were smaller than any of the other city merchants with the single exception of the peddlers, they frequently descended into the blue-collar ranks where many had originated. A few managed to survive through personal loans from family or friends; but, like other shopkeepers, their limited capital assets and meager profit margins all but precluded the possibility of attracting the necessary capital to carry them through periods of recession and depression.[23]

Not all merchant groups, defined either in terms of occupational status or ethnic grouping, suffered equally the ravages of property loss and occupational slippage. For example, the native-born merchants, who as a group commenced their San Francisco careers with more capital than their foreign-born counterparts, experienced the most severe property losses. Their mean property declined approximately 20 percent (from $29,500 to $23,500) in the 1850 decade, a reflection, as we have witnessed, of the substantial losses (both financial and occupational) suffered by the importer-wholesalers. The foreign-born, led by the Germans, actually experienced a net 10 percent increase (from $19,500 to $21,500). Once again, their property accumulation reflected their occupational strides in the 1850 decade.

Between 1851-52 and 1860, the Germans more than doubled their mean assets, from $11,500 to $31,500—a performance that far surpassed either the native-born or foreign-born merchants. Their San Francisco careers began in the lower-status merchant occupations where the Germans wisely utilized their limited savings to increase their financial resources through prudent investments in business enterprises. They were considered to be "frugal and industrious" and they seldom failed "to gradually accumulate capital when once established in a business, however small the beginnings may be.'' Their financial gains in the 1850s apparently resulted from their own merchant enterprises rather than from the more speculative investments in stocks and real estate, the two areas most severely affected by the depression. Not only were the Germans as a group and the Jews in particular less susceptible to the effects of the recessions, but in the midst of economic adversity they skillfully managed to increase their assets. [24]

Jacob and William Scholle, two German Jews who started as peddlers in Orange County, New York, and then opened a dry goods store in New York in 1846, not only survived the fires of San Francisco but together accumulated $200,000 by 1859. The Seligman brothers, also German Jews who began as peddlers in New York and Selma, Alabama, generated their initial profits exclusively from their dry goods business in the 1850s. Both the Scholle and Seligman brothers conformed to the pattern of the successful German merchants, who, shying away from nonmerchant speculative investments, insulated themselves from the catastrophic losses in stocks and real estate. [25]

The success of the German Jews must be seen as extraordinary when one considers the extreme difficulties and prejudices they encountered in obtaining working capital in a young city which lacked an adequate supply of it. Where the native-born had established commercial ties and hence ample credit lines from the East, the foreign-born (including the German Jews) possessed neither advantage.

Credit

A high credit rating within the community depended, in large measure, upon the merchant's capital assets. As table 4.1 indicates, there was a high correlation between property holdings and a favorable R. G. Dun evaluation.

The advantage clearly rested with the predominantly native-born importer-wholesalers. In a credit system where money begot money, the importer-wholesalers held the money, which assisted their credit rating which in turn attracted additional capital.

Merchant partnerships, too, were more likely to obtain a higher credit rating than were single proprietors. And it was certainly not by coincidence that virtually all of the import and commission houses in

Table 4.1. Credit rating and property, 1850-1880 (in percent).

Assets	No Credit	Fair	Good	Excellent	(N)
Under $10,000	36	40	20	4	(25)
$10,000-49,999	14	24	55	7	(29)
$50,000-99,999	3	16	59	22	(32)
$100,000-299,999	—	9	47	44	(34)
$300,000	—	12	13	75	(8)

SOURCE: R.G. Dun and Company, *Credit Reports.*

the city were legal partnerships, whereas most of the foreign-born shopkeepers conducted businesses as single proprietors. In 1860, when approximately 80 percent of the merchants listed in R. G. Dun and Company were in a partnership, no single proprietor was found to possess "excellent" credit and over 60 percent had either "fair" credit or "no credit" whatsoever. Part of the explanation for these lower credit ratings may be that the majority of these single proprietorships were in the clothing trade, traditionally considered a high risk business. However, well over half of the partnerships were rated either "good" or "excellent" for credit.

Partnerships were the preferred type of business arrangement for several reasons. First, the pooled funds of a partnership generated a larger volume of business than did the smaller assets of the single proprietor. And in times of recessions, partnerships were financially better equipped to sustain losses, in addition to having certain legal protection. An individual partner, for example, could not be held liable for losses beyond the percent of his ownership in the joint partnership. Partnership therefore attracted higher credit ratings, but only after the credit agencies carefully investigated each partner. "Silent partners" who had a history of business failures in San Francisco or back East often hid their contributing capital in partnership arrangements where the more reputable, though less affluent, member headed the partnership in name only. Approximately 30 percent of all merchants from the sample located in R. G. Dun were reported to have experienced at least one business failure *before* arriving in San Francisco. Therefore many, no doubt, wished to hide behind "blind" arrangements after they arrived in the city.

Credit ratings were also affected by the business or personal habits of individual partners. If one of the partners was known to be a gambler either at the faro table or in speculative stocks, his firm found it difficult to obtain credit. The merchants in these partnership agreements frequently established rules limiting the discretion of members to withdraw unlimited amounts of principal or income from the business. The partnership agreement between Albert Dibblee and Charles W. Crosby was perhaps typical of the precautionary measures taken by the affluent merchants to protect their own assets and the good name and reputation of their firm. Crosby contributed $15,000 and Dibblee $5,000 to an enterprise which was to have a trial period of one year. No partner was "to employ the funds or credit of the firm for his own individual use—nor to draw out more than two thousand dollars per annum for personal expenditures." In addition, each partner agreed not "to contract any individual liability or to engage in any separate business" during the life of the copartnership. Further, each could terminate the partnership upon notice to the other, with profits disbursed after all expenses were paid out, in proportion to original capital invested.[26]

These legal qualifications also served notice to a potential creditor that the partnership assets were, to the extent of tne agreement, invested in the legitimate trade of the business. Creditors not only verified these local agreements but checked out other partners who might be residing in the East. If the New York branch of the partnership was known to be in financial trouble, the credit of the San Francisco store suffered. Alternatively, if it were known that a San Francisco merchant house held close ties to a major source of secure eastern capital, an "excellent" rating might be granted in San Francisco. The J. W. Davidson and Co. of San Francisco received such ratings in the 1850s and 1860s because "they are looked upon as almost a branch house of Lazard Frères [of New York City] who make all their European purchases and pay for them." The safest money resided in the East, where San Francisco's native-born merchants maintained the strongest connections.[27]

But assets and eastern connections did not always guarantee automatic lines to credit. Character, that invisible ingredient so important in a society predicated on the Puritan ethic, counted and loomed large in credit calculations.

Jews were assumed not to possess character unless they proved otherwise. R. G. Dun almost always noted if a merchant was a "Jew" or "Israelite." If it was not accompanied with a positive qualifier such as "White Jew" or "an Israelite of the better classes," the religious affiliation more often than not carried with it the automatic assumption of poor credit. Not that all Jews were poor or unsuccessful—far from it. In terms of occupational attainment and property accumulation they were certainly as successful as non-Jews, and no doubt more so; lack of religious affiliation data prevented confirmation of this point. But the tell-tale notation by R. G. Dun that an individual was a Jew served as a signal to all prospective creditors. A credit report on two German Jews who owned rather substantial assets, warned: "They are Hebrews. May be good [for credit] *if well watched*; they are *tricky.*" This bias against Jews reflected a more general bias against the foreign-born.[28]

Because it was difficult to obtain capital and credit from San Francisco's traditional institutional sources, Jews borrowed money from abroad, particularly Germany, and after 1850 from other Jews within the city. Friends or family members advanced funds from Europe, while Jewish business associates offered short-term loans at interest rates generally lower than those offered to poor credit risks by local banks. One German Jew, Emanuel Goldstein, accumulated enough money in his grocery business to loan to friends. The interest on these loans allowed Goldstein to expand his merchant activities into the wholesaling business. The daughter of another Jewish merchant wrote about how her father conducted his finances: "Any capital not invested in Father's business was loaned to individuals or firms on personal notes. Later, when he was retired [1870s], all his capital was loaned in this way."[29]

If the Jews suffered for their religion, others, regardless of occupation or wealth, were condemned for their personal behavior. Two merchants received a "no credit" rating from R. G. Dun after they "were detected smuggling cigars and taking false oaths at the Custom House." Another merchant with reported assets of between $30,000 and $40,000 had "a very poor reputation and his credit is not in proportion to [his] means." A grocer was reported to have failed in 1857 because of "fast living," presumably because he was "living beyond his means" with "an extravagant wife." An import merchant was reported to be a frequent visitor to the numerous Chinese flesh palaces, usually accompanied by an out-of-town merchant. His credit rating, though perhaps not his out-of-town business contacts, suffered. Another businessman "indulged a little too much with women." Yet another merchant's credit problem was that his "*personal reputation is not good* . . . His moral character is considered bad, has a wife and children, has been accused of keeping for a long time past a mistress and of having a child by a servant girl." The message was clear. A "good family man" with moderate means rated a higher credit rating than a wealthy person whose personal behavior was deemed immoral. Property could not compensate for flaws in personal character as demonstrated through observed or reported behavior.[30]

An "excellent" credit rating, in large measure, increased the likelihood of property accumulation and further determined who would remain in San Francisco. For in a decade where the capital assets of the merchants declined, those with the least property—and hence those least likely to recoup losses through credit arrangements—were the first to depart San Francisco. One measure of the importance of credit is that of those merchants with "excellent" rating, only 13 percent departed the city by 1860. But well over one-quarter of the merchants with "fair" or "no credit" left the city before the close of the decade.

When property alone was reckoned, a similar pattern emerged. Approximately 85 percent of the affluent merchants with assets in excess of $50,000 remained in the city after 1860 while only two-thirds of those with property holdings of $10,000 or less persisted after 1860. And finally, where occupational status determined, in large measure, a person's capital assets, the affluent importer-wholesalers placed permanent roots in San Francisco far more frequently than did the small shopkeepers.[31]

Probably the single important economic factor that caused merchants to depart San Francisco was business failure. Well over half of the individuals reported by R. G. Dun to have experienced business failure in the 1850s had departed San Francisco by 1860. Their ultimate destinations were, for the most part, unknown. However, in those cases where destinations were noted, many merchants departed the city for the security of their own more permanent homes in the East or overseas, or to the satellite towns in the mining districts of the Sierras.[32]

No longer optimistic about the chances of surviving, much less profiting from the economic havoc of the 1850s, merchants expressed despair for their future in the city. One San Francisco merchant, S. Griffith Morgan, cautioned a friend at home in New Bedford against moving to San Francisco. "California for an immediate fortune, is out of the question," he warned, adding that the chances for economic success were better at home than in San Francisco. The disillusioned Morgan faced severe competition from other importers and suffered large losses in 1854, and he was not an isolated example of merchant disillusionment.[33] Another merchant warned his father back East against moving to San Francisco since there existed better "prospects in the States as here" and besides, "expenses for living are very large." Before returning home, he again cautioned his father: "the chances are instantly growing less for rapid fortunes." Two Irish merchants, formerly of Charleston, South Carolina, closed shop and departed because "they can do much better business in some other state with the amount of capital they have." Finally, one New Yorker expressed, no doubt, the spirit of the majority of departees from San Francisco when he noted sadly in his diary that by coming to San Francisco he "had hoped to have repeated benefits that would make me in a measure independent in the world." But he met with economic failure and broken health and returned to New York with "all my prospects blighted, all my hopes confoundedly smashed, squashed."[34]

At the same time that the San Francisco merchants questioned the economic vitality and future of their own city, they received communications from the East that further confirmed their own reservations. Morgan, who advised his friend to stay put in New Bedford, received this word from a business associate at home. "The majority of people that come [back] from California give an awful account of it—they are rejoiced to get home even without a cent. You said in your letter that California was a *humbug*; it was proven to be so to many while there are a few that are made rich. This has always been the way of the world; it holds out great inducements but there are few in comparison . . . [who] accumulate its wealth."[35] A New York merchant, upon learning of his brother's misfortunes in San Francisco, wrote that New York and not San Francisco would control the trade of the West Coast and urged his brother's return. "I feel now as I have for a long time, that . . . there is no place like this [New York]; all the houses that have done business here for the past five years, using ordinary care and prudence, and not overtrading, have made money and many became very rich. The trade here . . . keeps pace with the rapid increase of the Great West and South West, and with the general increase in population and their wants: all parts of the states pay tribute here and always will."[36]

Though the New York merchant may have exaggerated the importance and success of his city's merchant houses, the fact remained that the East, having put up most of the initial capital to finance the San Francisco merchants, wanted the profits to be returned East. So, in addition to those merchants who returned home because of business failure, others departed to carry profits back to eastern owners. Finally, for a class more accustomed to the comforts and luxuries of cities like New York, Boston, and Philadelphia, the frontier conditions of San Francisco, particularly the health hazards, fires, and the severe housing shortage, did not encourage permanent settlement in the 1850 decade.[37]

Even among the first monied men of San Francisco—92 percent of whom were employed in high white-collar occupations and more than half in merchant endeavors—the departure rate was surprisingly high. Generally, the more affluent persisted longer. The professionals, a bit less affluent than the importer-wholesalers or the managerial group of bankers, brokers, and manufacturers, persisted at a rate higher than any other occupational group among the monied elite. Only 16 percent had departed by 1860 while almost 70 percent remained twenty years or more. Even the original merchant elite of 1851-52—the importer-wholesalers and those few retail merchants whose assets exceeded $50,000—discovered that by 1860, their ranks had decreased by more than one-third, their financial assets by one-quarter, and of those from the original group who remained in the city, one-half had experienced occupational slippage. An original member of San Francisco's merchant elite commented from the perspective of a quarter of a century that "Most of the early pioneers here with few exceptions, have not been prosperous in the long run. They were prosperous at first, and I suppose with [the] idea that prosperity would last forever, became extravagant, and when times changed a little, they found themselves in bad condition."[38] No doubt a few of the very rich, after "accumulating a fortune," one observer reported, "followed the old stereotyped path—went to some other country to spend it." But there could be little doubt that the more common experience of the monied men was similar to that of the general merchants and importer-wholesalers of the city in the 1850-1860 decade—occupational slippage and signigicant property losses.[39]

Well over a third of the general merchants and importer-wholesalers experienced property losses in the 1850 decade. The importer-wholesalers' capital assets diminished by approximately one-quarter in value, and half of them lost occupational status in less than eight years. Of the general merchants, whose financial losses were less severe and within whose ranks one-fifth gained occupational status in the 1850 decade, almost half (46 percent) departed by 1860 due, in large part, to the adverse economic conditions prevailing in San Francisco. And finally the petty shopkeepers, who were the largest merchant group in numbers and possessed the least amount of capital to cushion the economic and occupational effects of the fires and recessions, experienced business failures and property losses. Those shopkeepers who could afford the relative luxury of remaining beyond 1860 in a city with the highest living expenses in the nation, discovered occupational opportunities that moved seven out of every ten into more prestigious occupations. But because of the relatively large capital resources needed to survive the severe economic dislocations of the decade, which few of them possessed, more than half chose not to remain and seek the twin goals of higher occupational status and increased financial security.

During the decade of the 1850s the initial generation of importer-wholesalers was vacating the monied ranks. But the petty shopkeepers, and to a lesser degree the general retail merchants, found it impossible to persist and fill the vacuum, pressed as they were by economic factors. As the decade progressed, a class of newcomers whose social origins differed significantly from the original merchant elite of 1850-51 began slowly to take up the vacant places. The replacement process, hastened by the recessions of the 1850s and the subsequent property losses, was apparent to certain members of the old merchant elite. A former commission merchant who wrote to a friend in New York about his personal and financial reverses observed: "Times have changed in California. The men of my own class have passed away: men to whom one could apply for five or ten thousand dollars and get it without a question. The money of the country is now held by men of small prosperity who never looked upon our large gains with any other feeling than envy, and who now rejoice in our reverses."[40]

As the merchants looked at their condition in the late 1850s, certainly the vast majority had not found the instant wealth that had lured them to San Francisco in the first place. For most, the perception of their individual condition in the late 1850s failed to match the exaggerated expectations they had once held at the beginning of the decade. The attendant loss of personal esteem no doubt added to the considerable emotional dislocations associated with the original transcontinental move to San Francisco. Some sought escape through alcohol, others were sent to the new mental asylum at Stockton, still others lost their physical health.[41]

Among those who persisted, the spirit of pessimism also prevailed. One merchant complained, "I never saw so hard a place to raise money as in California in my life . . . There are more damned cut throats here than [in] any five states in the Union." Even so affluent and prestigious a merchant as William Coleman, whose assets by 1860 were estimated to be well in excess of $100,000, could complain that "while great profits were realized in some instances, the average run of trade was not more profitable [in San Francisco] than in other [states] under a more settled state of affairs." "Losses," he lamented, "often over-balanced . . . excessive profits," and trying to conduct orderly business in San Francisco "was like playing a new game of hazard."[42]

In American society, where status has been directly related to income, the relative lack of occupational opportunities for the merchants in San Francisco in the 1850s was directly reflected in their accout books. There were few among the first generation of San Franciscans—merchant, clerk, tanner, porter, or servant—who would have disagreed with the observation of San Francisco's foremost banker and Civil War general, William T. Sherman, who lamented that California was "a great country for rich people, but death to a poor one."[43]

5

THE SOCIAL FABRIC

The San Francisco postmaster, housed on the ground floor of a leased wooden shack, complained in 1850 that the bundles of unclaimed letters to miners, merchants, seamen, and salesmen would soon engulf his single-room office. In this transient city, where the ships in the harbor far outnumbered the semipermanent structures on shore, there were no churches, hospitals, schools, or voluntary associations. Not even a fire company existed to protect the dingy collection of flammable canvas and wooden shanties that spread from the waterfront up towards the sand hills. Letters home in 1849 and 1850 detailed not the virtues of San Francisco, but individual anxiety and the miseries of the town—human and physical. In short, San Francisco was not a place where one wanted to settle permanently, raise a family, and worship God. The early economy of the city, fueled by gold from the mines, attracted a population whose optimism more often than not outlasted their good fortune; in fact, of the first adventurers who arrived before 1852, only one-quarter remained in the city through the end of the decade.[1] Yet optimism continued to be characteristic of the newcomers and of the pioneers who remained. From their ranks grew the nucleus of a permanent population and the beginning of the city's first elite.

San Franciscans, whose complaints coexisted with civic pride, perceived their city as one free of class structure, indeed, as the quintessential egalitarian society. Hubert Bancroft reflected on the social condition of the time when he wrote that the city's isolated location restricted its population to men whose "self-reliance and energy . . . verged on audacity." They were pragmatic and thus adaptable and they cared little for form and appearance. Unhampered by the conservatism of older communities, they "sought with flexible originality and subtle perception new and independent channels." Wit and muscle reigned supreme, and democratic equality leveled class aspirations. "The rapidity with which millionaires were made gave no time for covering the crudities of their humble origin. Yet the change was attended by little vulgar conceit, for the caprice of fortune continued to show itself in the making and unmaking of men within the day. Class distinctions gradually acquired some influence, but they have not yet reached the absurdities common in the east. Character and enterprise take a leading rank, but they must be practical and promising."[2]

In fact, however, San Francisco possessed an elite. It was perhaps less permanent than comparable elites in eastern communities, but the social origins of its members were not always so humble as the myth had it. At the pinnacle of San Francisco society, by virtue of their occupational status and affluence, were the city merchants, bankers, and brokers—those men who provided "the model by which the remainder of the community" were guided "in shaping their course through life."[3] Having sunk their financial resources into the commerce of the city, and being therefore cemented more securely to the city than more transient men, the men at the top invested their energies in making for themselves and their families permanent homes similar in structure to those of older cities. Occupying new jobs, adrift in a makeshift city lacking social institutions, separated in many cases from their family and friends, and geographically isolated on the western shores of a vast continent, the more permanent residents of San Francisco sought the associational networks and institutional arrangements that would provide them a sense of place in a new environment.

The city's elite, particularly the affluent importer-wholesalers and commission merchants, merely utilized their financial and occupational status in the community to establish and direct the associational life of San Francisco. As the elite perceived their status and role in the city, no one else possessed the legitimate right to challenge their leadership. And where in the single instance—politics—the reins of power failed to fall to the men of the elite, they would capture by undemocratic means what they had failed, out of sheer neglect, to control through the more democratic processes that were available.

Voluntary Associations

The voluntary associations provided the human cement that transformed San Francisco from a temporary stopover for peripatetic travelers to a permanent urban community. And for the individual participant or joiner, the voluntary associations offered an escape from the isolation of individualism that most early residents, geographically separated from family and friends, no doubt experienced. San Franciscans were no different from other Americans in this respect. Indeed, the formation of voluntary associations was a common activity, if not a habit, of nineteenth-century Americans. Alexis de Tocqueville described this unique American phenomenon. "In no country in the world has the principle of association been more successfully used or applied to a great multitude of objects than in America . . . Associations are established to promote the public safety, commerce, industry, morality, and religion. There is no end which the human will despair of attaining through the combined power of individuals united into society."[4]

The native-born merchants of the city carried the habit and memory of voluntary associations from the East Coast to the West. The San Francisco Chamber of Commerce, for example, modeled its by-laws after its New York predecessor. Fire and militia companies copied eastern models. In fact, with the important exception of the Vigilance Committees, there was no voluntary association in San Francisco in the 1850s which did not have its counterpart in New York, Boston, or Philadelphia.

Multiple office holding, or an "interlocking directorate" by the elite in voluntary associations, was as common in San Francisco as in other cities.[5] William D. M. Howard, one of San Francisco's most prominent commission merchants, sat as an appointed member of the first Town Council in 1849 and as one of the city's representatives at the California Constitutional Convention, donated the lot upon which his church congregation constructed a new edifice (appropriately named the Howard Street Presbyterian Church), captained the First California Guard (a militia company), promoted the Protestant Orphan Asylum, served as first president of the Society of California Pioneers, acted on the executive committee of the Vigilance Committee of 1851, and contributed a fire-pumper to the volunteer fire company that also bore his name.

In a city where fires raged through city blocks almost monthly and where annual property losses to the merchants averaged in excess of $1,000,000 during the period 1849-1855, merchants took the lead to organize volunteer fire companies. Their private subscriptions sustained the companies until 1854 when the city, with a $200,000 bond issue, provided financial assistance for the purchase of lots and equipment and the erection of fire houses. In 1866 the city replaced the volunteer companies with a department of full-time paid firemen. The San Francisco fire companies took for their model the volunteer companies of eastern cities where a considerable number of San Francisco volunteer firemen had trained. A San Francisco merchant recalled: "I was one of the organizers of the Empire Fire Company No. 1 . . . This [San Francisco] company was named after the Empire Fire Co. of New York of which I was a member. I brought out with me a copy of its by-laws which were the first and only laws at that time in the country [California]."[6]

Aside from the utilitarian duties of fighting fires, the volunteer companies in the 1850s served as exclusive social clubs in which "almost every gentlemen in town" was a member. Applicants for membership were reviewed by a committee which inquired "into the character and competency of all candidates for membership after they shall have been proposed." By limiting their membership to gentlemen, the San Francisco companies naturally insured that merchants, and particularly the wholesaler-importers, would be not only members but also the leaders of the volunteer fire associations.[7]

From a sample drawn from the early fire companies, a little less than half of the total membership of these companies were engaged in merchant occupations. In two organizations, the Empire and California Engine companies, merchant membership exceeded 60 percent. Merchants founded two other companies and in two additional fire houses they held a majority of the executive positions. Merchants also controlled the board of delegates, an organization of representatives from all the voluntary fire companies, which attempted to coordinate fire protection for the entire city. By limiting the majority of their membership to males employed in prestigious occupations, the fire companies conferred a certain degree of status on their members.[8]

Despite the occupational and class similarities, there were important distinctions between the companies which the members proudly guarded. One member noted that each fire company had its own special characteristics, "its pedigrees so to speak, its records and traditions. The Empires and Manhattans and Knickerbockers were New Yorkers. The Howards were Bostonians—the Monumentals were Bal-

The Monumental Fire Company, a two-story granite and freestone structure, founded by former residents of Baltimore, Maryland. The upstairs meeting rooms for members contained a 1,000-volume library.

timorians." Former New Orleans residents manned the Vigilant and Crescent companies while Frenchmen organized the LaFayette company. The companies competed for public attention and prestige by staging parades, fancy balls, banquets, and concerts. And when fires occurred, they rushed off to the conflagration in the most colorful uniforms hoping to arrive and extinguish the fire before a competing unit claimed credit for victory. Competition extended to the construction of luxurious fire houses. The Sansome company's building cost its members $24,000, was "furnished as well as any residence in the city," and housed a well-stocked library for its predominantly upper-class members. Additional subscription fees paid for the care of sick members and widows.[9]

Merchant participation and leadership extended to the local militia companies, which also afforded an environment for comradeship in the new city. In fact some of the local militia companies were off-spring of the fire companies. The Empire Guard, for example, was composed mainly of New Yorkers active in the Empire Engine company, and the majority of the Marion Rifles were Baltimorians active in the Monumental Engine company. William D. M. Howard, the merchant founder of the Howard Fire company, also helped establish San Francisco's first militia company, the First California Guard.

The militia companies were filled with proud citizen-soldiers, some of whom had served in the Mexican War or militia companies of eastern cities, and nearly all officers "ranked high in the social scale."[10] The merchants, again the importer-wholesalers, were heavily represented among the leadership ranks of the militia companies. In the National Lances in 1852, for example, half the officers were merchants, including the commanding officer, while 85 percent of the officers of the Eureka Light Horse Guard were employed in merchant occupations.

Serving as an auxiliary law-and-order agency in a city where the citizens, and particularly the merchants, complained vehemently about the "criminal element," the militia companies with their elite leadership performed certain quasi-military functions. They also served as a limited training ground for the Vigilance Committees of 1851 and 1856 and the Union Army. But the main factor that motivated the formation of volunteer militia companies was, despite their military appearance, primarily the fraternal desire for comradeship, and "the hope of social approval.''[11] Guard members gathered at the militia headquarters for the same reason volunteer firemen congregated at the fire house. Members proudly displayed their colorful and ornate uniforms on parades, at banquets, receptions, and target excursions. The armory served as a second home for many of the elite who, in a male-dominated city lacking the family structure of the older and more establsihed urban centers, sought the companionship of their social peers. Finally, the armory, like the fire companies, served as a clubhouse where young men, seeking an entree to the economic and social life of the city, established valuable business contacts and occupational opportunities.[12]

Merchants also carried the eastern model of religious affiliations to the West. San Francisco's first churches and synagogues were, in large measure, established and directed by the city's merchants. Organized ethnically and geographically, the German Jews were as separate from the Polish Jews as the New England Presbyterians were from their southern brethren. Church membership conferred status, particularly if one were a trustee of a ''respectable'' church.[13]

Protestant merchants who directed the volunteer fire and militia companies served also as trustees among the city's Protestant churches. Ira Rankin, a native of Pelham, Massachusetts, who commenced his business career as a clerk in a rural country store before opening a general commission house in San Francisco in 1852, served as an officer of a volunteer fire company and the president (moderator) of the First Congregational Church of San Francisco. Later in the decade, Rankin was elected president of the Mercantile Library Association and served on the prestigious committee of appeals of the city's Chamber of Commerce before his appointment as Collector of Customs. Another Massachusetts native, William Babcock, the son and grandson of a prominent Boston merchant family, lent his prestige to the board of vestrymen of San Francisco's Trinity Church and, in later years, to the presidency of the Chamber of Commerce. David Beck, descendant of an old Knickerbocker family, who left a dry goods store in New York in 1850 for a commission business in San Francisco, helped to found both the Manhattan Fire company and the First Presbyterian Church in San Francisco.[14] Finally, F. W. Macondray, a native of Raynham, Massachusetts, former ship's captain and one of San Francisco's leading commission merchants in the 1850s,

The Roman Catholic Orphan Asylum (circa 1860), home for 275 children. Next door is Saint Patrick's Church on Market Street, later the site for the elegant Palace Hotel in the 1870s.

served concurrently on the city's board of aldermen, as president of the Chamber of Commerce, chief benefactor to the Sansome Hook and Ladder company, and president of the First Unitarian Church of San Francisco.

Though there were few Catholics among the first merchant elite of the city, those who did move into the elite circles similarly performed leadership roles. For example, Joseph A. Donohoe gained his fame and fortune in dry goods, first in New York, then in Saint Louis, and eventually in San Francisco where in 1852 he served as an officer of the Chamber of Commerce and treasurer and trustee of the Catholic Orphan Asylum.

The Jewish merchants, who generally failed to gain entrance into the WASP-dominated fire and militia companies, organized the Jewish congregations and financed the structures which housed them. In the Jewish community, as among the Protestants, an interlocking directorate of wealthy merchants served as trustees for the synagogues and affiliated benevolent societies. August Helbing, a partner in the San Francisco wholesale dry goods firm of Meyer, Helbing & Co., helped found the Eureka Benevolent Society and the Pacific Hebrew Orphanage Association, and served as president of the People's Institute, the predecessor of the Mechanics Institute and Mercantile Library. The prominent Seligman brothers (Henry, Jesse, William, and Abraham) were instrumental in the formation of San Francisco's first synagogue, Temple Emanu-El. "Henry Seligman's greatest contribution to the communal life of San Francisco was in a field of Judaism," and according to Dr. Jacob Voorsanger, rabbi of the city's foremost Jewish house of worship, the Seligmans gave their unique administrative energy and leadership at a critical time. William was a charter member, Jesse loaned money to assist in the purchase of the city's first synagogue, and Abraham served as a trustee.[15]

Collectively as well as individually the merchants played a significant role in the religious life of the city. Merchants composed over half of the original founders of the First Congregational Church, First Baptist Church, First Unitarian Church, and Trinity Episcopal Church and over three-quarters of the founders of Temple Emanu-El and Sherith Israel. Of the twenty people appointed in 1854 to raise $75,000 for the construction of the Calvary Presbyterian Church on Bush Street, twelve were merchants. The merchants appeared to be less involved with the formation and leadership of various Roman Catholic churches of the city probably because there were fewer Roman Catholic merchants. By the close of the decade, a little over 50 percent of the leadership positions in the churches and synagogues of the city were occupied by merchants. In the Jewish congregations, 80 percent of their leaders earned their living in the city's merchant houses.[16]

The founders and early leaders of the quasi-religious benevolent societies were also predominantly merchants. Of the twelve original founders of the Eureka Benevolent Society, whose purpose was to aid German Jewish immigrants, eleven were merchants. Likewise, the wives of German Jewish merchants directed the activities of the Eureka's auxiliary, the German Hebrew Ladies Benevolent Society. Within the German General Benevolent Society (non-Jewish), merchants played a decidedly smaller role (approximately half of the founders were merchants) than their German-Jewish counterparts did in their organizations.[17]

A distinct social hierarchy existed in the San Francisco Jewish community. "The segregation of the Jews in classes takes place naturally; wealth decides the station in the synagogue and in society, and next to wealth is nationality. Bavarian, French and Alsatian Jews go one way, Russian and Polish another."[18] The Germans, the richer among the Jews, and those who sought reform of the Jewish ritual, congregated in Temple Emanu-El. Liberal in religious matters, they tended also to be socially exclusive. The Jewish merchant elite virtually monopolized Temple Emanu-El's board of directors. The less affluent Jews (some Germans but predominantly Polish, English, and later Russian Jews) congregated in Sherith Israel to practice their more conservative Judaism.[19] It was the German Jews who directed the Jewish charitable organizations of the city, much to the annoyance of the non-German congregation of Temple Sherith Israel. One observer noted:

The German Jews had a better sense of organization than the Jews from Russia, Poland and Roumania; and in San Francisco they were the first to undertake the organization of charitable institutions . . . although they were willing to cooperate with other ethnic groups, their consistent use of the German language, their adherence to old German traditions, and their separate social and cultural institutions made them a distinct group. Yet, among themselves, there was not accord. There was frequent dissention between Bavarian, Austrian, and German Jews. In 1849, the richer German Jews sought reform of the Jewish ritual. Revolving chiefly around Temple Emanu-El, these people sought seats on the board of trustees of the Eureka Benevolent Socity, the Hebrew Home for the Aged . . . and sought to take over the Hebrew Orphan Asylum. The English, Russian, and Polish Jews objected strenuously to this with the result that keen rivalry between Temple Emanu-El and Temple Sherith Israel ensued.[20]

The large Jewish population of San Francisco was looked upon as hard-working, frugal, and peace-abiding. The leading newspaper of the city, the *Alta California*, observed in 1853 that anyone who walked through the city's business district could not "fail to be struck with the fact that a very large fraction of our population is composed of Jews. They are good citizens . . . seldom is a Jew reported as drunk or disorderly."[21] Another observer noted the reasons why Jews were accorded a degree of respect by the non-Jewish population of San Francisco: "They are frugal and industrious, and seldom fail to gradually accumulate capital when once established in a business, however small the beginning may be. Few of them have any political aspirations, and it is a rare occurrence to find them occupying any official position, either municipal or state. Yet they take a lively interest in politics . . . there are a less number of Jews arraigned before the criminal tribunals of the city than any other class of citizens. In no instance has a Jew been before the courts of San Francisco to answer for the crime of murder."[22]

Visitors to the city also were surprised by the high esteem in which the Jews were held by the city residents, owing no doubt to the fact that Jewish merchants controlled a significant portion of the city's wholesale and retail trade. A Jewish visitor to San Francisco from the East in the mid-1850s noted:

The Jews are greatly respected by the non-Jews and it may well be said that nowhere else are they regarded with so much esteem by their non-Jewish brothers, and nowhere else are they so highly valued in social or political circles . . . Business, banking, as well as trade, is to a great extent in their hands. The market depends upon them completely, because they import the most, . . . and shipping and the forwarding business have them to thank for a great part of their flourishing business . . . the Jews are looked to first of all, because they are always willing to contribute, and such undertakings are generally successful because of their assistance. A large part of the wealth of California is in their hands; they have acquired it by thrift and sobriety, by steadfast industry and toil.[23]

Prejudice against the Jews, as well as other ethnic groups, did, of course, exist in California as in other sections of the nation. The caption of a lithograph in an early social history of San Francisco written in 1854 by three local residents referred to Latin American "greasers," "smelly" and "slant-eyed" Chinamen, and "hook-nosed" Jews. When a bill was introduced in the state legislature in March 1855, designed specifically against Jewish shopkeepers who traded on

Sundays, its sponsor, Speaker of the House William W. Stow of Santa Cruz, said that Jews "were a class of people who only came here to make money and leave as soon as they had effected their object." "They did not," argued Stow, "invest their money in the country or the cities." E. Gould Buffum, editor of the *Alta California* and one of San Francisco's representatives in the legislature, vigorously defended the Jews of his city. They "had built some of the finest edifices the city could boast, and their wealth, influence, and enterprise were as conspicuous and appreciated as anywhere in the world." The Jews of San Francisco were quick to defend themselves as well. A wealthy San Francisco Jewish lawyer, Henry J. Labatt, charged the speaker with "flagrant and malicious falsehood" and reminded him of the permanence and affluence of California Jews. In a scathing attack on Stow, Labatt asked rhetorically: "Are you ignorant of the number of [Jewish] families arriving on every steamer . . . [who wish] to make California their home? Are you ignorant of the brick synagogues erected in our cities for family worship? Are you ignorant of the permanent benevolent societies, which extend the hand of charity to their bereaved brethren, and relieve the state, county, and city of taxes for alms houses, hospitals, asylums? If you are ignorant of these facts, then you are basely ignorant; if not, you have greatly misrepresented facts, and you are a disgrace to the House over which you have the dishonor to preside."

The Jewish spokesman closed his letter by reminding the speaker that twenty San Francisco Jews paid taxes on over two million dollars of assessed property; he warned Stow: "A large and numerous body of voters of this state will remember these facts, and I trust every Jew will bear it in mind many a long day, for you cannot expel them from this state." "For myself," concluded Labatt, "I shall use every endeavor to keep it constantly before" the Jews of California. The Sunday Trading bill died and no one was heard to defend the speaker's proposal or to attack the defenders of San Francisco's Jewish population.[24]

As exemplified by Labatt's letter, the Jews of San Francisco and certainly the many affluent merchants among them, were secure in the knowledge that their publicly recognized accomplishments in business could overcome the infrequent and petty discriminations the Jews encountered in San Francisco. Led by their respected merchants, the

Jews of San Francisco probably faced less prejudice and carried forth into future decades the memory of fewer unpleasant experiences than the Jews of any city in the nation at midcentury. Although Jews were by no means fully integrated into the social fabric of the Gentiles, their very *immediate* business success, particularly in the merchant oc- cupations, served as clear evidence that they were allowed to conduct their lives relatively free of prejudicial barriers.[25]

Latin Americans, Australians (most of whom were mistakenly thought to be convicts), the Chinese, and certainly the blacks faced deeper and more ingrained prejudice than the Jews.[26] The 1852 California census counted some 2,200 blacks in California, approxi- mately 700 of whom resided in San Francisco with the remainder scat- tered throughout the mining districts of the Sierras. Almost all were free blacks who had migrated from northern and upper-southern states. A few were former slaves who had been freed by their masters in the gold fields. By 1860 the black population of San Francisco in- creased to 1,176, of whom 20 percent were employed as cooks and the other 80 percent worked as waiters, stewards, porters, barbers, shoe- blacks, and common laborers. Hinton Helper observed in 1855 that they "are in the same situation as their brethren in New York and Massachusetts, slaves to no single individual but to the entire com- munity. Like free negroes everywhere else, they inhabit the worst parts of the towns in California and live commonly in characteristic filth and degradation."[27]

Despite overwhelming prejudice, one black merchant was successful in San Francisco. Gold attracted Mifflin W. Gibbs, born a free man in Philadelphia in 1823. When he arrived in San Francisco, he found em- ployment as a carpenter, but when the white carpenters with whom he worked threatened to strike, he was fired. Gibbs saved money earned at odd jobs, and within a year joined in partnership with a white boot- maker, Peter Lester, to open the Pioneer Boot and Shoe Emporium which specialized in "fine imported boots and shoes" from Philadel- phia, London, and Paris. San Franciscans recognized the superior quality of the Emporium's inventory, for Gibbs and Lester reportedly had "without doubt the best customers for good boots in this city." Once when Gibbs refused to pay a poll tax for the dubious honor of not being allowed to vote, the city took possession of some goods from his store and put them up for auction. A southern white in-

Mifflin W. Gibbs, one of the few black merchants of San Francisco, owner of the Pioneer Boot and Shoe Emporium. He later became municipal judge in Little Rock, Arkansas, and then served as United States Consul to Madagascar.

formed the merchants assembled at the auction of the unjust confiscation and requested that Gibbs' goods be given a "terrible letting alone." No bids were received and the goods returned to the Pioneer Boot and Shoe Emporium. Gibbs, whose atypical career carried him from the black ghetto of Philadelphia to the white merchants' world of San Francisco, could say that "with thrift and a wise circumspection financially," the opportunities for blacks were "very good." But, he concluded, "from every other point of view, Blacks were ostracized, assaulted without redress, disenfranchised and denied their oath in a court of justice."[28]

Although the white merchants assisted a black colleague, they failed to aid more impoverished blacks. They would not employ blacks as clerks or bookkeepers, the apprenticeships for the merchant profession. Nor did they found, lead, or otherwise encourage voluntary associations or benevolent societies to assist blacks, an effort which they generally undertook for European immigrants. In general, San Franciscans treated their black residents with the same disregard and pervasive callousness as did most Americans everywhere. And finally, at a time when the "industrious" Germans, "useful" French, and "intelligent" native-born Americans (among other Nordics) controlled the city's social, economic and political networks, it was not surprising that they also viewed all Latins and Chinese with contempt.[29]

Vigilance Committee, 1851

The voluntary association to which the San Francisco merchants gave their greatest loyalty, energies, and money, was not the fire or militia company, church, benevolent society, or political party, but the Vigilance Committee. There were, in fact, two committees: the Vigilance Committee of 1851 and its bigger brother, the Vigilance Committee of 1856. Organized, led, and financed by the city's leading merchants, both committees demonstrated the elite's penchant for extralegal violence for which San Francisco earned a well-deserved national reputation in the 1850s.

The 1851 Vigilance Committee emerged suddenly and unexpectedly as a response by the "better classes of society" against the city's "criminal element." The inadequate protection by an undermanned city police force was compounded, the *Alta California* reported, by a corrupt court system which "instead of being a terror to evil doers, have proved themselves the protectors to villains and thus encouragers of crime." An agent for the DuPont Gunpowder Company of Wilmington, Delaware, whose product found eager purchasers throughout this frontier city in the 1850s, explained the situation in a letter to his family. In the first five months of 1851, thirty-six criminal cases awaited trial but, reported DuPont's agent, they were always postponed so "more profitable" civil cases could be heard. In the meantime, witnesses to the criminal cases departed San Francisco, and for lack of evidence, the "criminal let free." Between June 1850 and June 1851, fifty-four murders were committed in San Francisco, "not one of which has ever been punished."[30]

For the San Francisco merchants, crime was disruptive to a peaceful social fabric and a profitable business environment. It was enough to have to face unpredictable business recessions and fight indiscriminate fires without also tolerating crime. Thus in 1849 the merchants had organized a citizen group (the Regulators) to police their property and financial interests. Soon, however, the merchants lost control of their organization when "self-licensed robbers," calling themselves the Hounds, acted on behalf of the Regulators. By day the Hounds attacked the homes (tents) of recently arrived foreigners (mostly Peruvians, Mexicans, and Chileans) to rob them and extort money and valuables. By night the marauders robbed stores, taverns, and merchant warehouses.

And not only were minorities the victims. One woman complained in a letter to eastern relatives that "murders, robberies and accidents are 'very much in *vogue*'." And in another letter she reported that "there is usually an alarm of fire every day, one or two murders committed weekly, robberies happen every night." She freely admitted her anxiety: "I never feel safe." It seemed almost everyone, merchant or mechanic, carried a concealed weapon to protect himself against assault so common in the bars, gambling palaces, and city streets. Another observer noted: "Some scenes of a most savage and atrocious description, ending occasionally in death, took place between parties who were reputed to be of the first class of citizens . . . On the slightest occasion, at a look or touch, an oath, a single word of offence, the bowie-knife leaped from the sheath, and the loaded revolver from the breast pocket or the secret case, and death or severe wounds quickly closed the scene. The spectators often shared in the same wild feelings, and did not always seek to interfere. The law was powerless to prevent such personal conflicts."[31]

Lacking an efficient or responsive municipal government, local citizens, urged and led by the merchants, organized their own police force to capture and bring to trial members of the Hounds. The 230-man citizen police apprehended twenty members of the Hounds, detained them aboard the U.S.S. *Warren* for imprisonment, and convicted them before a citizen jury on charges of conspiracy, riot, robbery, and assault with intent to kill. Yet the harsh extralegal measures taken against the Hounds failed to discourage crime or "the criminal element."[32]

The incident that set the Vigilance Committee in motion occurred late in the evening of February 15, 1851. Two men entered the dry goods store of C. J. Jansen and robbed and beat him unconscious. The attack on the merchant, who was considered one of the leading citizens in the community, aroused the immediate anger of the merchants and the general citizenry. It was clear that most citizens believed the civil authorities were unwilling to ensure the safety of law-abiding citizens. To augment the city's small police force, the merchants formed a volunteer night patrol to protect their property. One member explained how the system worked. "The intention was that whoever had valuable property should take personal part in the patrol. Capt. F. W. Macondray [a commission merchant] was at the head of it, and there were about a hundred members . . . assigned to different districts, and were on duty about eight hours. I was out four times per month in this way. This was a regular police organization, with proper officers, established by ourselves for our protection; and the members were expected to and did personally perform duties required and [did] not delegate them to anyone else."[33]

But it was one thing to capture and arrest criminals and another to convict them in the San Francisco courts. The elected judges, the merchants believed, were all too susceptible to bribes. Mayor Geary pleaded that the local courts would try fairly the two men charged with the assault and robbery of Mr. Jansen. "Leave it to the courts," said the mayor. Sam Brannan, one of the city's leading merchants responded, "To hell with your courts. *We* are the courts—and the hangmen!" Another merchant, William Coleman, also responded to

Mayor Geary's plea: "We will *not* leave it to the courts. No! We will do no such thing. The people here have no confidence in your promises, and unfortunately they have no confidence in the execution of the law by its officers. Matters have gone too far. Patience is exhausted. I propose that the people here present form themselves into a court, to be organized within this building immediately."[34]

The merchants would tolerate an uncivilized environment only so long as their property and lives were not endangered. But by 1851 in the wake of a massive fire which had destroyed over one-fourth of the central business district and over $3,000,000 in property, the merchants of the city were in no mood to accept passively misfortune brought on by human hands. When the question came up, the merchants could, and would, control their own destiny. By organizing and supervising a Vigilance Committee for all to witness, the city's merchants gave clear warning that if the elected civil authorities could not keep social order, then the merchants would not only introduce order to the city, but maintain it through vigilante justice.

Under the initial leadership of Sam Brannan, the 1851 Vigilance Committee of San Francisco formed with the avowed purpose to "vigilantly watch and pursue the outlaws and criminals who were infesting the city, and bring them to justice, through the regularly constituted courts if that could be" or through a more "direct process" if need be. The committee would "sustain the laws when faithfully and properly administered" but, it warned, "we are determined that no thief, burglar, incendiary assassin (professed gambler and other disturbers of the peace) shall escape punishment either by the quibbles of the law, the insecurity of prisons, the carelessness or corruption of the police or a laxity of those who pretend to administer justice."[35]

Approximately 700 citizens joined the committee, half of whom were merchants; only 14 percent from the blue-collar ranks gained admittance to this overwhelmingly white-collar voluntary association.[36] Not only did the committee attract 86 percent of its members from the white-collar ranks, but two-thirds of them were employed in high status white-collar occupations. Among the merchant members, almost 40 percent were prestigious importer-wholesalers, who also filled over half of the positions in the Executive Committee.[37]

The committee, during its short one-month life, brought ninety men accused of crimes before its tribunal; charges were dropped on forty-

Table 5.1. Occupational distribution of the general city population and the 1851 Vigilance Committee (in percent).

Sector	General population (N = 669)	Vigilance Committee 1851 (N = 344)
Blue collar		
Nonskilled	20	4
Semiskilled	44	10
All blue collar	64	14
White collar		
Petty proprietors (nonmerchant)	5	1
Petty proprietors (merchant)	10	8
Clerical, sales	7	10
General merchants	3	22
Importer-wholesalers	2	19
Managers, large proprietors, manufacturers (nonmerchant)	3	18
Professional	6	8
All white collar	36	86

SOURCE: California State Census, 1852; Mary Floyd Williams, ed., *Papers of the 1851 San Francisco Committee of Vigilance;* San Francisco *City Directories,* 1851-1852.

five for lack of evidence, fifteen were handed over to the local authorities, fourteen were banished from the city, one was whipped before an enthusiastic audience and, amidst great fanfare and in the best frontier tradition, four men were publicly hanged from rope donated by a local merchant. When the committee disbanded, it was in the belief that it had brought law and order to San Francisco.

No one—including the mayor and the governor—publicly criticized the committee. The citizens of San Francisco enthusiastically congratulated it, heaped praise on its leaders, and defended the right of citizens to take whatever steps necessary, without regard to the law, to maintain law and order in the city. The "neck-tie" justice of the 1851 Vigilance Committee did have an immediate effect. The number of murders, assaults, and robberies in San Francisco declined, the police force was enlarged, and the courts prosecuted and convicted more vigorously those indicted on criminal charges. But while the committee was quick to capture, try, and execute petty criminals, it was, on the other hand, unconcerned with corruption in the city government. Local officials allowed valuable city property (2,000 acres) to pass into the hands of real estate speculators, many of whom were merchants, for less than its true value.[38]

Vigilance Committee, 1856

Within five years another Vigilance Committee emerged. The 1856 Vigilance Committee, with its 8,000 members, held the dubious distinction of being the largest such body in the long history of the American vigilante movement.[39] It was formed for complex reasons that went beyond a response to the reemergence of crime in the streets of San Francisco. Once again the merchants organized and led a vigilance movement for the avowed purpose of cleansing the social fabric of the criminal element. But in fact the 1856 movement was a political revolution by the merchants, many suffering financial and occupational losses, who attempted to restructure the political and economic order of the city so as to preserve their status in the community.

In the six years since statehood in 1850, San Francisco's government had failed to respond to the staggering fiscal problems caused by the city's rapid growth. The state in its initial 1850 charter to San Francisco had granted the city power "to make by-laws and ordinances not repugnant to the Constitution and laws of the United States or of this state." The state, in effect, allowed home rule, which left the city to the devices of its mayor and a legislative council composed of a board of sixteen aldermen and assistant aldermen. Other elective officials were a treasurer, comptroller, street commissioner, collector of taxes, marshall, city attorney, and two tax assessors for each of the eight wards. The city's fiscal extravagance led to immediate public demand for debt restraints which the local authorities either avoided or ignored. As early as 1851, the city was virtually bankrupt with a public debt of over $1,000,000. The *Alta California* pleaded with the citizens to "awake . . . the ship is sinking! Go on board and take command— seize the helm." The citizens responded with a succession of new city charters severely limiting the fiscal powers of the elected officials to incur further public debt, and made provision for reducing the existing debt and the salaries of city officials.[40]

The new charters had little effect, however. Taxes on real and personal property almost doubled between 1850-51 and 1855-56. And in the four years following the 1851 charter revision, city expenditures more than doubled while the city's debt increased another 40 percent. Fires destroyed the merchants' property, eastern shippers flooded the local markets with unwanted goods, gold production began to flag, causing two of the city's major banks to fail, and approximately one-third of the merchant establishments declared bankruptcy in the midst of the local 1855 depression. On top of this, the city imposed on the merchants' dwindling financial resources higher taxes and new license fees. Clearly, as the merchants viewed their world, city hall not only had failed to aid the beleaguered merchants, but the elected officials had acted against the best interests of the merchant class.[41]

In retrospect the merchants had only themselves to blame for their lack of influence in city politics. "The better class of men were so absorbed in business and were so sure they were not going to live here," reported one observer, "that they took little active interest in elections. Indeed, they would not stop to vote." A merchant, in a letter explaining the problems of the city, freely admitted the disinterest of his colleagues in the political process. "The merchant has considered politics of inferior importance," he wrote, "and has seldom taken the trouble to vote, and the consequence . . . unprincipled and untrusted men have the reins of government in their own hands and we have only to suffer for our neglect."[42]

Further, merchants frequently avoided jury duty, claiming that they could not take time from the commercial activities to attend court. The *Alta California* reported, "An aversion to the performance of jury duty has been so repeatedly exhibited by our business men and the course of justice so often impeded thereby, that frequent appeals to the patriotism of our citizens have been thought necessary to secure . . . the safety of civil interests."[43]

No evidence suggests that the merchants responded to these appeals.[44] They left the governance of the city to others because in the process of devoting their total energies to their own private businesses, they failed to recognize the potentially positive ways by which local government could be utilized to serve their own interests. The merchants became more active politically only as local government expanded its functions and as their economic fortunes declined. They were energized to act when they realized their fortunes and future could not be left to the dictates of others. The situation in San Francisco was not unlike that of rising, small eastern cities at that time. In Springfield, Massachusetts, a historian writes, "Government was of course becoming much more important to substantial businessmen and property owners. They feared the rising taxes and the soaring public debt, on the one hand, and on the other they were attracted by the government's new role in promoting prosperity, in building the city, and in increasing the value of their property through improvement. Because of this, because so much money and power had come to be at stake in public decisions, local affairs now required the more active participation of businessmen—as businessmen—to protect and further their own interests."[45]

Between 1850 and 1856 San Francisco's better class allowed the city's political affairs to be conducted by a Democratic machine headed by David C. Broderick, who served his political apprenticeship at Tammany Hall. Broderick and his machine, supported by political patronage, ballot-box stuffing, and the immigrant vote, were, so said the merchants, the cause of the city's ills. Unemployed eastern Democrats, those thrown out of office in 1849 by President Taylor, had "introduced the New York system of politics into San Francisco." The propertied classes charged Broderick and his Democratic machine with bankrupting San Francisco while convicted criminals walked the streets "without fear of being molested."[46]

Once again the spectre of lawlessness was raised but, beneath the rhetoric of "crime in the streets," the underlying issue was to have "good men" replace Broderick's machine. A commission merchant wrote that merchants must run for political office "for the purpose of reducing taxes on personal and real estate and [do] away . . . with the License Law. As a resident doing business and as a property holder," he continued, " it [is] necessary that good men should take the reins of government into their own hands to stop the enormous robbery which has been carried on in this state and city." Another commission merchant and former member of the 1851 Vigilance Committe, Captain F. W. Macondray, complained that "a horde of ruffians" controlled the ballot box, political "offices were sold out to the higher bidder," and "millions of the city's money had been plundered . . . and any man who dared to say aught was shot down like a dog." If "the people . . . framed the laws and the right of the government was derived originally from them," then the people, said Macondray, appealing to Lockean logic, possessed "the right to institute a new government [the Vigilance Committee] and new laws."[47]

There were periodic attempts to oust the Broderick machine. Whig would-be reformers replaced most local Democrats in 1851 and 1852. Never well organized, the Whigs, after the loss of federal patronage in 1853, transferred to the Americans, Republicans, and Democrats. In 1854, the local Know-Nothing party nominated a lawyer, Samuel P. Webb, for mayor after the anti-Catholic faction of the party succeeded in ousting a Roman Catholic merchant from the top of the municipal ticket. The Know-Nothing gained control for less than a year, however, only to lose to the Democrats in the 1855 election when "the issues . . . were between the Know-Nothings, or American Party, and the Anti-Know Nothings, comprising the foreign-born population of the city and the entire strength of the . . . Old Democratic Party."[48] Despite the Democrats' victory, three merchants who ran on the combined Whig-Know-Nothing ticket gained seats on the fifteen-man board of aldermen. But the city's merchants, many of whom were foreign-born and who distrusted the anti-foreign bias of the Know-Nothing Whigs (despite their reform rhetoric), failed to give their overwhelming support to any single party. On the eve of the formation of the 1856 Vigilance Committee, the merchants and the monied class of the city did have spokesmen in the councils of the city government but their influence was not strong enough to change the power structure of a political machine which had plunged the city into fiscal bankruptcy.

The incident that led to the formation of the 1856 Vigilance Committee was the murder of James King, editor of the San Francisco *Daily Evening Bulletin,* the paper which had constantly attacked the corruption of the Broderick machine. King himself epitomized not only the attitude but the economic plight of a majority of the city's elite. He had failed as a banker with Corcoran and Riggs in Washington, D.C., and began a new banking career in San Francisco in 1850. The local recession of 1854 forced him to merge with another bank, Adams and Company, but when they failed in the panic of 1855, so did King. He then started the *Bulletin,* a paper whose opinionated style and often exaggerated accounts of corruption in city politics gained for King a reputation as a volatile and outspoken editor.

King had charged that Broderick's party was not only responsible for the fatal shooting in November 1855 of a United States Marshall, William Richardson, but was also to blame for the hung jury that allowed "the murderer" Charles Cora to go free. Further, King charged, Broderick and his machine survived only through ballot-box stuffing. So when James P. Casey, a supporter and beneficiary of the Broderick machine, shot and fatally wounded King ouside his office on May 14, 1856, the attack only confirmed for the merchants the truth of King's recent charges. The following day, the city's leading merchants once again formed a vigilante committee.

Past history had demonstrated that the citizens of San Francisco could be galvanized to action and reform through appeals to law and order. Therefore in 1856 the merchants once again tested the response to law and order with the subtle intent of altering the city's political fabric. They did so for reasons going beyond their local needs. First, like merchants everywhere, they were careful to protect both their individual credit ratings and the general fiscal reputation of the city:

In the eyes of Eastern businessmen, San Francisco's economic stability was being jeopardized by the soaring municipal debt, rising taxes, and approaching bankruptcy under the Broderick machine. The spectre of municipal bankruptcy made eastern creditors fearful that the city was on the verge of economic chaos. The restoration of confidence in San Francisco's municipal and financial stability was a *sine qua non*. It had to be accomplished—and in such a way that would let Easterners know that conservative, right-thinking men had definitely gained control. Fiscal reform at the municipal level was thus basic to the vigilance movement. But in order to bring fiscal reform it was first necessary to smash David C. Broderick's machine.[49]

Second, by smashing Broderick's machine and restoring fiscal integrity to the city the merchants hoped to halt the corrosive effects of an economic recession that had caused the merchants, particularly the importer-wholesalers, general occupational slippage and severe financial losses. For if the Vigilance Committee succeeded in halting the city's economic deterioration, a number of the prestigious merchants might maintain, if not regain, their occupational status. Also, by the creation of a new political party, those displaced merchants might regain status through appointment or election to financially lucrative political offices.[50]

Between six and eight thousand people gained admittance to the committee. A ship's chandler and member of the executive committee explained his motive for joining.

I went into that Committee with as earnest a sense of duty as ever I embarked in anything in my life. The abuses were so great, political and physical too . . . that they had become unbearable, and the life, property and peace of the community were in danger . . . Gentlemen going along the street with their wives used to avoid the most public thoroughfares where these ruffians congregated . . . for fear . . . they would have daggers and pistols drawn on them. So I went into it as a religious duty to society, although I knew I was going antagonistic to the law of my city and state . . . I [wished] with my whole soul and determination to purge the city of these abominations. I, and my companions on the Executive Committee . . . were governed by the highest motives . . . Our only motive was to save our lives, property, and protect the community generally.[51]

The general membership of the committee, particularly the executive committe, was drawn from the "property owning class" of the city. William T. Coleman, an import merchant and president of the committee, explained: "The personnel of the Committee were men above the average. They were selected for their worth, integrity and good standing in the community, and no man was admitted whose record was not clean in these particulars . . . The largest element of the Committee was of northern and western men, chiefly representing the mercantile, manufacturing, and vested interests, but embracing every profession and pursuit."[52]

The merchant interests controlled the conduct of the Vigilance Committee through the forty-seven-member executive committee. Six of every ten members were merchants and of the merchants 90 percent were high status importer-wholesalers. In addition merchants served as president, vice-president, grand marshall (in charge of military operations), and treasurer. Thomas J. L. Smiley, the commission merchant elected vice-president, served also as prosecuting attorney, a position the committee was loath to give to any of the city's numerous lawyers.[53] Because of the city's poor record of criminal convictions, the Vigilance Committee believed the legal profession to be little concerned with the safety of local citizens and overly protective of the rights of the city's criminals. As the deputy grand marshall of the committee observed, the executive committee "was composed of our first merchants," but "the professional men were not so plentiful with us," particularly the legal profession who "were rather against us."[54]

The committee selected William T. Coleman as its president because of his active role in the 1851 vigilante group. For a man who held

William T. Coleman, prominent commission merchant and president of the 1856 Vigilance Committee and the 1877 Committee of Safety. Coleman also played a leading role in organizing the opposition to the Civil War draft riots in New York City.

absolute rule over a quasi-military organization the size of two army regiments, his background was distinctly nonmilitary. Born in 1824, the son of a Kentucky civil engineer, Coleman moved to Illinois in his early teens to work for an uncle who served as chief engineer of the state railroads of Illinois. At the age of sixteen, Coleman went to Saint Louis where he worked in an insurance company and later a lumber company before entering college. Having earned a B. S. degree, he served as overseer of an uncle's plantation in Baton Rouge, Louisiana. In the early 1840s he returned to his former lumber employer in Saint Louis to work as a purchasing agent in the Indian reservations on the northern Wisconsin frontier. When the California gold fever struck, Coleman with his brother took the overland journey to the Sierra mines. He made it as far as Sacramento where, as a contractor and builder, he commenced his long career in California. It was a trade in which, by his own admission, he "didn't know a fore-plane from a jack-plane." Soon a speculative venture in Osgood's Indian Chola-gogue, a popular fever remedy in the 1850s, netted Coleman $576 for an hour's work and set him to "thinking in a new direction: to weigh-ing cholagogue against carpenter work." Coleman concluded "that the mercantile business was more in my line than house building." And so he went to San Francisco to be a merchant. His ability to both calm and arouse a mob made him a friend of Sam Brannan, the leader of the 1851 committee, and he soon gained a wide circle of acquain-tances. With his status improved by marriage to the daughter of a wealthy San Francisco banker, and owning an importing and commis-sion business, it is not surprising that Coleman was approached by the city's merchants to head the 1856 committee.[55]

Coleman was thought to be perfect for the job. A self-made man (with a little help from a wealthy father-in-law), a merchant, and a pioneer (one who had arrived in California in 1849-50) rather than newcomer, Coleman had a flair for command and organization. A self-proclaimed admirer of Napoleon, Coleman demanded and re-ceived dictatorial powers as president of the Vigilance Committee. He admitted years later: "I would not undertake the organization of the Commitee, nor any direction, unless I had absolute control, unless what I said and did was accepted as authority and unquestioned. The reply was that I could have my own way, just say what it was . . . no dictator could have it more absolutely than I."[56]

Through his influence in the merchant community, Coleman was instrumental in raising necessary funds to purchase arms, a headquarters, and supplies. The merchants responded generously with money. Albert Dibblee, one of San Francisco's most respected merchants, contributed a "very liberal donation" to the committee. Others like Aaron Burns and Richard Jessup, merchants who served on the executive committee, proudly gave, in addition to money, their personal attention and active participation to the committee.   Burns later wrote: "We had the charge and control of all finances, the charge of the police department [of the committee, not the city], and all the prisoners that ever came in. Dick Jessup and I . . . took the business in hand. Jessup and I did the work. We were responsible for all the finances. Jessup and myself were also the commissaries, did the providing, spent all the money that was spent . . . purchasing the supplies and attending to the finances occupied all our time. It cost the members a good deal of money. It cost me four thousand dollars in money that I spent, besides the time."[57]

Indeed, business in the city came to a halt as merchant members did "nothing else but drill and march." The vice-president of the executive committee witnessed at least five committee members "with muskets in their hands, taking their turns at guard, not one of whom was worth less than half a million dollars." Certainly one of the major reasons why the businessmen of the city were so willing to leave their merchant shops for guard duty was the very cause for the creation of the committee: economic depression. William T. Sherman reported on local economic conditions in 1856: "Since I embarked in this scheme [banking in San Francisco in 1852], affairs have much changed. Almost every bank has failed. A large proportion of the wealthy have become embarassed and bankrupt. Real estate has fallen from an exaggerated rate to almost nothing . . . It has been a period of deep anxiety to me."[58]

Indeed all of San Francisco, particularly the merchants, lived in a state of anxiety. Incapable of controlling their market and local economy, the merchants responded with vigilantism. They took the law into their own hands by literally capturing Casey and Cora, the accused murderers of a United States Marshall and a local newspaper editor, from the civil authorities and transferring them to the committee headquarters. By such a daring and illegal maneuver, Coleman and his merchants challenged the authority not only of the mayor of San Francisco but the governor of California.[59]

Governor J. Neely Johnson reacted immediately, declaring San Francisco to be in a "state of insurrection," and ordered all the volunteer military companies to report to the newly appointed head of the state militia, Major General (and banker) William T. Sherman. Most of the volunteer militia companies, the majority of whose members either sympathized with the Vigilance Committee or were members of it, disbanded and transferred their arms to the Vigilance Committee. The city sheriff, under pressure from the Vigilance Committee, disarmed the city guard and rendered them impotent to perform military duties on behalf of the governor. The city guard then, like other volunteer militia companies, disbanded and reconstituted itself into an "independent" company free from state control. A number of militia company officers also accepted civil or military leadership positions in the Vigilance Committee.[60]

The committee, naturally anxious about how General Sherman and the governor would utilize the military forces of the state against San Francisco's civil insurrection, first acted to neutralize General Sherman. Personally and as an agent of the state of California, Sherman disagreed totally with the principles of the Vigilance Committee and recognized the violence that would certainly occur if the committee carried these principles into concerted action. On the other hand, as a member of the city's business community, he sympathized with the stated aims of the committee to cleanse the city of the criminal element. Sherman also recognized that "most of the rich men are contributing means and countenance sub rosa" to the committee.[61] These rich bankers and merchants also understood how to intimidate Sherman. For in addition to commanding the state militia, Sherman also remained head of the San Francisco branch of the Lucas, Turner & Co. bank. Silently, without public announcement, the city's businessmen gradually withdrew their accounts from his bank. They made it abundantly clear to Sherman: either he resign from the militia or, as one merchant delicately phrased it, his "banking house would be destroyed and the money lost." The general resigned his militia post to greet the return of deposits to his bank.[62]

Sherman claimed, and there is evidence to support his argument, that the resignation was prompted by his inability to obtain arms and supplies for the militia he commanded, and not by pressure from the business community. Governor Johnson had requested the United States Secretary of War to furnish Sherman's troops with arms from the federal arsenal across the Bay at Benicia. Washington refused Governor Johnson's request on legal grounds, though the real reason may have been political—a Democratic President who wished to embarrass a Know-Nothing governor. And when the United States Army attempted to transfer some arms from Benicia to a storehouse in San Francisco, the Vigilance Committee "appointed a party who . . . captured the sloop with everything on board." Without arms, and with little or no organized public support to oppose the Vigilance Committee, Sherman resigned his state militia post. Governor Johnson, with his unarmed troops and no support from Washington, found himself powerless to counteract the "insurrection" in San Francisco.[63]

The mild and generally ineffective opposition in San Francisco to the Vigilance Committee came from the loosely organized Law and Order party (The Vigilance Committee referred to them as the Law and Murder party). The party was composed for the most part of a number of lawyers, many southerners, a portion of the foreign-born population of the city, and political office holders loyal to the Broderick machine. Those bold enough to express publicly their opposition to the committee, and they were few indeed, usually opposed the lawlessness of Coleman's organization rather than the political objectives of the vigilantes. One member of the Young Men's Democratic Club and a printer employed by the San Francisco *Herald,* the only paper which opposed the Vigilance Committee, attacked the "extra legal" body "composed of men who by neglect of their duty . . . were responsible for whatever lawlessness they offered as an excuse for the organization."[64]

The Vigilance Committee, however, brought none-too-subtle pressures to bear upon its critics. One prominent insurance agent "at first came out strongly against the Vigilance Committee" but, as a committee member reported, when the agent discovered "that nearly the entire business community were in league with the Committee and that a great feeling was growing [against] him, he hauled in his horns and now professes moderation." Committee members had informed the insurance agent, the leading one in the city, that if he did not moderate his views, he "would surely lose half his business."[65]

The volunteer associations of the city offered no resistance, in fact they gave their wholehearted assistance to the vigilantes. A number of militia companies supplied arms and men, fire company members rushed to enlist, and the clergy anointed the committee with "divine authority." The pastor of the Washington Street Baptist Church proclaimed from the pulpit that "self-protection is a right above all forms of law," and concluded: "If the ends of justice are to be defeated by the treachery of men in office, or the over-awing influence of a band of desperadoes, . . . or by the quibbling of lawyers, or the dishonesty of perjured jurymen—then heaven . . . has left no alternative but such as the Vigilance Committee supplies."[66]

The single cleric who dared to raise his voice against the committee, Reverend William A. Scott, a native of Tennessee and pastor of the Calvary Presbyterian Church, blamed San Francisco's problems on the breakdown of the family ("the separation of parents from their children"), and the failure of the city's voluntary associations (like churches, schools, bible societies, benevolent societies and the YMCA) for "pandering to the popular cry for blood." Scott asked,

What is the influence of our Lyceums, Mercantile Library, and Mechanical Associations, our public schools and our *thirty-one* churches, with their Sabboth schools, if now the city cannot be governed without a Lynch Law court? . . . And to my mind it is perfectly preposterous as to contend that the many thousands of men and money wielded by the Committee, could not have secured in a lawful manner the purity of our elections and the faithful execution of the laws as far as perfection in such things can be obtained in human courts. If they could not, then our republican institutions are a failure. Indeed, I have not yet seen a plea in justification of mob law that is not a blow at Republicanism.[67]

San Franciscans responded to Scott's moderate pleas by hanging him in effigy at about the same time as the Vigilance Committee hanged its four victims. No counterforce existed either before or during the height of the committee's activities to check the extralegal activities of the vigilantes. The local government of San Francisco had never exercised control in the city before the arrival of the 1856 Vigilance Committee; and during the summer of 1856, when the committee ruled the city, the local government ceased to exist and the state government was rendered impotent by Washington's failure to supply Governor Johnson with arms.

"Fort Gunnybags," headquarters of the 1856 Vigilance Committee, near the corner of Sacramento and Front streets. It is flanked by Mills & Valtine, importers of wines and liquors.

And so the committee arrested citizens (among them a disproportionate number of Irish) for questioning, searched private premises without warrants, conducted trials with rigged juries, and threatened critics with physical violence and economic boycotts. In addition to the four men executed, twenty-five were deported and others were ordered to leave the city, forbidden to return under penalty of death, "a lesson which led to the departure of [an additional] 800 malefactors and vagabonds." By August of 1856, three months after its formation, the violent phase of the Vigilance Committee had ended.[68]

Vigilantism, the Political Phase

In the midst of performing its military police functions, the Vigilance Committee assured the citizens that as soon as "law and order"

Six vigilante sharpshooters of the Thirtieth Infantry Company, Fourth Regiment.

had been restored and the "criminal element" eliminated, the committee would disband, as it had in 1851, and return the cleansed city to its inhabitants. But before disbanding, and to ensure the success of its efforts, the Vigilance Committee selected from among the most trusted members a Commitee of 21 to nominate candidates for a new political party ordained by the vigilantes, the People's party. Controlled by the business elite of the city, the Committe of 21 selected a slate of candidates that appealed "to the commercial occupations of the city rather than to religious or ethnic groups." Charles Doane, the commander of the Vigilance Committee's 5,000-man military force, was nominated for sheriff, while other trusted members received nominations for chief of police, alderman, and state representative.[69]

In the local election that immediately followed the formal disbanding of the Vigilance Committee, six of the twelve aldermen (now called supervisors) were up for election. The People's party nominated merchants for four of these positions. All four reformers won the election as the People's party defeated the Democrats and Know Nothings.[70] But more important, a wholesale merchant and a respected member of the business community, Ephram W. Burr, now occupied the mayor's office. Burr, the son of a Unitarian druggist-physician from Warren, Rhode Island, had clerked for merchants in Warren and Providence before he arrived in 1849 at the age of forty in San Francisco. With profits from his wholesale grocery business, Burr had helped found with another merchant, in 1855, the San Francisco Accumulating Fund Association, a hybrid bank and savings and loan association which catered to the city's merchants. Before 1856 the business community had failed to exert the effort necessary to control local politics; by November 1856 it had captured the mayor's office, over half the seats on the board of supervisors, and the important offices of sheriff, chief of police, assessor, and United States Marshall for San Francisco.

The revolution was complete. The merchants had established a local government which would institute those changes—lower taxes and reduced local expenditures—that they felt were mandatory for their livelihood. By consolidating the administrative functions of the city and county and by making major budget changes, the city expenditures dropped from $2.6 million in 1855 to $353,000 in 1857; these measures helped to restore the city's credit rating. And much to the relief of the business community, taxes declined 40 percent. With subsequent victories of the People's party, the political phase of the committee lasted another ten years. There was, however, no evidence to suggest that the incidence of crime declined with the arrival of the new administration. But then that was not the primary purpose of the Vigilance Committee or its surrogate, the People's party.[71]

But why did the merchants embrace vigilantism? Their violence cannot be explained by the elite's attempt to regain political power in San Francisco. They had not in fact held the reins of government before 1856; nor had they, as evidenced by their general failure to vote, demonstrated anything other than apathy toward local politics. When the members of the city's elite in the years 1852 to 1856 experienced sudden and dramatic shifts in their careers, they selected vigilantism as the solution to their plight, unaccustomed as they were to working with the democratic procedures available. In a frontier city where the occupational and financial status of men changed so suddenly, the elite reacted with violence not because of class "challenges from below," as suggested by one historian, but out of impatience and frustration with injurious economic forces, both external and internal to the city, which severely altered their fortunes. The formation of the Vigilance Committee of 1856 was in itself an admission by the elite of their failure to maintain their occupational and financial status in the community. And having once successfully tested the vigilante model (but for different reasons) in 1851, the city's elite in 1856 captured, through violent means and the tactics of intimidation, that which they believed rightfully belonged to them because of their high status and that which could preserve their position in the community: the political machinery of the city.[72]

The Vigilance Committee successfully halted the process of occupational and financial erosion of the city's business elite. Most members of the executive committee, the majority of whom were importer-wholesalers, either gained occupational status or, at a minimum, maintained their occupational position. And taking all committee members who held either civil or military executive positions in the Vigilance Committee, 70 percent of whom were either high-status general merchants, importer-wholesalers, bankers, brokers, manufacturers or professionals, over 80 percent either maintained or improved their occupational status. They did, in fact, outperform the merchant and general populations of the city in the years 1852-1860. Apparently an executive position in the Vigilance Committee eased the climb up, or at the very least, halted the slide down the occupational ladder.[73]

Most committee members remained in their traditional lines of employment. But a surprisingly large number (a quarter of the vigilante executives) moved in to fill the new political positions in the new People's party. By 1860 former executives of the Vigilance Committee occupied the following city posts: alderman, city assessor, chief of police, city sheriff, under-sheriff, deputy sheriff, deputy district attorney, harbormaster, city gauger and city treasurer, as well as other minor positions. Through the People's party and the reelection of the mayor, merchant Ephram Burr in 1858 and 1860, the business elite maintained their control of the political machinery of the city. And the new occupational opportunities in the People's party provided an alternate route for status advancement for a number of the city's business elite who, prior to 1856, had experienced large losses in occupational prestige.

Unlike the 1851 vigilante movement, which existed solely for the purpose of eliminating crime in the city, the 1856 Vigilance Committee initiated a political revolution. And the leaders of this revolution remained in San Francisco to oversee its completion and reap its benefits.[74] For having attained political power, the elite plotted and maneuvered to guarantee the permanence of the revolution they had wrought. Albert Dibblee, one of the city's most prestigious merchants, best illustrated the new involvement of the business elite in the city's political affairs. Acting on behalf of the business elite through the People's party, Dibblee, in conjunction with merchant associates, selected candidates for local and state political office. Dibblee, in explaining his new responsibility, commented: "Have had to look after Public Matters of late, to get all right for the city election in September. A few of us have to 'fix' things right before hand, select men and etc.—but always keeping ourselves in the background."[75]

That San Francisco's business elite requested Dibblee to act as their political filter was, considering his status among them, not at all surprising. The son of a New York merchant and alderman, Dibblee was first of all a very successful pioneer commission merchant who retained excellent commercial and credit connections in Boston, New York, and throughout the West. He helped found the city's most prestigious militia company, the San Francisco Guard, contributed time and money to the Vigilance Committee, and concurrent with his leadership in the People's party, served as president of the San Francisco Chamber of Commerce. Before 1856, like other city merchants, Dibblee failed to participate in the city's political affairs. But as the economic recessions of the mid-1850s became more frequent and severe, and the beleaguered merchants were burdened with ever-increasing taxes assessed by a political machine that failed to either represent or assist them, Dibblee, with other city merchants, turned to politics. He worked through the Chamber of Commerce to obtain federal assistance for harbor improvements, the construction of bonded warehouses, and more equitable excise duties. Dibblee's actions represented the merchants' new perception of government (local, state, and national) in San Francisco. For too long had the powers of government been utilized against the best interests of the business elite. And, said these businessmen, the blame for the misfortunes of the city rested clearly with a "corrupt" political machine which gained power by ballot-box stuffing while allowing the "criminal element" free rein to intimidate the "better classes" of the city. Of course, the city's elite would not admit to either their own former political apathy or to the undemocratic vigilante tactics by which they exchanged one political machine for another after 1856. And so to preserve the revolution of 1856, the business leaders of the city participated directly and indirectly, through merchant leaders like Dibblee, in controlling the political, and hence economic, institutions of San Francisco. Dibblee explained to his brother in New York his own political involvement and the all-pervasive influence of his business associates.

My attentive friends have crowded a new duty upon me;—I have been forced to go into the People's [party] Nominating Convention of which I was chosen President, and now have a levee every day of men of every class and condition, from highest to lowest, soliciting office or recommending their friends . . . our people have the city offices (including Judgeships) in their power, so all office seekers are after us. After I get out of this convention I mean to back out of everything for a while, but it is the hardest kind of work to keep in the background. A set of my friends have the lead here in many respects in local matters and when a new work is carried through, everyone is expected to do some work towards it. If I try to shirk, there will be so many to follow around, urging and pressing, that it is almost impossible for me to do as I wish.[76]

By 1860 the revolution was complete and the merchants and their allies monopolized the social, economic, and political fabric of the city. Despite the illegal methods, violence, and impatience with democratic procedures, San Francisco's elite would proclaim not only the wonders of their revolution but the ultimate wisdom of their methods. San Francisco was in 1859 the "best governed city in the nation," boasted her leading newspaper. Just look at Baltimore and her problems with "rowdyism." What Baltimore needed was an efficient San Francisco-style Vigilance Committee! For "was it not better," asked the *Alta California*, "that the people of this city should resort to revolution than that today San Francisco should be classed with Baltimore?"[77]

Poor Baltimore would have to suffer the inefficiencies of democracy. But not San Francisco—at least so thought the city's elite. The other citizens, if critical of the committee, remained silent. The memory of vigilante justice had permeated all levels of San Francisco's citizenry.[78]

PART TWO

THE SECOND GENERATION

6

THE CIVIL WAR, RAILROADS, AND MANUFACTURING

Before an investigation of the careers of San Francisco's second generation of merchants, it may be helpful to review the events and human decisions of the 1860s and 1870s that transformed the economic environment of this commercial seaport. For the very magnitude of change in the city's economic structure presented the merchants with new challenges to which they would have to readjust their mode of business operation.

Civil War Boom

The 1860 decade opened in a spirit of optimism. "No complaint is heard of 'hard times' among the industrial classes, of whatever denomination," reported the *Alta California,* "and cases of industrial misfortune have, for some time past, been exceedingly rare." The increasing agricultural production of the state, particularly wheat, found overseas buyers. The farmers, city millers, laborers, wholesale and shipping merchants all profited. Indeed "the employment this [foreign] demand . . . has given to thousands, and the consequent diffusion of ready cash among the people . . . has permeated every avenue of business and imparted a stimulus to every industrial pursuit."[1]

The explosion in the agricultural production of the state accounted for much of the city's prosperity. By 1860 California ranked fourteenth in the nation in beef production, twelfth in wheat, and sixth in the production of wool; and with the outbreak of the Civil War and the disruption of port trade along the East Coast, Great Britain sought California's new agricultural production. San Francisco was the chief beneficiary of this new demand. Exports to Great Britain grew from $29,000 in 1859 to almost $3,000,000 in 1861; and general trade, which showed a marked decline along the East Coast during the war, actually increased in San Francisco during the span of the Civil War. Between 1858 and 1866, imports into the city more than doubled while exports expanded from approximately $5 million to over $17 million. San Francisco's geographical isolation, her deep-water port close to and tied with the agricultural areas of the state, and a merchant network which could efficiently handle the financial and administrative details for this trade, all directly aided the relative prosperity of the city during the Civil War.[2]

The city remained loyal to the cause of the Union from the very start of the war. Slavery had been outlawed in California in the Compromise of 1850, and the institution could find few spokesmen willing publicly to defend it in a city overwhelmingly populated with migrants from the northern states. During the course of the war there were only occasional expressions of dissent, and "no indications that any great proportion of the inhabitants entertained unpatriotic sentiments or approved the manifestations of such sentiments elsewhere."[3]

The merchants were particularly concerned about the spread of slavery into California; as one of them wrote at the outset of the war: "I am for the Union as long as we can keep slavery in the southern states, but am not for allowing the slaveholders to take their slaves through or into the northern states while travelling—or at any other time. If they want slaves let them keep them at home. We—or *I* do not want them under our noses. They will have their sins to account for—not we."[4] The major concern of the city was not disloyalty among its own ranks but the danger that confederate sympathizers from the southern counties of California might stir up trouble or elect a governor sympathetic to the cause of the Confederacy.

The city merchants immediately organized a voluntary association, the Home Guard, to counter these threats. Founded in May 1861, the Home Guard signed up approximately 3,000 citizens for the avowed purpose of detecting and suppressing "any treasonable combinations or conspiracies against the Union and the public peace." Merchants James Otis, a city supervisor, and Albert Dibblee, president of the Chamber of Commerce, put the organization together. Dibblee served as chairman of the five-man executive committee while Lucius Allen, a graduate of West Point and for many years an officer in the United States Army, was appointed to command the guard. Fearful that the Confederacy might organize an armed force in Southern California, Dibblee in 1860 urged Washington to send federal troops to Los Angeles and a naval detachment to San Francisco. But an invasion from Southern California, or a blockade of the harbor, or the election of an unsympathetic governor, never materialized. With overwhelming support in San Francisco, and with a war governor firm in his support of the Union, Lincoln was elected. The Guard immediately disbanded, and for the rest of the war the city never wavered in its support of the Union.[5]

Besides supporting the war and profiting indirectly from the increased trade at the port, the city merchants also amassed large profits from currency transactions which favored the bearers of gold at the expense of those who traded in greenbacks. In San Francisco, business was generally conducted with specie; in the East, merchants accepted paper currency as payment in most financial transactions. Thus, for example, a San Francisco merchant demanded that his bills be paid only in United States gold coin, and exchanged the specie for discounted greenbacks in the East where he purchased goods or paid off debts. The merchant then had the goods shipped to California "and sold them at a gross profit of 50 percent at wholesale and 100 percent at retail, in gold." Gold, at its highest, reached about $2.50 in currency, and as one of the innumerable merchants who profited from such transactions admitted, "we made more in selling our gold when buying eastern exchange than we did in our goods." Even at more equitable exchange rates, the West Coast merchant profited handsomely. With the gold dollar worth $1.70 in greenbacks in New York, the San Francisco merchant could purchase $10,000 worth of goods with $5,877.00 in gold. A single import house, Janson, Bond and Co., reportedly made $1,500,000 from currency transactions during the war, and R. G. Dun and Company reported that a cigar dealer who "has silently been eng'd in 'Greenback' operation & advancing money on mining stocks & c.[certificates] & has been very successful—is considered worth fully $15[thousand]."[6]

In conjunction with the favorable exchange rate, merchant profits during the Civil War were often also enhanced by an occasional and fortuitous supply shortage in the San Francisco market. For example, in 1863, when greenbacks were worth fifty cents in gold, one coal merchant purchased coal in the East with currency and then sold his shipment in San Francisco for coin.

My coal oil cost me fifty cents per gallon in Boston, payable in currency. The freight was also payable in currency . . . my coal oil cost me a little over twenty-five cents per gallon laid down in San Francisco.

About 1863 there was an unusual demand for coal oil . . . consequently the market price went up very rapidly until it reached $1.50
and $1.75 per gallon. The result was that I sold all I had in the ware-
house and [that which was] on the way around the Horn . . . I do not
look upon these speculations as any foresight of mine, but the change
of circumstances and conditions of the market.[7]

To ensure that the favorable "circumstances and conditions" did
not change, the city merchants met in November 1862 to protect themselves against the possibility that greenbacks might filter into the local
currency and be forced upon them for the payment of merchandise or
debts. They expressed their intention to adhere to gold as a standard
and resolved not to "pay out or receive the legal tenders at any but the
merchant value." The agreement further stipulated: "If any refuse, or
after agreeing to pay for goods in gold, pay in greenbacks at par instead, then his name will be entered into the agreement [and] notified
that whenever he may thereafter deal, he will have to pay for his goods
in yellow gold *in advance*."[8]

As assurance of the continuance and legal permanence of this practice, the city merchants actively and successfully lobbied at the state
capital for the Specific Contract Law. Passed in 1863, the law stated
that parties could contract among themselves as to the type of money
to be used in the course of certain business transactions. Merchants
naturally specified gold payment, excluding the payment of debts in
greenbacks. The state legislature repealed the law after the Civil War,
but for the duration of the war the merchants, particularly the wholesalers and importers who purchased in the East, greatly prospered
from the currency exchange.

Critics claimed the San Francisco merchants "milked" the nation
of war profits while others fought their battles. The city merchants
found the currency exchange so lucrative, charged one critic, "that
they kept one of their members constantly attendant on the Gold
Board in Wall Street to take advantage . . . of the good or bad news
received from the operations of the hostile armies in the field." Further, the military situation only served the "cupidity of our traders by
enabling them to 'milk' the community of its gold in order that they
might reap exorbitant profits from their merchandize. It was a peddling advantage taken out of the throes of a great nation."[9]

Defenders of the merchants claimed that the currency profits benefited the community, since the merchants emerged from the war "not only free from obligations, but with established credit" in the East. They argued that their stronger financial position vis-a-vis the East would insure greater prosperity for the city and encourage eastern investment in San Francisco. More important, the new prosperity of the merchants would soon "diffuse itself through every department of the Commonwealth."[10]

Actually no evidence suggests that the general population of the city profited directly or indirectly from the new merchant prosperity. The generally healthy economy of San Francisco and California, however, helped to attract investment capital from the East. But the San Francisco merchants did not invest their excess capital in the new opportunities opening in the city and the state—manufacturing and the railroads—but rather in real estate, or, more commonly, in the new silver mines in Montana and Utah. The city merchants, from the time of the gold discovery in 1849, had derived their business profits directly and indirectly from the mines; and conditioned as they were to their past experience, they would not, out of habit, consider in the late 1860s other investment alternatives.

The Silver Rush and Other Speculations

News of the silver discoveries in the Comstock Lode activated once again the city merchants' gambling instincts. Before the late 1850s mines were owned by joint partnerships; by the mid-1860s, joint-stock companies and corporations had become the preferred form of business arrangement. In April 1863 over 300 mining companies were incorporated with a capital stock of $50 million, and during the preceding three months, more than $200 million worth of mining stocks had been offered for sale in the market. The *Alta California* estimated in late 1863 that city residents "own silver stock to the value of about $25,000,000 and perhaps one-tenth as much gold stock." "Not only the capitalist and banker" owned shares in the silver mines, but also "the wholesale and retail merchant, the carpenter and black-smith . . . "[11] Mark Twain, a city resident in the late 1860s, confirmed the widespread involvement of all classes in the speculative mania. "Stocks went rising; speculation went mad; bankers, merchants, law-yers, doctors, mechanics, laborers, even the very washer-women and servant girls, were putting up their earnings on silver stocks, and every sun that rose in the morning went down on paupers enriched and rich men beggared. What a gambling carnival it was."[12]

At the height of the speculative boom, the city merchants inadvertently flooded the local market with goods. But in mid-1864 the market broke, stock prices plummeted about 50 percent, and merchants had to seek buyers at the auction house for their over-abundant supply of goods. "The great tumble in mining stocks," a merchant complained, "is one cause why trade is not more brisk . . . plenty of men who once thought themselves rich are now quite poor."[13]

As the recession hit the city, merchants sought new and distant markets that they might control and monopolize. One trading area which had always gripped the imagination of the city merchants was the "opulent" Orient. As early as the mid-1850s the San Francisco business community imagined China as a new market for American goods. The anticipated expansion of the import and export trade with China, with a little help from Washington, would more than compensate for the declining trade with the California mining towns. Thus, the San Francisco Chamber of Commerce in 1861 called upon Congress to finance a fleet of mail steamships which "will give to American merchants the advantages of more rapid communication of commercial intelligence than will be possessed by [our] European competitors." Further, "a line of steamers across the Pacific, while extending and strengthening our own commerce, would direct the trade, passengers and commerce of other nations to our ports, and to the benefit of our ships and people." To the San Francisco merchant community, the federal government existed to serve the interests of American commerce in general and the San Francisco merchants in particular. "We believe it desirable to use our steam navy in forwarding the interests of commerce," declared the San Francisco Chamber of Commerce, and if not the navy, then San Francisco must at the very least have access to subsidized steamers to China "whose efficiency for warlike purposes may be insured by frequent official inspections." It was an enticing suggestion and Washington readily accepted it.[14]

With an annual federal subsidy of $500,000 the Pacific Mail and Steamship Co. in 1866 began operating monthly steamship packets to Hong Kong, Honolulu, the Sandwich Islands, and Kanagawa, Japan. The government had opened the way for trade, and it was now up to the merchants to take full advantage of this opportunity for "opulent traffic." As a city spokesman declared, the steamship company and the government can only "furnish facilities for the business of our mercantile community," they cannot "originate or conduct your operations." Appealing to the instincts of Manifest Destiny, the spokesman implored the city merchants: "You, our merchants, our bankers, our businessmen must . . . enter into honorable competition for this opulent traffic. You must . . . strike out new paths, to infuse new ideas, to create new markets for American produce and American manufacturers, and to teach the asiatic world that we, too [like the British] are of that great dominant race, the Anglo-Saxon, that Anglo-Saxon ability, vigor, and enterprise, and even Anglo-Saxon aggression, finds with us its best and highest development."[15]

With the possible exception of tea, the imports of which rose from approximately $300,000 in 1860 to over $1,000,000 in 1870, trade with the Far East never fulfilled the expectations of the city merchants. China with its underdeveloped economy never became the lucrative consumer market envisioned by California's farmers, merchants, or manufacturers; indeed, the main reason for continuing the packet service was to transport Chinese "coolies" to San Francisco to fill the demand for cheap labor generated by the railroads and city manufacturers.[16]

Having achieved only limited success in Asia, the city merchants sought to expand their trading network to the new mining districts in Utah, Colorado, and Montana. Conditioned by the experience of 1849-50 when mass immigration followed the discovery of gold in the Sierras, the merchants fully expected a similar immigration to follow the discovery of silver in the Rockies. The *Alta California* urged the city merchants to control the growing trade of Montana before Saint Louis spread her commercial tentacles into the Comstock Lode. All that was needed was "a little energy and expense." The Montana trade alone, advised the *Alta,* would guarantee to San Francisco "at least a share of business now amounting to several millions a year and continually on the increase." In the Utah territory, San Francisco merchants evisioned 125,000 potential customers for dry goods groceries, hardwares, and teas. The city also admitted that "the whole of this trade . . . is enjoyed by New York, Chicago, and St. Louis, simply because the people of these cities take hold and make the most of every advantage given them."[17]

San Francisco saw itself locked in a battle to capture a portion, if not all, of the lucrative trade of Montana, Colorado, and Utah. Los Angeles, so dependent upon San Francisco trade in the 1850s and 1860s, managed to send approximately $150,000 in merchandise to Salt Lake City between November 1863 and May 1864, while eastern merchants shipped 16 million tons of merchandise to Utah in 1864. A California newspaper warned the San Francisco merchants that if they did not act quickly to control the trade of the new mining areas, then the entire wealth from this new trade would automatically "flow to New York, Boston, Chicago, and St. Louis." "There is one very important fact which the San Francisco merchants seem to forget. There is a movement among Eastern capitalists to build a railroad from Lake Superior to the navigable waters of the Columbia River. The prize these enterprising capitalists are grasping for is the Montana gold and trade. Boston as well as all the Northwestern cities, are interested in this great movement—striving to do what our San Francisco merchants should do, cut off St. Louis."[18]

New York, the San Francisco merchants learned, was "offering every inducement" to the merchants of the Utah territory. Chicago and St. Louis "coveted the wealth of this same commerce, and look with ardent anticipation to the day when the Pacific Railroad shall secure to them the object of their desire." Colorado and Arizona, a "land of gold" with a "future of resplendent prosperity," must be brought into the San Francisco commercial orbit. San Francisco merchants, therefore, must not repose "in supine indifference while those distant, but more enterprising cities . . . snatch . . . the wealth" of these rich territories.[19]

The city merchants immediately responded to this call for action. But rather than directing their attention and financial resources toward the building of railroads, a course that eastern merchants enthusiastically supported, they financed joint-stock steamship companies to navigate the Colorado River. The opening of "this great highway" for the transportation of passengers and merchandise to Utah, Colorado, and Montana, the local merchants confidently believed, would insure that these "populous regions will at once become [a] tributary to San Francisco."[20]

Navigating the Colorado River had always captured the imagination of various explorers, miners, and government officials. But it was left to the San Francisco merchants to finance and put into actual operation this disastrous commercial venture. A group of city merchants met in early 1864, formed a company, and, on an experimental basis, sent the steamer *Esmeralda* from the Sacramento River to the Colorado River to compete with two other independent companies each operating one vessel on the Colorado. In March 1865 the *Esmeralda* successfully ascended the Colorado to within 400 miles of Salt Lake City. On the basis of this "encouraging news," a San Francisco importer put together the Pacific and Colorado Steam Navigation Company. Capitalized at $200,000 (fifty dollars per share), the company was directed by a group of prominent San Francisco merchants and manufacturers. The city's Chamber of Commerce also lent its enthusiastic blessing.

> The Pacific and Colorado Steam Navigation Company has demonstrated during the past year the entire practicability of the navigation of the Colorado River to Callville—a point to within 400 miles of Great Salt Lake City.
> It is a matter of surprise that the trade of 100,000 people, for the last ten years so nearly connected to us by this great water channel of communication, should have been so entirely monopolized by cities thousands of miles distant, without scarcely an effort on our part to secure it . . . The vast extent of country made accessible by the free opening of navigation on the Colorado cannot well be overestimated, and while the community at large are devising methods of attraction for an immigration to our State, would it not be well for the merchants of San Francisco to secure all the trade possible from the population now within their reach?[21]

The Colorado water follies attracted additional merchant capital but the scheme had been doomed to failure from the start. The volume of water through the Colorado River, and its shoals and currents, defied easy, much less profitable, navigation. And even if boat captains were skillful enough to reach Callville, merchants still had to transport their merchandise an additional 400 miles by land to Salt Lake City and then another 450 miles to Montana. Finally, the Colorado River scheme was doomed by the organizational efforts and vision of a group of Sacramento merchants. While Albert Dibblee and his merchant associates in San Francisco tinkered with their boats, Charles Crocker and his merchant associates in Sacramento built a transcontinental railroad.[22]

One of the initial organizers and investors of the Pacific and Colorado Navigation Company admitted to its failure when in 1869 he called upon the city merchants to support the efforts of the Central Pacific Railroad management to construct a railroad east from Missouri to San Francisco. Then and only then "can we largely control . . . the trade of Utah, Colorado and Montana . . . From some investigations recently made, I am decidedly of the opinion that another population, almost equal to that on the immediate coast, may be made tributary to our commerce by proper exertion on our part."[23]

The Transcontinental Railroad

Ever since a transcontinental railroad was first proposed, San Francisco had supported the idea. "This scheme for a giant Pacific Railroad is all right and proper," reported a local newspaper in 1851, "and we should like to see the government at once commence the construction." The city merchants had continually petitioned Congress for improved communications and transportation facilities to break San Francisco's geographic isolation and thereby improve her commerce. They requested subsidized steamer lines, more frequent mail service, improved navigational aids and harbor facilities, and an overland telegraph.[24]

Compared with the early 1850s, communications with the East had vastly improved by the mid-1860s. Faster ships on a more regular schedule from the larger eastern ports serviced the West Coast, but the danger, expense, and unpredictable nature of sea transportation remained. What the West needed and demanded was safe, cheap, and efficient overland transportation. The Overland California Mail bill in 1857 provided more dependable stagecoach service. A liberal government subsidy was awarded to the Butterfield Overland Mail Co., that connected San Francisco with Saint Louis with intermediate stops at El Paso, Tucson, Yuma, and Los Angeles. The trip averaged twenty-five days, passengers paid $200 (which also paid for forty pounds of baggage), mail cost three and a half cents per half-ounce, and the service operated throughout the year. The service ended, however, when the company's equipment fell into the hands of the Confederate Army. The Pony Express provided relatively fast mail service but it was also too expensive. Riders carrying fifteen pounds of mail departed twice a week from the western edge of the railroad at Saint Joseph, Missouri, for San Francisco, 2,000 miles away. A letter posted in New York could be delivered in San Francisco thirteen days later, but the charge of five dollars for half an ounce discouraged wide use. After the Civil War, Ben Holliday, with a million-dollar government mail contract, operated a coach line between Atchison, Kansas, and Sacramento. But again this service proved expensive and in the end, unprofitable. What was needed, said the merchants, was a railroad that would not only carry mail and immigrants to California but would also open new trade areas to the San Francisco merchants. The merchants' spokesman, the *Alta California,* declared in 1860:

Build the [rail]road, and our business ceases to be Californian only and local; we become distributors, our merchants and their imports will provide not only for California but for the whole interior of the continent; our producers will grow not only for home consumption, but for other states and populations, for cities and towns now in embryo, but ready to be awakened into life by the whistle of the locomotive . . . If San Francisco is to be the New York of the Pacific, we must have the road . . . If our producers desire fair market rates for their produce, corresponding with those obtained on the Atlantic, it must be from a more expanded market, from an added population to California, and from new peoples in every fertile spot west of the Rocky Mountains.[25]

Besides allowing San Francisco merchants to compete with eastern cities for the Mississippi Valley and western territorial trade, the railroad would guarantee San Francisco's future role as the "financial center of the monetary exchanges between Europe and China." With the new steamer connections to the Far East, "there is no improbability in the supposition," reported the *Alta,* "that all the silver shipments intended to settle the accounts between London and Paris on one side and India and China on the other, will go through this city." And as terminus of the transcontinental railroad, San Francisco "will rank in the first rank of cities as a centre of population, wealth, commerce and luxury, and also, it is to be hoped and expected, of art, science and literature." Finally, and to further inflate the expected benefits which would naturally derive from the rail connection, "intelligence will be increased, society liberalized by intercourse, and extemporaneous adventure driven out by better industries, as in the olden time the temple of God was cleared of money-changers by the presence of a superior spirit." The railroad would transport to the West Coast metropolis new immigrants attracted not by "the dangerous and corrupting passion of gold" but industrious and civilized souls who represented "the best forms of society."[26]

One unemployed local resident was not so optimistic about the beneficence of the railroad. Henry George predicted in 1868 that the railroad would radically alter San Francisco and California society which heretofore had been characterized by a spirit of "cosmopolitanism," "diffused proprietorship," and the absence of fixed classes. "The truth is," contended George, "the completion of the railroad and the consequent great increase of business and population, will not be a benefit to all of us, but only to a portion." "As a general rule," George concluded, "those who *have*, it will make wealthier, for those who *have not*, it will make it more difficult to get." That George correctly predicted San Francisco's future (though for the wrong reason) is less significant than the fact that he stood virtually alone in doubting the benefits of the transcontinental railroad.[27]

For all their enthusiasm the merchants demonstrated little willingness to help finance the railroad or otherwise directly encourage its construction. Yes, they wanted the railroad, but someone else would have to risk financing and building it while the merchants speculated in mining stocks. The merchants represented, no doubt, the general feeling of the city. For when the Big Four (Charles Crocker, Colis Huntington, Leland Stanford, and Mark Hopkins) requested that San Francisco subsidize the construction of a rail line to link the city with the transcontinental route, only one-third of the city's registered voters cared enough to vote on the million-dollar bond issue which was defeated by a small margin.[28]

Independent of any substantial financial assistance from San Francisco or her merchants, but with considerable financial subsidies from the federal government, the Sacramento Big Four built the western section of the transcontinental railroad. On the occasion of its completion in 1869, the San Francisco merchants and the Chamber of Commerce euphorically predicted a new and immediate prosperity with the ending of "the isolated position we have occupied since our admission as a State." Future recessions could now be forever ended by shipping surpluses to new markets opened by the railroad. "It would be folly to say that quick communication will not stimulate trade," reported a local newspaper, and no longer would San Francisco be "isolated from the rest of the Union"; the railroad that "changed the condition of the Mississippi Valley and made it an empire," would similarly transform California.[29]

The city's business community also envisioned a linear relationship between the opening of the railroad and mass immigration to the West Coast. City manufacturers could expect the arrival of a new cheap labor pool from which to profit. Real estate speculation would benefit from the new immigration regardless of the immigrant's occupation or ethnicity. And merchants, besides gaining access to an enlarged trading area throughout the trans-Mississippi region, would profit from the expanded California consumer market.

The San Francisco business community, therefore, immediately organized and financed the California Immigrant Union to advertise in Europe and in eastern cities the salubrious climate, beauty, and high wages of San Francisco. Headed by William T. Coleman, import merchant and former president of the 1856 Vigilance Committee, the Immigrant Union raised money from local businessmen and sent agents to the East Coast to "lecture upon the 'Inducements to Immigration' offered by California." The union also printed a pamphlet entitled *All about California* and distributed it throughout northern Europe and the East Coast. The immediate results of the advertising campaign were not encouraging; no immediate mass immigration occurred, and those who did journey to California preferred the slower but cheaper ships of the Pacific Mail Steamship Co. to the more expensive Central Pacific Railroad.[30]

Problems in the Wake of the Railroad

In fact, the railroad that was once expected to bring about a state of economic bliss, brought instead competition from eastern merchants and unemployment. After the construction of the railroad, Chinese workers flooded the local labor market. And many items once consigned to the interior towns of the Far West by way of San Francisco harbor and the city merchants, now were sent overland and routed directly to their destinations. Sacramento merchants no longer placed their orders exclusively through San Francisco but often dealt directly with eastern suppliers. And Los Angeles, once totally dependent upon San Francisco for virtually everything except livestock, could trade directly with her suppliers and thus save costs that formerly accrued to the merchants of San Francisco.[31] Finally, merchants from Chicago, with their aggressive marketing techniques, frequently outwitted their San Francisco competitors. An economic historian noted that, "Almost before its [the railroad] construction had begun, the merchants and manufacturers of Chicago, more energetic than those of San Francisco, had realized the vast possibilities that were to be opened up. As the Union Pacific Railway was pushed . . . westward, agents representing the Chicago houses followed close behind and secured trade and customers. The San Francisco *Chronicle* of June 12, 1870 pointedly declared, that when 'the junction was made at Promontory Point . . . Chicago was there represented by her agents, while San Francisco down by the sea, was reading accounts of the event.' "[32]

The San Francisco *Evening Bulletin* indirectly criticized the city merchants when it reported that eastern merchants "acted as though new gold mines of fabulous wealth had been opened up to them on the coast." Easterners, the newspaper reported, "canvassed the coast thoroughly, not forgetting the smallest retail establishment . . . and as a reward for their perseverance . . . they secured a number of orders and subsequently forwarded a large quantity of goods in response to such orders and for speculative account. As a result of these operations, our [San Francisco] markets, which were already well stocked, were overburdened with goods, and stagnation was the inevitable consequence."[33]

The railroad, by tying San Francisco to a national market and opening up the Mountain states to eastern merchants, had in effect weakened San Francisco's trading preeminence in the western territories; and worse, it forever destroyed San Francisco's geographic isolation and hence disrupted the West Coast trade network that San Francisco had so fortuitously monopolized for twenty years. The city and its merchants had no alternative but to accept the consequences that the railroad wrought—the loss of a trading monopoly which coincided with the city's integration into the national marketplace. But the city would not passively accept the arbitrary and unfair disadvantage of unequal rates imposed upon it by the railroads. A local newspaper complained in the early 1870s: "There is no equality of competition between the merchants of Chicago and those of San Francisco and

Sacramento so long as freight charges and passenger travel are two and three-quarters times as much per mile over the California as over the eastern end of the road . . . that Chicago, under this rule, can deliver flour, heavy groceries, machinery for agriculture and mining, even boots and shoes, blankets and clothing, at Salt Lake cheaper than our merchants can, even if they form combinations to sell at bare cost."[34]

A San Francisco tea importer complained that his Chicago clients "did not wish to buy four or five hundred packages and get them to Chicago and then have the freight dropped on them." Another merchant lamented, "it costs me more to send my merchandise from San Francisco to Reno than from New York to San Francisco." He further complained that the railroad would not tolerate competition from water carriers. The railroad threatened the city merchants that if they failed to ship all their freight, rather than a portion of it, via the Central Pacific Railroad, then freight rates would be doubled.[35] One merchant described the ways of the railroad:

A short time since one of our Front Street merchants received a letter from railroad headquarters, notifying him that the Argus-eyed official charged with the duty of watching such matters, had discovered on a certain ship, that on her voyage from New York to San Francisco, there were some packages consigned to him and requested an explanation. Another merchant received a similar missive, appraised that he had purchased some merchandise which had been brought aroung Cape Horn, and if the offense was repeated the company would terminate his contract and charge him double rates. . . . The time had come when we will no longer permit that merchandise shall be brought from the city of Louisville, or from Cincinnati . . . and be carried past our doors and delivered in Arizona Territory at less than we pay for the transportation of the same goods from San Francisco to the same . . . destination.[36]

The Central Pacific Railroad consolidated its monopoly when it purchased the California Steam Navigation Company and thereby controlled river transportation to Sacramento, Stockton, and the interior towns; and second, by an arrangement with the Pacific Mail Steamship Co., the shipping company agreed to raise its rates in proportion to those of the Central Pacific in return for a rebate from the railroad.

The merchants responded in a weak and ineffectual fashion. They attempted no concerted action either in the form of a boycott or petitions to Congress. In fact the San Francisco Chamber of Commerce appeared more concerned with the income of the "debt-ridden railroad" than the losses suffered by the city merchants. The chamber stirred itself to draw up a bill to create a Board of Transportation Commissioners for overseeing the operation of the railroad, but it was so mild and ineffectual that the Central Pacific failed even to oppose it.[37]

The city merchants did, however, organize a committee to investigate the feasibility of a federally sponsored trans-Isthmus canal. The committee complained about the "want of cheap transportation" and recommended to Congress the immediate construction of a canal through Nicaragua which would ensure "cheap freights" and "permanent relief." "The millions of Europe and our country men on our Eastern seaboard want the varied products of our soils," the committee reported, "but we are debarred from the benefit which should thereby accrue" by the expanse of the continent, the long voyage around the Horn and the railroads. The canal would free the city of the railroad and "the fetters of expensive transportation." Then, and only then, would the railroads "learn to regard their local business as a factor of great importance."[38]

Despite disclaimers to the contrary, however, San Francisco gained some immediate benefits from the railroad. First, the freight distance from New York to San Francisco was shortened greatly, from 6,100 miles by sea to 3,400 miles by rail. The distance reduction favored large wholesalers who controlled large market areas, thus yielding to them greater absolute cost savings. Second, the railroad and its feeder lines connected and opened up new interior markets for the San Francisco merchant. In some places, particularly within the Sacramento and San Joaquin Valleys, rate advantages did not rest with midwestern or eastern cities. Compared to San Francisco, the communities most handicapped by discriminatory rates were those midwestern towns intermediate between Pacific terminals and the East. "Prices slightly higher west of the Rockies" was (and remains so today) an obscene charge to westerners. But the railroad eventually provided cost savings even to them, when after the 1880s rates to the entire West Coast dropped significantly with the arrival of the Northern Pacific in Portland and Tacoma, and the completion of the Southern Pacific to Los Angeles and eventually San Francisco.[39]

Even before the city gained equitable rates, the railroad helped transform San Francisco from an isolated mercantile community into a major industrial metropolis. The initial manufacturing advantage that San Francisco held in California (and the West Coast) in 1860 was heightened a decade later with the arrival of the railroad, which expanded the city's market possibilities. But the new industries would complete a process which the railroads began—the ultimate undermining of a predominately mercantile economy.

Early Manufacture and the Impact of the Civil War

San Francisco was not without manufacturing establishments in the early 1850s. The first industries—mostly foundry and machine shops —repaired the fleet of ocean and river steamboats that cluttered the local harbor. However, the first real growth of local manufacturers occurred in the late 1850s with the transition from placer to quartz and hydraulic mining. The demand for new equipment from the mines required stamp mills, rope, wire, blasting powder, concentrators, amalgamators, and an assortment of heavy tools. Items that could not be imported economically from the East were manufactured locally by such companies as the Union Iron Works and the Pacific Foundry. And with the rise of agricultural production in California, saw mills and local food processing plants made their appearance in San Francisco in addition to those establishments which produced for local consumption items like bricks, malt liquors, bread. Also there were the custom manufacturers of products for specialized local usage— wagons and carts, tin, copper, sheet-iron ware and ore-mining machinery. Finally a few manufacturers were combined with retailing, like boots and shoes, rope, saddlery and harness. In 1860, San Francisco actually ranked ninth of all American cities in the value of production. But this was misleading "since over half [52 percent] of San Francisco's value," one investigator of the city's manufacturers noted, "was derived from 'gold mining' [refining] of which only 10 percent was value added and in which only 15 workers were employed." Moreover, the value of San Francisco's manufacturing was inflated by the city's wage rates which were "three times those prevailing in cities of the Middle Atlantic Region in 1860." A more realistic perspective showed that only 1,564 city workers were employed in manufacturing, or 1.6 per thousand population, compared to 5 per thousand population in the United States as a whole. And in terms of the percent of the city population employed in manufacturing, San Francisco ranked behind Washington, D.C., and New Orleans. The city, with only 2.6 percent of its population employed in workshops and small factories as of 1860, nonetheless "accounted for 25 percent of the state's industrial employment and 40 percent of its value added by manufactures."[40]

As in the mercantile cities of Boston, New York, Philadelphia and Baltimore, where in the 1830s manufacturing was the handmaiden of commerce, in San Francisco small manufacturing plants in the 1850s were intimately associated with the city's commerce. The industries of eastern mercantile cities, an economic geographer noted, "processed import and export commodities that could be distributed through established channels to known markets; or provided printed materials, ships and other capital goods and services vital to the perpetuation of trade with . . . coastal points, and the interial hinterland; or catered to the household and construction demands of the local mercantile population and the classes serving that population." San Francisco manufacturers in the 1850s performed similar functions.[41]

The low level of industrialization in San Francisco in the 1850s was the result of high labor costs (compared to the East Coast) caused by a critical shortage of skilled labor. Most laborers preferred to test their luck in the gold mines rather than sell their skills in the marketplace. But even if an adequate labor supply had existed in San Francisco in the 1850s, it is doubtful that manufacturing output would have increased significantly. Few capitalists were willing to invest in new manufacturing ventures which could not reasonably be expected to show a profit in anything less than two years. Investment opportunities, in the opinion of the city merchants and others with available funds, were far superior in real estate, mining stocks, or in one's own company.[42]

Capital began flowing to San Francisco during the Civil War. In an economic climate where greenbacks did not circulate (and hence inflation was checked), eastern and foreign capital sought new investment opportunities and capital returns in San Francisco. In a single week in November 1864, eastern financiers reportedly transferred over $600,000 to the city. Five British banks established offices in San Francisco during the war period to take advantage of new investment opportunities.[43]

The Civil War had another effect upon San Francisco and her industrial development. With shipping lanes disrupted and transportation costs exorbitantly high, few prospective purchasers of industrial goods were willing either to risk capture at sea or pay the costs of goods imported from eastern manufacturers. Further, a high protective tariff discouraged foreign imports. One advocate of manufacturing remarked in 1864: "We are situated at so great a distance from the manufacturing centers of the world that the cost of transportation is equivalent to a profit." In the end, the Civil War enforced upon the city an industrial self-reliance. But before full industrialization could be realized, a cheap labor supply was needed.[44]

The Chinese filled the labor vacuum and completed the profitable equation. Spokesmen for the manufacturing interests who complained about the high costs for raw materials, power, and transportation, argued that if San Francisco was to diversify its economy through industrialization then cheap labor must be employed to balance the costs. Diversity of the economy and a move away from total reliance upon merchandising and mining were deemed essential to the survival of the city. The two obstacles to the development of manufacturing in San Francisco were, said an advocate of the new manufacturing class, "the prejudice entertained by a portion of our people against the influx of the only kind of labor that can make . . . industry successful, and . . . the national predilection of our people to follow in the old beaten track of their ancestors."[45]

The merchants, for the most part, never did give up "the old beaten track of their ancestors" nor did they immediately oppose the influx of Chinese and foreign labor from overseas or the railroad camps. By 1870 there was an abundance of cheap labor. Manufacturers said they needed inexpensive labor to compensate for the high cost of importing raw materials by rail so as to compete with eastern manufacturers. A rope manufacturer explained that "had it not been for Chinese cheap labor" there would have been no manufacturing in San Francisco in the 1860s and 1870s. "White labor costs two or three dollars a day," he noted, "and we could not have established a factory here at that time against the same labor in the East at $1.50 per day. We employ cheap Chinese labor and it has enabled us to distribute millions of money among the white people here."[46] That "millions" actually filtered down from the city's industrial self-styled philanthropists to the

The Kimball Carriage Company, one of the many local manufacturing companies that expanded its operation after the Civil War. The plant, like most others, was located in the district south of Market Street.

workers is less clear than the fact that the Chinese (and, no doubt, a large portion of the European immigrants) were exploited by their employers. Those industries that competed with eastern and European products (clothing and textiles) hired, for the most part, Chinese labor. White laborers, mostly European immigrants, were employed in those industries (saw and planing mills, sash factories, box factories, foundries, machine shops, gold and silver quartz mills, printing and publishing houses) that faced high transportation costs for raw materials or intense external competition.[47]

The existence of a large number of Chinese and European laborers did force wage rates down, but it did not automatically guarantee to the San Francisco manufacturer a condition of parity with eastern competitors. Wage rates in California relative to the rest of the nation, and hence labor costs, remained approximately 40 percent higher than the average wages paid in the Middle Atlantic states. For example, the average weekly wage for blue-collar workers (skilled and nonskilled) in 1878 was $18.22, far higher than the $12.07 paid in New York. Still, the regional wage differential did narrow between 1860 and 1880. With the large increase in the relative and absolute number of blue-collar workers in San Francisco during the two decades, labor costs to the local manufacturer had declined.[48]

The railroad actually protected the city's manufacturers from eastern competition. The Central Pacific charged the highest freight rates of any major railroad in the country in the 1870s (fifty dollars per ton for dry goods, the same rate charged by the clipper ships in the early 1850s). Although the manufacturers could not export to national markets, neither could the eastern manufacturers profitably export to West Coast markets. Initially the high railroad rates acted in much the same manner as a protective tariff and allowed the San Francisco manufacturer to monopolize California's consumer market, at least until railroad rates declined in the 1880s.

The three factors needed for profitable manufacturing were sufficiently established by the late 1860s to allow San Francisco to begin its industrial transformation. The infusion of "foreign capital," easier access to local raw materials, and a decline in labor costs relative to the East, encouraged manufacturing output in San Francisco between 1860 and 1880. The per capita increase in manufacturing output within California in the two decades was two and one-half times that of the United States as a whole. And whereas San Francisco accounted for 40 percent of California's manufacturing output (measured by "value added") in 1860, the city accounted for almost 70 percent of the state's industrial production in 1880.[49]

Unlike the 1850s, when San Francisco manufacturing was primarily geared to the production of mining equipment and therefore susceptible to the unpredictable economic cycles of the mining industry, manufacturing in 1880 was broadly based in terms of products. The six leading industries were: slaughtering and meat packing; sugar refining; boots and shoes; foundries, machinery; men's clothing; tobacco and cigars. In addition, printing, liquor distilleries, carpentering, and flour and grist milling added significantly to the value of the city's manufacturing production.[50]

By 1890 manufacturing in San Francisco had expanded so considerably that 16 percent of the city's population was employed in manufacturing enterprises compared with only 2.6 percent in 1860. Already by 1880 more people were employed in manufacturing than were employed in the combined activities of trade and transportation. San Francisco was, in fact, the ninth leading manufacturing city in the nation measured both in terms of industrial output (value added) and percent of the city's population employed in manufacturing.[51]

This change in the economic structure of the city—from a mercantile community to a major industrial metropolis—eventually challenged the traditional trading and distribution function of the merchants and threatened their economic preeminence in the city. As manufacturing became more concentrated and formed larger producing units, manufacturers came increasingly to assume the function of the wholesalers. This process was no doubt hastened by the city merchants' reluctance to invest in new manufacturing enterprises. Manufacturers in the 1860s and 1870s were no longer dependent upon credit extended to them by wholesalers acting as their suppliers and distributors. Capable of financing their own expansion from retained earnings or from eastern or foreign sources, manufacturers sought capital independent of the mercantile community. More significantly, manufacturers began in the late 1870s and 1880 to adopt the "strategies of vertical integration" whereby they obtained raw materials directly. The importance of the merchant middleman as a supplier of these raw materials declined. Finally, manufacturing corporations initiated their own marketing organizations—complete with advertising, sales, installation, and repair technicians—which sold directly to retail outlets. The merchant middleman could not handle, even if he was willing to do so—and many were not—the complexities of new market techniques. New skills and services were demanded which the conventional merchant simply "could not provide as efficiently as the manufacturers themselves."[52]

The rise of manufacturing in San Francisco between 1860 and 1880 altered the city's occupational structure. San Francisco by 1880 had reached an industrial threshold, one urban geographer noted, that had the effect of creating "a host of new business, service, trade, construction [houses, streets, sewers and water mains, schools and other public buildings, stores and business establishments], transportation, professional and miscellaneous white-collar jobs."[53] Among the blue-collar positions, most of the new jobs required industrial or mechanical skills; there was a corresponding decline in the demand for unskilled laborers. Of the white-collar jobs, the most significant change occurred in the clerical positions, which proportionately doubled between 1852 and 1880. The percent of managers, company officials, and manufacturers also doubled, and important increases occurred in the professions.

Merchant occupations moved counter to the general white-collar trend. Whereas the merchant occupations accounted for 14 percent of the city's occupations in 1852, they represented only 8 percent in 1880. The one-man shop was giving way to the larger retail stores which employed almost all of the city's 7,775 clerks.[54] But despite this shrinkage in the relative number of merchants, the proportion of merchants in the city's overall occupational structure was still second only to Brooklyn when compared with other American cities. The new level of industrialization altered San Francisco's occupational structure so that in 1880 a more even balance existed between the manufacturing-industrial sector and the wholesaling-trading complex. San Francisco in 1880 was an industrial city, but it had not yet lost its mercantile heritage (see table 3.2).

A significant reordering of the city's occupational structure occurred, therefore, after the Civil War. Encouraged in part by the war and indirectly by the railroad, manufacturers emerged to challenge the preeminence of the merchant establishment. Though by no means a local phenomenon limited to San Francisco, the response of the San Francisco merchants to this challenge would determine their ultimate fate.

7

A NEW MERCHANT
GENERATION

"Where are they now," Mark Twain asked in the early 1870s
of all the enterprising young pioneers who twenty years ago migrated
to the West Coast in search of instant wealth. "Scattered to the ends
of the earth—or permanently aged and decrepit—or shot or stabbed in
street affrays—or dead of disappointed hopes and broken-hearts—all
gone, or nearly all—victims devoted upon the altar of the golden calf
—the noblest holocaust that ever wafted its sacrificial incense heaven-
ward. It is painful to think upon."[1]

Disillusioned with the California Dream, some unwilling and others
incapable of surviving the economic dislocations of the 1850s, most of
San Francisco's first generation of residents—merchants and nonmerchants alike—had departed the city within eight years after their arrival. Only about two out of every ten merchants, a persistence rate
twice that of the city's pioneer general population, remained in San
Francisco through 1880.

Yet the disappointments of one generation did not discourage the
mass migration to San Francisco of a second generation. Although
they held less exalted expectations, the later arrivals sought the same
substantive occupational and financial opportunities that had generated the pioneer migration in the 1850s.

Who among the second generation occupied the merchant positions
in the city? Did they experience a higher degree of social mobility in
terms of careers than the pioneer merchants? Or did the challenges of
a new industrial city prevent them from attaining the limited gains of
the first merchant generation? Finally, was the social system as it
operated in San Francisco in the 1870s and 1880s any more open than
that of certain eastern cities in the late nineteenth century?

Population Growth and Turnover

The city's population grew 160 percent in the Civil War decade and
another 56 percent in the 1870s so that by 1880 San Francisco ranked
as the ninth largest city in the nation. The pattern of migration to San

Francisco after the Civil War, however, had changed considerably. Whereas four of every ten city residents in 1852 were born in or near the Eastern Seaboard states, less than two out of ten of the residents in 1880 were born in New England or the mid-Atlantic states. Also by 1880, 35 percent of all San Franciscans were born west of the Mississippi (virtually all native Californians), compared to one percent of the 1850 pioneer generation.

The number of foreign-born males in the city declined steadily from 53 percent of the total in 1852 to 45 percent in 1880. Still, the percent of foreign-born in San Francisco (male and female) was the second highest in the nation (behind Fall River, Massachusetts); and in absolute terms only New York, Chicago, Philadelphia, Brooklyn, Boston, and Saint Louis had more foreign-born than did San Francisco. While the percentage of San Francisco's population born abroad remained relatively stable, the ethnic composition of the city changed significantly between 1850 and 1880. The English and French who together composed almost a quarter of the city's total residents in 1852, but who were the first to depart San Francisco in the 1850s, numbered only 6 percent of the population in 1880. The Irish, on the other hand, whose departure rate among the first generation of city residents was also high, maintained their relative proportion in the city through the constant influx of Irish-born immigrants in the 1860s and 1870s. Meanwhile, the Chinese, who were less than 1 percent in 1852, grew to 9 percent of the city's population in 1880, and East and South Europeans (particularly Italians), similarly few in the 1850s, grew to approximately 4 percent of the city's residents.

From a systematic sample of the city's employed male population in 1880, only 30 percent resided in San Francisco ten years earlier and less than 10 percent lived there in 1860. Thus, over three-quarters of the native-born and two-thirds of the foreign-born had migrated to San Francisco sometime during the decade of the 1870s—the South and East Europeans the most recent arrivals among the foreign-born. The Irish, among the second generation of residents, had resided longest in the city.

Occupational Structure and Origins, 1880

Not only a new generation of residents but a new group of merchants had emerged in industrial San Francisco in less than two decades. Only a little more than 10 percent of the merchants could claim two decades of local residence, a figure slightly higher than the average for other San Franciscans; the majority of the merchants, like the general population, had resided in the city less than a decade.[2] But the new merchants differed significantly from both their midcentury predecessors and from the general population of the 1880 city.

The principal change within the merchant class was that the second generation, unlike the first, was predominantly foreign-born. This in itself was not surprising considering that the foreign-born outnumbered the native-born in the city's male employed population almost three to two. The foreign-born were almost 60 percent of the total male employed working force (excluding the Chinese), but they occupied over three-quarters of the merchant positions. Whereas the native-born had occupied well over half the merchant positions in the city in 1852, they accounted for less than a quarter of these merchant jobs in 1880. There were also very important ethnic differences in the occupational distributions.

The Germans continued to cluster heavily in merchant ranks. By 1880, they were two times more likely to be working as merchants than in any other occupation within the city. They controlled the clothing, dry goods, and cigar trades, both wholesale and retail. Probably well over a half of the Germans were Jews who, one observer noted, were "leaders in and controlled, to a great extent, the principal mercantile businesses. The clothing trade—here as elsewhere—is monopolized by them, and the principal dry-goods houses, and crockery and jewelry establishments, belong to Jews."[3]

The Irish, the second largest group of foreign-born merchants, had yet to reach demographic parity in the merchant occupations by 1880. For the most part they were petty shopkeepers (grocers, wine and liquor shops) and occupied the lower status retail merchant positions.[4]

As a group the Italians also clustered in the petty shopkeeper ranks as peddlers, fish mongers, and fruit and vegetable dealers. Most of the Italian merchants of the city had progressed in their geographical transfer to the United States from farms or the ranks of the urban unemployed in Italy. They viewed the United States as a promised land, where they could forget the ineradicable physical hardship of their homeland. "Southern Europe," one historian noted, "simply offered too few inducements for the city unemployed, young or old," with the result that the urban as well as the rural poor looked to "foreign

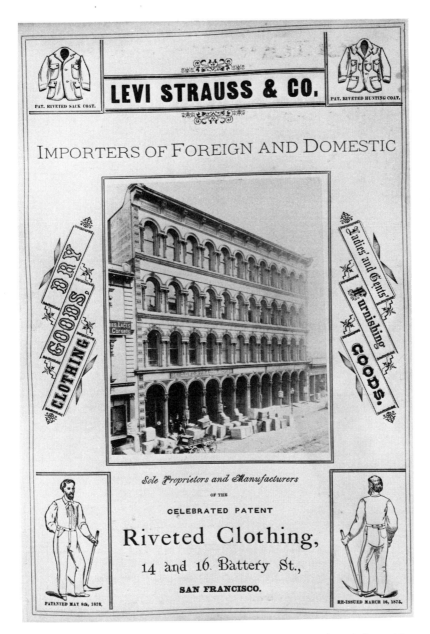

Levi Strauss' work clothes, hand-crafted from canvas shipped from New York in 1849, were manufactured in San Francisco by the 1870s.

shores for their vision of the future.'' Depending upon the district in Italy in which immigrants were born, the wages paid the Chinese in San Francisco were two to three times higher than those prevailing in Italy in 1880. Although few were believed to have had any merchant experience in Italy, the Italians in San Francisco were three times more numerous in the merchant occupations than in the city's employed male population.[5]

As a general rule, the higher the occupational status, the greater the representation of the native-born (taking into account the disproportionate number of foreigners in the merchant sector). The foreign-born clustered within the lower-status white and blue-collar occupations. The less prestigious merchant occupations, for example, tended to be reserved, as they had been in the 1850s for the Irish and the Germans, and after 1870, for the newly arrived Italians. The general trend over the three decades was that while the native-born continued to hold a large portion (36 percent) of the higher-status merchant positions in 1880, the foreign-born, and particularly the Germans, had more than doubled their representation within the importer-wholesaler ranks—from 26 percent in 1852 to 64 percent in 1880.

An index of representation demonstrates the disparity between the

Table 7.1. Ethnic distribution of employed males in merchant occupations, 1852 and 1880 (in percent).

	1852 Generation		1880 Generation	
Nativity	Merchants (N = 643)	General population (N = 669)	Merchants (N = 958)	General population (N = 731)
All native-born	62	47	24	41
All Foreign-born	38	53	76	59
English-Scottish	11	14	6	7
Irish	4	12	15	20
German	14	7	34	15
French	3	9	5	3
Italian	—	1	7	2
Other	6	11[a]	9[b]	12[c]

SOURCE: California State Census, 1852; Federal Census, 1880.

a. Latin America, Mexico: 4%.

b. Norway, Sweden, Denmark: 1%; Poland 2%.

c. Norway, Sweden, Denmark: 4%; Poland 1%.

native-born and foreign-born in the city's labor force. A score of 100 indicates the nativity group has attained parity at a particular occupational level and is therefore receiving its share of such jobs; a score of 200 indicates that twice as many members of a nativity group are employed at an occupational level as would be expected if jobs were allocated without regard to native origin; similarly, a score of 50 indicates that a nativity group holds only half as many jobs as expected.[6]

Clearly the higher the status of an occupation, the more likely it was to find a native American employed within it. There was one important exception to the finding. Among the city's male clerical force, which in terms of status ranked below bankers, manufacturers, and the general retail merchants (those who employed the majority of city clerks), the native-born far outnumbered the foreign-born. This may perhaps be explained by the fact that a clerkship was considered the training ground for future promotion into the high status white-collar occupations. In the 1870s clerks were reportedly an "educated and gentlemanly" group in San Francisco. "The clerk and salesman of

Table 7.2. Index of occupational representation by nativity, 1880.

Occupation	Native-born	Foreign-born	Percent of total labor force
White-collar			
Professionals	145	68	9
Manufacturers; managers; government officials; bankers, brokers	130	78	6
Importer-wholesalers[a]	88	108	1
General merchants[a]	70	120	3
Clerks	146	68	15
Saloon, boarding house, restaurant keepers	69	121	6
Petty shopkeepers[a]	37	143	4
All white-collar	113	90	44
Blue collar			
Skilled laborers	95	103	46
Nonskilled laborers	65	125	10
All blue-collar	89	107	56

a. This category is prepared from 1880 merchant sample (N = 958); others are from 1880 sample of the city's employed male population (N = 731). The Chinese are excluded from both samples.

today," reported the San Francisco *Bulletin*, "is the merchant of tomorrow."[7]

More second generation merchants, however, were recruited from the working class than from the clerical and sales force, a recruitment pattern which suggests a relatively high degree of occupational mobility in the 1870s between the blue-collar trades and the merchant occupations.[8] Also one-fourth of the second generation of petty shopkeepers had worked in a blue-collar position as their first job in San Francisco. Even among the importers, one-fifth had emerged from the working class. But merchant experience seemed more important for advancement in the merchant class. Of the second generation merchants who resided in San Francisco for at least ten years and for whom at least one previous occupation could be verified, six of every ten held as their first job a merchant occupation.

Nativity differences in recruitment into the merchant occupations reflected the native-born/foreign-born differences in the city's overall occupational structure. Approximately one-quarter of the foreign-born merchants emerged from the blue-collar ranks where the majority of the city's foreign-born were employed; and from the clerical ranks, which were predominantly native-born, emerged approximately one-quarter of the native-born merchants.

The merchants tended, therefore, to move from the occupational pools that reflected their own nativity and that in terms of occupational status were closest to them. For example, the American-born merchants (the majority of whom occupied high-status merchant positions) recruited more heavily within the predominantly native-born clerical ranks than from among the pool of foreign-born blue-collar workers. For the foreign-born merchants, those who predominated within the petty shopkeeper ranks, the recruitment pattern was reversed.

Considered from the perspective of occupational origins, the second merchant generation experienced somewhat less occupational mobility and considerably more job stability than the pioneer merchants. Of the pioneer merchants almost half moved up the occupational ladder between the time they departed their former jobs in an eastern city and the time (1852) of their first occupation in San Francisco. Yet of the second generation, only a little more than a third experienced upward mobility between 1870 and 1880. The downward rates were approximately the same.[9]

Table 7.3. Comparison of mobility from original occupations for first and second generation merchants (in percent).

Merchant Category	First Generation (c. 1846-1852)				Second Generation (c. 1870-1880)			
	Upward	Same	Down-ward	(N)	Upward	Same	Down-ward	(N)
Petty shopkeepers	26	26	48	(20)	27	53	20	(148)
General merchants	49	45	6	(68)	39	58	3	(218)
Importer-wholesalers	75	25	—	(40)	62	36	2	(39)
All merchants	54	36	10	(128)	37	54	9	(405)

SOURCE: California State Census, 1852; Federal Census, 1880.

Social mobility for the merchant class, as measured by occupational movement, declined somewhat over the span of three decades. The first generation had experienced high rates of shipboard mobility on their way to a merchant occupation in San Francisco.[10] And although they had, for the most part, experienced rough times in the 1850s, those who persisted through the 1860 decade profited financially and advanced occupationally during the war decade. But in the 1870s the second generation merchants faced intense competition from each other, and more importantly, from the merchandizing offices of the new manufacturers.

Failure and Competition

The high rate of business failures reflected difficulties faced by the merchants in the 1870s. Bankruptcy among merchants was three times as high in the 1870s as in the 1860s.[11] And to shield themselves against financial losses, merchants in the late 1860s began to utilize the services of new credit collection associations. A group of importers, wholesalers, and commission merchants, for example, formed the San Francisco Commercial and Trade Association for the purpose of "mutual protection against fraudulent debtors and the collection of debts." Members reported $1,500,000 of unpaid debts in the first nine months of operation. The association managed to recover in its first year $500,000 through 82 court cases. A group of merchants in 1871 formed the Grocers Protective Union, an association to collect bad debts and to print yearly a list of delinquent accounts owed to association members. Another group of 260 merchants hired a small merchant company, Dunbar Bros. and Company, to act as their collection agent. For a fee, Dunbar published a monthly confidential report listing San Francisco residents who owed money to the members. The report, said Dunbar, "will be worth more for reference than the membership fees."[12]

In the late 1870s another merchant collection agency, the Merchants Protective Association, was formed. Composed mainly of general merchants, it warned its members that "if more discrimination was exercised by you in giving credit, both as to the party's means and moral character, you would have fewer failures, less losses and this Association less business." The association also urged its members to put a halt to the practice of "dishonest failures." "Most failures," the association observed, "occur for the express purpose of making money by a compromise, and it should be your aim . . . to stamp out this practice . . . The bankruptcy law works an injustice to the creditor, it provides that a debtor may surrender his estate, and by paying 30 percent [of his debts], be discharged of all debts."[13]

Regardless of what the association thought to be lenient grounds for bankruptcy, merchants realized, as did their creditors, that a declared bankruptcy would adversely affect their credit ratings in the community. Credit was the life-blood of the merchant's world and to declare bankruptcy was to admit failure publicly. The high rate of business failures for merchants in the 1870s was evidence less of the leniency of the bankruptcy laws than of the severe competition.[14]

The city's new manufacturing establishments offered both an opportunity and a competitive challenge to the merchants. When manufacturers expanded their sales departments, they threatened to usurp the merchant's traditional trading function and network. On the other hand, manufacturing offered the merchants an alternative investment opportunity by which they might profit and hence cushion themselves against the loss of trade to the manufacturers. The general failure of the second merchant generation to match the performance of the pioneers was caused as much by that generation's failure to recognize or adjust to the city's industrial transformation, as by the structural dislocations brought by this change.

The San Francisco merchants responded to the new opportunities of the industrial revolution with a distinct lack of enthusiasm or imagination. Whereas eastern merchants acted as the catalysts for the industrial transformation of their communities, the San Francisco merchants remained shackled to their traditional faith in the mining industry and the trade which the mines generated. The Boston merchants, for example, invested in the Waltham and Lowell textile mills in the 1820s. Pittsburgh and Baltimore merchants somewhat later were leaders in the development of their local iron mills. Having traditionally functioned as investment and commercial bankers and having mastered "the art of doing business over long distances with a polyglot assortment of currencies and commercial paper," these eastern merchants, two economic historians noted, "routinely performed all the functions later institutionalized in formal agencies such as banks, credit bureaus and factoring companies." In short, the financial versatility of the eastern merchants, developed in a preindustrial economy, "proved readily adaptable to manufacturing."[15]

Unlike the eastern merchants, the San Francisco merchants failed to play an "indispensable part in American industrialization." Acting more like the New York merchants on the eve of the Revolution, the West Coast merchant in the 1860s and 1870s believed an investment in manufacturing enterprises to be "a third choice at best." Conditioned to the myths of the early 1850s, when a few merchants garnered huge fortunes through trade with or speculative investments in the mines, they continued to trust their future to an older mercantile economy which derived its life-blood from "the diggings."[16]

Immediately following the Civil War, spokesmen within the city's business community urged the merchants to forego their time-honored fascination for the mining trade and turn to industry. A local insurance company executive warned the merchant-dominated Chamber of Commerce that unless San Francisco changed its priorities from mining to manufacturing "our permanent prosperity will remain in abeyance." The city's future lay not with speculation in or trade with the cyclical and unpredictable mining industry but in the "encouragement of diversified industry."[17]

In 1873 the mayor asked the city to "offer every encouragement to capitalists abroad to send their surplus funds here for investment in the manufacturing and other enterprises which are needed to quicken the settlement and enhance the prosperity of the State." And the mayor's successor in city hall, James Otis, one of San Francisco's foremost commission merchants, advised his merchant colleagues "we need manufacturers of all kinds." Rather than ordering industrial products from the East Coast or Europe, "let us make [them] at our own door." The merchant-capitalist must be willing to invest in manufacturing a portion of his money, and the result, advised the merchant-mayor, will be a fair return on his capital in addition to "furnishing employment to thousands who are now idle or non-producing." Otis indirectly admonished the merchant community for their past investment practices when he concluded: "Your money invested in some good manufacturing enterprise will pay better than invested in some sandheap, waiting for the tide of population to sweep over it and make you rich without labor, a condition which by the laws of God cannot be arrived at."[18]

The merchants and the Chamber of Commerce responded with indifference. They continued fussing and fuming to Washington about the inadequate navigational aids in the San Francisco harbor, and reserved most of their enthusiasm for a scheme to encourage English investors to purchase and reclaim swamp lands in the San Joaquin and Sacramento Valleys for the purpose of European colonization. In fact as late as 1878, when the city's industrial production ranked ninth in the nation, the chamber's president boastfully proclaimed to his colleagues: "We are, over and above everything else, a mining people, and it affords me the highest satisfaction to . . . report that whatever may have been the failures or shortcomings of the season in other respects [they were considerable], this great [mining] interest is in a most exceptional healthy state."[19]

Merchant Investments

The business and personal ventures in which San Francisco merchants invested their excess capital indicated clearly their vision of the future. They did possess ample capital for investment, for the losses of the 1850 decade were more than made up during the Civil War years when San Francisco merchants profited from their relative isolation and a favorable currency exchange vis-a-vis the East. By 1870 the general merchants, and particularly the importer-wholesalers, possessed the capital assets with which to finance, if they so wished, the future manufacturing industries of the city.[20]

Affluent merchants also received the higher credit ratings which allowed them to borrow capital from lending institutions for their businesses or for investment purposes. The general merchants and importer-wholesalers, for example, were four times more likely to receive a "good" or "excellent" credit rating than were the petty shopkeepers in the 1860s and 1870s. And by 1880, of those merchants with assets in excess of $50,000, over 80 percent received "good" or "excellent" ratings. Lending institutions were, however, somewhat more cautious with their loans in the 1870s than in the 1850s. R. G. Dun and Company, for example, granted fewer high credit ratings in the 1870 decade than they had twenty years earlier. Conditioned by the speculative mania which constantly pervaded the San Francisco marketplace, R. G. Dun and no doubt local banks too investigated more thoroughly the financial background of their clients before issuing either a higher credit rating or a substantial loan. Whereas approximately 40 percent of the merchants who could be located in the R. G. Dun credit reports in 1880 received a "good" or "excellent" rating, 65 percent in the early 1850s were granted a similar rating. Still the merchants had accumulated the capital assets by 1870 which to borrow and invest and therefore encourage manufacturing if they so wished.[21]

Rather than investing in manufacturing, the merchants preferred to purchase larger inventories, new retail outlets, and to extend further lines of credit to consumers. Or, addicted as they were to mining and speculative enterprises, a habit carried over from the 1850s, they invested in real estate or mining stocks which they believed offered quick profits with a minimum risk. The myriad of mining stocks which appeared on the market in the 1870s was a particularly popular attraction. A number of these mining companies were organized by San Francisco businessmen. William C. Ralston, a city banker, organized the Union Mill and Mining Company to uncover the Comstock Lode. Also locally organized was the Virginia Consolidated Mining Company, formed by James G. Fair, James C. Flood, William S. O'Brien, and John W. Mackay.

With the opening of the Comstock area to mining, a speculative mania engulfed the whole city. Merchants "who had hitherto been content with the comparatively moderate profits of legitimate trade" invested heavily, as did saloon keepers, hostelers, and traders, to whom the merchants "would scarcely grant a month's credit."[22] A visitor to the city reported: "Money, wealth, is everything here with everybody . . . as with the laboring class. A million is the unit in estimating a man's wealth, and the rich man is also the great man, the good man, in fact THE MAN. Others are of little account. Hence everybody feels the necessity of getting rich, very rich, because he wants to be somebody. Therefore this universal stock gambling in which everybody and his nurse or hosteler, and all women of all positions are engaged . . . Wealth being everything, it must be gained by everybody, and those who fail are in a constant state of despair."[23]

The volatile stock prices of the mining stocks moved in gigantic spurts up and down. In January 1872, the shares of the thirteen leading mines of the Comstock Lode were valued at $17 million. In June their market value was $80 million. By the end of August, the stocks had plummeted to $20 million. A weekly movement of 25 percent in a single stock was not uncommon. By 1875 losses in mining stocks caused bankruptcies, bank runs, and the failure of the Bank of California—the dominant bank on the West Coast. In January 1877 another panic occurred when the Consolidated Virginia Mining Company failed to pay its monthly dividend. The extent to which San Francisco was affected by the stock collapse, one historian observed, "is appreciated only when one realized that the loss actually amounted to $1,000 for each adult male in San Francisco."[24] Within all levels of San Francisco's society, men experienced financial losses. But the group that suffered most were the small investors. Uneducated to the machinations of the market, they sold out only after insiders had exacted high profits through stock manipulations.

The stock market, despite local advertisements to the contrary, was not a generator of social mobility. From a sample of people owning personal property in excess of $20,000, not a single one could be traced to a blue-collar occupation at any time during the entire span of his occupational career in San Francisco. Nor was there any evidence to suggest that the reportedly large number of blue-collar workers who invested their small earnings in silver stocks were brought to new heights of affluence. Although the sample was not representative of the general population of the city, it did suggest that there were distinct class differentiations among the beneficiaries of the stock market. Not only did stocks comprise a higher percentage of the total property assets of the more affluent, but the stockholders in 1880 accumulated five times as much capital between 1874 and 1880 as those who didn't own stocks. Also the profits accrued on stocks by this sample far exceeded the property accumulations of the more representative R. G. Dun merchant sample in the 1870 decade.[25]

Like the earlier harvests from the gold mines, the stock profits from the silver mines filtered back to a very few wealthy investors. A local city newspaper reported in 1879 that the last "five years have brought disaster and money famine to the masses, notwithstanding the enormous field of precious metals." Capital, one report noted, was no longer "generally distributed" but "concentrated in colossal fortunes." Robert Louis Stevenson referred to the stock exchange as "the heart of San Francisco" which continually pumped up "the savings of the lower quarter into the pockets of millionaires upon the hill." And as one historian of the mining frontier has observed: "The distribution of wealth in California was visibly more unequal after the Comstock boom than before it."[26]

As for the merchants, they were no more successful than the average investor in the stock market. A few importer-wholesalers were known to have profited handsomely, but there was no evidence to suggest that the luck of a few represented the fortunes of an occupational group. R. G. Dun looked with disfavor upon merchants known to be playing the market and so they played surreptitiously. If a merchant was known to be a heavy speculator in mining stocks, "his commercial credit was instantly lowered"; bankers refused him loans and other merchants "declined to credit him."[27]

Merchants also invested a considerable portion of their capital assets in real estate. They purchased vacant lots in anticipation that the transcontinental railroad would flood the city with thousands of new residents. During one period of a minor recession and declining trade (1867 to 1870), a number of Jewish merchants were reported to have invested over 80 percent of their personal property in real estate. One Jewish merchant, Martin Heller, a former peddler from New Jersey, invested his dry goods profits after the Civil War in fourteen buildings which he had constructed between 1867 and 1872, at a total cost of $115,000. Well over three-quarters of the merchants traced in R. G. Dun were reported to own (with the aid of mortgages) at least one piece of real estate.[28]

The affluent American-born merchants, rather than investing in city real estate, preferred to purchase huge tracts of land far from San Francisco on which to ranch and build country estates. Albert Dibblee, a commission merchant, owned large tracts of land in Santa Barbara and Los Angeles counties; Henry Newhall, another commission merchant, invested his profits from auctioneering in real estate spread throughout four separate counties, including Los Angeles. The present-day city of Newhall spreads out over his former ranch. Denis J. Oliver, a paint and oil merchant, invested his excess capital in San Mateo County grazing land and named his ranch Menlo Park after a town near his native birthplace in Ireland.[29] These were in some cases profitable enterprises. Dibblee, for example, continued to exchange his merchant profits for more land, cattle, and sheep. In the three years between 1870 and 1873. Albert Dibblee and his brother Thomas each received from their ranch's operation approximately a 10 percent annual return from their original investment of $300,000.[30] More attracted to the model of the leisured landed gentry than to the opportunities of the urban entrepreneur, the wealthy native-born merchants left to others the task of building an industrial city.

Merchant capital did participate in the industrial transformation of the city but, given the capital assets, not to the degree it might have been expected. One reason, no doubt, was that merchants were uncertain as to the immediate profitability of new manufacturing enterprises. As in all lines of business endeavors, there were instances of failures and bankruptcies within the city's industrial sector.[31] Yet the level of the city's industrial production had more than doubled between 1860 and 1880, suggesting that capital investment had flowed to the industrial sector even if the lead had not come from the merchant class.

One study of the sources of capital for the city's manufacturing establishments discovered that most of the capital derived from non-merchant sources. Of the thirty-six manufacturing partnerships investigated, the capital sources for seventy of the eighty partners indicated that "twenty of them accumulated their capital through merchandizing activities, ten saved money from their wages, ten had no capital except their skill, and thirty of the partners obtained their capital from such sources as farming, loans, sales of assets, and capital brought into California." The merchants reflected, no doubt, the apparent reluctance of most city banks to invest in local manufacturing. The San Francisco Savings Union, for example, issued loans only on real estate and top grade securities, a policy which encouraged land speculation and similarly reduced the amount of capital available for investment in manufacturing establishments. Manufacturing was not the favored investment compared with either mining or real estate.[32]

The San Francisco Bank of California, one of the most important financial institutions in the state, was an enthusiastic supporter of local industries. "A friend to every home industry," its president, William Ralston, "personally assisted various leading industrial enterprises" in San Francisco. His own personal assets, estimated at "several millions," and those of his bank, were liberally invested in local enterprises. A business associate of Ralston's reported that "it was a great hobby with him to build up home industries and to develop home resources." For if California prospered, thought Raltson, "the Bank will prosper—we shall all prosper."[33]

Among the Bank of California investments were local industries producing carriages, agricultural implements, furniture, locks, silk, cigars, woolen goods, watches, and sugar. In addition, Ralston financed the opulent Palace Hotel, the California Theatre, and the Union Mill and Mining Company. "You might say," reported his brother, "that he was the center figure and the one to whom they all came with propositions for the promotion of enterprises . . . and that he promoted them to an extent that no other individual did or could do." Ralston represented, in essence, the quintessential spirit of local entrepreneurship. He, typical of city boosters elsewhere, envisioned for San Francisco not only a healthy local economy based on manufacturing, but theatres, libraries, and grand hotels which would ensure San Francisco's future as the leading industrial and cultural center in the nation. Unfortunately for the city, the Bank of California failed in 1875, dragging down with it a number of smaller establishments. A few hours after Ralston was asked to resign, his drowned body washed ashore on North Beach—an apparent suicide.[34]

The city merchants were, at best, ambivalent to Ralston's enthusiasm for local industry. His "wild speculations" were not models to follow but objects of ridicule; as one of the city's most respected commission merchants said of Ralston: "He had ambition to control not only all banking business, but the politics and other affairs of the country." He spent large sums of money and devoted "much time to effect his ambition.'' In addition his ''character was that of a very ambitious man—desirous of wealth, not so much for its own sake, as for the power its possession gave him.''[35] Yet at a public meeting to pay tribute to Ralston's memory shortly after his death, a spokesman for a new generation eulogized:

He was the life of all enterprise, the vigor of all progress, the epitome and representative of all that is broadening and expansive and uplifting in the life of California . . . Did you wish to forward a public or private charity? Ralston headed the subscription list. Would you develop a new industry to enlarge the resources of the city, start a new manufacture, add wealth to the state, and furnish hundreds of husbands and fathers with contented and well-paid toil? You went to Ralston for advice and assistance . . . of all her public possessions the commonwealth of California never owned anything more valuable than this man's life; of all her public disasters she has had none greater than his death.[36]

In contrast to Ralston's enthusiastic encouragement of the city's industrialization, the merchants were slow to respond either to the investment opportunities in manufacturing or to transforming their own businesses from exclusive mercantile establishments to enterprises which combined trade with manufacturing. For example, of the San Francisco manufactures listing assets over $50,000, approximately 35 percent of the listed owners or company managers had at one time in their occupational careers in San Francisco worked in a blue-collar trade. Former merchants accounted for 20 percent of the 1880 manufacturers, former clerks for 17 percent, and those who had combined manufacturing with either a retail or wholesale function accounted for an additional 11 percent. The remainder, for the most part, had worked in or were associated with manufacturing establishments throughout their occupational careers in the city. Considering that at least 60 percent of the manufacturing firms performed, in addition to their industrial production, either a retail or wholesale function, former merchants and merchant-manufacturers were underrepresented in the ranks of the city's manufacturers.[37]

Merchandizing and Manufacturing

Because over half of the city's manufacturers combined a retail or wholesale function with industrial production, it was surprising that so few former merchants opened quasi-industrial operations to strengthen their relative competitive position in the local marketplace. San Francisco's industrial production, like that of New York, Boston, and Baltimore, was connected to a former mercantile economy and specialized in producing the very goods which the merchants traded and with which they were most familiar.[38]

When merchants did transfer into manufacturing, they inevitably produced the consumer goods they had traded as full-time merchants. Those, for example, who dealt in iron stoves and doors, opened foundries, while bookstore owners and printers, like the Bancroft brothers, went into paper manufacturing, publishing, and large-order printing. Domingo Ghirardelli, an Italian by birth who came to California in 1849 after residing in Lima and Montevideo, commenced his career as a general merchant in Stockton. After moving to San Francisco in the late 1850s he specialized in wines, chocolate, coffee, and spices; after 1870 he confined himself entirely to the manufacturing of chocolate. The brothers Hiram and Alfred Tubbs, both importers and dealers in ship chandlery, found it cheaper and more profitable in the 1850s to manufacture their own rope. By the late 1870s, Tubbs and Co. was exclusively a cordage manufacturer. Wholesale and retail furniture merchants, who in the 1850s and early 1860s imported furniture from the East in "knocked-down" form and assembled it locally, began in the late 1860s to manufacture certain items in San Francisco. Levi Strauss' canvas pants became so popular that he no longer had them produced in New York by his brother but manufactured them himself in San Francisco. By combining the production and sales departments under one roof, Strauss, like others, profited from the savings in labor and transportation costs.[39]

When a merchant lacked the technical competence to transfer into manufacturing, he hired or took into partnership someone who could direct that portion of the business. The hardware house of Merrill, Holbrook and Co., one of the largest wholesale distributors in the city, accepted a new partner, J. W. Brittan, who combined his manufacturing skills with the already developed hardware business.[40]

To counter the loss of their traditional trade network to the growing sales departments of local and national manufacturers, merchants increasingly acted as manufacturers' agents. G. M. Josselyn and Co., importers and wholesale dealers in ship chandlery were, by 1880, agents for the Taunton (Massachusetts) Sheathing Metal Manufacturing Company. William T. Coleman's commission house, which grew from a staff of two in 1851 to thirty-five employees by 1883, in addition to its normal wholesale mercantile trade, acted as commission agents for numerous manufacturers.[41]

Coleman's business was illustrative of the merchant diversification made necessary by the rise of industry and the modern corporation. The company was organized into departments, each responsible for a certain line of products or commercial function. The canned goods department served as agents for numerous fruit and salmon canneries in and around San Francisco. The shipping department acted as agents for clippers arriving from Australia, China, and South America, and for chartered ships bearing English and Australian coal. The insurance department handled the San Francisco business of the Globe Marine Insurance Company of London and the Chinese Insurance Company of Hong Kong. The commission department was the agent for Royal and Standard baking powder, Walter Baker and Co. chocolate, Kingsford Oswego starch, Armor lard and canned meats, Emery and Sons candles and oriental teas. The coal, iron, metals, and borax department acted as the headquarters for all the borax deposits on the West Coast. Coleman also exported wheat to Europe and England, imported foreign liquors, exported barley to eastern brewers, besides handling local cooperage stocks, Japanese sulphur, China oil, canned fruits, and barreled salmon.[42]

Coleman illustrated the successful adjustment of a merchant to the city's industrial transformation, but he was an atypical case among his class in 1880. A native-born pioneer who arrived in the early 1850s, he survived and progressed in San Francisco from a general merchant of modest means to become one of the wealthiest men in the city. When not in residence on Nob Hill, he lived at his spacious country home in San Mateo County or visited his branch offices in New York, Chicago, or London. He had persisted in the city for three decades, unlike the vast majority of his merchant generation who had either died or, more likely, had long departed San Francisco in search of other opportunities. Coleman had reached the pinnacle of San Francisco society when as a prestigious and wealthy commission merchant he led the Vigilance Committee of 1856, and continued to maintain his status in the community by constantly adapting to the ever-shifting structure of the city.

Occupational Mobility

The vast majority of Coleman's merchant colleagues in 1880—well over three-quarters of whom were of the second generation—failed to match the occupational gains of the first merchant generation. When intragenerational mobility is viewed from the perspective of occupational destinations, the experience of the second generation differed considerably from that of the first.

The petty shopkeepers' first generation could boast in 1860 that seven of every ten within their ranks had progressed up the occupational ladder. By 1890 three-quarters of the second generation had failed to move up the occupational scale or, worse, had dropped in occupational status. After 1870 the small grocery stores and the one-man shops were having to compete with the larger and more efficient retail stores and also faced intense competition within their own ranks. There were, reported the San Francisco *Commercial Herald and Market Review,* "too many traders and too few producers" in the city. One grocer complained that competition was "so strong in our line that none of the retail grocers can make anything of their retail trade." "We sell our goods," he said, "down to cost price to draw customers, and depend on the back bar for the profits."[43]

The general merchants of the second generation fared even worse

Table 7.4. Comparison of occupational mobility (destinations) for first and second generation merchants (in percent).

Merchant category	First Generation (1852-1860)				Second Generation (1880-1890)			
	Upward	Same	Down-ward	(N)	Upward	Same	Down-ward	(N)
Petty shopkeepers	72	24	4	(47)	26	64	10	(113)
General merchants	21	67	12	(178)	19	52	29	(183)
Importer-wholesaler	1	49	50	(82)	9	61	30	(23)
All merchants	26	53	21	(307)	21	56	23	(319)

SOURCE: California State Census, 1852; Federal Census, 1880.

than the petty shopkeepers. Three out of ten experienced occupational slippage in the 1880s, a rate twice that of the first generation of merchants.

The second generation importer-wholesalers also experienced a similar rate of occupational slippage, though they were far less downwardly mobile in comparison with the first generation. With their capital assets, the small group that persisted in the city in the 1880 decade managed either to maintain their occupational status by connecting with a manufacturing firm as agent, opening a small manufacturing plant to operate in conjunction with their traditional wholesale function, transferring into a nonmerchant managerial position, or moving up into one of the professions. But in spite of these maneuvers and substantial financial assets, almost a third of them had slipped in occupational status in ten years or less.

Of the second generation merchants who persisted in San Francisco through the 1880 decade, three-quarters remained in a merchant occupation. But compared with the occupational destinations of the 1850 merchant generation (where 84 percent of the persisters maintained their merchant affiliation for at least ten years), the second generation moved more rapidly away from the merchant occupations and toward other white-collar callings during the 1880s. The petty shopkeepers who had neither the skills nor the capital to move into higher white-collar occupations were the most likely to remain either as shopkeepers or to slip into the blue-collar ranks. Approximately three-quarters of the general merchants remained merchants ten years later, though 30 percent had lost occupational status in the decade. The importer-wholesalers were considerably more successful than their first-generation counterparts. Over 20 percent, three times the rate of the first generation importers, transferred into equally high status jobs as managers, manufacturers, bankers, brokers, or government officials. In fact, the higher the occupational status of the second generation merchant, the more likely it was that he had moved away from a merchant occupation by the end of the 1880 decade.

It is understandable that, at a time when the merchant class was having to meet intense competition in an expanding industrial city, and when manufacturing firms were preempting the traditional functions of the importer-wholesalers, these high-status merchants were not only the most downwardly mobile of all city merchants but also

Table 7.5. Occupational destinations of first (1852-1860) and second (1880-1890) generation merchants (in percent).

Generation sample	Blue-collar	Petty proprietors nonmerchant	Petty proprietors merchant	Clerical-sales	General merchants	Importer-wholesalers	Managers, manufacturers, brokers, capitalists	Professionals	(N)
1852									
Petty shopkeepers	4	0	23	6	54	6	6	0	(47)
General merchants	2	0	4	5	67	13	7	2	(178)
Importer-wholesalers	2	0	4	4	40	42	7	1	(82)
Sample mean[a]	3	0	7	5	58	19	7	1	(307)
1880									
Petty shopkeepers	10	3	61	5	14	3	4	0	(113)
General merchants	6	2	15	6	52	8	9	2	(183)
Importer-wholesalers	4	0	0	4	22	39	22	9	(23)
Sample mean[b]	8	2	30	6	36	8	8	2	(319)

SOURCE: California State Census, 1852; Federal Census, 1880.
a. 1850 merchants in merchant occupation in 1860: 84 percent.
b. 1880 merchants in merchant occupation in 1890: 74 percent.

the most likely, with their considerable capital and skills, to transfer to a nonmerchant white-collar occupation. With the possible exception of the relatively small group of importers who as a group maintained or improved their occupational status in the 1880s at a somewhat higher rate than the first generation, it could not be said that San Francisco in the 1870s and 1880s offered better opportunities than those which existed in the 1850s. A young Harvard graduate best summed up the occupational opportunities in San Francisco when he complained in a letter to his mother in Boston, "influence and favoritism (not to mention nepotism) are just as rife here as in the East, and without them a young fellow stands no show."[44]

The decline in occupational opportunities within the San Francisco merchant class over time was also confirmed by an intergenerational investigation—the degree to which merchant fathers transferred their occupational status to their sons. Sons of the second merchant generation, for example, not only discovered that it was more difficult for them to follow their fathers' occupations than it had been for sons of the first generation, but a far higher percentage of them were forced to enter a blue-collar trade. For both generations, however, the higher the merchant occupational status of the father, the more likely was the son to enter a white-collar position as his first job.[45]

The sons of wealthy importers frequently moved into their fathers' businesses or, with the assistance of a family inheritance, quickly positioned themselves within the managerial class. Albert Kelly handed over to Albert, Jr., his oil and paint importing house. Claus Spreckels, who progressed from a farm laborer in Hanover, Germany to retail grocer in Charleston, S. C., to sugar magnate in San Francisco, gave half a million dollars to each of his three sons to expand the family shipping business. William T. Coleman's son, Carleton, became a partner in his father's wholesale business, which no doubt helped finance his "fondness for race horses." Webster Jones and William Kruge both gave their sons partnerships in their wholesale grocery firms. The three sons of Alfred Tubbs, the cordage manufacturer and merchant, when not hunting, held managerial positions in their father's company. The eldest son of an exporter took charge of his father's shipping interests in San Francisco while the younger son managed the family's real estate holdings across the bay. All the merchant sons, with their high-status jobs and the financial resources of

their family securely behind them, were active members of San Francisco high society, and if not married, were considered the most eligible bachelors in the city.[46]

The sons of the petty shopkeepers were less fortunate. The experience of one grocer, and the fate of his son, was typical of a number of
shopkeepers. Robert Croskey, Irish-born, came to San Francisco in
the mid-1850s and found employment as a pattern maker at the Vul-
can Iron Works. With his savings he opened a grocery store, and operated it with his son assisting as bookkeeper and clerk until 1876, when
he was forced by his partner to sell out. The next year he bought another store for $1,500, added $500 of liquors and purchased an additional $500 of stock on credit. But even after selling off a small parcel
of real estate for $2,200, Croskey could not turn a profit. Five months
after he opened his second grocery business, he filed for bankruptcy
listing assets of $1,445 and liabilities of $1,900. Robert, Jr. went to
work in a factory.[47]

Out-Migration in the 1880s

The high rate of out-migration from San Francisco of the second
merchant generation additionally confirmed the bleak occupational
opportunities. From tracings in the city directory, two-thirds of the
1880 merchant generation could not be located in 1890. The second
generation apparently fled San Francisco at a far higher rate than had
the disillusioned first generation. Though some nine years older on the
average than the 1850 generation (thirty-seven years compared to
twenty-eight years), the second generation departure rates, even after
controlling for age, remained far higher than those of the first.[48]

Studies of other communities suggest that persistence increased with
occupational status and success; the merchant exodus from San Francisco in the 1880s must thus be explained in large measure by occupational failure. Neither occupational status, property, nor ethnicity
could explain, as they had for the 1850 generation, persistence in or
departure from the city. Even compared to the general population of
the city (the majority of whom were blue-collar workers), of which
only one-third of all employed males remained in San Francisco at least
through 1890, the merchant departure rate must be viewed as particularly high. And compared with rates for white-collar occupations in

other cities, the departure rates among the San Francisco merchants were extraordinarily high.[49]

Compared with other cities, San Francisco apparently offered fewer opportunities than eastern cities in the 1870s and 1880s, and fewer than it had offered in the 1850s. In the 1870s, for example, the rate of slippage from white-collar to blue-collar jobs in San Francisco was somewhat lower than the experience of white-collar workers in Poughkeepsie, and Altanta, Georgia. But the rate of blue-collar workers climbing to white-collar positions was no higher in San Francisco than Poughkeepsie and considerably lower than Atlanta. In the 1880s, the white-collar slippage rate of the San Francisco merchants into the blue-collar ranks was somewhat less than that of all white-collar workers in Boston, though higher than the white-collar slippage rate in Atlanta and Omaha.

The fate of the merchants in San Francisco, as in other urban centers, was directly related to the rise of industry. Manufacturing establishments had usurped, in large part, the trade of the merchants. New technology demanded new skills which a largely foreign-born second influx was either incapable of performing or had not had the opportunity to learn. Further, San Francisco's rate of growth, relative to California as a whole and to other western cities, showed a marked decline. The city could no longer sustain the overcrowded merchant sector.[50]

Table 7.6. Career mobility rates in selected urban communities, 1870-1890 (in percent).

Community	Decade	Blue-collar workers climbing to white-collar	(N)	White-collar workers skidding to blue-collar	(N)
San Francisco	(1870-80)	13	(127)	6	(370)
Poughkeepsie	(1870-80)	13	(1661)	9	(866)
Atlanta	(1870-80)	19	(188)	12	(250)
San Francisco	(1880-90)	15	(150)	8	(319)
Boston	(1880-90)	12	(334)	12	(309)
Omaha	(1880-90)	21	(n.a.)	2	(n.a.)
Atlanta	(1880-90)	22	(299)	7	(435)

SOURCE: Poughkeepsie, Atlanta, Boston and Omaha data from Stephan Thernstrom, *The Other Bostonians* (Cambridge, Mass., 1973).

The once prestigious merchant class was being eroded by a new industrial order. Manufacturers could profitably market their own goods without the assistance of the merchant middlemen. Industrial sales departments slowly emerged to replace wholesale distributors, large department stores came to replace the one-man shops, and a decline in the city's growth rate placed further competitive pressures on an already crowded occupation. Those who had the capital to invest in the new industrial order and thus preserve their competitive position in the market place, preferred instead the habit of gambling in real estate or mining stocks. Some importer-wholesalers maintained, and even a few less affluent merchants attained, elite status. But the merchant ranks were no longer the primary recruiting ground for the city's elite.

8

A SOCIAL GEOGRAPHY OF THE URBAN LANDSCAPE

The manner in which populations distribute themselves in space, as Robert Park, the urban sociologist, observed, "tends to assume definite and typical patterns." Historians, sociologists, and geographers have attempted over the years to bring some explicable order to these patterns, but scholars have by no means agreed among themselves how to describe, much less interpret, their investigations of urban social space. There is a general consensus, however, that a rational spatial ordering of residences and business establishments exists within a city. The location of person's residence is believed to be generally an accurate reflection of his social status in the community.[1]
The contemporary San Francisco banker, for example, does not reside in the Hunter Point working-class district but in a spacious, well-appointed residence in one of the intracity or suburban upper-middle class neighborhoods. On the other hand, today's businessmen seek economical locations for their offices, stores, plants, and warehouses to effect maximum savings and profits. Assuming that there is a geographical social order in the city today, did there also exist in the nineteenth century discernible spatial patterns? How was social status transplanted onto the urban landscape? Did any significant spatial reordering of the city's social space occur over the time, and what were the characteristics and the dynamics of change? To answer these questions, the discussion of San Francisco's social geography will focus primarily upon class residential patterns (and their symbiotic relationship to the central business district) as measured by the variables of occupation, property, nativity, and family status.

Instant Spatial Ordering

Certainly one important, perhaps unique, feature of San Francisco's urban space at midcentury was the *speed* with which this West Coast city sorted itself out on the ground. While Boston and New

York had taken over half a century to develop a spatial ordering of their central business districts by economic functions, San Francisco, by comparison, accomplished this complicated task almost instantaneously.[2] The basic patterns of San Francisco's social geography, patterns that would continue for at least the next thirty years, were present in the city three years after the first flood of migrants began. As early as 1852 there emerged in San Francisco a few distinct residential neighborhoods and a clearly defined central business district.[3]

The city's business center was bounded by water on the east, Market Street on the south, and extended to the Pacific Street wharf on the north and to Montgomery Street on the west. The district included within its thirteen blocks almost all large business establishments of the city, including 70 percent of all merchant shops, offices, and warehouses.

The commission merchants arranged themselves geographically according to their own specialization. A recent study by an urban geographer located shipping and commission merchants primarily on the Jackson and Clay Street wharfs. Wholesale grocers and merchants dealing in produce, wine, and liquor were found mainly at the foot of Washington Street near the bay. The importer and commission merchants who specialized in dry and fancy goods were situated on or adjacent to Montgomery near the intersection of Sacramento, and those who dealt in lumber and building materials clustered outside the business district south of Market Street. As a general rule, the commission merchants and wholesaler-importers occupied the more expensive space closest to the city's wharfs within the business district.[4]

Between the wholesalers and the surrounding middle class residential area, the retailers occupied the space adjacent to the business district north toward the base of Telegraph Hill, west to Dupont and Stockton Street, and south below Market Street. The clothing, dry goods, fancy goods, and millinery stores clustered in specific areas within the business district but they were not as concentrated as the importers, jobbers, and wholesalers. And unlike the wholesaler arrangement, there was not always a spatial relationship between retail stores trading in related items. Clothing, dry and fancy goods, and millinery stores were generally not located in the same section of the business district, while the "ladies' ware shops were located farthest from the business center and the men's clothing closer to the center."[5]

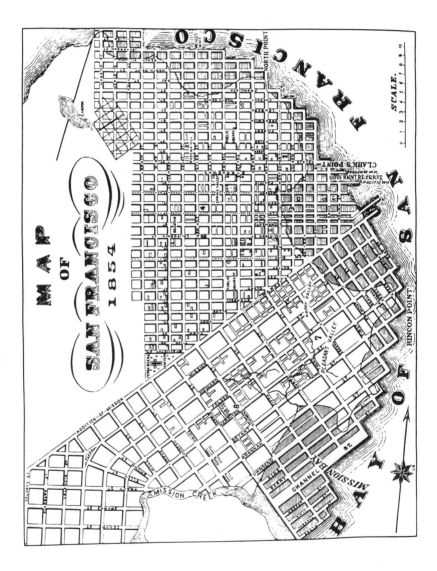

Map 3: Density of San Francisco Merchant Business Establishments, 1852.

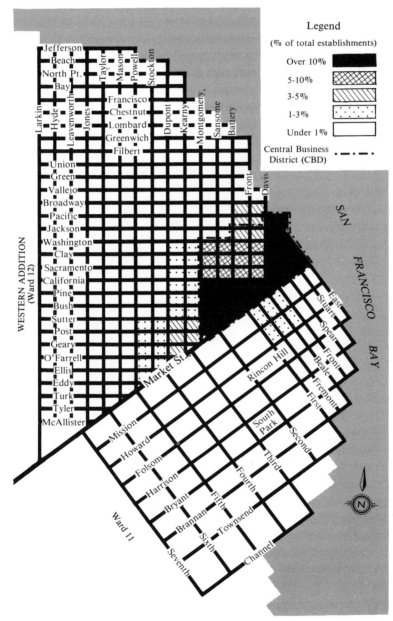

Legend
(% of total establishments)

Over 10%
5-10%
3-5%
1-3%
Under 1%

Central Business
District (CBD)

Retail grocers were dispersed throughout the limited geographical area of the city, usually on street corners within the residential districts or in the less accessible, and therefore less expensive locations within the business district. Real estate, stock, merchandise, and money brokers, bankers, and lawyers shared the central space of the business district with the commission and import merchants. The few manufacturing establishments shared space within a working-class district south of Market Street with the ship builders, saw mills, flour mills, foundries, and breweries.[6]

There were also some discernible residential patterns in San Francisco by 1852.

Approximately half of all blue-collar workers resided north of Market Street and east of Dupont Street, the boundary between the working-class and middle-class neighborhoods. Here the working class huddled in inaccessible and congested pockets around the outside perimeter of the high-rent business district. At first (1849-1851) district ethnic enclaves existed within the blue-collar district. The Australians and Latin Americans resided north of the business center's Jackson Street boundary toward the base of Telegraph Hill. The French quarter (later the heart of Chinatown) lay along the western edge of the business district but still east of the Dupont Street boundary. And along the southern fringe of the business district was German Town. These ethnic spatial arrangements of the working class were only temporary, however, as fires constantly ravaged the area north of Market Street. After the fires, the working class either resettled in the same general areas (but not in noticeably ethnic neighborhoods) or migrated to the districts south of Market Street.

The merchants were only somewhat less likely to live east of Dupont Street, in or near the central business district, than either the blue-collar workers or the general working population of the city. The relatively high concentration of merchant residences in 1852 in close proximity to both the business district and the working-class neighborhoods can be explained by a number of factors. First, most of the pioneer merchants initially had not planned to reside permanently in San Francisco. They wanted only to make substantial profits and return home. Consequently they sought only a temporary room in one of the numerous hotels and boarding houses which immediately surrounded the business district. The fashionable hotels, spread along the

Table 8.1. Residential distribution by occupation, 1852-1860 (in percent).

| Location | General Population | | | | | | Merchants | | Monied men |
| | Blue-collar | | White-collar | | Sample mean | | All occupations | | All occupations |
	1852 (N=55)	1860 (N=61)	1852 (N=48)	1860 (N=46)	1852 (N=107)	1860 (N=110)	1852 (N=164)	1860 (N=190)	1852 (N=90)
East of Dupont	49	39	46	28	47	37	44	25	46
West of Dupont	22	25	35	50	29	36	41	49	42
South of Market	29	36	19	22	24	27	15	26	12

SOURCE: San Francisco *City Directories*, 1852-53, 1860-61.

western fringe of the business district, provided adequate meals, comfortable rooms, and congenial surroundings, usually at high cost to the resident. The less expensive boarding houses, somewhat farther from the heart of the business district, similarly attracted a large number of merchants seeking a temporary home away from home.[7]

Even if they had initially decided to make San Francisco their home, the less affluent merchants did not possess the financial resources to build, purchase, or even rent a family home in the residential areas outside the business district. The shortage of lumber, the high cost of labor, and the exorbitant price of real estate confined the petty shopkeepers to the working-class districts adjacent to the city's business center. They frequently shared a room over their shop with a clerk or lived in a boarding house. One shopkeeper's wife complained of this boarding-house life. "I'm tired of having nothing to do and threatened Edwin I will go home unless we commence housekeeping. He says I may go [back to Dover, Mass.] if I'll go without him, and remain there six months or a year. I can't make up my mind to do so, but perhaps I shall. Don't report such a story for I may not start [back]. If we commence housekeeping, I shall not."[8]

But even the more affluent merchants desired, at least initially, to be as close to the business center of the city as possible. By temporarily foregoing the luxury of a more spacious and expensive residence, the accrued savings allowed excess capital to be reinvested in their merchant businesses rather than tied up in a nonliquid and more speculative investment. Also the downtown area was not yet so congested as to encourage residential migration to outlying areas. Thus half of those owning assets in excess of $25,000 lived adjacent to or within the central business district. And among the monied elite over half the bankers, capitalists, and professionals lived within or close to the business center (and the working class), usually in the Tehama House or Oriental Hotel, the gathering place for "gay [high] society." A majority of the affluent class, it appeared, preferred the convenience of a nearby hotel to the outlying residential spaces which, if they desired, they certainly could afford.[9]

Finally, the high concentration of merchants in or near the business district may be further explained by the fact that 85 percent of the city merchants were either single or their wives had not accompanied them to the West Coast. In 1852 San Francisco was not a community of nuclear families but a collection of young single men. Rather than owning private residences in the more sedate residential districts, they preferred makeshift quarters over their shops or in hotels or they lived in boarding houses close to the gambling and prostitution houses along the northern and western edges of the city's business district.

If a merchant lived with his family in the city and could afford a single-family dwelling in the early 1850s, he more often than not resided in one of the middle-class neighborhoods west of the business district and the working-class residential belt, in the area out beyond Dupont Street. One such fashionable residential area in the 1850s was Stockton Street. Along this north-south axis lived approximately one-quarter of the city merchants, most of them wholesaler-importers and general merchants with families. A local newspaper reported that "handsome private residences" lined Stockton Street and persons who sought and could afford "at once a pleasant and fashionable abode, bought building lots in this vicinity."[10]

Rincon Hill, once covered with small oaks, heavy brush, and a plentiful growth of poison oak, also attracted the merchant and professional classes. This area, which extended from Folsom Street to Bryant and from Spear to Third, was considered the Nob Hill of the Fifties and Sixties and was the first residential experiment which successfully conquered the steep hills of San Francisco.[11] Below Rincon Hill to the north was Pleasant Valley and nearer to Market Street, Happy Valley, both upper-class residential neighborhoods.

For men who had used eastern models for their business establishments, it was natural to look to the East and Europe for guidance in laying out their living space. In 1856 Rincon Hill was enhanced by the construction of South Park, a twelve-acre residential area designed by an Englishman, George Gordon, after Berkeley Square in London. Promoted as "the only level spot of land free from sand in the city limits," the park itself was enclosed by gates to which only residents owned keys. The houses in and around the park were large, usually ten to twelve rooms (dining room, kitchen, servants' rooms, two basement pantries, two parlors and another small room on the first floor, and five bedrooms on the second floor) and were all of similar design. The trust deed of the property, framed after that of Gramercy Park in New York, prohibited the erection of buildings other than brick or stone. "For quiet, economical family residences, free from risks or annoyances of contiguous shops or stores," South Park furnished, said an advertisement, "the most elegant sites in the city." Here, in the security and attractive setting of a planned community, resided many of the city's upper-class citizens. And with the planking of Third Street in 1854 and the opening of an omnibus line between South Park and the business district, merchants, capitalists, and professionals were within comfortable commuting distance to their offices.[12]

Within the Rincon Hill-South Park complex, considered an "island of Victorian respectability," lived some of the city's most prominent businessmen. Peter Donahue, president of the Union Iron Works, built a forty-room mansion at the corner of Bryant and Second Streets. Isaac Friedlander, the grain merchant, lived nearby, as did shipping and lumber merchant, John A. Hooper, bankers Pedar Sather, John Parrott, and Joseph Donohoe, General William T. Sherman, and future governor and U. S. Senator Milton Latham.[13]

To serve and service the neighborhood, local residents financed the erection of Union Hall (for social events), the South Park and Rincon Hose Companies (fire stations), a college, two private schools, two hospitals, and three churches. Like the Stockton Street area to the north, the Rincon Hill-South Park community attracted the affluent middle class and their voluntary associations in the 1850s.

One measure that provides a further description of middle-class social space in nineteenth-century San Francisco is the commuting distance between place of residence and business. Up to a certain point distance correlated with occupation. The importer-wholesalers commuted the longest distance (an average of approximately 1100 yards) while the shopkeepers, many of whom lived over their shops, traveled the shortest distance (800 yards). The bankers, brokers, capitalists, and professionals—the wealthiest monied men at the apex of the occupational structure—clustered closer (a commuting distance of 750 yards) to the central business district and the working-class residential areas. The middle class, defined both in terms of occupation and wealth, tended to reside away from the downtown business center. (See table 8.4.)

Finally, the location of one's residence appeared to be a fairly accurate prediction of whether or not an individual would remain in the city throughout the 1850 decade. For example, the importer-wholesalers who resided and owned homes in the South Park-Rincon Hill complex or along the Stockton Street axis, were twice as likely to remain in the city throughout the decade as were those importer-wholesalers, bankers, capitalists and other rich men who rented rooms in hotels or boarding houses in or near the central business district. The residential neighborhoods, where most merchants owned their own homes, attracted those who for one reason or other had decided to remain in San Francisco. Also the financial commitment to invest in a private home in a residential, family neighborhood served as a further inducement to remain in this transient city. The higher rate of persistence among the residential property owners, however, may very well have been related less to their status as home owners than to the probable higher marriage rates among those who chose in the first place to reside in the city's residential neighborhood. Incomplete marriage data in 1852, however, makes it impossible to weigh this factor.

In addition to the factors of occupation and property ownership, nativity influenced San Francisco's spatial arrangements in the early 1850s. Although the foreign-born among the general population did not segregate themselves significantly in any one of the three city districts out of proportion to the native-born general population, there were some differences within the merchant population.

The foreign-born merchants clustered more heavily in the area west of Dupont Street. Here a majority of the German merchants, including most of the affluent German Jews, resided close to their voluntary associations—the German Turn Verein Hall, the Hebrew and Eureka Benevolent Societies, and the city's two synagogues. The foreign-born merchants were less likely to live in or near the central business district than the native-born merchants, and if they chose to live south of Market Street, it was outside the confines of the Rincon Hill-South Park community. (See table 8.2.)

To what degree did the merchants segregate in the 1850s and what were the factors, if any, which influenced residential segregation among the merchant class? To measure the difference between the spatial distribution of merchant residences and those of the city's employed male population at a given time, a segregation (or dissimilarity) index was utilized. The underlying rationale of the index is: assuming that a person's occupation or any other factors affecting residential location (place of birth, wealth, family size) did not influence his choice of residence, then no neighborhood (however defined) would be all merchants or all blue-collar workers but each class would be represented in each neighborhood in approximately the same proportion as represented in the entire city. Thus, in a city where merchants represented 10 percent of the total male employed population, one of every ten residences in a particular neighborhood might be expected to be a merchant. This would represent a completely even distribution of merchants within each city neighborhood. In this case the segregation index assumes a value of zero, indicating no occupational residential segregation whatsoever. The opposite situation, that of a completely uneven or segregated distribution, occurs when there is no residential integration of merchants within the neighborhoods of the city. Operationally, this description holds if a section of the city contains only merchants but no representatives from the city's general employed male population. For this situation, the segregation index assumes a value of 100, indicating a maximum degree of residential segregation.[14]

When the city was divided into 87 districts of approximately equal size, the segregation indexes for the merchants, compared with the general population, were: all merchants, 42; native-born merchants, 37; foreign-born merchants, 62. Even though it might be expected that the native-born merchants would be more residentially segregated in a city where the foreign-born outnumbered the native-born (53 percent to 47 percent), the reverse situation occurred. Nativity considerations in the early 1850s, however, appeared to have exerted less influence upon the location of one's residence than did one's occupational affiliation.[15]

In sum, the most important observation about San Francisco's social geography was that as early as the 1850s social divisions within the city had been clearly transplanted upon the landscape. The earliest pattern of spatial separation was by occupation, wealth, and nativity, and surprisingly, it was a pattern traditionally associated with the modern industrial city.

Development upon a Basic Pattern

Between 1852 and 1860, with the addition of some 20,000 residents to the city, the central business district increased in density and size by about a third. Our result was that by 1860 much of the residential housing in or adjacent to the business district was replaced by offices, warehouses, and new industries. Whereas almost half of the city's population lived east of Dupont Street in 1852, less than a third resided there in 1860. And of the first generation of merchants who remained in the city throughout the 1850s, only a quarter resided in the vicinity of the city's business district. Almost half of these merchants by 1860 inhabited the residential area west of Dupont Street.

The working class, the least geographically mobile during the 1850s, moved to the district south of Market Street which was slowly emerging as the city's manufacturing area. The merchants, the most mobile in terms of in-city migration, also demonstrated a slight preference for the area south of Market. However, although the merchants and blue-collar workers migrated into the same general space, the merchants moved toward the Rincon Hill-South Park community while the workers clustered in the lowland blue-collar district close to Market Street and near the wharves. (For 1860 spatial distributions by occupation see table 8.1.)

The intracity mobility patterns of the native-born and foreign-born followed the general occupational trend, though with some noticeable highlights. For example, well over two-thirds of the native-born merchants moved to the southern section of town while three-quarters of the foreign-born merchants migrated to the western residential districts. Of the general foreign-born population who moved out of the business district, most migrated south of Market into the working-class neighborhoods. Throughout the city in the 1850 decade the native-born in both the blue- and white-collar ranks shifted around at twice the rate of the foreign-born. Yet after all this in-city movement during the 1850 decade, the merchants remained segregated from the general population to about the same degree in 1860 as they had been in 1852 though they became somewhat more segregated from the blue-collar workers. And, compared with the residential distribution of the city's general population, the foreign-born, regardless of occupation or class, remained more segregated than the native-born throughout the decade. Indeed, by 1860 nativity played a more important role than it had in the early 1850s in determining the selection of one's residential location.[16]

The commuting distance from place of residence to place of business for the merchants changed very little between 1852 and 1860. For

Map 4: Density of San Francisco Merchant Business Establishments, 1860.

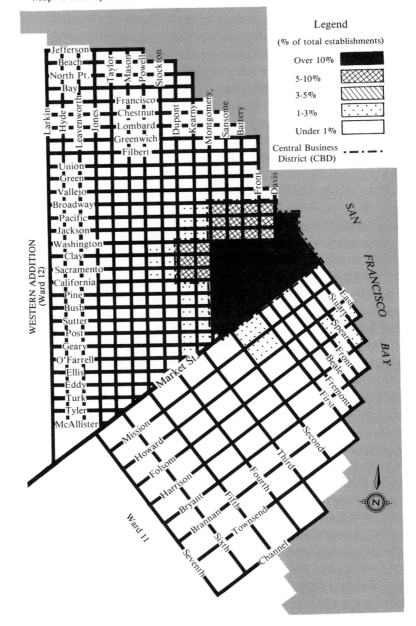

Table 8.2. Residential distribution by nativity, 1852-1860 (in percent).

	General Sample						Merchant sample					
	Native-born		Foreign-born		Sample mean		Native-born		Foreign-born		Sample mean	
Location	1852 (N=56)	1860 (N=69)	1852 (N=50)	1860 (N=52)	1852 (N=106)	1860 (N=121)	1852 (N=126)	1860 (N=119)	1852 (N=38)	1860 (N=71)	1852 (N=164)	1860 (N=190)
East of Dupont	47	30	48	40	47	37	45	24	37	28	44	25
West of Dupont	30	42	28	27	29	36	40	46	45	52	41	49
South of Market	23	28	24	33	24	27	15	30	18	20	15	26

SOURCE: San Francisco *City Directories*, 1852-53, 1860-61.

despite considerable in-city migration, the movement occurred within the same general perimeter which had defined the outer limits of the city's space in 1852. Also, the amount of one's wealth no more influenced commuting distance in 1860 than it had in 1852. But compared with the blue-collar workers whose residences were located in close proximity to their respective work place, the merchant's commuting distance was almost two times greater than that of the workingmen.[17]

The merchants could afford the expense of commuting from the city's "middle landscape" to the business district. If they did not own a horse and carriage (a distinct luxury), they traveled downtown on one of the six omnibus lines. Most merchants could leave to their assistants (clerks, salesmen, and bookkeepers) the time-consuming chores associated with their businesses, a luxury which allowed them more time to commute from their private residences.

When a merchant selected a residence in a pleasant neighborhood, he demonstrated to the public (and confirmed to himself) his membership in the middle class. To reside along the Stockton Street axis or in the Rincon Hill-South Park community was for a merchant, banker, broker, or professional to be among "your own." These two areas attracted an increasing number of middle-class families between 1852 and 1860 and constituted the apex of elegance and comfort as "the only places in those days where one could be born respectably."[18]

The Immigration of Women

The number of families residing in San Francisco in the 1850s was small, however, compared to the number of young single males. But the arrival of more women and children, and simultaneously, the introduction of an intracity transportation system after the Civil War, radically altered the city's boundaries and hence its social geography.

Although the *Alta California* reported in 1851 that "each succeeding steamer is bringing to California the wives and families of our merchants and mechanics who have preceeded them and built for them a home amongst us," only about 15 percent of the adult male population had wives living with them in San Francisco in 1852.[19] An equal number no doubt had left their families on the East Coast with the intention of either returning home within a year or two or sending for their families after they established themselves in San Francisco.

The foreign-born, however, were twice as likely to bring their wives to San Francisco, at least in the early 1850s, as the native-born. In fact, among the foreign-born, the lower the occupational status the more likely the chances that a man's wife accompanied him to the West Coast. Thus over 30 percent of the foreign-born nonskilled workers of the city had wives with them in San Francisco, but only 15 percent of the foreign-born import merchants were listed in the census as living with their wives. For the native-born, the trend was reversed. Less than 5 percent of the nonskilled workers and 15 percent of the import merchants were married. A possible explanation for the nativity differences may be that the native-born intended to remain in San Francisco but a brief time in search of fortune, and were therefore less likely to move their families across the continent. Also, more affluent than the foreign-born, the native Americans possessed the financial resources to maintain a second household. The foreign-born, and particularly the blue-collar workers (those geographically most mobile in nineteenth-century America in search of employment) could ill afford the luxury of two separate households. Nor did they possess an extensive family to look after their spouses while they awaited passage money to San Francisco.[20]

Between 1852 and 1860 the number of women in the city increased significantly, a fact which influenced household structure and hence the city's residential patterns. Whereas the male to female ratio for people over twenty-one years of age was approximately 6.5 males for every female in 1852, by 1860 the ratio stood at 2.5 males for every female, again with native-born females far more numerous than foreign-born females. Finally, by 1880, the male-female ratio of the city had about evened out, though among the older adult population (ages twenty-nine to sixty-five), males still outnumbered females three to two.[21]

As the relative and absolute number of women increased in the city between 1852 and 1880, so too did the number of families. By 1880 two-thirds of all the merchants and over 40 percent of the total male population resided in family households. Unlike the 1850s, marriage rates increased with occupational status within both nativity groups, with the foreign-born more likely to be married than the native-born. Finally, as in previous decades, the higher the occupational status of an individual the less likely it was for a native-born male to marry a foreign-born female—a reflection of the stronger class identity which prevailed in the higher occupational categories.[22]

No longer a town of bachelors, San Francisco by 1880 was a more permanent community of families. The average number of children per couple increased from 2.5 in 1852 to 3.2 in 1880. In the 1870 decade alone the population grew 56 percent (from 149,000 to 233,000), and San Francisco ranked in 1880 as the ninth largest city in the nation.[23] Within the same decade the number of physical dwellings increased 31 percent, well below the 43 percent rise in the absolute number of families. Construction had not kept pace with the demographic pressures so that crowding resulted. In 1880 the average size of the family residential unit, for example, increased to a point where it was one of the highest in the nation.[24]

Urban Transportation and the Expanding City

Partially as a result of the demographic changes in San Francisco, a fully developed intracity transportation system emerged by 1870 to serve new residential areas and alter the scale of the city. The transportation companies spread an interconnecting network of street cars out to the residential neighborhoods so that by 1864-65 the city residents had access to five horse- or steam-powered rail lines in addition to ferry service to Oakland and Marin County. By 1870 eight railroad companies were operating over thirty-five miles of single track. No longer was San Francisco a "walking city." The horse car was among "the most indispensable conditions of modern growth," the *City Directory* observed. "In these modern days of fashionable effeminacy and flabby feebleness," the city population "never walks when it can possibly ride." The horse car "virtually fixed the ultimate limits of suburban growth."[25]

The invention of the cable car in 1873 further increased the area available for residential space. The first cable line, built at a cost of $68,000 per mile of single track, ran up the Clay Street grade from Kearny Street to Leavenworth. Two years later the California Street Cable Railroad extended commuting service from Kearny Street over the imposing California Street slope out to Fillmore Street into the Western Addition—the Pacific Heights area lying within the boundaries of Jackson and Filbert Street, Van Ness Avenue and the Presi-

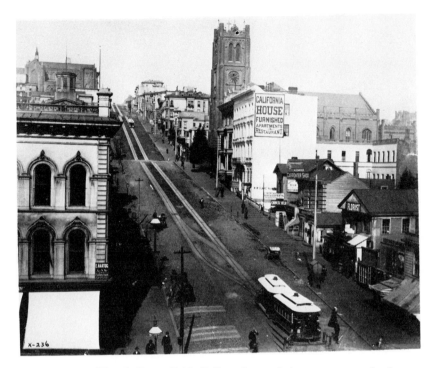

In 1875, the California Street Cable Railroad extended commuter service from Kearny Street out to the western addition.

dio. By 1880 the Western Addition was serviced by another cable line which ran along the Geary Street east-west axis from Kearny out to Presidio Avenue, and at the same time Leland Stanford and his associates took over the Market Street Railroad, modernized the equipment, and extended service well into the southern districts of the city.

The development of an urban transportation system only reflected San Francisco's spectacular industrial growth in the 1870s. For with the arrival of new manufacturing plants, warehouses, and the rail lines which serviced them, San Francisco's landscape was again altered. Industry, which placed a premium on central location for purposes of transportation economics, demanded and received space immediately south of the business district adjacent to the fashionable South Park-Rincon Hill area. As one historical geographer observed: "Industry was able to demand almost any land in the city. Such was its bidding

South Park, modeled after Gramercy Park in New York City, was a fashionable residential district in the 1850s, before manufacturing plants moved into the area in the 1870s.

power, and such was the utility which manufacturing gave to the land.'' But for the middle class that had first settled in this once fashionable section of town, the arrival of industrial plants (and the railroads and steamship wharfs which served them) meant only noise, congestion, and filth. What in the 1850s had been San Francisco's most respectable residential neighborhood, came to be in the late 1870s and early 1880s an industrial complex and one of the largest residential areas for workingmen. When the city leveled Rincon Hill to provide better access from Market Street to the railroad yards, the middle class, with a modern urban transportation system at its disposal, sought suburban alternatives to living within sight or smell of industry's new central location.[26]

Residential neighborhoods soon spread westward beyond Van Ness Avenue, the Gough Street slope, and out to the Western Addition (ward 12). Here, far away from the city's industrial center, and in the districts west of Dupont Street, half of the merchants, including three-quarters of the importer-wholesalers, located new residences. The area east of Dupont—the business district and its immediate vicinity—was being vacated by all classes, particularly the middle class. Whereas in

1852 the downtown area housed almost half the city's population, only 15 percent resided there in 1880.

The working classes, on the other hand, were attracted to the cheaper housing within the industrial section south of Market and its adjacent areas—ward 11 and the southern section of the business district. Here the vast majority of immigrant blue-collar workers lived in close proximity to their work places. The city's industrial sector "offered the largest and most diverse source of unskilled employment opportunities," one urban geographer noted, "and the adjacent districts provided uncomfortable but conveniently located residential quarters which were within the limited financial means of new immigrants."[27]

In blue-collar districts the percent of resident merchants decreased among the more prestigious merchant occupations. Wherever blue-collar workers clustered the elite were less likely to reside, a change from the 1850s when the native-born elite and foreign-born, blue-collar workers lived within close proximity to each other either south of Market Street or in the vicinity of the city's business district. Finally, in the three areas of the city in 1880 (ward 11, east of Dupont and south of Market) where 93 percent of all major manufacturing plants were situated, the higher the merchants' occupational status, the lower the proportion of merchants living in these districts.[28]

Middle-Class Residences

As the original residents deserted South Park in the late 1860s, everything south of Market Street came to be considered "unfashionable." Many of the wealthy residents of South Park moved to the Western Addition or to the southern slopes of Russian and Nob Hills. The Nob, which in the 1870s eclipsed "all other localities in [the] extravagant display of riches," was the site for William T. Coleman's white Roman villa and the ornate mansions of James Flood, Leland Stanford, Mark Hopkins, and Charles Crocker. Along the slopes of Nob Hill the elite, including a number of the city's wealthiest merchants, modeled their "truly palatial" mansions after European castles so as to identify themselves with old world nobility. This neighborhood, with all of its aristocratic pretensions, offered what one resident referred to as "country quiet within city bounds."[29]

Map 5: Density of San Francisco Merchant Business Establishments, 1880.

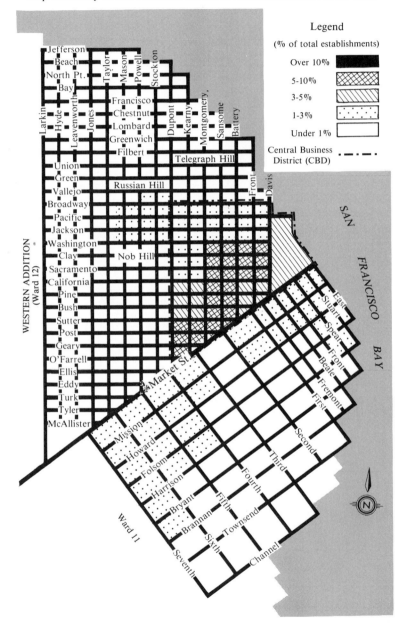

Table 8.3. Residential distribution by occupation, 1880 (in percent).

Location	General sample			Merchant sample				Elite[a]
	Blue-collar (N=392)	White-collar (N=308)	Sample mean (N=700)	Petty shopkeepers (N=398)	General merchants (N=474)	Importer wholesalers (N=76)	Sample mean (N=948)	All occupations (N=288)
Ward 11	21	19	20	22	17	10	18	7
Ward 12	10	19	14	17	24	22	21	28
Outside city	0	1	1	0	1	0	1	5
West of Dupont	17	27	21	26	26	49	28	36
East of Dupont	18	13	16	12	11	4	11	8
South of Market	34	21	28	23	21	15	21	16
Percent of total	56	44	100	42	50	8	100	100

SOURCE: San Francisco *City Directory*, 1880-1881.
a. Sample drawn from the San Francisco *Elite Directory*, 1879.

Home of Claus Spreckels on Van Ness Avenue, mid-1880s. A native of Hanover, Germany, he was a grocer in Charleston, South Carolina, before arriving in San Francisco in 1856. Spreckels later made a fortune in sugar refining.

The physical structures which housed the elite in 1880 were impressive, at least in terms of size. Built of the most expensive materials—granite, brownstone, and sometimes marble—the homes were fit for the aristocracy; "at present," boasted the *Elite Directory* of the city, "the families of our wealthiest citizens are more luxuriously housed than most European princes." The interiors similarly were lavishly decorated to reflect the owners' affluence and "appreciation" of the arts. William T. Coleman bought at Solomon Gump's Emporium wholesale shipments of art work "imported directly from Italy." Hanging beside an Italian master however, would be a mounted deer's head, recently stuffed after a hunting trip in the mountains. A visitor to Leland Stanford's Nob Hill mansion observed that it "looked as if the old palaces of Europe had been ransacked of their art and other treasures to embellish" the interior rooms.[30]

Home of Milton Latham on Rincon Hill, 1870. Latham was a prominent city attorney and later governor of California.

In the 1870s and 1880s a small segment (5 percent) of the elite began to build their spacious homes beyond the city limits in Marin and San Mateo Counties and across the bay in Oakland. The homes at first served as weekend and summer retreats, but as rail and ferry service improved, a number of the wealthy—bankers William Ralston and D. O. Mills, merchants Frederick Macondray and Albert Dibblee, and capitalist James Flood—preferred the luxury of suburban space. Dibblee, for example, built a comfortable, well-furnished mansion in Ross Valley, Marin County. He worked in his orchards and gardens before breakfast, traveled by carriage to the ferry slip in Sausalito, and arrived at his downtown office by nine-thirty. The commuting time for Dibblee was shortened considerably in the mid-1870s when the railroad established a direct line to the ferry through his property. The railroad acquired the right of way, however, only after Dibblee

An interior view (library) of Latham's home.

wisely extracted a promise from the company "to slow any of its trains north on which Mr. Albert Dibblee is a passenger so as to allow him to get off such train in front of his place in Ross Valley."[31]

Dibblee explained in a letter to his brother what it was he sought in a country residence. "I have had a longing for a larger place, say 100 or 200 acres of good soil and a climate like that of Santa Barbara [where Dibblee owned a large cattle and sheep ranch] where I could plant orchards and vineyards and perhaps raise a little fine stock for amusement sake. You know how a city man will long for a country life and a country home, where he can walk over his own broad acres and see around him all that makes up the beauty and the pleasure of life in the country and all of his creating."[32]

The elite homes both in the city and the country also housed a bevy of house servants, cooks, Chinese launderers, coachmen, and footmen. The daughter of a middle-class Jewish shopkeeper described the scene one night outside the elegant residence of John Mackay, the mining magnate: ". . . carriages stood constantly before the door, barouche, coupe and high stanhope, wooden coachman sat in aristocratic nobility, footmen sprang like acrobats from the seats to hand out the ladies of the house . . . On the night of the ball the elite of the city stepped, if they were women, or sprang, if they were men, from the carriages to a crimson velvet carpet, which glowed from the street to the entrance door."[33]

The individual expenses of one import-wholesale merchant may give some idea as to the financing of the internal household and the escalating life style of the city's elite in the 1870s. Albert L. Bancroft, a wealthy book and stationery importer, withdrew $5,300 from his business partnership in 1868 to cover his $400 monthly household and personal expenses which included food, $46; utilities, $20; cook, $30; nurse, $20; horse and buggy, $35; pew rent and charities, $25; and wife's allowance, $25. In addition, Bancroft spent considerable sums on amusements, doctors, travel (to his hunting lodge), life insurance premiums, and new household furniture. By the end of the decade and with his business flourishing, Bancroft vacationed with his family in Europe where his expenses jumped to $650 a month, in part explained by the luxurious purchases of a diamond ring for his wife and a gold watch and diamond studs for himself. Upon his return to San Francisco, his life style became even costlier. In 1872 he withdrew $9,250 from his business partnership. Expenses that year included a $450 piano, a substantial addition to his house, an expanded sidewalk, two house servants, a nurse, a gardener, new furniture, art work, carpets, riding crops, a gold cane, wedding presents, club dues, and an advance of $168 for passage of two Scottish servant girls; for his children he paid for allowances, drawing, elocution, and German lessons. In 1875 Bancroft built a new residence for $10,300, financed by a 6 percent loan of $10,000 which he paid off four years later. Clearly as Bancroft's business prospered, he, no doubt like other merchants of his class, spent increasing sums of money on his household—a reflection of his more elevated life style and perceived status.[34]

Some of the elite in the 1870s, as in the 1850s, preferred the convenience of a downtown hotel. Both the Palace Hotel and Lick House catered to their every need. The Palace apartments consisted of a drawing room, one or two spacious bedrooms, a dressing room, bath, and buzzers to summon servants. If the Irish chambermaid or Chinese

The inner court of the Palace Hotel. Financed by William Ralston's bank, the hotel was home for some of the city's elite in the 1870s and 1880s.

waiter was slow to respond, there were rubber tubes through which to bark orders so as to hasten their arrival. The Lick House dining room was reputed to be "the most elegant in the United States." It was roofed over with "an immense elliptical cupola, and graced with columns and porticos. Its great windows gave the effect of a large crystal ball . . ." A spacious gallery above the dining floor accommodated an orchestra for special occasions.[35]

The middle-class merchants dwelled in more modest and less pretentious structures, though to the extent of their financial resources they aped the style of the Nob Hill moguls. Constructed for the most part of wood, the houses were square, usually two stories high, with the front entrance bisecting two small windows on the ground floor and balconied windows jutting out from the second story. The houses

Middle-class homes along Bush Street (1868) in a residential neighborhood west of the central business district.

were painted in light shades of buff, yellow, or brown, and like most homes in the city, displayed well-tended and colorful flower beds by the entrance.[36]

The interiors of the middle-class homes displayed a well-ordered neatness, meticulously maintained frequently with assistance of children and servants. The parlor took on great symbolic importance since it hosted guests and visitors on special occasions. In the parlor a large mirror, which served as an excuse for an ornate frame, hung over a nonfunctioning fireplace. The wool carpet displayed a flower design and the heavy satin curtains hid the interior shutters. Oil portraits of husband and wife usually glared at each other from opposite walls displaying a symmetry typical of most middle-class homes. "Each piece of furniture lived under the observation of its double. A walnut armchair with seat and back of crimson brocade was here against the eastern wall and there against the western. A cushioned taboret stood on this side of the slender onyx table in the center of the room, and again on that side. Two long high-backed sofas austerely regarded each other from opposite walls; even the bronze chandeliers were twins. Along the same wall, balancing the first mantel, a second mantel owed its reputation to the baby turtles clustered on a mossy green stump under two oval glass globes."[37]

To one side of the parlor was the music room. The ceiling of one such room was described as having "a lattice of bamboo intertwined with garlands of tea roses and autumn leaves, and burnished birds of copper and blue winging their flight across the area of the firmament not occupied by the base of the chandelier." Here, beneath such celestial activity, might be found a handsome mahogany Steinway on which a young daughter performed a Chopin piece after dinner.[38]

The dining room, complete with matching table, chairs, and sideboard, and the kitchen, filled the remainder of the ground floor. The visitors to the kitchen door represented a multi-ethnic composition of the city. To one merchant's back door came "many nations and races to furnish with our supplies. The baker was German; the fish man, Italian; the grocer, a Jew; the butcher, Irish; the steam laundryman, a New Englander. The vegetable vendor and the regular laundryman . . . were Chinese." The live-in servant, a luxury which 18 percent of the merchants could afford, was more likely than not Irish and lived in a back room off the kitchen. Upstairs the master bedroom faced the front of the house while the children shared the back bedrooms. All in all, they were comfortable family homes and the middle class spent a considerable portion of their income to finance and maintain them.[39]

The residential life-style that separated the middle-class merchants from the working classes did not, however, automatically guarantee that the two classes would be totally separated in space. For example, in 1852 and 1860 the merchants resided almost twice as far from their place of work as the working class, but by 1880 the difference in commuting distance between the two classes was relatively insignificant. Between 1860 and 1880 the commuting distance for the blue-collar workers increased by almost a third; between 1852 and 1880 the commuting distance for the petty shopkeepers declined by almost a half. In the same period, the general merchants commuted approximately the same distance; only for the city's elite had the distance between place of work and residence increased significantly.[40]

Despite the increase in commuting distance for blue-collar workers, they continued to live close to the city's manufacturing establishments where residential property values remained low. The relatively short commuting distance of the petty shopkeepers (mostly grocers) can be explained by the fact that they, like their shops, were physically dispersed throughout the city. About half resided over the shop while most of the others lived nearby in order to open their shops early and close late. The importer-wholesalers on the other hand, commuted a distance three times that of the petty shopkeepers.[41]

A minor consideration for the majority of merchants, but a major

Table 8.4. Commuting distance by occupation, 1852-1880 (in yards).

Sample group	1852-60	(N)	1880	(N)
Blue-collar	540	(295)	690	(2214)
Petty shopkeepers	810	(14)	460	(35)
General merchants	960	(90)	920	(119)
Importer-wholesalers	1070	(69)	1470	(73)
Bankers, capitalists brokers and professionals	750	(27)	1290	(97)

SOURCES: San Francisco *City Directories,* 1852-53, 1860-61, 1880-81; blue-collar figures from Elgie, "The Development of San Francisco Manufacturing, 1848-1880: An Analysis of Regional Locational Factors and Urban Spacial Structure," M.A. thesis, Univ. of California, Berkeley, 1966.

Home and shop of a local grocer in the working-class district south of Market Street.

expense for the working class, was the cost of commutation. The state legislature in the mid-1870s had fixed the fare on all San Francisco streetcars at five cents, but even this relatively small expenditure directly influenced the commuting distance of the blue-collar worker. One study discovered that where the cost of a rail commutation absorbed a higher percentage of a worker's weekly wage, the mean commuting distance declined.[42]

Other Aspects of Spatial Ordering

There was, in addition to occupational differentiations in space, some spatial ordering by family and household size in 1880. Married men, for example, commuted a distance approximately 15 percent to

20 percent greater than did bachelors regardless of occupation.[43] The married merchants with the larger families, be they shopkeepers or importers, tended to live farthest from the business district and to commute the longest distance. But there appeared to be an upper limit to this generalization. In merchant families of six or more children the commuting distance for the father dropped considerably when compared with families of less than six children. A similar pattern emerged when commuting distance was compared with household size. The distance increased with household size up to seven but in larger households the distance declined. No doubt the expense of sustaining a large family precluded the luxury of living in and commuting from the affluent suburbs. This was particularly true among the foreign-born merchants who, with generally larger families and smaller financial resources than the native-born, lived closer to their place of work. The city's native-born population taken as a whole commuted a distance 30 percent greater than the commuting distance of the foreign-born; and among the merchants the difference exceeded 50 percent.[44]

What is statistically significant is not so much the small differences in commuting distances between the general population and merchant samples but rather the difference between the native-born and the foreign-born in each sample. It might be expected that since the foreign-born clustered in the lower status occupations in both the blue- and white-collar ranks, their shorter commuting distance bore a direct relationship to their occupation and income. But when occupation was controlled for, the native-born merchants at all three occupational levels commuted a distance 20 percent to 30 percent farther than that traveled by the foreign-born. And within the blue-collar ranks a similar pattern had emerged. Spatial differentiation by nativity group was clearly in evidence in 1880, a change from the 1850s when no such distinct pattern could be discerned. The foreign-born generally resided in the districts closest to the city's business center while the native-born gravitated to the outlying areas.

Utilizing a six-district index of dissimilarity for table 8.5, the segregation index for the native-born merchants, compared to the general population, was somewhat higher (17) than that for the foreign-born merchants (12). Surprisingly, the native merchants were more segregated than their foreign-born colleagues in what had become by 1880 a predominantly (53 percent) native-born city. In the span of three dec-

Table 8.5. Residential distribution by nativity, 1880 (in percent).

	General sample			Merchant sample		
Location	Native-born (N = 289)	Foreign-born (N = 415)	Sample mean (N = 704)	Native-born (N = 216)	Foreign-born (N = 725)	Sample mean (N = 941)
Ward 11	23	19	20	18	18	18
Ward 12	17	12	14	21	21	21
Outside city	1	0	1	2	0	1
West of Dupont	22	21	21	31	27	28
East of Dupont	11	17	16	9	14	12
South of Market	25	31	28	19	20	20

SOURCE: San Francisco *City Directory,* 1880-81.

ades the nativity segregation pattern had reversed itself to a point where the foreign-born merchants were somewhat more residentially integrated within the city. In other cities, the predominant nativity group has usually been the one least segregated within the community.[45]

Also, and of particular significance, occupational status in 1880 continued to influence (as it had in the 1850s) residential segregation patterns. The importer-wholesalers and the city's elite were at least two and three times more segregated than the general merchants and petty shopkeepers respectively, and as occupational status increased, so did the segregation indexes for the two nativity groups.[46] In other words, the higher an individual's occupational status the more likely he was to be segregated not only among his own occupational class but within and among his own nativity group. Of the two variables—occupation and nativity—the former appeared to be more influential in determining the location of one's residence.[47]

Finally, the amount of personal property a man owned influenced to a considerable degree the location of his residence and hence the segregation patterns of the city in 1880. Merchants with assets in excess of $50,000 were far more segregated than those with assets under $10,000. Unlike the 1850s, the majority of the wealthy elite no longer chose to live in or close to the central business district and the blue-collar residential neighborhoods but by 1880 had segregated

themselves to a considerable extent in their own exclusive neighborhoods.

An important question remains. Was San Francisco any more segregated in 1880 than in 1852? Utilizing the index of segregation where
residential distributions were calculated on the basis of 87 city districts
and which allowed for fairly precise horizontal measurement, the
segregation index for all merchants actually declined from approximately 40 in 1852 to 20 in 1880. The merchants, regardless of occupational status or nativity affiliation, were more residentially integrated
in 1880 than they had been in 1852. Only the elite continued their preference for horizontal segregation.

Certainly the trend towards residential integration cannot be explained by any proportionate decrease in class consciousness within
the city. If anything, class consciousness had magnified to the point
where in 1879, the same year Henry George's *Progress and Poverty*
appeared, the city's elite published its first social register detailing the
rules of conduct expected of its "genteel" membership. The *Elite Directory* admitted to the lack of socially distinct geographical sections
in the city and said that where they did exist, they overlapped "at the
edges." The *Directory* observed, however, that when the city is viewed
from the perspective of "superimposed strata, the composition of the
lower changes insensibly into the next higher, and so on to the aristocratic capstone. It is not always easy to see where the adventurer
merges into the gambler, the gambler into the stock-sharp, the stock-
sharp into the regular broker, the broker into the man who follows
occupations of greater certainty, until we reach the summit of wealthy
leisure and unexceptional gentility. In reply to this it may be urged
that it is changing rapidly. The lines are year by year more tightly
drawn."[48]

If the elite mistakenly perceived in San Francisco an egalitarian
past, they had by 1880 realistically recognized their own socially strati-
fied existence. And when the social geography was investigated from
the vertical perspective of "superimposed strata," as suggested by the
Elite Directory, rather than measured by a segregation index on a horizontal plane, very possibly the spatial trend in San Francisco was not
toward residential integration but rather towards continued segregation. When, for example, class residential locations were plotted by

altitude within the city, there emerged a clear pattern of social distance. Simply stated, the affluent classes lived on the slopes or atop the numerous hills of the city, while the workingmen resided at the lower levels. From this perspective, the city's social and physical topography were one and the same.[49]

With the advent of the cable car in the mid-1870s, the city's hills and slopes could be totally conquered and hence built upon. The elite had climbed Rincon Hill by horse and carriage in the 1850s but only the cable car dared approach the steeper city slopes and hills. Technology allowed the affluent classes to segregate themselves by altitude, a pattern which began in the 1850s and was completed in the 1880s. The city's *Social Register* of 1884 described in part the reason for the vertical segregation. "The city has grown beyond original expectation. The lower part was by [c. 1870] . . . crowded with business houses. There was no longer any suitable neighborhood for residences east of Stockton, nor in much of the region south of Market Street."[50] One resident described the process of vertical segregation upon San Francisco's social topography in which "the guilded migration has been from early fashionable Stockton Street . . . to Rincon Hill and South Park to the south slope of Russian Hill to Nob Hill to Sea Cliff and Pacific Heights . . . a climb almost steadily upward socially and topographically." The great mansions of the wealthy dominated the higher elevations of San Francisco, one architectural historian noted, like "castles of the Old World."[51] San Francisco's capitalist princes, like those in other American communities, merely transplanted their perceived superiority to the higher elevations in this New World city.

It is no coincidence that the most imposing natural feature of the San Francisco landscape and that upon which the super-rich built their palatial mansions was once known as Snob Hill. And although the descendents may have sanitized the memory of their forefathers by renaming the Nob, still to this day it remains the location of elite residence and worship.

9

A VIEW TOWARD THE NOB

For all of the city's spectacular physical beauty, there was a harshness to life in San Francisco, "an ethos of survival of the fittest which began in the Gold Rush and continued throughout the century."[1] Associated with this selection process, an elite surfaced in the 1880s to control the city's power structure in much the same way as their mansions dominated the uppermost reaches of the urban landscape.

The presence of an elite, the process by which that elite had risen, and their leadership role in the city had not changed in thirty years. The only differences were the composition and size of the 1880 group. For as San Francisco grew from a medium-sized trading center of less than 25,000 in the early 1850s to an industrial metropolis of over 200,000 residents in 1880, the merchants no longer monopolized the upper echelons of San Francisco society. In large part, they were cast into a lesser role by the new industrial managers—those who directed and financially profited from the city's industrial transformation in the 1860s and 1870s. Like the merchants before them, industry's leaders quickly transferred their high occupational status and substantial new wealth into positions of power within the social fabric of San Francisco.

The social composition of the new elite reflected the altered economic structure of the city, and their behavior suggested a further demarcation of class lines in San Francisco in 1880. They felt compelled to define further their high status and exclusive social boundaries through the visual display of material possessions, new modes of social behavior, and the publication (for the first time) of a social register. They did so less out of fear that their social position would be challenged from below than to provide public evidence and personal reassurance of success. For at a time when social mobility rates in the city had declined, what better way to demonstrate their own firm belief in the survival of the fittest ideology than to identify publicly the winners of the struggle and to display ostentatiously the evidence of their lofty position.

Who, then, were the members of the elite of San Francisco in 1880, to what degree did they exert their status-power in the community, and did their careers in this relatively young city suggest what E. Digby Baltzell terms an "open elite "—one based "on the American ideal of equality of opportunity?"[2]

Elite Characteristics

In 1879 San Francisco's upper class published its first complete membership list. The *Elite Directory for San Francisco and Oakland* contained the names and addresses of 2,341 men, women, and children (1.2 percent of the city's total population) arranged alphabetically by family. Also included within the *Directory* were the membership lists of those private clubs which through their selection process defined, maintained, and renewed their exclusive ranks. One was the Pacific Club, founded in 1852, and the oldest social club in the city. It was considered to be "the most exclusive and dignified, its members being confined mostly to the upper crust millionaires and merchants." In addition to other Christian clubs, there was the Concordia Club, entirely Jewish in membership but only for "the elite of the Hebrew residents of the city," composed chiefly of wholesale merchants.[3]

The *Directory* listed virtually every known millionaire in San Francisco: the Central Pacific Big Four (Charles Crocker, Leland Stanford, Collis Huntington, and Mark Hopkins), the Mining Kings (James Fair, James Flood, William O'Brien and John Mackay), and the presidents and owners of the city's largest industrial and commercial enterprises with fortunes of less gigantic proportions. The *Directory* compilers failed to state by what criteria an individual was included in the publication. But it must be assumed from an investigation of the listed members that high occupational status and substantial financial assests were the most important prerequisites.

When the occupations of the 1879 *Directory* members are compared with the 1851 *Monied Men of San Francisco,* it is apparent that the ranks of the city's elite had changed significantly in the three decades. Whereas the merchants dominated the 1851 list, their representation among the 1879 elite had diminished by almost one half.[4]

Table 9.1. Occupational distribution of the San Francisco elite in 1851 and 1880 (in percent).

Occupation	1851 (N = 144)	1880 (N = 302)
Blue-collar	1	—
Petty proprietors (nonmerchant)	1	1
Petty shopkeepers	5	3
Clerical, sales	3	6
General merchants	24	21
Importer wholesalers	33	9
Capitalists, brokers, managers, manufacturers	16	38
Professionals	17	22

SOURCES: Cooke, Lecount Booksellers, *A "Pile" or a Glance at the Wealth of the Monied Men of San Francisco and Sacramento* (San Francisco, 1851); *Elite Dictionary* (1879).

Almost two-thirds of the 1851 elite were merchants, but by 1880 this percentage shrank to one-third. Manufacturers, stockbrokers, capitalists, high government officials, real estate speculators, and company executives composed over a third of the elite membership. Professionals, primarily attorneys and physicians, accounted for an additional 20 percent. The rest, for the most part, were younger sons who served in clerical positions.

A local observer in the late 1870s recognized the importance of occupation and wealth as the main requirements for elite membership. "It is natural that in a community so largely made up of fortune hunters, wealth should be a controlling social power; but it would be unjust to say that wealth is the sole standard of social position. Occupation, how one lives, and where one lives have something to do with it. There is a story of a rich man . . . who had a large circle of acquaintances, but he could not invite everybody. 'We must draw the line somewhere, you know,' he said, and he drew it bravely between wholesale and retail. The man who sold soap and candles by the box was decreed to be within the 'sacred pale' of the society's most elect. The man who sold soap and candles by the pound was voted a social Philistine."[5] That a wholesaler was included among the elite in 1880 was not in itself surprising, for, in fact, importers and wholesalers had always been included within the "sacred pale." The change from the 1850s was that class social boundaries were more clearly drawn.

There were others among the elite who represented San Francisco's more diverse metropolitan character. A few from the bohemian crowd gained entrance—artists Charles Rolo Peters and Julian Rix, writer Ambrose Bierce, the city's poet-laureate Charles Warren Stoddard, and the Berkeley scientist-philosopher Joseph Le Conte—but they were exceptions. The elite probably agreed with Ambrose Bierce's definition of the typical San Francisco bohemian whom he described in the local journal *The Wasp* as "a lazy, loaferish, gluttonous, crapulent and dishonest duffer, who according to the bent of his incapacity —the nature of the talents that heaven has liberally denied—scandalizes society, disgraces literature, debauches art, and is an irreclaimable, inexpressible and incapable nuisance."[6] Writers so excluded were Robert Lewis Stevenson, Brett Harte, and, of course, Henry George. Two historians, Hubert H. Bancroft and John Hittell, were admitted to the select circle; but civic historians who glorified the wonders of the city were hardly bohemians. Other exceptions to the general predominance of businessmen were the clergy—but only those whose Sunday flock included the elite—and high ranking military officers stationed in San Francisco.

Finally, a few gained elite affiliation because of their family background and despite their relatively low occupational status. One of them was Edward Howe, the son of a prominent Boston family and graduate of Harvard, who quit his superintendent's job in a Massachusetts smelting plant to seek new opportunities in San Francisco. He bounced from job to job, first as a clerk in a telegraph office, then to a similar position in a hardware store, and later to a supervisory position in the local Eureka Smelting Works. Throughout the period of moving from one relatively menial job to another, the transplanted Bostonian was a frequent guest at elite social functions. When not working, he taught German to the children of the upper class, attended their Unitarian Church, participated in an amateur theatre group, the choral society, the Mercantile Library Association, and attended monthly meetings of the local Harvard Club. He finally quit the Eureka Smelting Works ("I don't like 12 long hours of work") and emerged, by his own admission, "a gentleman loafer." Such an occupation was by no means unique among the elite, many of whom had retired; only the age at which the Harvard graduate had decided upon his newfound leisure was surprising.[7]

Besides their lofty occupational position and substantial financial resources, elite members prided themselves on their "pedigree, 'old stock' . . . exclusiveness." "Old stock" to San Franciscans in 1880 was measured in two ways. Judging from an impressionistic study of the surnames in the Christian elite list, old stock equaled Anglo-Saxon. Status was also no doubt improved and directly related to length of residence in the city. Since San Francisco in 1880 had little history to play with, three decades was the functional equivalent of three centuries in New England. A San Francisco pioneer, hard put to trace his lineage back to the *Mayflower,* could at the very least boastfully claim passage from Boston to San Francisco in 1849 on, say, the *California.* One observer noted that "to be a pioneer is to assert a claim to aristocracy, as absolute as attaches to a descendant of the Knickerbockers in New York, or to a resident of Boston who traces his ancestry in the passenger list of the *Mayflower.*" From the vantage point of an easterner, this would be considered a perverse sense of history. But by San Francisco standards, thirty years constituted the sum total of the city's rather raucous history.[8]

By comparison with the elite, the average resident of the city was a newcomer in 1880. Seven out of every ten employed males in the city had arrived in San Francisco after 1870, and less than 8 percent could boast over twenty years of residence. The elite, by comparison, were long-term residents—70 percent of them had lived in the city at least ten years.[9] Thus, despite San Francisco's relatively late industrial transformation, this was not exclusively an elite of the "arrivistes." Over 40 percent of the elite had resided in the city twenty years or more, and of the largest occupational group within the upper class (the capitalists, brokers, manufacturers, corporate executives), one-half claimed two decades or more of local residence. In a city where less than one in ten of the city's employed males could boast similar residential longevity, the elite corps was filled with those who had participated in and provided the leadership for San Francisco's industrial transformation. William Alvord, president of the Pacific Rolling Mill; Horace Davis, owner of the Golden State Flour Mill; Joseph Donohoe, bank president; John Fry, president of the Mission and Pacific Woolen Mills; Martin Heller, president of the Odd Fellows' Savings

Bank; Nicholas Kittle, commission merchant; capitalists Mark Livingston and D. O. Mills, were but a few of the long-time residents who had invested their capital and energy in the city's future for over two decades.

After the pioneers about 30 percent of the upper class had only "recently arrived." This group included corporation executives, who in their geographical transfer to San Francisco carried elite affiliations from their former community. Also included were the nouveaux riches (the mining and railroad moguls), who gained their wealth elsewhere but moved to San Francisco to spend it.[10]

From Rags to Riches?

The speedily acquired wealth of the nouveaux riches and their almost instantaneous elevation to elite status served to popularize and perpetuate the local rags-to-riches ideology. One believer described San Francisco society in the 1870s as "greatly changed for the better within the past few years, but is still somewhat 'mixed.' " "The lines of class," he observed, "are often vague and shadowy. Your coachman of yesterday may be your landlord today. The man who supplied you with vegetables a few years ago may now rank with you socially."[11] A local historian in 1879, and elite member himself, similarly propounded the theory of free and open access for all to San Francisco high society.

In no place is society more free and cordial . . . nobody cares whether he [the newcomer to San Francisco] belongs to a distinguished family, has moved in a fashionable circle, or possesses wealthy or influential friends or relatives . . . The course of business is such that no profession has all the wealth. There are rich men of all occupations and some of the mechanical trades are now . . . profitable . . . , as are the learned professions. Those who were rich in older states, and received a thorough education and a polished training, may be poor, while those who came here poor and ignorant may now be rich. Besides, the changes are so rapid that our neighbor who is poor today may be rich tomorrow, and the neighbor who is rich today may be poor tomorrow.[12]

The locally published "mug" books, which made their initial appearance in the 1870s, also perpetuated the ideal of the self-made man. These collective biographies glorified the wondrous achievements of men born in rags who, through true grit, rose to local and even national prominence.[13] Too often, however, the accounts were exaggerated either by the author to boost sales or by the subject to inflate his achievements and hence status. The author of one such book, *Representative Men of San Francisco,* let it be known that "it would be advisable that each person whose biography it contained, should agree to take a large number of copies, or pay a small amount for having the sketch published." The author, reportedly "a brilliant blackmailer," charged between $500 and $3,000 for inclusion.[14] By advertising their success, the elite wished to legitimize the system which generated their rise and maintained their high status. It is not without significance, also, that the mug books perpetuated the rags-to-riches gospel at the very time classes were in open conflict in the city streets and occupational opportunities were on the decline.

Examination of the occupational origins of San Francisco's 1880 elite failed to reveal a rags-to-riches mobility pattern. The elite did experience, however, considerable occupational mobility within the range of the white-collar world. Of the bankers, brokers, capitalists, corporate executives, import merchants, manufacturers, and professionals, who together composed two-thirds of all elite positions, 45 percent had experienced occupational advancement from less prestigious jobs between the time of their first job in San Francisco and 1880. As a group, they were considerably more mobile than the general employed population of the city though, to some degree, the higher mobility rate of the elite was partially a result of longer residence in the city. But even when time was controlled for, the elite outperformed the general population in the 1870 decade.[15]

Patterns of Mobility of the Elite, Merchants, and Workers

The performance of the elite was better revealed when judged by the occupational distance traveled during the span of their careers in San Francisco. By assigning prestige scores to each occupation and comparing the mean occupational prestige score of the first job with the job held in 1880, the direction and distance of the elite's occupational mobility could be determined. The same calculations were computed for the second generation 1880 merchants and the general employed population of the city.[16] Compared with these two samples, the elite outperformed both the city merchants and the general employed population. In one sense this was to be expected, since to travel to the top of the occupational ladder implied distance. The important point, however, is that the elite did, to some degree, climb the occupational ladder *in San Francisco* and did not automatically gain their high status positions through a lateral occupational transfer, or by virtue of family ties. True, their first jobs were relatively high on the occupational scale, but the occupational distance traveled by the elite as compared with both the merchants and the general population suggests a degree of openness within the elite ranks.[17]

The best proof that the elite of San Francisco in 1880 was an open one is the *Directory* itself. It was divided into two parts: the Calling and Address List, and the Jewish List. The second included 455 names, or approximately 19 percent of the total listings. With an estimated 16,000 Jews residing in the city in 1880 (7 percent of the population), Jewish representation in the elite ranks must be considered extraordinarily high. The curious anomaly was that a few Jews—Levi Strauss, the canvas pants manufacturer, and Abraham Weil, dry goods importer, two known cases—were included on the Christian Calling and Address List but not the Jewish List. By what criterion they were listed with the Christians is not known, but it must be surmised that the Christian elite ranks were fluid enough to accept at least two prominent Jewish merchants who served as leaders within their own religious community.[18]

Since the 1850s the more affluent members of the San Francisco Jewish community had rarely experienced the religious barriers which guarded the ranks of eastern urban elites. Gertrude Atherton, a local

Table 9.2. Occupational mobility: first job to 1880 job (in prestige scores).

Sample	First job	1880 job	Difference	(N)
Blue-collar	31.8	32.7	+0.9	(117)
General population	36.5	40.1	+3.6	(205)
Merchants	40.6	43.1	+2.5	(404)
Elite	51.3	55.7	+4.4	(202)

SOURCE: San Francisco *City Directories,* 1852-53, 1860-61, 1870-71, 1880-81.

writer herself to-the-manor-born, observed in the 1870s that "San Francisco has always prided herself on having the finest class of Jews of any city in the United States." "They are, and always have been," she continued, "highly educated, travelled, dignified, elegant, public-spirited and of outstanding ability." As "gracious patrons" they were active in charities, the women patronized "the fashionable dress-makers in San Francisco, New York and Paris," and their children attended "the exclusive private schools." In addition, their city and suburban homes were "as handsome as any" in San Francisco and Burlingame, "but without ostentation." In short, despite their "clan-nish" proclivity to "form an inner group of their own," the affluent Jewish community performed all the correct rituals expected of them by the predominantly WASP elite and hence were "welcome members of the 'best society.' " These remarks failed to mask a deeper anti-Semitism present within San Francisco's "best society." For despite the notable exceptions, Jews continued to be excluded from virtually all the city's principal social clubs until the 1960s.[19]

The new elite of 1880 was in a very real sense the product of the city's industrialization process. However, these occupational advance-ments were limited to the white-collar sector. Mobility from the blue-collar world into either the white-collar occupations or the elite ranks declined significantly after the 1850s. Only 5 percent of the 1880 elite had worn a blue collar in their first San Francisco job, a far smaller group than the 16 percent of the first merchant generation (the elite of the 1850s) who emerged from the ranks of workingmen.[20] The trend toward more constricted mobility was also reflected throughout the city's entire work force. For example, in the 1850 decade, the oppor-tunities for occupational advancement were considerably higher among the city's first generation of employed males (the majority of whom were blue-collar workers) than those prevailing in the 1870s for the second generation. From whatever perspective occupational mo-bility is measured (prestige scores or the movement along the scale of occupational groupings) there were very significant differences in occupational mobility rates before and after the city's industrial trans-formation. The lot of the average city worker did not improve with or after industrialization. Only the elite appears to have prospered.

The merchants, whose occupational opportunities and status de-clined significantly over the span of three decades, continued during

Table 9.3. Occupational mobility before and after industrialization: employed males, all occupations (in percent).

Age cohort	Before industrialization: first generation, 1852-1860				After industrialization: second generation, 1870-1880			
	Upward	Same	Down-ward	(N)	Upward	Same	Down-ward	(N)
20-29	38	55	7	(73)	26	67	7	(55)
30-39	32	57	11	(47)	30	66	4	(71)
40-49	40	55	5	(20)	33	56	11	(45)

SOURCE: California State Census [San Francisco], 1852; Federal Census, 1880; San Francisco *City Directories,* 1852-53, 1860-61, 1870-71, 1880-81.

the remainder of the century to disappear from society listings. Those who maintained their elite affiliation in 1880 managed to do so either because they had altered their merchant businesses to conform to the new industrial order, or because their "pioneer" status and early fortunes allowed them to maintain their elite membership. The group of pioneer merchants who survived and persisted in the city's elite ranks in the 1870s and early 1880s viewed with alarm the industrial process which, because it had displaced them, they could neither understand nor accept. They were conservative but also obstructive. One observer described the typical pioneer as a "California Bourbon." "He lives wholly in the past. He dates the creation of the world from the discovery of gold at Sutter's Mill, and Deluge from the great flood at Sacramento. He went to sleep immediately after the collapse of the Vigilance Committee, and has been asleep ever since. The world has moved on; the city has increased in population sixfold; a new race of men has come upon the stage, but he knows it not."[21]

Some first generation merchants did adapt to change. They conformed to the demands of industrialization with new manufacturing, distributing, and marketing arrangements. One such man, illustrative of others from the first merchant generation, was Alfred L. Tubbs. Born on a farm in Derry, New Hampshire, in 1827, Tubbs in his teens clerked for merchants in Concord, Baltimore, and later Boston. A Boston merchant firm sent Tubbs to San Francisco with two cargoes of goods in 1849. He never returned East except to pass through on his way to vacations in Europe. A member of the executive committee of the 1856 Vigilance Committee and trustee of numerous city voluntary associations, Tubbs had by the age of twenty-nine become the leading cordage manufacturer in the city. His company continued to thrive throughout the 1860s and 1870s when he combined merchandising with manufacturing. After the Civil War, he served as a state senator, and through his friendship with Governor Leland Stanford, served on the board of trustees of Stanford's new junior college in Palo Alto. Tubbs' sons went East to Harvard, but returned to assist their father in his three business endeavors: the rope factory, the wholesale outlet, and a vineyard in the Napa Valley.

Elite Leadership and Values

Tubbs maintained his status and power in the city, but the preeminent social position of his pioneer merchant generation gradually passed to men who represented the new industrial city. Whereas, for example, merchants dominated the leadership positions of the city's voluntary associations in the 1850s, the industrial managers had replaced them by 1880. By then, the trustees of San Francisco's exclusive Pacific-Union Club were, with the exception of one merchant, all bankers and capitalists.[22] The board of trustees of the First Unitarian Church, led by merchants in the 1850s, was by 1880 headed by the local agent of the Davis Sewing Machine Company. Other trustees included an insurance company agent, a wire manufacturer, a real estate investor, and a capitalist. In 1880, elders of the Calvary Presbyterian Church had no merchants among them either, whereas in 1856 they had composed over half of the board. Even the Chamber of Commerce, which for over two decades had served as the private preserve of the city's importers, had on its board of trustees in 1880 more manufacturers than merchants.[23]

Only in the Jewish voluntary associations did merchants continue to dominate the leadership positions—a situation that reflected the continued clustering of the Jews in the merchant occupations and their relatively slow transfer into nonmerchant related activities. Merchants continued in 1880 to monopolize the leadership positions in Temple Emanu-El as they had in the 1850s. Similarly, merchants outnumbered nonmerchants among the trustees and officers of the Pacific Hebrew Orphan Asylum.[24]

As in the 1850s, when the propertied classes controlled the city's social, political, and economic structure, so the elite in the 1880s exerted their influence throughout San Francisco's social fabric. They maintained their control of the important political and judicial positions in 1879-80, despite organized challenges from Dennis Kearney and his Workingmen's party. The city's mayor, five of the twelve supervisors, the president of the board of education, and three of the four police commissioners were all elite members. And to insure that upper-class justice prevailed in the city, they dominated virtually all of the state and federal judgeships (whose jurisdiction encompassed San Francisco), and half of all judges on the local Superior Court.

The only change that occurred over time was the greater dispersal of leadership posts to a larger number of elite members. Whereas in the 1850s there were scores of city merchants and bankers who served as an interlocking directorate for the city, by 1880 there were few upper-class members who held more than two leadership posts. As the city increased in size, and there were more executive positions to fill in the voluntary associations, the absolute number of members of the elite in these offices increased. Some members devoted their status and energies to directing the affairs of their churches, some to politics, while others confined themselves strictly to business affairs. There was a greater parceling out of the leadership posts among the elite in the 1870s than in the 1850s, not because the "better classes" were any less willing to serve and lead the myriad of voluntary associations, nor because of any effective public pressure to democratize the city's leadership ranks, but simply because few elite members possessed all the specialized skills, or even time, demanded of leadership in a period of increased specialization.[25]

Participation in and the leadership of voluntary associations, however, was only part of a larger responsibility which the elite demanded of their members. High social status carried with it the expectation that individual social behavior conform to established standards. Too busy gathering their fortunes, the early monied men of the 1850s possessed neither the time nor the self-confidence in their newly acquired social position to delineate unique class rituals. But by 1880, with the assurance that their status and fortunes (self-made or inherited) were firmly secure in a more settled social order, the elite detailed for themselves (and their lower-class audience) distinct modes of behavior.[26]

They engaged in social activities, hosted lavish parties (preferably with music), contributed to and led voluntary associations (particularly the church), and if young, participated in an upper-class sport (yachting, hunting, or horses). Of course, one dressed the role and lived in a pretentious residence or fashionable club (Bohemian, Pacific-Union) or hotel (Occidental, Palace, The Baldwin, Grand, Lick House) where the elite clustered. It was assumed that if an elite member did not engage in an occupation, at least he possessed the financial resources to sustain a lavish life style. Servants, private schooling and tutors for his children, trips to the East Coast and Europe, and a country home, not to mention proper clothes, residence, household furnishing, and an exquisite dinner table (to include vintage wines), all added up to a hefty annual elite maintenance fee. The aristocratic aspirations of the San Francisco elite were also suggested by the accounts of fathers scouring Europe for titled aristocrats for their eligible daughters. The formula for forging an alliance between democratic capitalism and aristocratic nobility was simple: "The old man furnishes the coin, the girl the love, and the distinguished foreigner the title." Apparently British noblemen were most in demand, followed in descending order by the French, Russians, Italians, Spanish, and finally the least noble Germans.[27]

The prevalent mode of living was luxurious and the habits of the rich extravagant. From their large incomes they saved very little, as one historian noted, preferring "to enjoy their gains as they go along." The elite admitted to squandering their money with "little thought taken for the future or the morrow," and those who had gained (even if by luck) a fortune in a year, were rather excited by the possibility of spending a good portion of the proceeds in a month. The "luxury, and comfort, and associations" were considered, the *Elite Directory* noted, "ample compensation for the outlay."[28]

There were, of course, certain taboos. Males should not frequent the city's numerous flesh palaces, but if they insisted on doing so (as many did), such "scandalous visits to the tenderloin" should be hidden from public view. An elite member did not work with his hands nor live among those who did. Neither did his wife except within the household and there only in tasks thought too important to be detailed to a foreign servant. Of course the wives assisted their favorite voluntary associations but that was charity, not work. After the mid-1850s

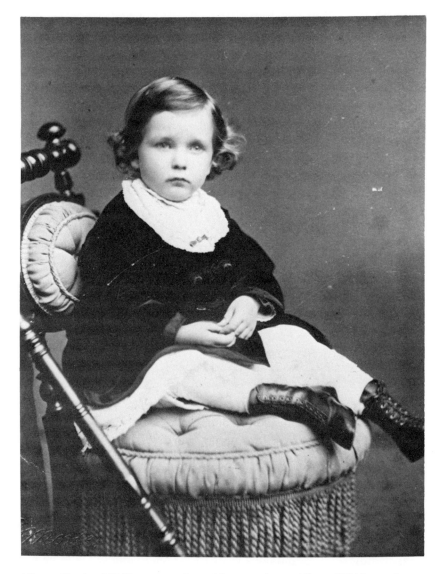

Albert Charles Dibblee, son of wealthy merchant Albert Dibblee, whose mother accompanied him each fall to Cambridge, Massachusetts, so that he might receive a "proper and fashionable" education at the Browne and Nichols school. Young Dibblee later attended Harvard and practiced law in San Francisco.

the men did not gamble, and if they did, would never admit to it in polite society. Gambling, however, did not by definition exclude playing the stock market. A purchase of Consolidated Virginia was rather an "investment" despite the fact that so few profited from these speculative ventures. Drinking, but never in excess, was reserved for the holiday outing, over lunch, or at the exclusive men's club where could be found "good food, luxurious surroundings, an opportunity to meet intelligence, . . . wealth . . . wit on an equal footing.[29]

The Vigilantes Return

The upper class shared a network of common values despite the large range of skills recruited into their ranks and the wide diversity of leadership roles they performed. When, for example, other classes challenged their propertied interests, members of the upper class acted in concert to meet the threat. Mayor James Otis, a pioneer commission merchant, indirectly referred to the city's class antagonisms when in 1873 he called for "a little more unity and harmony of action; more forbearance towards one another; less jealousy of individual success; and a more liberal feeling and spirit" so as to increase "the welfare and advancement of the whole people."[30] And when in 1877 Dennis Kearney organized thousands of city workingmen to protest against local labor conditions (unemployment, low wages, and competition from cheap Chinese labor) which resulted from the inequities of the industrial system, the city's elite countered with the time honored solution—the vigilante committee.

William T. Coleman, former leader of the 1856 Vigilance Committee, once again sounded the law-and-order whistle, warning the city, and particularly the upper class, that "the safety or destruction of the city hangs on the pivot." Unless the "better classes" organized and "pledged themselves and their money" to protect their "wives, children and fortunes," the city would stand in ruin from this "socialist" threat. At a public meeting Coleman outlined the need for a Committee of Safety.[31] "The purpose of the organization is to sustain the constituted authorities, undertaking no duty not immediately connected with securing the safety of life and property . . . however desirable it may appear that this disturbing element [Kearneyism] should finally be withdrawn and removed from our midst, we are unanimous in the conviction that violence will not hasten its proper adjustment, and may produce incalculable injury to all. The public peace and security to life and property in this city shall be maintained and protected at all hazards."[32]

Proclaiming a dire need for a vigilante organization automatically appealed to the city's ruling class. One lady expressed her assurance that "mob violence" could be averted by Coleman and his business colleagues when she wrote: "When the strong, quick-thinking, self-reliant and totally fearless men of [San Francisco] . . . rouse themselves, use their brains and superior powers of organization, they will put down the worst form of mob violence that could threaten our city." They may "sacrifice blood and money," she added, "but they will do the work." Fortunately, there is always present on the local scene "a William T. Coleman, a man of the hour."[33] "The Lion of

COMMITTEE OF SAFETY.
EXECUTIVE MEMBERS.

Executive members of the Committee of Safety, 1877, all prominent business and civic leaders, headed by the "Lion of the Vigilantes," William T. Coleman.

the Vigilantes" and his executive committee invited all those who opposed mob rule to join with them in the Committee of Safety. Signature rolls were set up in the rooms of the Chamber of Commerce (the committee headquarters) and within two days over 5,000 enlistees had enrolled to support yet another local venture in law and order. The U. S. Army provided 8,000 firearms and 80,000 rounds of ammunition as well as a general to advise the executive committee. The U. S. Navy also responded to Coleman's request for military assistance by placing three war ships in the harbor to keep watchful eyes and guns on the potentially dangerous situation.[34]

Reportedly, the majority of those who joined the Committee of Safety were mechanics who, though they shared the general working class concern for the labor problems in San Francisco, cared not at all for Dennis Kearney or his solutions. The committee, however, was controlled, organized, and financed by the city's elite in much the same manner as the better class had dominated the vigilance committees of 1851 and 1856. "In 1877 the same people [class]," said committee president William Coleman, "in the same place, under different conditions and yet in some respects the same, determined to act in the spirit of the law." The same poor economic conditions prevailed locally in 1877 as had existed at the time of the Vigilance Committee of 1856.[35] Also a few of the 1877 leaders had earned their law and order reputations in 1856—particularly Coleman. The main similarity was elite leadership; for while the individuals within the elite ranks had changed over time, the upper class remained in constant control of the city's social fabric. As William Coleman reminded his flock, "The better class of people in California now [1877] do not feel the necessity of a mob[;] on the contrary they have turned against it. They are ready and prepared to organize and form military forces, if necessary, to meet a mob, to dispense with it, and if the civil and judicial authorities are not sufficiently active, they will furnish the power to supply their peace."[36]

The leadership to "furnish the power" came from the executive committee who pledged "to preserve the peace and well being of the city" with their "money and persons." Well over half the executive committee were also members of the city elite. They included, among others, James Flood, the mining magnate of the Comstock Lode, Charles Crocker, president of the Pacific Railroad, two bankers, a score of manufacturers, corporate executives, capitalists, and import merchants, all of whom rejected Kearney's attacks against the Chinese, the rich on Nob Hill, the railroads, and the police. And after Kearney threatened to give Springfield rifles to men who would "hang, shoot, or cut the capitalists to pieces," not surprisingly "the business men and property owners of the city," one participant observed, "responded nobly and furnished all the means [$75,000] that were necessary" to carry out the objectives of the executive committee.[37]

To put down, disperse, and ultimately disband the mobs, the Committee of Safety sent companies of 100 men each into the streets. In order to be at the right place at the right time, to meet an assemblage of unarmed laborers with a counterforce of armed committee members, the executive committee used informers within the ranks of Kearney's followers. "Information has been recieved at these headquarters," the committee communicated with the police, "that a meeting and procession of the longshoremen will be held in this city tomorrow night. It is desirable that we should have some reliable information on the subject."[38]

When the longshoremen attempted to march out of the working class district up toward a middle-class residential neighborhood, the city police with the assistance of 1,500 committee members (armed with hickory pick handles) clubbed the demonstrators into submission. Coleman and his lieutenants witnessed the beatings from the security of Nob Hill. The vigilantes so intimidated Kearney's group with arrests, beatings, and general harassment, that the workers abandoned the streets to carry the fight into the court and the ballot box. Immediately after the victory of the "pickhandle brigade," the state legislature, at Coleman's urging, passed a "gag" law making it a felony to incite a riot. When Kearney next spoke at a public gathering, a local judge jailed him. And to insure the permanence of their victory, the elite nominated five of their own to run for the board of supervisors. All five were elected, while candidates of the Workingmen's party gained not a single seat. Finally, when the bankers of San Francisco offered to advance the city $10,000 for the purpose of doubling from 150 to 300 the number of city policemen (to be selected by the Committee of Safety), and the board of supervisors accepted the offer, the committee members returned to their normal occupations and left the streets to the police.[39]

The defeat of the workingmen was, said the daughter of one committee member, "a magnificent demonstration of what can be accomplished in a republic by a superior class of citizens over demagogues and their mistaken followers—the lawless element of a city." How lovely and peaceful it was, she added, that here amidst a democracy our ways were so "vastly different . . . from the tyrannies of European states ruled by militarism. In republics agitators merely lie for their own purposes when they assert that all men's chances are not equal." The daughter of the elite finally admitted to a more realistic and less homogenized assessment of the social system when she asserted: "Cream will rise to the top until the day of doom."[40]

Henry George, another local observer but one who never did "rise to the top" (at least not in San Francisco) expressed a different view of the city's social structure. He once believed San Francisco to be "more thoroughly Americanized" than any eastern city, more orderly, and possessing "greater mobility of society than in older communities." But with the new concentrations of economic power in the hands of the railroad and the rise of large corporations during the 1870s, George radically revised his earlier observations. "The class who can live sumptuously on their incomes has steadily grown; there are rich men beside whom the richest of the earlier years would seem little better than paupers—in short, there are on every hand the most striking and conclusive evidences that the production and consumption of wealth have increased with even greater rapidity than the increase in the population, and that if any class obtains less it is solely because of the greater inequity of distribution."[41] "There are plenty of millionaires in this city," another observer noted, but he hastened to add, "there are also many poor men." As for the distribution of wealth, "the [city] is monopolized by a few, and the large capital is in the hands of a few."[42] The "cream" had indeed risen to the top!

10

CONCLUSION

Recent historical studies have demonstrated that there were more similarities than differences in the social mobility and persistence rates for nineteenth-century cities, regardless of size, location, or even age. These are important and significant findings. However, the commonality claimed for the American experience hides, and can distort, some important variations within particular communities—variations which, if recognized, provide a different perspective of the forces and processes described by historians to explain the similarities over time and space. We know from other studies that there were significant differences in the career mobility patterns for various racial, religious, and ethnic groups within individual cities. Beneath San Francisco's overall mobility pattern, one which did in some important way conform to other nineteenth-century cities, there too existed major class differences in the mobility rates, both between the blue-collar and white-collar classes and also within the white-collar sector itself. These dissimilar class experiences have important consequences within a community.

The internal differences, if recognized at all by historians, are too often described only through statistical measures and techniques. Rarely are they explained within the social context in which they occur. This context includes the hopes, aspirations, and anxieties of those whose lives are being measured. To exclude these considerations, through the exclusive use of quantitative techniques, is to disregard how individuals perceive their own reality and to preclude any normative judgments regarding social mobility in a society. How the merchants perceived their own life chances given their personal expectations, as measured against their actual performance in the city's social system, is a far different and considerably more interesting question than how white-collar mobility rates in San Francisco compared with similar groups in other cities. Such an investigation, still far from complete, may not in the end be particularly important.

The social context to which I refer was determined to a large degree by one very important symbolic act performed by the pioneers immediately after their arrival in Yerba Buena village in the late 1840s. They changed the town's name to San Francisco and the result had important consequences. The new designation immediately attracted to this deep-water port ships with gold-seekers bound for the San Francisco Bay, away from rival ports in the vicinity. Simultaneously, money-seekers and money-changers invaded this Spanish village and swiftly eradicated a religious community while simultaneously erecting a commercial city. From the very beginning of the mid-nineteenth-century migration, it was evident that San Francisco was not settled by Christian souls seeking to establish a covenanted community, but inundated by a multinational invasion of profiteers who, if they worshipped God at all, did so to implore Him to enrich their pockets. This was a city that worshipped at the high altar of Mammon, and its most revered and respected citizens defined themselves as "merchant capitalists." Horatio Alger, the hero of the nineteenth-century American success story, aspired to be a businessman, not a military general, government civil servant, or great landowner in the European tradition. And no city at midcentury so optimistically proclaimed the opportunity to succeed in that career as did San Francisco.

To the thousands of American citizens and foreign immigrants who flocked westward to fetch the gold at the end of the continental rainbow, San Francisco represented El Dorado—a frontier city not only abundant in natural beauty but one offering opportunities far superior to the "life chances" they left "back home." Expectations of immediate gratification, material and psychological, mobilized a transcontinental and transoceanic migration of young businessmen, clerks, artisans, and laborers who sought escape from what they perceived to be the social and economic stratifications and conflicts of the Eastern Seaboard and Europe. "Goin' to Frisco" also offered, no doubt, adventure and a relief from personal boredom in an age that expected and sought excitement. What was surprising, given the distances traveled and the expenses involved, was not that native-born Americans and immigrants alike accepted the golden fairy tales emanating from California which were so uncritically repeated by the eastern and European press, but rather that so many, with such meager resources and information, actually sought to capture the California Dream.

The early illusion of making quick fortunes vanished in the face of disastrous economic conditions in the years immediately following the boom. The pot of gold disappeared upon close investigation in the clear, unfiltered light of experience. Still the city continued to attract thousands of transcontinental migrants each year. The new arrivals with their high expectations debarked from the ships as the disillusioned passed through the turnstile for home. A few remained in the city because their home never existed or because, like the roulette player, they gambled on Lady Luck to enrich them. They stayed and played and even prayed because the joyous laughter of the few winners overshadowed the more silent despair of the many losers. They were engaged, they thought, in a "chance game" where "some won golden nuggets" while others "won poverty and death." "They were all gamblers," wrote one observer, "they had heard that the 'stake' was here to be won, and they took a 'hand' and 'played.' But it was not skill in those days that carried off the prize, sheer luck gave victory."[1]

The first generation merchants served as the human pool from which "the chance game" had plucked its first San Francisco victims and beneficiaries. The more fortunate would advertise the beneficence of the selection system and emphasize the rewards of hard work —the keystone to the structure which supported the capitalist ethic. What was not admitted, for by doing so would weaken the ethic, were the advantages of native blood, an adequate bank account, and a few well-placed business and family connections. But even these advantages, as everyone knew too well, did not by any means guarantee success; they only lowered the odds against failure. Everyone, the victims and the beneficiaries, accepted that one unknown element in the selection process—chance. As one of the more successful native-born, affluent, eastern-connected San Francisco commission merchants admitted in the late 1850s, "all is still a lottery."

The merchants and the city constantly strove to eradicate the element of chance from their collective destiny. But about the time San Francisco rationalized her commercial sea trade with those unscrupulous easterners who flooded local markets with unwanted goods, the railroad broke the regional monopoly the city had so dearly protected and cultivated. In this situation, although the merchants had the opportunity to use their accumulated capital to control their

own destiny, they lacked the imagination to either adapt to or participate in the city's industrialization. The legacy of the gold rush was all
too pervasive. Conditioned as they were in the 1850s to the mines and
the wealth which profited a few among them, the pioneer merchants
continued to place their faith in the "diggings." In the end, industrialization and its new capital arrangements had destroyed the merchant
class which had ruled the local roost since pioneer days. They had
founded a city, provided the initial social glue, but in the end they
could not understand the forces which sustained and transformed
their own creation.

Disillusionment, as might be expected, was the most common feeling expressed by the merchants. Such a sense of despair was, however,
by no means unique to San Francisco. The American democratic ideology, as Tocqueville reminded us, so raised the level of individual
expectations that a moderate advancement in a person's economic or
social position was perceived to be, considering the enthusiastic acceptance of the egalitarian ideology, no advancement whatsoever. "It
cannot be denied that democratic institutions strongly tend to promote the feeling of envy in the human heart; not so much because they
afford to everyone the means of rising to the same level with others, as
because these means perpetually disappoint the persons who employ
them. Democratic institutions awaken and foster a passion for equality which they can never entirely satisfy."[2]

It is within this context of high expectations in the United States
generally, and in San Francisco particularly, that any judgments
about the degree of social mobility must be assessed. Throughout the
period covered by this study, for example, San Francisco residents
experienced no occupational gains (with the exception of the early
1850s) which surpassed the career opportunities of populations in the
eastern cities, despite the fact that in a new and dynamic city it might
be expected to be otherwise. A sense of personal failure, disillusionment, and despair was more strongly felt in San Francisco, I suspect,
because the opportunities were thought to be so much superior in the
Golden Gate City. Certainly in many cases the personal goals and
aims of those in search of a golden future were unrealistic, and only
obtainable in some imagined utopia. Accordingly, the carping tone of
personal diaries and letters of those who migrated to California "to
seek the elephant" reflect the tears of a crocodile. But too many con-

firmed cases, particularly those who sought nothing more than the opportunity to improve their condition only marginally, foundered (after some initial successes) upon harsh economic and occupational failure. The sense of disillusionment was for them the result of personal experiences which cannot easily be dismissed as an exaggerated sense of self-pity. Succeeding generations would construct institutional devices to protect themselves against panics and depressions and the catastrophic captial losses which resulted. But amidst the economic chaos in this instant city, the 1850s offered few personal protections against downward mobility. Henry George was among the city's many unemployed workers who experienced a sense of disillusionment after having lost both his job and his life-savings. He wrote in 1864 that California would soon possess a large population, but he went on to express the question others felt with equal keeness: "Will she have more wealth . . . will it be so evenly distributed? She will have more luxury and refinement and culture; but will she have such general comfort, so little squalor and misery; so little of the grinding, hopeless poverty that chills and cramps the souls of men, and converts them into brutes?" To George, California (and particularly San Francisco) represented a social failure because it had promised so much. Maybe that was what Thoreau meant when he wrote: "Going to California. It is only three thousand miles nearer to hell."[3]

Associated with this disillusionment was the extraodinary degree of social fluidity in the city, particularly during the 1850s. This occupational and property instability, however, was far more common within the white-collar occupations than within the working class, a not surprising finding given the wider range of occupational opportunities available outside the confines of a relatively immobile working class. The consequences of this instability within San Francisco's social fabric profoundly affected the whole city. For beneath the exaggerated advertisements proclaiming a serene civic and economic environment in San Francisco, where one could pocket a personal bonanza, there existed a harsh competitiveness as violent and debilitating as in any town or city in nineteenth-century America. For example, even though a third of the higher-status city merchants (those who commanded the wealth and power in the city) lost both occupational status and large amounts of capital assets in the 1850s, they nevertheless still possessed the capacity, which they enthusiastically exercised, to cause considerable social havoc. Through the Vigilance Committee, an institutional arrangement which represented the city's business leaders, the merchants attempted to preserve their social status. It was not so much that the businessmen were being challenged and replaced by upwardly mobile workingmen, as that those whose fortunes were threatened by unpredictable panics and recessions felt the need to rationalize the city's economic and political machinery and bring it under their direct control. The merchants thought that if they only could control the city's political machinery, they would be able to preserve the extraordinary wealth they had so quickly accumulated since 1849. Once again, in the economically troubled 1870s, the city fell victim to the vigilante justice administered by merchants and industrialists unable to maintain their status or economic position in the new industrial city. Three vigilance committees in three decades is evidence enough of the harshness of the system.

The occupational and economic instability which the merchants experienced, and the vigilantism which all too often resulted, suggest that the causes for urban violence may not always rest with a disgruntled, angry working class. In San Francisco, those who attempted to preserve social, political, and economic order through violent means were the very ones who had both gained and then lost the most status and wealth in the city's "root, hog or die" capitalist system. What they could not preserve through more democratic procedures, they would capture through more violent means.[4]

What stands out, amidst all the economic and social chaos of San Francisco's phenomenal growth in the three decades, is how quickly class lines formed and how rapidly they were institutionalized through voluntary associations at all levels of society. The vigilance committees, the most powerful and highly structured of the city's associations, best demonstrated the class consciousness of the middle class. Workingmen and a large segment of the foreign-born population who worked in the lower status white-collar occupations were excluded from the vigilance committees and other elite organizations because of ethnic and religious biases among the "better classes." More specifically, the predominant native-born elite excluded them because workers and foreigners lacked the necessary capital resources thought necessary for economic and political leadership of the city. San Franciscans, like residents of other emerging western cities, carried with them from older communities in the East familiar habits and attitudes, political loyalties, economic forms, and social institutions which they modified hardly at all on the urban frontier. To a large degree, the political, economic, and social arrangements of the middle class were patterned after those institutions which could be found in the communities from which San Franciscans had moved westward. As one historian has reminded us, "A large part of western opportunity was the opportunity to imitate an older society."[5]

The city's residential patterns also reflected a class consciousness that was not unique to the West. The spatial arrangements by which city residents separated themselves were part and parcel of the cultural baggage carried out from the East. The San Francisco elite lived in what Rudyard Kipling termed "aggressive luxury," segregated from the working-class residential neighborhoods and the city's industrial sections. Again, the speed with which social classes separated and arranged themselves suggests that New York's Grammercy Park, Bos-

A view from Nob Hill toward downtown and the harbor, in mid-1870.

ton's Beacon Hill, and Philadelphia's Society Hill served as convenient models for transfer onto the San Francisco topography. Even the standard grid pattern of eastern city streets failed to be modified in its transcontinental migration; it was transposed rigorously, and rather impractically, to the hills and nobs of San Francisco. Gertrude Atherton, novelist, biographer, and member of San Francisco's hilltop elite who wrote (by her own admission) for that social "stratum which had acquired enough intellectual snobbery to be contemptuous of Edgar Rice Burroughs, but cannot palate the refinement of Henry James," summed it up best for her audience when she observed, "What are any of us but the logical results of tradition."[6]

The class divisions which so quickly took root in the city during the 1850s did not, of course, prevent people of varied status from amassing quick fortunes. Despite deep cracks and crevices in the social fabric, these individual success stories kept alive the California Dream. People did make it to the top, not always by cunning, unethical behavior or luck but by intelligence, energy, skill, and personal sacrifice—characteristics found throughout all segments of the population. But among the merchants, and no doubt all other occupations, one ingredient for success seemed to be paramount—the ability to obtain capital resources.

In an economic environment which placed a premium upon growth and expansion, those who possessed ample capital or who managed to borrow in times of hardship from business associates, relatives, or lending institutions gained an immediate and distinct advantage. The inability to raise capital almost always guaranteed personal disaster during the frequent panics, recessions, and depressions which struck the city. The native-born sons of eastern merchants usually had little trouble in arranging a family loan. The German merchants borrowed extensively among themselves or from friends and relatives in eastern cities. But others, whose connections were less secure or affluent, encountered severe difficulties. The R. G. Dun and Company credit reports, which today read like FBI dossiers, detailed the obstacles which thousands of city residents encountered in obtaining capital resources. But far more important, the tone and prejudices reflected in the reports strongly suggested the middle-class values and standards one had to possess or achieve in order to receive credit, and hence capital, in San Francisco.

The credit company, and no doubt others like it throughout the nation, served as a clearing house through which passed applicants of diverse origin who sought credentials into the middle class. While financial criteria (amount of capital, debts outstanding, type of business) were important considerations, they were far less significant to R. G. Dun than "personal character." It was this item, the most subjective of all the criteria, that received the greatest importance. Character included one's ethnic, religious, and racial background, personal dedication to the Protestant work ethic, moral and ethical behavior. Irishmen, Jews, blacks—to name but a few—were deemed less worthy of credit than their Anglo-Saxon counterparts. The credit reviews served as a convenient filter system through which the middle class selected its own new recruits in an effective if slightly circular fashion, excluding groups and individuals prejudged to be sick, lazy, promiscuous, or worse. The importance that lending institutions in San Francisco attached to a high credit rating suggests also the power and influence of a middle-class value system as defined exclusively by a WASP institution, founded by New York merchants and headquartered there. Once again, an eastern institution served the purposes of those westerners intent upon shaping a city which mirrored the stratifications of more familiar and comfortable environments. That certain groups in San Francisco, particularly the German Jews, attained economic success in spite of the ethnic and religious barriers placed before them, is testimony to their perseverance and group cohesiveness rather than to the weakness of the institutional arrangements. The ethnic, racial, and religious slurs in the reports too often coincide with individual credit ratings which conclude "not good for credit." The fact that R. G. Dun and Company was the largest and most powerful credit-rating agency in the nation also suggests the possible influence and power of these middle-class entrance requirements throughout the nation.

It is little wonder, therefore, that those who arrived in San Francisco in the 1860s and 1870s, predominantly a foreign-born generation seeking new and improved life chances, found that opportunities for better jobs and material comfort were no better and in some respects even worse than they had been for their pioneer predecessors. And despite the proclamations from the city's business community that industrialization would revitalize the Jeffersonian ideal of meritocracy, entrance to and mobility within the middle class was made increasingly more difficult. The social system had atrophied not because of mechanistic or deterministic explanations which blamed industrialization. It stagnated because people at the top arranged, defined, and administered the entrance requirements to, and the speed of, the social escalator which might lead to the top. Those who controlled these mechanisms rationalized the procedures and institutionalized the values in their own image and had, therefore, changed the rules. The "life game" remained the survival-of-the-fittest but, having surrounded and insulated themselves with new institutional arrangements, the winners legitimized and protected their position at the top. No longer need they worry, as people did in the 1850s, about the unexpected panic, depression, or even social upheaval. The odds against downward mobility had been lowered. The elite through their institutions had succeeded in immobilizing a social system which at one brief time had demonstrated considerable openness and fluidity. If the system had really remained open, the social composition of the city's 1880 elite would have included fewer pioneer sons, considerably more Italians, Germans, Poles, and Irish, and a far larger proportion of people who had, at one time in their life, worked with their hands.

No wonder a sense of disillusionment pervaded San Francisco in the late nineteenth century. An English observer described for his Tory audience at home the Spencerian process grinding away in San Francisco.

San Francisco is full of social wrecks—wrecks more complete and miserable than any possible in calmer seas. There is said to be a greater proportion of suicides here than anywhere else in the civilized world. No wonder. A society so new that its members are bound to each by few and slight ties—a society so new that has in general lost all old faith and found no new faith in God or man—it foams on like a battle, like a riot towards its ends. Quarter is neither given or expected. Victory! victory or nothing! . . . That ghastly eternal slaughter, that grim war-game of fates, called selection-of-the-fittest, goes on here like a frontier war, without convention, without checks, without mercy; not with circumstances of deliberate cruelty, but worse—amid panic.[7]

Industrialization had not ameliorated class divisions in the city; it had not offered opportunities to the average city resident which were superior to those of earlier days when San Francisco, in its splendid isolation, monopolized the trade of the West Coast and the surrounding interior; nor could it be said that the San Francisco experience was much different from the opportunities which pertained in other cities in the second half of the nineteenth century. Thousands who escaped to San Francisco in search of better opportunities found little improvement in the quality of their lives. The tragedy of frustrated ambitions, intensified class-consciousness, and bitter social and economic antagonisms that accompanied nineteenth-century urban growth elsewhere in America, was more apparent in San Francisco than city fathers or new arrivals liked to admit. Perhaps nothing summarizes the presence of these harsh forces more clearly than a petty but highly symbolic incident involving Charles Crocker, the former dry goods merchant who had risen to become a railroad magnate.

"One man works hard all his life and ends up a pauper," Crocker once stated; "another man, no smarter, makes twenty million. Luck has a hell of alot to do with it."[8] But this central notion that good fortunes depend largely upon good fortune, however predictable, typical, and reassuring it may be, serves to obscure more truth about the social system than it conveys. In the enjoyment of his good fortune, Charles Crocker, opulent and powerful, was living in an insulated position on Nob Hill in 1877. Desiring to set himself off still further in physical and social terms, Crocker aspired to own the entire block upon which his mansion was situated. When his neighbor, a Chinese undertaker named Yung, refused to sell, Crocker then proceeded to build around Yung's cottage a thirty-foot high board fence. Some months later, amidst the labor disturbances, Dennis Kearney led three thousand followers to Nob Hill and staged a mass protest against Crocker's "spite fence," an example to the city's workingmen of the arrogance and permanence of great wealth. To protect Crocker and his fence, middle-class vigilantes (the Committee of Safety) arrived to chase and club the protesters back down the hill. The spite fence remained intact and stood as an infuriating symbol of the less visible, but no less permanent and effective barriers that have persisted in San Francisco society, and other American cities, far into the twentieth century.

Charles Crocker's mansion on Nob Hill and the "spite fence" he built to surround the property of his Chinese neighbor, Mr. Yung.

APPENDIXES

NOTES

INDEX

APPENDIX A

Methodological Notes

The Samples

Five major samples were used for this study. Because the Federal Census of 1850 for San Francisco was "lost at sea," the two samples utilized for the 1850s (chapters 3, 4, and 8) were drawn from the California State Census of 1852 for the County of San Francisco. One sample (N = 643) was composed exclusively of persons who gave as their occupation "merchant" or a similar designation. (For a complete listing of "merchant" occupational designations, see Appendix B). A second random sample (N = 669) of the general population, employed males sixteen years old and older, was also drawn from the 1852 California Census. In chapters 7 and 8, the "second generation" samples (merchants, N = 958; general population, N = 731) were randomly drawn from the 1880 Federal Census. The elite sample (N = 288) for chapters 8 and 9 was systematically selected from the 1879 San Francisco *Elite Directory*.

Because the 1852 merchant sample presented certain unexpected difficulties, it should be explained in some detail. Approximately 3,100 people listed themselves as merchants in the 1852 California State Census for San Francisco. But because of the way the census was conducted in San Francisco, many people were picked up two and sometimes three times by the census taker. Of the original 3,100 listed, 643 could be located and verified in the 1852 or 1854 San Francisco *Directory* as being employed in a merchant occupation. This group of 643 became the merchant sample for the study of the first generation of San Francisco merchants.

It was decided to work with the group of 643 rather than the larger total of 3,100 merchants for a number of reasons. First, approximately 15 percent of the 3,100 group were not merchants and if it had been possible to verify all the occupations in the city directories, no doubt the percentage of nonmerchants would have been higher. Second, in order to be as precise as possible about someone's specific merchant function at the beginning of his occupational career in San Francisco, it was necessary to locate the man in a city directory not only to verify if he was a merchant but, more important, to know what type of merchant activity he engaged in (wholesale or retail, and kind of merchandise). The California Census, like the Federal Census for 1850, failed to list occupation in any precise manner. The city directories were not very precise either, but they were an improvement over the censuses. Finally, because San Francisco was in the early 1850s a port of entry for the entire state of California and most of the West Coast, a considerable number of the 3,100 picked up by the census taker in 1852 were in the city at the time of the census but gone to the interior towns a month or so later. Many were, in fact, only temporarily in San Francisco as they made preparations to take up residence elsewhere. These transients were therefore dropped from the sample. If occupational and property mobility and residential patterns were to be studied, then the sample had to be of residents who were known to be merchants, whose type of merchant activity could be verified, and who were known to work in the city.

However, by selecting this sample a definite bias occurred. A sample which included only those merchants listed in the city directory would be heavily weighted towards the larger and more prestigious merchants. Unlike the importers and wholesalers, the small shopkeepers (peddlers and traders) were not included in the city directories in proportion to their number in the merchant occupations. For example, when the merchants were categorized into three classifications: petty shopkeepers, general merchant and importer-wholesalers, the distribution of my merchant sample was definitely biased in favor of the general merchants and importer-wholesalers.

From a random sample of the general male population of the city, it was discovered that of those who gave their occupation as "merchant," 70 percent of the ones whose occupation could be verified in the city directory were, in fact, petty shopkeepers. Yet only 20 percent of my merchant sample were petty shopkeepers. Similar biases existed in the general merchant and importer-wholesaler categories. The bias of the merchant sample, therefore, prevented me from making certain generalizations, particularly with regard to occupational mobility, about *all* first generation San Francisco merchants. Mobility rates were computed for each merchant category (petty, general, and importer-wholesaler) but not for all merchants based on the combined sample.

Persistence

Persistence rates were calculated on the basis of whether or not an individual was listed in the city directories of San Francisco for 1852-54, 1860-61, 1870-71 and 1880-81. If someone could not be located, for example, in the 1860-61 directory, it was assumed he had departed the city or died. However, if that person was located in the city directory for 1870-71 (but not 1860), it was assumed that he persisted in the city from 1852 to 1870. Individuals living outside the city (Oakland, Sausalito, or other nearby places) but working in San Francisco were counted as persisters.

There was, of course, the bias of early city directories to exclude men of low status, particularly blue-collar workers; the city directories became more inclusive with time so that by 1880 most blue-collar workers were included. The early bias, however, affected to some degree the persistence rates of the general sample but had little effect upon the merchant sample. If a merchant was included in the directory of 1852 or 1854 (all were, since this was a criterion of the merchant sample) and if the individual worked or resided in San Francisco in 1860, 1870, or 1880, there was an excellent chance he would be included in the directory for those years.

Property and Credit

The property data for chapter 4 and chapter 7 were gathered from the credit reports in the Dun and Bradstreet Collection, in the Baker Library, Harvard Business School, Cambridge, Massachusetts. The company was earlier called R. G. Dun and Company and is referred to by that name throughout the book. The collection consists of approximately 2,500 volumes of confidential credit reports on over 3 million people from the mid-1840s to approximately 1890. The volumes are indexed by county and city and, where there are foreign reports, by country. The indexes are, however, not always complete. Boston, for example, is incomplete for the 1840s and 1850s and, unfortunately, the New York City index was lost in the transfer from Dun and Bradstreet to Harvard. A new index for New York is now being assembled at Baker Library.

A brief history of Dun and Bradstreet and a description of the credit reports may give some idea of the richness of the collection and its value to economic and social historians. The Mercantile Agency (later R. G. Dun and Company), the forerunner of Dun and Bradstreet, was founded in 1841 by Lewis Tappan, a New York City merchant. He, as well as other merchants during and immediately following the Panic of 1837, found that considerable sums owed to them by debt-ridden city merchants could not be repaid. To prevent the recurrence of extending credit to merchants whose assets were generally unknown, Tappan founded the Mercantile Agency for the purpose of investigating individual merchant credit. The reports were then passed on in written form or, as was the more common practice in the earlier years of the agency, verbally to those merchants subscribing to the agency. The agency appealed "to every solvent and upright merchant in the community."

Information on individuals was gathered from "attorneys, cashiers of banks, old merchants and other competent persons." The agency advertised that the greatest care was taken "to have agents of intelligence, good judgement, extensive information and integrity" and assured its customers that the information was "imparted to the subscribers confidentially so as not to injure anyone."[1]

Initially the agency reported only on New York City merchants, but almost immediately after its founding Tappan recognized the need (and demand) to investigate merchants outside New York with whom most Gotham merchants had commercial contacts. By 1850 the agency's network of correspondents and agents were reporting back to New York on "merchants, blacksmiths, wagon-makers, brokers, millers, grocers, bankers, printers and manufacturers" in every major city in the country (states and territories) who "under any circumstances would ask for credit away from home.'' The agents were asked to report:

(1) Length of time in business, (2) Amount of own capital in business, (3) Amount of net worth after deducting all liabilities of every nature, (4) of what is estimated wealth composed? (viz: real estate less incumbrances, capital in business, personal property, which includes bonds and mortgages, stocks, notes, etc., etc.), (5) Character? very good, good, medium, poor, (7) Business qualifications? very good, good, medium, poor, (8) Prospects of success. good, fair, medium, poor, (9) Succeeded whom? if any person of firm, state whom; (10) Give individual names of partners, with age. [2]

The reports in the 1840s were brief and stated in only general terms the assets and credit of a partnership or individual, as, for example, ''doing a fair retail trade in tobacco; good for moderate amounts.'' By midcentury the reports were more thorough, particularly on merchants in the larger cities, and when possible the individual accounts followed the list of instructions. In smaller towns and cities or in new communities, such as San Francisco, the reports were sparse on actual property data but did give some indication of credit standing. As San Francisco grew both in terms of numbers and commercial importance, the individual credit reports became more thorough and the percentage of individuals included in the R. G. Dun reports increased over time.

A definite bias existed as to who was included and who was excluded by Dun & Company. The men who were commercially active in a community, be they merchants, manufacturers, brokers, bankers, or large farmers—depending upon the economic environment in which they worked—were more heavily represented in the credit reports than persons with limited capital resources transacting a small volume of business. For example, where 23 percent of the 1850 merchant sample were importer-wholesalers, over one-third of the sample located in Dun's San Francisco volumes were employed in importer-wholesaler occupations. Similarly, only 5 percent of the petty shopkeepers from the sample were reported by the credit company yet they composed one-fifth of my 1852 merchant sample.

The company agents, who identified themselves in individual reports by a code number, sent their credit reports back to New York where the ledgers were maintained. The company constantly updated their individual reports so that, for example, a merchant who worked in San Francisco between 1850 and 1880 might have ten or more entries in the credit ledgers during the span of his occupational career. The agents investigated the promptness with which a merchant paid his bills, his outstanding debts, and ''accounts receivable.'' If allowed to do so, the agent might also study the account books of the merchant firm for an estimate of assets, the annual dollar volume of business, and a profit and loss accounting. Sometimes the partnership agreements were read to note capital participation and liability arrangements. There might have been a notation of where a particular merchant had previously engaged in business (with volume and page number to another R. G. Dun & Co. city ledger book), the success or lack thereof in a former business, the marital status and ethnicity of the individual. If the agent estimated the net worth of the individual, he stated the basis for determining the dollar figure.

Although the credit reports are not totally accurate, they were thought to be more accurate than the personal and real property figures which were reported in the 1860 and 1870 Federal Census. The census marshalls expended little effort, since they not were so required, to make a detailed investigation of personal and real property. In addition, it was common knowledge that when asked the amount of their property by a tax assessor or census taker the respondents pleaded poverty or undervalued their assets anywhere from 30 to 100 percent.[3] One San Francisco resident explained her family's fear and suspicion of the investigating tax assessors of San Francisco.

What the Assyrian had been to the Babylonians, and the Persians to the Assyrians, what the Huns had been to Rome, and the Indians to the American colonists, the assessors were to us . . . From house to house they went, extracting data after battles with the tenants. Sometimes they were fine men . . . But they were more likely to be mean fellows, unyielding to persuasion . . . the mission of the assessor was to uncover, to seize, to consume. I felt that no secret was secure from his eagle eye. He could see through matresses and closet doors. When he appeared, standards were reversed; pride or ownership shrank into fear of detection. He poised a pencil and fate hung trembling with admission . . . the questions he asked about purchases and prices were those gentlemen never asked. His coming was catastrophic . . . Furs, velvet coats, feather neckpieces, were gathered from closets and rushed to old canvas-covered trunks. The diamond rings vanished from mother's fingers to hallowed places beneath her bodice . . . We dismantled as the locust eats. In a few minutes everything that made for opulence had been removed, and the rooms were reduced, as far as possible, to a semblance of shabbiness and poverty.
"Any jewelry, diamonds?"
"Diamonds?" mother laughed heartily, "One is lucky to have shoes this year."[4]

Such was the reaction to the tax assessor, and to a similar degree, the census marshall. But the Dun and Company agent's job was made easier because persons who sought credit were more likely to admit the extent of their assets to a credit investigator than to a tax assessor. True, the values were in certain instances inflated, but the credit agent did have at his disposal methods of verifying personal assets. And when possible, these methods were scrupulously followed. The reputation of the company depended upon the accuracy of their estimates of personal wealth and hence credit. So while the Dun and Company estimates of personal wealth may have been inflated and the census estimates undervalued, on balance it seemed that the former estimates reflected more accurately the true assets of an individual.[5] The census concerned itself primarily with counting people; R. G. Dun and Company earned its high reputation by estimating wealth.

The relationship between occupation and property is suggested by table A.1, compiled from the data in the R. G. Dun credit ledgers. The inclusion rate in the credit reports of the three merchant occupational groups confirmed the rank-ordering of the occupational groups by property. R. G. Dun and Company biased their coverage toward the more affluent. The percent of importer-wholesalers always exceeded the percent of either the petty or general merchants included in the reports, despite the fact that the latter two groups were more numerous in the total merchant population of the city.

To verify the rank-ordering of the merchant occupations by property, I utilized a substitute variable for capital assets—servants in the household. Whereas 5 percent of the importer-wholesalers and 3 percent of the general merchants and live-in servants in 1852, no petty shopkeeper from the sample was discovered to have the luxury of a live-in servant.

Table. A.1. Occupation ranking by mean property of San Francisco merchants, 1850-1880[a] (in thousands of dollars).

Sample group	1850	1860	1870	1880
Petty merchants	inc. data	3.8	4.9	8.5
General merchants	23.5	17.5	25.5	31.5
Importer-wholesalers	33.5	25.5	56.2	41.2
(N)	(64)	(97)	(144)	(147)

a. The 1850 and 1860 data are for individuals in the 1852 merchant sample, and the 1870 and 1880 data are for those in the 1880 sample. Individuals in each sample were traced in the R. G. Dun & Co. credit reports.

APPENDIX B
Occupational Classifications

Listed below are the occupational classifications used throughout this study:

I. High White Collar. *Professionals:* apothecary/pharmacist; architect; artist; dentist; doctor/physician; engineer; editor; lawyer; minister; scientist; ship's captain; surveyor; teacher; writer/author; *Major Proprietors, Managers and Officials* (nonmerchants): banker (to include cashier); broker; capitalist; company executive; gentleman; government official (tax collector, customs inspector, county clerk, sheriff); manager (branch manager, union official); manufacturer; real estate broker; stock/money broker; *Major Proprietors, Managers and Officials* (merchants): commission merchant; importer; jobber; manufacturer/merchant; merchandise broker; retired merchant; shipping merchant; wholesaler; wholesaler/retailer; *General Merchant* (retailer): books; stationery; bricks; lime cement; clothing; crockery, glass, stoneware; dry goods; fancy goods; feed; grains; fuel (oil, coal, wood); furniture, furnishings; general merchandise; hardware; hides, leather; lumber; merchant agent; merchant (unspecified); metals (iron, copper, tin); paints and oils; produce; provisions; saddlery-harness; ship chandler; stock (beef, chickens, horses); storage; sugar; tea, coffe; wines and liquors; wool, cotton.

II. Low White Collar. *Clerks and Salesmen:* agent (insurance, real estate, purchase); auctioneer/appraiser; bookkeeper/accountant; buyer; city, county or federal employee; clerk; collector; dispatcher; letter or mail carrier; office worker; salesman; telephone/telegraph operator; teller; transportation conductor; *Petty Proprietors, Managers and Officials* (nonmerchants): bar/saloon keeper; boarding house owner; conductor; station master; contractor/builder; farmer; miner; florist; foreman/supervisor/overseer; huckster; restaurant keeper; *Petty Proprietors, Managers and Officials* (merchants): boots and shoes; cigars and tobacco; confectioner; dealer (unspecified); fish; fruit/vegetable; grocer; hats and caps; junk/rags; market; peddler; trader; variety store; wines and liquor (saloon).

III. Skilled, Semiskilled and Service, Blue-Collar. Apprentice; baker; barber; bartender; blacksmith; boatman; boilermaker; bookbinder; bricklayer; butcher; cabinet/furniture maker; carman/coachman; longshoreman; lumber worker (mill worker); machine operator; machinist; mariner; mason; mechanic; metal worker (smelter, melter, caster, moulder); milkman; miller-wright: other skilled worker (artisan, sailmaker, etc.); carpenter, joiner;

chemical worker; cigar maker; construction worker; cook; cooper; drayman; engraver; expressman; factory worker; farm hand; gardener; milker; fireman; fisherman; food processor (sugar, grains, coffee, wine); glass-bottle worker; hatter and milliner; janitor; jeweller (goldsmith, silversmith); launderer; leather goods maker (and repair); waiter; warehouseman; watch/clock maker; packer; painter/varnisher; paper hanger; paper maker; plasterer; policeman; printer/pressman; railroad worker; seaman/sailor; service worker, other (bellboy, doorman, etc.); servant; steelmetal worker; shipwright; shoemaker (and repair); tailor; teamster; textile worker (spinner, weaver, knitter, etc.); toolmaker; truckman; upholsterer; watchman; wharfinger.

IV. Low Manual (Nonskilled) Blue-Collar. Boatman; laborer; gardener; porter; hostler; lumberman.

Excluded from the merchant categories (and also from the samples) were those who, though they traded in a specific item, were either quasi-professionals (traders in drugs and medicines, optical equipment), or skilled artisans (jewellers, merchant tailors, cabinetware). Also excluded were pawnbrokers and hucksters. Though they too traded in specific commodities, the hucksters and pawnbrokers, unlike the peddlers, were not considered by their contemporaries to be merchants. A strong case could, however, be made for their inclusion. But with the inclusion of peddlers in the sample, it was felt that the lower staus merchant occupations were fully represented.

NOTES

Abbreviations:
Bancroft Library, University of California, Berkeley (BL, UC)
California Historical Society, San Francisco (CHS)
California State Library, Sacramento (CSL)
New York Public Library, New York (NYPL)
R. G. Dun & Co. (RGD)

1. The Westward Migration

1. Warren S. Tryon, *A Mirror for Americans* (Chicago, 1952), III, 680. See also Samuel E. Morison, *Maritime History of Massachusetts, 1783-1860* (Boston, 1941). For the hide and tallow trade see William Heath Davis, *Seventy-Five Years in California* (San Francisco, 1967). See also Adele Ogden, "Boston Hide Droughers along California Shores," *CHS Quarterly,* vol. VIII, no. 4 (1929), 289-305.

2. Richard Henry Dana, *Two Years before the Mast* (New York, 1940), p. 243.

3. Quotes from John P. Young, *San Francisco: A History of the Pacific Coast Metropolis,* 2 vols. (San Francisco, 1912), I, 38-39.

4. Thomas Larkin to Moses Yale Beach, May 28, 1848, in George P. Hammond, ed., *The Larkin Papers,* 10 vols. (Berkeley, Calif., 1951-1964), IV, 201.

5. Thomas Larkin, "Description of California," April 20, 1846, in *Larkin Papers,* IV. Interested observers of the California coast should also read the published accounts of John C. Fremont.

6. Frank Soule, John H. Gihon, and James Nisbet, *The Annals of San Francisco* (New York, 1856), p. 178; Young, *San Francisco,* I, 114; and W. B. Osborn, "Narrative", ms. (BL, UC).

7. Rachel and Sherman Thorndike, eds., *The Memoirs of William T. Sherman* (New York: Scribner & Sons, 1894), pp. 83-84. A contemporary on the scene in the early 1850s said Yerba Buena changed its name to San Francisco because "the local name of Yerba Buena . . . is unknown beyond the district." It was changed, the observer said, "to prevent confusion and mistakes in public documents, and that the town may have the advantage of the name given on the public maps." Frank M. Smith, ed., *San Francisco Vigilance Committee of 1856 . . . Sketches of Events Succeeding 1846* (San Francisco, 1883), p. 5.

8. Polk's Presidential Message of December 6, 1848, *New York Tribune,* December 8, 1848. Accompanying the message was Colonel R. B. Mason's documentation of the high quality of the gold discoveries. A day later in the

Tribune appeared two letters from Thomas Larkin to Secretary of State Buchanan reporting the extensive gold discoveries and the "unusual purity" of the gold.

9. *New York Tribune,* April 5, 1849.

10. Letter printed in the *New York Tribune* (n.d.) and pasted in the travel diary of Dr. I. G. Shaw, "Miscellaneous Scrapbooks," ms. (CSL). See also Francis E. Pinto "Diary," ms. (NYPL). The Missouri letters are included in Wyman Walker's *California Emigrant Letters* (n.d.), pp. 25, 77.

11. *New York Tribune,* April 5, 1849. Many of the diaries kept by the gold rush adventurers have pasted in them newspaper clippings describing the mines, and the best land and sea routes from the eastern states to California.

12. Letter, June 11, 1848, in "Mellus & Howard Correspondence and Papers," ms. (BL, UC).

13. See S. Griffiths Morgan to T. L. Hathaway, October 1850; Morgan to his uncle, Charles W. Morgan, October 31, 1850; and Morgan to Richard Paxton, Jr., November 1850. Charles W. Morgan, "Business Records," ms. (Baker Library, Harvard University), vol. 15; also Henry Hunter Peters, July 12, 1852, to his brother H. H. Peters, "Correspondence and Papers," ms. (NYPL).

14. Dr. I. G. Shaw folder, "Miscellaneous Scrapbooks," ms. (CSL), George S. Hellman, "The Story of the Seligmans," ms., n.d. (New York Historical Society), p. 40; Alfred L. Tubbs, "Dictation," ms. (BL, UC), p. 5; Levi Strauss' tent canvas would soon be cast into the first pair of "Levis."

15. Rudolf Glanz, "The Immigration of German Jews up to 1880," *Yivo Annual of Jewish Social Science,* II and III (1947-1948), 81-99.

16. Fred L. Strodtbeck, "Jewish and Italian Immigration and Subsequent Status Mobility," in David McClelland et al., *Talent and Society* (Princeton, N. J. 1960), pp. 259-268; see also "Diaries" in the Bancroft and California state libraries which have posted articles from German newspapers.

17. Reported in *Merchants Magazine and Commercial Review,* 23 (September 1850), 698.

18. Hubert H. Bancroft stated that the cost of passage alone tended to filter out the poor. See Bancroft, *History of California,* 7 vols. (San Francisco, 1884-1890), VI, 120, 123, 124; Samuel E. Morison, *Maritime History of Massachusetts* (Boston, Mass., 1941), p. 332; James Truslow Adams, *Memorials of Old Bridgehampton* (Port Washington, N.Y., 1962), chapter 13.

19. John H. Cornelison "Diary," ms. (NYPL); see also "Stock Notices," *New York Tribune,* December 9, 1848.

20. Caleb Fay, "Statement," ms. (BL, UC); from an advertisement in the *New York Tribune,* December 13, 1848: "A young man, with the best of references, wants to mortgage real estate in the country worth $1,000, for money enough to pay his passage to California. He would like to join a company of young men."

21. *New York Tribune,* December 19, 1848.

22. See A. G. Benson's "Supercargo Agreement" with Robert A. Parker, ms. (BL, UC).

23. Selecting from the 1852 merchant sample (N = 643) all those individuals who in the California state census listed their "prior residence" as New York, they were searched in the 1847-48 New York City *Doggett's Directory, Merchants Business Directory,* and *Mercantile Register.* Seventy-one individuals with their business or residence addresses were located. The New York City tax records were then searched, utilizing the addresses noted, for the assessed valuation. Estimating wealth from tax assessments inherently involves a number of pitfalls, chiefly the undervaluation of property. More extensive use of the tax records led one scholar to believe that the real estate valuations were undervalued by "considerably more than half" and that personal property, "regarded by tax authorities and insiders as typically equal in value to real," was almost "totally masked." Tax officials "bemoaned the practice of great merchants, men known to be owners of vast real-estate holdings and substantial shareholders in banks and insurance companies, coolly to swear that they possessed no personal wealth whatsoever." See Edward Pessen, "The Egalitarian Myth," *American Historical Review,* 76.4 (October 1971): 995-997. The lack of capital of the San Francisco merchant sample may also be accounted for by their relatively young (28) age (average).

24. S. R. Throckmorton to Peter Roach, in New York, August 10, 1852. Throckmorton, "Letters" ms. (BL, UC).

25. To learn of the capital resources of San Francisco's first generation of merchants, I searched members of the 1852 merchant sample in the earliest San Francisco R. G. Dun & Co. volume, "California," vol. A. Frequently at the beginning of the narrative account there would appear a cross reference (volume and page number) to another city, indicating a business connection prior to arrival in San Francisco. For example, on page 71 of "California," vol. A, the narrative credit report of William T. Coleman (a dry goods and commission merchant who came to California in the early 1850s and married the daughter of one of San Francisco's earliest and most successful bankers, D. D. Page) notes: "whose assistance enabled Coleman to make a Fortune." At the beginning of the narrative there is a notation "N. Y. Vol 7/992," indicating an entry in the New York City ledger, vol. 7, p. 992, which indicates an earlier entry on page 300 of the same volume. It was possible to determine that Coleman, prior to arrival in San Francisco, had been a commission merchant in New York and St. Louis, with little capital of his own. The RGD reports were also useful in establishing former occupations of other San Francisco merchants. For further discussion of RGD materials, see Methodological Notes in Appendix A.

26. Bernard Bailyn, *The New England Merchants in the Seventeenth Century* (Gloucester, Mass., 1955), pp. 34-35. See in the Alsop & Co., "Correspondence and Papers," ms. (BL, UC), the power of attorney agreement between Alsop & Co. of San Francisco and the New York City firm of Duncan, Sherman & Co.; see also Samuel R. Throckmorton, "Letters," ms. (BL, UC).

27. J. F. Marshall of the Graeffenburg Co. of New York City to Alfred Robinson. See Alfred Robinson, "Papers and Correspondence," ms. (BL, UC), folder 3.

28. Philip T. Southworth to his brother A. B. Southworth, October 27, 1850, in Philip T. Southworth, "Papers," ms. (CSL).

29. There were of course some Jewish merchants with lines of credit. R. G. Dun & Co. reported that the Seligman brothers in New York used credit extensively, paid off promptly all debts and were considered in New York City as "one of the best houses among the Hebrews." RGD, "New York," vol. 198, p. 137. See also RGD, "New York," vol. 320, p. 583.

30. *New York Tribune,* December 13, 1848; John Taylor, "Statement," ms. (BL, UC). The cigars were later sold in San Francisco for $15 and $45 per thousand.

31. *New York Tribune,* January 1, 1849.

32. Jesse and Leopold Seligman, who took the S.S. *Northerner* from Panama City to San Francisco in 1849, witnessed the death of half of their 16 fellow passengers from the Panama Fever. Leopold himself contracted the fever and as he lay stricken below decks, Jesse watched above as they buried the dead passengers at sea. Hellman, "Story of the Seligmans."

33. Robert G. Albion, *The Rise of New York Port, 1815-1860* (New York, 1967), p. 356. One vessel, the *Water Witch* out of Boston, encountered a three-month delay in Rio—one month to unload the cargo and two months for repairs and the bureaucratic red tape of the Brazilian authorities. See also Mary S. D. Smith, "Letters," ms. (CHS).

34. Albert Bee, "Diary" ms. (CHS).

35. Francis Cassin, *"Dictation and Statement,"* ms. (BL, UC), p. 3-4.

36. W. W. Call, "Recollections," ms. (BL, UC).

37. Albion, *The Rise of New York Port,* pp. 354-357. See also *The Merchants Magazine and Commercial Review,* vol. 22, p. 208. Over 60 percent of the ship clearances for San Francisco departed from the six ports of New York, Boston, New Bedford, Baltimore, Philadelphia, and Salem, Mass. The freight rates on the clippers ($60 per ton) were more than double the $25 per ton rate charged by the larger, but slower, packets. See J. G. B. Hutchins, *American Maritime Industry and Public Policy, 1789-1914* (Cambridge, Mass., 1941), p. 317.

38. In the 1852 California state census the census enumerator asked the individual the state, territory, or country of "prior residence." Percentages are based on the merchant sample of 1852 (N = 643) and the general sample of the male working population of San Franciso in 1852 (N = 669). In addition to a possible sampling error, some respondents no doubt gave as their prior residence the port of embarkation where, if they resided at all, it was for a month or so while awaiting transportation to California. In any event, there is no doubt a 5 percent error in the calculations. *New England:* Me., N. H., Vt., R.I., Conn.; *Mid-Atlantic:* N. Y., N. J., Pa., Del., Md., D. C.; *South:* N. C., S. C., Va., Ky., Tenn., Ga., Fla., Ala., Miss.; *Old Northwest:* Ohio, Ill., Ind., Mich., Wisc.; *New West:* Minn., Iowa, Neb., Mo., Ark., La., Texas, Kan., Mont., Nev., Utah, N. M., Colo., Idaho, Wash., Ore., Calif.

39. The difficulty of distinguishing between an urban or rural prior residence is caused by the fact that only the state of the prior residence is given on

the census schedule. However, in a number of cases a city would be designated, though with no apparent consistency. Sample members were selected who gave as their former residence New York, Massachusetts, Pennsylvania, Maryland, Ohio, Missouri and Louisiana. Those who were over 18 years of age in 1847-48 were searched in the New York City, Boston, Philadelphia, Baltimore, Cincinnati, St. Louis, and New Orleans city directories. Thirty percent of the subsample in these seven cities were located. Many more may have resided in these cities, but for one reason or another were not included in the directories. Had the search continued through other city directories in those seven states, no doubt a higher percentage would have been located. A conservative estimate is that 50 to 60 percent of the merchants formerly resided in cities larger than 10,000.

40. Native-born, foreign-born percentage distributions in 1850:

Place	Native-Born	Foreign-Born
U.S.	89 percent	11 percent
N.Y.	79	21
California	76	24
La.	74	26
Wisc.	64	36
S. F. 1852	47	53

New Orleans, with 56 percent foreign-born, was similar to San Francisco.

41. See Clyde Griffen, "Workers Divided: The Effect of Craft and Ethnic Differences in Poughkeepsie, New York, 1850-1880," and Stuart Blumin, "Mobility and Change in Ante-Bellum Philadelphia," in Stephan Thernstrom and Richard Sennett, eds., *Nineteenth-Century Cities: Essays in the New Urban History* (New Haven, 1969). Both authors demonstrate that the native-born were generally more occupationally mobile than the foreign-born. Given the fact that the more mobile native-born also accumulated more capital than the foreign-born, it would therefore follow that the native-born could more readily afford the expense of moving to San Francisco.

42. Doris M. Wright, "The Making of Cosmopolitan California: An Analysis of Immigration, 1848-1870," *CHS Quarterly,* XIX (December 1940), 341.

43. Randolph Barnes to Dr. Julius S. Barnes, June 25, 1849, item VFM 117 (Mystic Seaport Marine Historical Association Museum). See also C. L. Ross, "Dictation," ms. (BL, UC).

44. The "central place" theory is discussed in Beverly Duncan and Stanley Lieberson, *Metropolis and Region* (Beverly Hills, Calif., 1970), chap. 3. An early visitor to San Francisco reported, "the city supports the country, instead of the country nurturing and sustaining the city; and this will continue . . . so long as the country is under the necessity of importing whatever she requires to use." Hinton R. Helper, *The Land of Gold* (Baltimore, 1855), pp. 44-45.

45. From a trace of the San Francisco census in 1852, approximately 3,100

individuals gave as their occupation Merchant, or a similar designation. Of the total population of San Francisco in 1852 (34,776), 8 percent were children under the age of 16, and 7 percent were estimated to be nonworking women. Subtracting the children and nonworking women from the total population gives a total work force of 29,560. Based on the type of merchant covered in this study, approximately 3.5 percent of the occupational structure of the United States were engaged in similar merchant occupations. The only state with a higher proportion of merchants per capita than California in 1850 was Louisiana. My estimates are based on occupational distribution figures in J. D. B. DeBow, *Statistical View of the United States . . . Seventh Census* (Washington, D.C., 1852); quote is by James E. Vance, Jr., *Geography and Urban Evolution in the San Francisco Bay Area* (Berkeley, Calif., 1964), pp. 9-10.

46. The concept of the "metropolitan economy" is developed by Norman S. B. Gras, *An Introduction to Economic History* (New York, 1922) and discussed by Julius Rubin in his essay, "Urban Growth and Regional Development," in David T. Gilchrist, ed., *The Growth of the Seaport Cities, 1790-1825* (Charlottesville, Va., 1967), pp. 3-21. Rubin states that the central concept of the "metropolitan economy" is that of "metropolitan dominance, in which the metropolis is the center of the trade and transportation of the region and the provider of a host of specialized goods and services of the region."

47. *Alta California,* May 24, 1850.

2. The 1850s

1. Estimates from Doris M. Wright, "The Making of Cosmopolitan California: An Analysis of Immigration, 1848-1870," *CHS Quarterly,* XIX (December 1940), 323-343.

2. Exports, 1860, in millions of dollars: New York, $117; New Orleans, $101; Charleston, $28; Boston, $18; Mobile, $17; San Francisco, $15.

3. The merchants performed a similar role in the eastern states. See Allan Pred, "Manufacturing, 1800-1840," *Annals of the Association of American Geographers,* 56 (June 1966) 307-338; Caspar T. Hopkins, "The California Recollections of Caspar T. Hopkins," *CHS Quarterly,* XXVI, 63.

4. In 1850 31 percent of the United States population was between the ages of 20 and 40. *Seventh U. S. Census* (Washington, D. C., 1852).

5. Franklin A. Buck, *A Yankee Trader in the Gold Rush* (Cambridge, Mass., 1930), pp. 46-47.

6. Soule, *Annals,* pp. 52-54, 499; Alfred Robinson, "Letterbook," ms. (CHS). "There is a man here," wrote the Dupont Gunpowder Co. agent in San Francisco in 1850, "who takes the dirty clothes, makes you out a bill of lading for them, insures them, sends them there [to the Sandwich Islands], brings them back for about two or three dolls. per doz: about half of what it can be done for here." Letter of Robert L. Lammot to his brother Dan, January 13, 1850. Lammot, "Family Letters," ms. (BL, UC).

7. Soule, *Annals,* p. 213. The wage rates in California were the highest in the nation in 1850. For example, a laborer received a daily wage of $5.00 in California, 90 cents in New York, and $1.38 in Massachusetts. A carpenter received $7.60, $1.09, and $1.45 respectively. See J. D. B. Debow, *Statistical View of the United States: A Compendium of the Seventh Census (1850)* (Washington, D.C., 1852).

8. H. Bancroft, *History of California,* vol. 7, pp. 106-107, 111.

9. Alex Mayer to his uncle, Lazarus Mayer, November or December 1850, in Albert H. Freidenberg, "Letters of a California Pioneer," *Publications of the American Jewish Historical Society,* no. 31, pp. 139-140.

10. Milton Hall to his father, April 25, 1852. Milton Hall, "Letters," ms. (BL, UC).

11. The number of overland immigrants also declined from between 40,000-50,000 in 1852 to approximately 15,000 in 1853. Estimates from D. M. Wright, "The Making of Cosmopolitan California," Appendixes C and D, pp. 341-342. San Francisco *Prices Current,* December 20, 1853, quoted in Ira Cross, *Financing of an Empire: A History of Banking in California* (San Francisco, 1927), I, 171. Tonnage figures for the port of San Francisco from Benjamin C. Wright, *San Francisco's Ocean Trade: Past and Future* (San Francisco, 1911), pp. 211-212. Wages in May 1853 from *Merchants' Magazine and Commercial Review,* 29 (1853); 131; see also Young, *History of San Francisco,* I, 246.

12. Cross, *Financing an Empire,* I, 196; also John S. Hittell, *A History of the City of San Francisco* (San Francisco, 1878), pp. 208-232.

13. Albert Dibblee, "Letters and Correspondence," ms. (BL, UC) and Frederick W. Macondray & Co., "Papers," ms. (CHS).

14. *Alta California,* February 25, 1850.

15. The San Francisco merchants planned on increased demand for goods from the miners in the winter months when they stockpiled for the summer months. Perishable goods, however, were in constant demand. See Samuel Gray, "Letters," ms. (BL, UC); also Patrice Dillon, "La Californie dans les derniers mois de 1849," trans. and ed. by A. P. Nasatir, *French Activities in California* (Stanford, Calif., 1945), p. 551; for quote see Hubert H. Bancroft, "Scraps," ms. (BL, UC), vol. 12, part 1, p. 4. (There is no date on the paper but it is included in the section with clippings from early 1850s.) See also Alexander Stott, "Letterbook," ms. (BL, UC), February 1856.

16. S. Griffith Morgan, "Papers," in Charles Morgan, "Business Records," ms. (Baker Library, Harvard Univ.) vol. 15.

17. Samuel Throckmorton to Peter R. Roach in New York City, October 1, 1850, in Throckmorton, "Letters," ms. (BL, UC).

18. Robert L. Lammot to Dan, January 13, 1850, in Lammot, "Family Letters," ms. (BL, UC). A. P. Nasatir, ed., *A French Journalist in the California Gold Rush: The Letters of Etienne Derbec* (Georgetown, Calif., 1964), pp. 207-208; see also letter of J. F. Osgood to George Strang, June 10, 1850. J. F. Osgood, "Letters," ms. (BL, UC).

19. Alfred Robinson, "Letterbook," ms. (CHS), p. 28-29.

20. Letter in the *New York Herald,* June 6, 1851, quoted by Hubert H. Bancroft, *California Inter Pocula* (San Francisco, 1880), p. 352.

21. *Alta California,* May 31, 1856; see also Caspar T. Hopkins, "The California Recollections," p. 63.

22. Robert L. Lammot to Dan, January 13, 1850, in Lammot, "Family Letters." For an example of the unlimited optimism generated by the belief in the eternal blessings of a growth economy, see Godeffroy, Sillem & Co. (San Francisco commission merchants), "Reports," in Rodman Price, "Correspondence," ms. (BL, UC).

23. San Francisco citizens, "Memorial to Congress . . . for the Establishment of a Branch Mint" (Washington, D.C., 1851), p. 4; see also *Alta California,* March 14, 1851.

24. George Hussey, "Journal Book," ms., invoice no. 1 (Baker Library, Harvard Univ.).

25. Soule, *Annals,* p. 303. See also letter of Alex Mayer to his uncle, Lazarus Mayer, in Philadelphia, dated May 1, 1851, in Freidenberg, "Letters of a California Pioneer," p. 148; Benjamin Richardson, "Diary," ms. (BL, UC).

26. Cassin, "Statement," ms. (BL, UC), pp. 13-14.

27. George E. Schenck, "Statement," ms. (BL, UC), p. 19.

28. Estimates of fire damage in San Francisco: in 1849, $1,250,000; in 1850, $10,000,000; and in 1851, $14,500,000; total, $25,750,000. See *Merchants Magazine and Commercial Review,* 31 (1854), 114; and H. H. Bancroft, *History of California,* 6, 202-209. Insurance costs in the 1850s were between 5 percent and 10 percent of assessed value. Only foreign companies offered insurance coverage for San Francisco. Because of the high rates, few merchants availed themselves of property insurance. See also Henry Schmiedell, "Statement," ms. (BL, UC).

29. Pinto, "Diary," p. 148.

30. Alex Mayer to Lazarus Mayer, June 30, 1851, in Freidenberg, "Letters of a California Pioneer," pp. 157-159.

31. Owen P. Sutton, "Statement," ms. (BL, UC), p. 10.

32. Thomas O. Larkin to Daniel C. Baker in Boston, June 29, 1850, in *Larkin Papers,* VIII, 329; see also Aaron Holmes, "Letters," ms. (BL, UC); and Hellman, "Story of the Seligmans."

33. Letter dated May 12, 1851. Typed copy of letter from collection of S. Knapp of New York City in Macondray & Co., "Papers," ms. (CHS).

34. Roger Lotchin, *San Francisco, 1846-1856: From Hamlet to City* (New York, 1974). Lotchin believes the numerous fires forced San Franciscans, who thought of the city as only a temporary residence, to build more substantial structures. This increased capital investment committed the original generation of San Franciscans to a more permanent residence in the city.

35. One New Yorker best summed up the reason for the absence of small coins in San Francisco: "at home we should think more of two cents than a bit here, which is twelve and a half cents—a New York shilling—some call it,

others, a shilling. There's no smaller coin used than a bit. Ten cents is a bit, also if you pay within two bits of what they ask you, it's all the same, either two bits over or two less . . ." Mary Smith, "Letters," ms. (CHS), p. 80; see also J. F. Osgood, "Letters," ms. (BL, UC); see letter of June 10, 1850, from Osgood to George Strang.

36. See Hubert H. Bancroft, "Biographical Sketch of William Coleman," ms., folder 1, (BL, UC), p. 48.

37. William T. Sherman, *Memoirs of William T. Sherman,* 2 vols. (New York, 1875), 1, 101, and his *"Home Letters"* (New York, 1909), p. 146. In 1850 Albert Dibblee, a successful San Francisco commission merchant, was offered a $25,000 loan from James Lee & Co. of New York. Dibblee wrote back to New York to say that credit, if he needed it, was available in San Francisco. See letter of Albert Dibblee to James Lee & Co., September 15, 1850, in Albert Dibblee, "Private Letters," ms. (private collection of Arthur Mejia, Jr., San Francisco). For a thorough discussion of banking in San Francisco in the 1850s, see Dwight L. Clarke, *William T. Sherman: Gold Rush Banker* (San Francisco, 1969).

38. See Albert Dibblee's "Biography," ms. (CHS); see also Albion, *Rise of New York Port,* p. 229. The stated function of the San Francisco Chamber of Commerce was to "promote integrity and good faith, just and equitable principles of business; discover and correct abuses; establish and maintain uniformity in commercial usages; acquire, preserve and disseminate valuable business statistics and information, prevent or adjust controversies and misunderstandings; and generally to foster, protect and advance the commercial, mercantile and manufacturing interests of the city." *By-Laws and Rules of the Chamber of Commerce of San Francisco* (San Francisco, 1857), pp. 11-19. See also Bradford F. Luchingham, "Associational Life on the Urban Frontier; San Francisco, 1848-1856," (PhD. diss., University of California, Davis, 1968), chap. 4; *Alta California,* September 9, 1849, and Samuel Colville, *San Francisco Directory* (1856). For commission rates, see *Merchants Magazine and Commercial Review,* 24, 631-632.

39. "Memorial to Congress from the San Francisco Chamber of Commerce," dated February 5, 1856, in San Francisco Chamber of Commerce, "Papers," ms. (CHS).

40. Helper, *Land of Gold,* p. 58.

41. See J. H. Meussdorffer & Sons, "Papers," ms. (Society of California Pioneers, San Francisco); Charles W. Morgan, "Business Records," S. G. Morgan file; and Alfred Robinson, "Papers and Correspondence," ms. (CHS).

42. Lammot, "Family Letters," ms. (BL, UC); Hellman, "The Story of the Seligmans," and letters of Alex Mayer to his uncle Lazarus Mayer, March 2, 1851, and March 31, 1851, in A. M. Freidenberg, "Letters of A California Pioneer," pp. 142-144.

43. For examples of advisory letters from San Francisco merchants to colleagues in the East see letter from Alfred Robinson (San Francisco) to Peter

Roach (New York) of 1852, in Alfred Robinson, "Letters," ms. (BL, UC); Albert Dibblee, "Collection," ms. (BL, UC); William H. Davis, "Collection," ms. (CSL); F. W. Macondray, "Papers," ms. (CHS); W. D. M. Howard, "Papers," ms. (CHS); White and Burr, "Papers," ms. (Baker Library, Harvard Univ.); Elihu Spicer, "Papers," ms. (Mystic Seaport Marine Historical Assoc.).

44. Faxton D. Atherton, "Papers," ms. (CHS); see also letter from Henry H. Peters to his brother, June 30, 1852, in Henry Peters, "Correspondence and Papers," ms. (NYPL). See also letter of S. Griffith Morgan to William F. Bryant, November 1, 1853, and to R. Rodman, January 14, 1854, in Charles Morgan, "Business Records," vol. 20.

45. James Neall, "Dictation," ms. (BL, UC). Rodman Price, "Correspondence and Papers," ms. (BL, UC). Cross, *Financing an Empire,* I: 38-39, 41, 74-76.

46. James E. Vance, Jr., *Geography and Urban Evolution in the San Francisco Bay Region* (Berkeley, 1964), p. 15; see also William H. Davis, "Papers," ms. (CSL); Albert Dibblee, "Collection"; William M. Howard, "Papers"; and Gertrude H. Whitwell, "W. D. M. Howard," *CHS Quarterly,* XXVII, 105-113, 319-332.

47. William T. Coleman, "Statement," ms. (BL, UC), p. 43. This specialization process also occurred among the eastern merchant class but over a period of approximately 45 years as opposed to only 10 years in San Francisco. The general trend across the nation served to cement "the merchant's role as coordinators, movers and shakers of the American economy." For a discussion on this point see Glen Porter and Harold Livesay, *Merchants and Manufacturers* (Baltimore, 1971), chap. 2.

48. *Merchants Magazine and Commercial Review,* 24 (1851), 23.

49. Letter dated August 23, 1849. J. K. Osgood, "Letters," *Alta California,* January 22 and 26, 1854.

50. J. H. Clay Mudd to Secretary of the Treasury Thomas Corwin, February 13, 1851; see also U. S. Customs Collector F. Butler King to Secretary Corwin, July 14, 1852, U. S. National Archives, "Correspondence," ms. (microfilm copy in BL, UC).

51. William T. Coleman, "Statement," folder C-D.

52. James R. Garniss, "Statement," ms. (BL, UC), pp. 10, 24-25. Francis Cassin, "Statement," ms. (BL, UC), p. 17.

53. Quote from William T. Coleman, "Statement"; see also John C. Hewlett, "Dictation" in "California Miscellaneous, 1883," ms. (BL, UC).

54. Howard C. Gardner, *In Pursuit of the Golden Dream,* p. 115.

55. Caleb Fay, "Statement," ms. (BL, UC); J. O. Earll, "Statement," ms. (BL, UC). Charles Wooley, "Letterbook," ms. (CHS), pp. 7-8.

56. Pinto, "Diary," pp. 161-162.

57. James Hunnewell (Boston) to William H. Davis (San Francisco), June 11, 1850; see also Hunnewell to Davis, November 25, 1850, in W. H. Davis, "Papers."

58. Dana quote from Oscar Lewis, *This Was San Francisco* (New York, 1962), pp. 155-156.

59. Hubert H. Bancroft, *Chronicles of the Builders of the Commonwealth,* 7 vols. (San Francisco, 1891-92), 6: 521; quote from William Sherman, letter of June 30, 1853, in *Home Letters,* p. 135; see also Caspar Hopkins, "The California Recollections of Caspar T. Hopkins," p. 63.

3. Occupational Mobility

1. Quote is from S. M. Lipset and H. L. Zetterberg, "A Theory of Social Mobility," in Stuart Blumin's article, "The Historical Study of Vertical Mobility," *Historical Methods Newsletter,* I (1968), 1-13. Stephan Thernstrom says that "occupation may be only one variable in a comprehensive theory of class, but it is the variable which includes more, which sets more limits on the other variables than any other criterion of status." Thernstrom, *Poverty and Progress: Social Mobility in a Nineteenth Century City* (Cambridge, Mass., 1964), p. 84.

2. Michael Katz, "Occupational Classification in History," *Journal of Interdisciplinary History*, III (Summer 1972), 63-64. See also last section of Thernstrom's "Notes on the Historical Study of Social Mobility," *Comparative Studies in Society and History*, 10 (January 1968).

3. Katz, "Occupational Classification," p. 63. For an incisive discussion of the problems of occupational classification, see Clyde Griffen, "Occupational Mobility in 19th Century America: Problems and Possibilities," *Journal of Social History* (Spring 1972), pp. 311-330.

4. San Francisco *Evening Bulletin,* July 29, 1862 editorial upon the death of Capt. F. W. Macondray.

5. James E. Vance, Jr., *The Merchant World* (Englewood, N. J., 1970), p. 15; *Alta California*, January 10, 1853.

6. B. E. Lloyd, *Lights and Shades in San Francisco* (San Francisco, 1876), p. 184. See also Charles Warren Stoddard, *The Footprints of the Padres* (San Francisco, 1912), p. 45.

7. The occupational classification scheme utilized for this study attempted to categorize merchant occupations on the basis of how the merchants themselves and the general population of San Francisco perceived the status and prestige of individual merchant occupations. The classifications scheme was assembled without regard to the variable of property. It turned out, however, that property was highly correlated with this occupational scale (see chap. 4).

8. Alba M. Edwards, "A Social Economic Grouping of the Gainful Works of the United States," *Journal of the American Statistical Association*, XXVII (1933), 377-387. The Edwards scale has been utilized by Stephan Thernstrom, Clyde Griffen, Stuart Blumin, Peter Knights, and others in their mobility studies. Where others have separated semiskilled and service workers from skilled workers, I have grouped them together since no intraclass (blue-collar) comparisons are made in this study. The few semiprofessionals who

appeared in my sample were grouped with professionals rather than in a separate occupational category.

9. Frank Soule, John H. Gihon, and James Nisbet, *The Annals of San Francisco* (New York, 1856), p. 246.

10. Milton Hall writing from Green Mountain Bar, in the Sierras) to his father, August 15, 1852. Milton Hall, "Letters," ms. (BL, UC); for similar reports of discouragement in the mines, see Fay Family "Papers," ms. (CSL); William McCollom, in *California As I Saw It*, Dale L. Morgan, ed. (Los Gatos, California, 1960), pp. 156-157; and Howard Gardner, in *In Pursuit of the Golden Dream: Reminiscences of San Francisco and the Northern and Southern Mines, 1849-1852*, Dale L. Morgan, ed. (Stoughton, Ma., 1970).

11. Francis E. Pinto, "Diary," ms. (NYPL).

12. Owen Sutton, "Statement," ms. (BL, UC), pp. 4-5.

13. McCollum, *California As I Saw It*, pp. 155-156; J. K. Osgood, "Letters," ms. (BL, UC). John Taylor, "Statement," ms. (BL, UC); Robert S. Lammot to his father, December 30, 1849: "Jim Eddy [formerly a retail grocer in Philadelphia] . . . went to the mines, made a little money, came here [San Francisco] and opened a retail grocery store; he is making lots of money," in Lammot, "Family Letters," ms. (BL, UC).

14. Francis Cassin, "Statement," ms. (BL, UC), p. 12.

15. From the merchant sample of 643 the "prior residence" of each person was noted. The people were then searched in the respective city directories for 1847-48 to determine their former occupations before moving to San Francisco. Twenty percent of the sample (128) were found in the following directories: New York, 50; Boston, 29; Philadelphia, 16; New Orleans, 17; Baltimore, 5; St. Louis, 5; Newburyport, 3; Louisville, 1; Charleston, S. C., 1; Providence, 1; total: 128.

Considering the bias of nineteenth-century city directories to exclude blue-collar workers from their lists, the percent of San Francisco merchants with former occupations in the blue-collar ranks is no doubt higher than 18 percent —probably somewhere between 20 and 25 percent. The numbers for each individual city were too small to allow for any valid intercity comparisons, except to say that of the New Yorkers, the foreign-born displayed a higher rate of occupational mobility in their geographical move from the blue-collar ranks of New York into merchant occupations in San Francisco—22 percent of the foreign-born were upwardly mobile, compared with 14 percent of the native-born New York residents who moved to San Francisco before 1852.

16. One scholar who has written about immigrants and the relationship between occupation and migration observed that "neither the immigrant agricultural workers nor the immigrant skilled workers followed their former occupations to a large extent after coming to the United States. The fact that many occupations show an increase of foreign born entirely disproportionate to the number of immigrants of the same occupation who came to this country, indicates that immigrants chose an occupation without much regard to their previous training and experience." Louis Block, "Occupations of Immi-

grants before and after Coming to the United States," quoted in E. P. Hutchinson, *Immigrants and Their Children* (New York, 1956), p. 64. Block is referring mostly to blue-collar workers. My findings are based on data calculated on the previous occupations of the foreign-born *after* their arrival in the United States, but before moving to San Francisco.

For the importance of clerical training as an aid to movement into the merchant occupations, see Robert G. Albion, *The Rise of New York Post* (New York, 1967), and Lewis E. Atherton, "Pioneer Merchant in Mid-America," *The University of Missouri Studies,* vol. XIV, no. 2 (April 1939).

17. Cassin, "Statement," p. 7.

18. Previous occupations of 55 men in the general male sample (8 percent of the 669 in the sample) were located. The entry rate of the blue-collar into white-collar jobs was 18 percent, the same rate of blue-collar entry into merchant occupations within the merchant sample. The slippage rate (former white-collar occupants who took up blue-collar occupations in San Francisco) was 4 percent. Again, this figure is, no doubt, low considering the strong bias of the early San Francisco directories to exclude blue-collar workers. It is estimated that approximately one in every ten San Francisco residents between 1849 and 1854 who held a white-collar job prior to his arrival in the city entered a blue-collar position as his first job in San Francisco.

19. S. Griffith Morgan to Francis Hathaway, August 30, 1852. S. G. Morgan "Papers" in the Charles Morgan "Business Records," ms. (Baker Library, Harvard Univ.); Thomas E. Farish, *The Gold Hunters of California* (Chicago, 1904), pp. 27-28.

20. Albion, *Rise of New York Port,* p. 237. From the merchant sample the occupations of only 18 fathers were determined, 16 of whom were merchants —a sample too small from which to generalize.

21. Data for Boston and Poughkeepsie "traced men from first known occupation held prior to age 30 to last known occupation held later than age 30. Poughkeepsie sample members were born between 1820 and 1850, Boston men between 1850 and 1859, so that the time period is only roughly, not precisely, comparable." Stephan Thernstrom, *The Other Bostonians* (Cambridge, Mass., 1973). The San Francisco data is based on men born, for the most part, between 1810 and 1830. "High white collar" for San Francisco are the importer-wholesalers and general merchants from the merchant sample; "low white-collar" are the petty merchants from the merchant sample; "skilled" are the skilled and semiskilled from the general sample; and "low manual" are the nonskilled from the general sample.

22. Because of a bias within the merchant sample, no occupational mobility rates were computed for the total merchant sample. The petty merchants, for example, were underrepresented in the sample due to the fact that their occupations could not be verified in the 1852 city directory, which tended to exclude them.

23. Community persistence rates, 1850-1860: Boston, 39 percent; Philadelphia, 32 percent; Waltham, 44 percent; Northampton, 53 percent; Wapello

County, Iowa, 30 percent; Trampeateau County, Wisconsin, 1860-1870, 25 percent; San Francisco, 24 percent. All figures except San Francisco are from Thernstrom, *The Other Bostonians,* p. 222.

24. The scale was based upon a standard international occupational scale constructed from 60 different countries which discovered high international similarities in the ranking of occupations according to prestige. Each individual, based upon his occupation at a given time (1852, 1860, 1870, 1880), was assigned a prestige score according to the international scale. Mean Prestige scores for occupational groups (such as petty merchants, nonskilled laborers, and others), can be computed and compared over time. See "The Validity of the 'Standard International Occupational Prestige Scale' For Historical Data" by Donald Treiman, a paper delivered at the Conference on International Comparisons of Social Mobility in Past Societies, Institute for Advanced Studies, Princeton, N.J., June 15-17, 1972 (sponsored by the Mathematical Social Science Board).

25. Cassin, "Statement," p. 12.

26. Bonestell & Co., *Centennial* (San Francisco, 1952), p. 14. For another example of numerous occupational changes during his career, see James Wadsworth, "Dictation," ms. (BL, UC).

27. Albion, *Rise of New York Port,* p. 243. One investigator of merchants in the Midwest found that approximately 46 percent of the merchants he studied began their careers as clerks. See Lewis E. Atherton, *Pioneer Merchants,* p. 31. Ackerman Brothers, *Rules for Governing Clerks* (San Francisco, 1874), p. 4.

28. Thernstrom, *The Other Bostonians,* last chap.

29. See Thernstrom, *Poverty and Progress;* Griffen, "Workers Divided: The Effect of Craft and Ethnic Differences in Poughkeepsie, New York, 1850-1880," in Stephan Thernstrom and Richard Sennett, eds., *Nineteenth-Century Cities: Essays in the New Urban History* (New Haven, 1969).

30. Harriet Levy, *920 O'Farrell Street* (Garden City, 1942), p. 12; see also Egal Feldman, "Jews in the Early Growth of New York's Men's Clothing Trade," *American Jewish Archives,* vol. 12, no. 1, pp. 3-15; Albion, *Rise of New York Port,* p. 59; John Meussdorfer, a German Jew who owned a hat and cap shop in San Francisco, used his branch store in Marysville as a training ground for his younger brothers. He lent them money, supplied them with goods and considerable advice about bookkeeping, credit, taxes, advertising, discount sales, and how best to beat the local competition. When the brothers were trained to his satisfaction, he transferred them to San Francisco to work in the main store. John Meussdorfer, "Papers," ms. (Society of California Pioneers, San Francisco).

31. See Rudolf Glanz, *The Jews of California from the Discovery of Gold until 1880* (New York, 1960), p. 5; in another study, Glanz estimated the percentage of Jews among the Germans employed in certain trades in San Francisco during the 1850s: clothing, 94 percent; cigars, 66 percent; and dry goods, 58 percent; see R. Glanz, "German Jewish Names in America," *Jewish Social*

Studies, vol. 23, no. 3, p. 150; also Glanz, "Notes on Early Jewish Peddling," *Jewish Social Studies,* vol. 7; Gustar A. Danziger and K. M. Nesfield, "The Jews in San Francisco," *Overland Monthly,* ser. 2, vol. 25, no. 146 (February 1895), pp. 384, 410-411; Israel J. Benjamin, *Three Years in America, 1859-1862* (Philadelphia, 1956), I, 232-233; Michael Zarchin, *Glimpses of Jewish Life in San Francisco* (Oakland, 1964).

32. Blue-collar to white-collar mobility for the native-born was almost twice the rate as that of the foreign-born—26 percent as opposed to 14 percent for the foreign-born (N = 91).

33. See Glanz, "Notes on Early Jewish Peddling," and Atherton, *The Pioneer Merchant in Mid-America.*

34. Meussdorfer, "Papers."

35. Lloyd, *Lights and Shades in San Francisco,* pp. 401-402. The West Coast fur trade was monopolized in the 1860s-1870s by the Alaska Commercial Company, the president of which was Lewis Gerstle. A German Jew, Gerstle had migrated from Louisville, Kentucky, and commenced his successful career in San Francisco as a fruit stand operator in 1850. See Mark L. Gerstle, "Memoirs," ms. (BL, UC).

36. To verify that there was a positive relationship between occupational success and persistence among the German petty merchants, more individual cases would need to be investigated. Even if there were a positive relationship for the Germans, this would still leave unanswered the question of the low persistence rate among the petty merchants as a group. It may have been that the Irish were the most unsuccessful in this occupational category, and because of their relatively high representation in the petty merchant occupations, they skewed downward the persistence rate for the petty merchant group. The size of the petty merchant group within the merchant sample was too small, unfortunately, to make valid intra-ethnic comparisons.

From a list of 110 Jews who arrived in San Francisco between 1849 and 1852, almost all merchants, 44 percent persisted in San Francisco to 1860. During this decade, 30 percent had moved up in occupational status, 64 percent remained the same, and only 6 percent had declined. Again, there appeared to be some relationship between occupational success and persistence, but this may well have been a characteristic unique to the Jews or Germans. The experience of the Irish or Catholics, English or Protestants, may have been much different. List from Isaac Markens, *The Hebrews in America* (New York, 1888), pp. 336-337.

37. Percent of foreign-born merchants residing in San Francisco thirty years: English-Scot, 7 percent; French, 23 percent; German, 32 percent; Irish, 11 percent; other, 20 percent; N = 243. Unfortunately there were not enough cases to calculate prestige mobility rates for other ethnic groups within each occupational subgroup to further investigate the connection between occupational mobility and persistence patterns. The reasons why, for example, the French and the English were the first to leave the city, or why the English and Irish were the least likely to persist, must remain unanswered.

38. S. Griffith Morgan to G. Nye, Jr., May 5, 1854, in Charles Morgan, "Business Records," vol. 20. See also Alfred Tubbs, "Dictation," ms. (BL, UC), p. 5.

39. Pinto, "Diary."

40. No way has yet been devised to trace systematically the geographical (and hence occupational) destinations of out-migrants from a city. The possibility exists, but was not fully explored, through the use of the Dun & Bradstreet (formerly R. G. Dun and Company) Credit Ledgers at the Harvard Business School Library. A man found to be in the San Francisco volume for the 1850s would have a cross-reference to the city volume where he moved to after his residence in San Francisco. From reading over 200 individual accounts of those merchants who came to San Francisco from New York and who did not persist in San Francisco through 1860, I conclude that the vast majority returned to New York.

Place of prior residence appeared to have little effect on persistence. The only sectional variation was among those who came to San Francisco from the South, of whom 62 percent had departed San Francisco by 1860. This might be explained by the anti-slavery bias of the San Francisco population which produced an environment unattractive to the southerners. Those who had moved to San Francisco from a foreign country (with the exception of the Germans) were somewhat more likely to be the first to leave the city and the least likely to remain than those who moved to San Francisco from a prior residence within the United States. There was no significant variation in occupational mobility when prior residence was controlled.

41. Albert Dibblee, "Letters and Correspondence," ms. (BL, UC).

4. Property, Credit, and Persistence

1. For a discussion of the relationship between occupation and property in social mobility studies, see Stuart Blumin, "Mobility and Change in Ante-Bellum Philadelphia," in Stephan Thernstrom and Richard Sennett, eds., *Nineteenth-Century Cities: Essays in the New Urban History* (New Haven, 1969), Appendix B; and Michael Katz, "Occupational Classification in History," *Journal of Interdisciplinary History,* III (Summer 1972), 68. Katz also proposes a unique occupational scale which incorporates property data.

2. See Houghton, "Collection," ms. (CSL); Milo Hoadley, "Account Book and Journal," ms. (Huntington Library, San Marino, Calif.); Charles and Edward Hosmer, "Correspondence," ms. (Stanford University Library). The expectations of profits were high. A New York merchant, Thomas J. Stewart, who shipped saddles to Alfred Robinson in San Francisco, wrote to Robinson about a recent shipment of goods: "I hope they won't be sold for less than five hundred per cent profit . . . however, I leave it with you to do the best for me you can." Thomas J. Stewart to Alfred Robinson, March 3, 1849. Alfred Robinson, "Papers and Correspondence," ms. (CHS), folders no. 3, 6.

3. Frank Soule, John H. Gihon and, James Nisbet, *The Annals of San Francisco* (New York, 1856), pp. 498-500; C. L. Ross, "Dictation," ms. (BL, UC), p. 14.

4. *A 'Pile' or a Glance at the Wealth of the Monied Men of San Francisco and Sacramento City* (San Francisco, 1851). Real estate values were in some cases included in the individual estimates at the "cash price in the market, and not at the estimation in which it is held by those who are its acknowledged owners." No information is given by the publishers (Cooke, LeCount Booksellers of San Francisco) as to who assembled the list and how the estimates of personal property were derived or by whom. In the few cases where R. G. Dun & Co. had estimates of wealth on the same people, the *'Pile'* estimates did not vary significantly. However, more individual cases would need to be studied to verify this assertion. The total wealth of the 570 men listed was $19,162,000. Individual entries varied from as little as $5,000 to as much as $750,000 (James Lick, a real estate speculator). In cases where partnerships were named, the total figure for the partnership was divided by the number of listed partners. Sixty-three individual entries were derived in this manner.

A precise total assessment for the city of San Francisco in 1851 could not be determined. However the amount of taxable property in San Francisco in 1855 was reported to be $32,841,000; see *Merchants Magazine and Commercial Review,* 34 (1856), 347. In 1850 it was estimated to be $20,000,000. I would therefore estimate approximately $25,000,000 for 1851, though this may be high considering the fires of 1850-51. John S. Hittell, *A History of the City of San Francisco* (San Francisco, 1878), estimates taxable property in 1851 to be $22,000,000.

5. See Edward Pessen, "The Egalitarian Myth," *American Historical Review,* 76 (October 1971), 989-1034. The distribution of wealth in San Francisco in 1851 was that 2 percent of the population owned 75 percent of the wealth. Comparable figures for other cities were: New York in 1845, 4 percent owned 66 percent; Boston in 1848, 4 percent owned 64 percent; and Brooklyn in 1841, 3 percent owned 59 percent. The inequity in the distribution of wealth was found to exist also on the rural frontier. See George Blackburn and Sherman L. Richards, Jr., "A Demographic History of the West: Manistee County, Michigan, 1860," in the *Journal of American History,* 57 (1970), 613, 618.

6. Occupations from the 1852 and 1854 San Francisco *City Directories* were determined for 144 of the 570 people, or 25 percent.

7. Henry Peters to his brother, Joseph Peters, July 30, 1852. See also H. Peters to J. Peters, July 22, 1852. Henry Peters, "Correspondence and Papers," ms. (NYPL); see also Julia C. Altrocchi, "Paradox Town, San Francisco in 1851," *CHS Quarterly,* 28 (1949), 43.

8. Ernest de Massey, "Some Phases of French Society in San Francisco in the 'Fifties'," *CHS Quarterly,* 32 (1953), 118. Another San Franciscan observed that the prostitutes "were quite shameless, often scrawling their names and reception hours in big letters on their doors . . . all in all, the women of

easy virtue here earn a tremendous amount of money . . . A whole night costs from $200 to $400." Bernard de Russailh, *Last Adventures,* pp. 28-29.

9. Unfortunately, the state census of 1852 failed to list individual property. For a rank ordering of the merchant occupations by property, see table A.1. in Appendix A.

10. B. E. Lloyd, *Lights and Shades in San Francisco* (San Francisco, 1876), p. 350; Mary Smith, "Letters," ms. (CHS).

11. Data on 79 merchants (from original sample of 643), whose assets could be verified for 1852 and 1860 in the RGD, "Credit Ledgers," ms. (Harvard Business School), "Calif." vol. A, pp. 1-101.

12. Hubert H. Bancroft, *California Inter Pocula* (San Francisco, 1880), p. 341; and *Merchants Magazine and Commercial Review,* 44 (1861), 520; for a list of applicants for bankruptcy see *Merchants Magazine,* 34 (1856), 470-471. Further discussion of the causes for failure may be found in chap. 2 above; see also J. S. Hittell, *A History of San Francisco,* pp. 208-330; Theodore H. Hittell, *A History of California,* 4 vols. (San Francisco, 1885-1897) III, 423-459; Hubert H. Bancroft, *A History of California,* 7 vols. (San Francisco, 1884-1890), VI, chaps. 23-26, and III, chap. 8; Josiah Royce, *California From Conquest in 1846 to the Second Committee* (Boston, 1886), pp. 377-501.

13. RGD, "Calif." vol. A., p. 62; William T. Sherman, *Memoirs of William T. Sherman,* 2 vols. (New York, 1875), vol. I, p. 130, 132.

14. J. O. Earll, "Statement," ms. (BL, UC); RGD, "Calif." vol. A., p. 19.

15. S. B. Throckmorton to Peter R. Roach, June 6, 1857, in S. B. Throckmorton, "Letters," ms. (BL, UC); see also letters from Throckmorton to Roach of May 5, 1857 and September 19, 1857.

16. RGD, "New York City," vol. 2, p. 167. Mining stocks attracted a wide range of investors in the 1850s. "Lawyers, doctors, preachers, bankers, merchants, clerks, bookkeepers, mechanics, and in fact persons in every occupation," one reporter observed, "are allured into this speculation . . . The merchant will reduce his capital stock to raise a sum for investment." Lloyd, *Lights and Shades,* pp. 40-41. For examples of stock speculations by merchants in the 1850s, see J. W. Allyne, "Papers," ms. (CHS) and Epes Ellery, "Papers," ms. (CHS).

17. Insurance for a ship's cargo averaged approximately 5 percent of the total cost. For these and other expenses incurred by a San Francisco importer, see Alfred Robinson, "Letterbook," ms. (CHS); for port charges, San Francisco, 1851, see *Merchants Magazine and Commercial Review,* 24 (1851), 232. License fees, San Francisco, 1855, are listed in the *San Francisco Manual of the Corporation of the City* (San Francisco, 1856), pp. 30-38.

18. "Expenses and Profits of San Francisco Merchants," *Merchant Magazine and Commercial Review,* 36 (1857), 136. One merchant-manufacturer estimated his business expenses to be 40 percent of his monthly profits. See John C. Meussdorfer, "Account Books" (1852-53), ms. (Society of California Pioneers).

19. Alfred Robinson, "Letterbook," ms. (CHS), pp. 14-15.

20. See Cherney, Souther and Co., "Ledger," ms. (BL, UC), and RGD, "Calif." vol. A, p. 279.

21. Mary Harker, " 'Honest Harry' Meiggs," *California Historical Society Quarterly,* 17 (1938). Once Meiggs was established in Latin America, the Peruvian government invited him to engineer the construction of the Trans-Andean Railroad. The railroad was built with a labor force of over 20,000 workers, to the immense satisfaction and pride of the Peruvian authorities.

22. See RGD, "Calif." vol. A., pp. 3, 7.

23. RGD reported that "grocers generally are not worth as much as other dealers, who have been here a long time . . . their profits being small." See report on R. E. Brewster, "Calif." vol. A, p. 15.

24. Lloyd, *Lights and Shades,* p. 402. I encountered no Germans in the RGD credit reports who failed because of speculations outside their own businesses. For a discussion of the Jewish merchants' success during the late 1850s and early 1860s, see Henry J. Labatt, "Jewish Business Interests in California, 1861," in Morris U. Schappes, ed., *A Documentary History of the Jews in the United States, 1654-1875* (New York, 1952), pp. 441-444.

25. RGD, "New York City," vol. 198, p. 154, and vol. 199, p. 232; also George S. Hellman, "The Story of the Seligmans," ms. (NYPL).

26. Losses were to be shared by each in proportion to their individual capital contribution. But Dibblee, who contributed only 25 percent of the total initial capital, was to recieve 37.5 percent of the profits. Apparently the advantage rested with Dibblee because of the business contacts ("friends") whom he brought to the partnership. Crosby received 50 percent of the profits and his son, Frederick, received 12.5 percent "in lieu of salary for his services as clerk in the store." See "Partnership Agreement between Albert Dibblee and Charles W. Crosby," in Albert Dibblee, "Private Papers," ms. (private collection of Dibblee's great-grandson, Arthur Mejia, Jr., San Francisco, Calif.)

27. RGD "Calif." vol. I, p. 300.

28. See report for William Langerman, a German Jew, in RGD, "Calif." vol. A, p. 76, and "Coosa County, Alabama," p. 129; see also A. Rich and Brother in RGD, "Calif." vol. A, p. 92. Although the mean property for the foreign-born merchants located in RGD for 1960 was actually higher than the mean property of the native-born, only 58 percent of the foreign-born received a "good" or "excellent" credit rating whereas 73 percent of the native-born sample received such ratings.

29. Tillie Ackerman, "The Biography of Our Grandfather," ms. (Magnus Library, Berkeley, Calif.). Harriet L. Levy, *920 O'Farrell Street* (Garden City, N. Y., 1947), p. 163. Berry Supple in "A Business Elite: German Jewish Financiers in 19th Century New York," *Business History Reviews,* vol. 31 (Summer 1957) states that the Germans "were able, through cultural, social and linguistic affinities to draw upon German capital across the Atlantic," p. 176.

30. RGD, "Calif." vol. A, p. 19; vol. I, p. 251; vol. A, p. 62; vol. A, p. 10; vol. A, p. 102.

31. For persistence rates calculated by occupational status see chap. 3. The persistence pattern of the affluent class in San Francisco was similar to the pattern for the propertied class in Boston. See Peter Knights and Stephan Thernstrom, "Men in Motion," *Journal of Interdisciplinary History* vol. I (1970), pp. 29-30.

32. RGD, "Calif." vol. A, pp. 1-101; see also A. P. Nasatir, *A French Journalist in the California Gold Rush: The Letters of Etienne Derbec* (Georgetown, Calif., 1964), p. 8; A. M. Freidenberg, "Letters of a California Pioneer," *Publications of the American Jewish Historical Society,* no. 31; M. V. B. Fowler, "Diary," ms. (University of California, Los Angeles). Some, particularly Jewish shopkeepers, believed the interior mining towns to hold out superior economic opportunities because the capital requirements for expansion were less demanding. See Robert E. Levinson, "The Jews in the California Gold Rush," Ph.D. diss. (University of Oregon, Eugene, Oregon, 1968).

33. S. Griffith Morgan to T. L. Hathway, New Bedford, Mass., September 30, 1850, in S. G. Morgan, "Papers," vol. 15; see also S. G. Morgan to G. Nye, Jr., May 5, 1854, in Charles Morgan, "Business Records," vol. 20; Morgan figured his profits to be $72,000 from February 1852 to April 1860, or $9,000 a year. His best year was 1852-53 when between February 1852 and April 1853 he earned, by his own accounts, a profit of approximately $37,000. Yet between January and October 1854, in the midst of the depression, he lost $10,000. See S. Griffith Morgan, "Papers," vol. 5, Ledger Book.

34. Joseph G. Eastland to his father, March 31, 1853 and May 24, 1853. Joseph G. Eastland, "Letters," ms. (CHS). See also RGD, "Calif." vol. A, p. 8; and John Cornelison, "Diary," ms. (NYPL).

35. Charles Staffard, New Bedford, Mass. to S. Griffith Morgan of San Francisco, December 7, 1850, in Charles Morgan, "Business Records," vol. 44.

36. Philip T. Southworth of New York City to his brother, A. B. Southworth of San Francisco, January 4, 1856, in Philip T. Southworth, "Papers," ms. (CSL).

37. Hubert Bancroft makes the point that frequent visits to the East were the custom of the merchant class. Bancroft, *Inter Pocula,* p. 177. This was certainly true of the more affluent merchants; however, there were many more who left for the East in the early 1850s and never again returned to San Francisco.

38. Henry Schmiedell, "Dictation," ms. (BL, UC), p. 6.

39. T. A. Barry and B. A. Patton, *Men and Memories of San Francisco in the "Spring of '50"* (San Francisco, 1873), p. 215. Among the monied elite, 29 percent were downwardly mobile in occupation between 1850 and 1860, 68 percent remained at the same occupational level, and only 3 percent moved ahead. The pattern was similar to the merchant sample where, in terms of oc-

cupational prestige, the general merchants gained occupational status between their first job and last job, whereas the importer-wholesalers declined significant in prestige. The greatest loss, in terms of occupational distance, for a single occupational group among the monied men was experienced by the nonmerchant managers (bankers, brokers, and manufacturers). Combining *all* occupations for the monied men, their occupational prestige declined between first job and last job with the largest losses occurring in the 1850-1860 decade. For lack of data it was impossible to determine the property of the monied men in 1860 (except in a few isolated cases) in order to estimate if collectively they, like the merchants, lost property in the 1850 decade. But since the experience for the high-status merchants (general and importer-wholesalers) from the merchant sample was known to be one of property loss, it is reasonable to expect that the experience of the monied men mirrored that of the merchants.

40. S. R. Throckmorton in San Francisco to Peter R. Roach in New York City, October 4, 1858. Throckmorton, "Letters," ms. (BL, UC).

41. "Don't think that everyone can blithely come here [San Francisco] and adjust himself to this completely new existence. I've seen men go mad, and many others lose hope and drink themselves to death . . . " Bernard de Russailh, *Last Adventure,* p. 10.

42. Alex Warfield, "Correspondence," letter dated December 31, 1862, included in Cowan, "Collection," ms. (University of California at Los Angeles). William T. Coleman, "Statement," ms. (BL, UC), Folder C-D, 755, p. 1.

43. Letter of June 30, 1853, from Sherman's "Home Letters," p. 135.

5. The Social Fabric

1. Hubert H. Bancroft, *History of California,* 7 vols. (San Francisco, 1884-1890), VII, 714-715.

2. Certain immigrants and blue-collar workers had entered the elite ranks, and it may have appeared that San Francisco society was less rigid than older East Coast communities because some newcomers gained easy access to the elite community. But in a new city only newcomers could fill these ranks. The appearance rather than the reality of social fluidity is suggested by Gunther Barth in "Metropolitanism in the Far West," in Frederick C. Jaker, ed., *Industrialism in America* (New York, 1968), p. 63.

3. *Alta California,* December 10, 1857.

4. For a discussion of anomie in a city, see Louis Wirth, "Urbanism as a Way of Life," *American Journal of Sociology,* 44 (July 1938). Alexis de Tocqueville, *Democracy in America,* ed. Phillips Bradley, 2 vols. (New York, 1945), I, 198-9; II, 110.

5. For a study of voluntary associations and their relation to the "functional organization of communities," see Walter S. Glazer, "Participation and Power: Voluntary Associations and the Functional Organization of Cin-

cinnati in 1840," *Historical Methods Newsletter,* 5 (September 1972), 151-168.

6. James C. Wadsworth, "Dictation," ms. (BL, UC).

7. Robert Lammot to his brother Dan, March 2, 1851, in Robert Lammot, "Family Letters," ms. (BL, UC); see also the "Constitution and By-Laws of the Knickerbocker Engine Company (No. 5)" (San Francisco, 1854), ms. (CHS). The Knickerbocker Company limited its membership to American citizens.

8. Sample drawn from five of the nine fire companies in 1852; see also Bradford F. Luckingham, "Associational Life on the Urban Frontier: 1848-56," Ph.D. diss. (University of California, Davis, 1968), p. 34.

9. F. J. Bowlen, "Materials Relating to the San Francisco Fire Department," 4 vols., ms. (BL, UC), vol. 4, p. 130; John P. Young, *San Francisco: A History of the Pacific Coast Metropolis,* 2 vols. (San Francisco, 1912), I, p. 256.

10. B. E. Lloyd, *Lights and Shades in San Francisco* (San Francisco, 1876), p. 129.

11. Dello G. Dayton, "California Militia, 1850-1866," Ph.D. diss. (University of California, Berkeley, 1951), p. 93.

12. The militia company headquarters, like the volunteer fire houses, were among the more prestigious buildings in San Francisco in the early 1850s. The First California Guards raised $30,000 (through a joint-stock company arrangement of selling to members 300 shares at $100 each) to construct at the corner of Dupont and Jackson Streets a two-and-a-half story armory complete with drill room, billiard saloon, library, and arms room. See Frank Soule, John H. Gihon, and James Nisbet, *The Annals of San Francisco* (New York, 1856), p. 703. For a discussion of the militia company as a social institution, see Dennis Van Essendelft's forthcoming study of nineteenth-century militia.

13. One observer noted that it was cheaper to go to the theater in San Francisco "than to hire a seat in a respectable church." Laura Smith, "Letters," ms. (Huntington Library, San Marino, California), letter to sister Helen, November 12, 1856.

14. See William F. Babcock and David Beck, "Sketch(es)," ms. (BL, UC).

15. Edgar M. Kahn, "Early San Francisco Jewry" ms. (BL, UC), pp. 10-13. George S. Hellman, "The Story of the Seligmans," ms. (NYPL) p. 56.

16. From a sample of seven churches and two synagogues: First Baptist Church, First Congregational Church, Episcopal Grace Church, Episcopal Trinity Church, German Evangelical Church, First Presbyterian Church, First Unitarian Church, Congregation Sherith Israel, and Congregation Emanu-El. Officers of these churches are listed in the 1860 *San Francisco City Directory,* (San Francisco, Langley and Co., 1861). The officers' occupations were then searched in the same directory. Percentage is based on known or listed occupations.

17. Michael M. Zarchin, *Glimpses of Jewish Life in San Francisco* (Oak-

land, 1964), pp. 105, 146; Rudolf Glanz, "German-Jewish Names in America," *Jewish Social Studies,* vol. 23, no. 3 (July 1961), p. 147. Heinrich Kaufman, *Sixty Years of the German Benevolent Society,* (San Francisco, 1914), pp. 2-13.

18. Gustar A. Danziger and K. M. Nesfield, "The Jew in San Francisco," in *Overland Monthly,* ser. 2, vol. 25, no. 146 (February 1895), p. 391.

19. See Luckingham, "Associational Life on the Urban Frontier," chap. 3, fn. 10-12.

20. Zarchin, *Glimpses of Jewish Life in San Francisco,* p. 153.

21. The *Alta California,* May 16, 1853.

22. Lloyd, *Lights and Shades,* pp. 401-402. In the mining areas of California, where Jews owned many of the smaller shops and general stores, there was a distinct lack of prejudice against them. See Robert E. Levinson, "The Jews in the California Gold Rush," Ph.D. diss. (University of Oregon, Eugene, 1968).

23. Israel J. Benjamin, *Three Years in America,* 2 vols. (Philadelphia, 1956), I, 233.

24. "Anti-Jewish Sentiment in California, 1855," *The American Jewish Archives,* vol. 12, no. 1 (April 1960), pp. 19-23. Labatt served as president of the Hebrew Young Men's Debating Society, secretary of the Congregation Emanu-El and the Hebrew Benevolent Society, and editor of the Anglo-Jewish periodical *The Voice of Israel.* For additional evidence of anti-Semitism see Hinton Helper, *Hand of Gold* (Baltimore, 1855), p. 54.

25. For examples of anti-Jewish business prejudice, see the discussion of credit ratings and Jews in chap. 4. As Jews quickly accumulated capital in San Francisco, they soon bypassed non-Jewish institutional sources and borrowed instead from other more affluent Jews in San Francisco or the Jewish communities in the eastern states and Europe.

26. Soule, *Annals,* p. 506.

27. See Rudolph M. Lapp, "The Negro in the Gold Rush," *Journal of Negro History,* XLIX (April 1964), 83-85. The California state census (1852) indicated the "color" of each person. Only three blacks could be located among the total (3,100) merchant population of San Francisco in the 1852 census. Hinton Helper, *Land of Gold,* p. 275.

28. RGD, "Calif." vol. A, p. 87. The partnership assets were estimated at $10,000. Mifflin Gibbs, *Shadow and Light* (Washington, D. C., 1902), pp. 46-50. Gibbs left California in 1858 for Frazer River, British Columbia, to seek gold. Unsuccessful, he returned to the United States in the late 1860s, studied law, and was appointed municipal judge in Little Rock, Arkansas. Gibbs closed out his distinguished career as U. S. Consul to Madagascar. A short biography of Gibbs is included in Sue Bailey Thurmann, *Pioneers of Negro Origin in California* (San Francisco, 1952).

29. One observer in the 1850s commented that "all Mexicans and Chileans, like the people of negro descent, were only of the commonest description." As for the Chinese, "there is a strong feeling,—prejudice it may be,—existing in

California against all Chinamen . . . they are nicknamed, cuffed about and treated very unceremoniously by every other class." Soule, *Annals,* pp. 378-379, 412. For the treatment of blacks in other cities, see Richard Wade, *Slavery in the Cities* (Chicago, 1961); Gunther Barth's *Bitter Strength* (Cambridge, Mass., 1964) discusses the prejudice against the Chinese in California.

30. *Alta California,* February 24, 1851. Lammot "Letters," ms. (BL, UC).

31. Mary Smith, "Letters," ms. (CHS), pp. 86-102; Soule, *Annals,* pp. 364-365, 399.

32. Soule, *Annals,* pp. 277, 553-561. The Hounds were reported by Soule to be Australian convicts and ex-members of the regiment of the New York volunteers who had fought in the Mexican War. It was a common myth in San Francisco that all Australians were ex-convicts. Actually most were free immigrants and only a little over 10 percent of the Sydney immigrants to San Francisco (1849-50) were known convicts. See Charles Bateson, *Gold Fleet for California* (East Lansing, 1964), p. 122; see also John Henry Brown, *Reminiscences* (San Francisco, 1933), pp. 102-103.

33. George E. Schenck, "Statement," ms. (BL, UC), pp. 34-35.

34. James A. B. Scherer, *The Lion of the Vigilantes: William T. Coleman* (New York, 1939), pp. 101-102; Soule, *Annals,* p. 317.

35. Scherer, *The Lion of the Vigilantes,* p. 108. See also the constitution of the 1851 Vigilance Committee, in Mary Floyd Williams, ed., *Papers of the 1851 San Francisco Committee of Vigilance,* Publications of the Academy of Pacific Coast History, vol. 4 (Berkeley, Calif., 1919), p. 1.

36. Of the 711 members of the 1851 Committee, the occupations for 344, or 48 percent of the total membership, could be determined from tracings in the 1852 *San Francisco City Directory.*

37. Based on a list of the 44 members of the executive committee in Williams, ed., *Papers of the 1851 San Francisco Committee of Vigilance.*

38. For an estimate of the effect of the 1851 committee on crime in San Francisco, see Mary Floyd Williams, *History of the San Francisco Committee of Vigilance of 1851* (New York, 1969), pp. 389-390. The issue of corruption in the city government is discussed in Roger Olmsted, "San Francisco and the Vigilance Style," *American West,* vol. 7, no. 1 (1970), pp. 63-64.

39. Richard Maxwell Brown lists a total of 327 vigilante movements which occurred in the eighteenth and nineteenth century. Brown's list is an appendix in Hugh D. Graham and Ted Gurr, *The History of Violence in America: A Report to the National Commission on the Causes and Prevention of Violence* (New York, 1969), pp. 218-226. Though the 1856 San Francisco Vigilance Committee was by no means the most violent, at least in terms of the number of victims killed, it was with its 6,000 to 8,000 membership by far the largest of the vigilante committees. John Hittell placed the membership at 9,000 out of an adult white male population in 1856 of 12,000. See Hittell, *Resources of California,* p. 371. Bancroft places the membership at 8,000 in *History of California,* vol. VI, p. 747.

40. *Alta California,* February 27, 1851. For detailed provisions of the 1851

charter see Lewis F. Byington, *A History of San Francisco,* 3 vols. (Chicago, 1931), I, 211. See also Bernard Moses, *The Establishment of Municipal Government in San Francisco* (Baltimore, 1889).

41. See tax, revenue expenditure, and debts schedules in City of San Francisco, *Municipal Report for the Fiscal Year 1863-1864* (San Francisco, 1864), Appendix, pp. 325-340. For discussion of the merchants' economic problems on the eve of the 1856 Vigilance Committee, see chap. 2; see also John Hittell, *History of San Francisco,* pp. 208-330; T. H. Hittell, *California,* vol. III, pp. 423-459; Bancroft, *History of California,* vol. VI, chaps. 23-26; Josiah Royce, *California* (New York, 1948), pp. 333-340.

42. S. H. Willey, *Thirty Years in California* (San Francisco, 1879), pp. 45, 49. J. K. Osgood, "Letters," ms. (BL, UC). Letter dated June 10, 1850.

43. *Alta California,* January 21, 1853.

44. The merchants' neglect of city politics and civic responsibilities prior to 1856 cannot be attributed to the factor of geographical mobility. The merchants, particularly the importer-wholesalers who by their occupational and financial status were in the most advantageous position to influence the political system of the city had they chosen to do so, were in fact among the most geographically persistent of the city's residents. See chap. 3 for merchant persistence rates. Lloyd Warner in *Big Business Leaders in America* (New York, 1955) has suggested that when a young man leaves the community that reared him "before learning or recognizing or accepting the kinds of social and personal debts the rearing has incurred—he is not likely to feel the sense of community indebtedness in his new community that could make him a responsible and serious community leader." The self-made man in a new community feels no responsibility to his new place of residence. In addition, "restlessness leading to movement may also foster restlessness social and emotional. The consequences in the behavior and attitudes of some of the men who occupy elite positions may well be indifference to the values and beliefs of the past, and to the needs and debts they owe their communities." (p. 195). In San Francisco however, the business leaders were active in the voluntary associations of the city and thus not lacking a sense of "community indebtedness." Only in politics, and only before 1856, did the elite demonstrate a general lack of interest and participation.

45. Michael H. Frisch, "The Community Elite and the Emergence of Urban Politics: Springfield, Massachusetts, 1840-1880," in Stephan Thernstrom and Richard Sennett, eds., *Nineteenth-Century American Cities* (New Haven, 1969), p. 285. Sam B. Warner in *The Private City* (Philadelphia, 1968), suggests that once nineteenth-century businessmen realized "that the city was not important to their daily lives," after midcentury when their businesses became national in scope, the "business leaders became ignorant of their city and abandoned politics." And as the businessmen of Philadelphia dropped out of politics, new political professionals stepped in "to make careers of public office." In San Francisco, the reverse occurred. Businessmen replaced professionals, who once again gained political control in the 1870s.

46. From the *New York Herald* quoted in the *Alta California,* July 16, 1856. Francis E. Pinto, "Diary," ms. (NYPL), p. 167.

47. Charles L. Heiser to Christopher Heiser, quoted by Earl Pomeroy, "California, 1846-1860: Politics of a Representative Frontier State," *California Historical Society Quarterly*, vol. 32 (1953), pp. 296-297. F. W. Macondray, "Papers," ms. (CHS); see also his "Statement on the Vigilance Committee," ibid.

48. *Alta California*, May 26, 1855. Pomeroy writes that the Know-Nothing party in California was a direct reflection of nativist sentiment which pervaded California politics from 1846 to 1860; "indeed, discrimination against foreigners has been a major theme in California politics from time to time since mining districts first outlawed Mexicans and Chinese." In San Francisco in 1854-55 nativist sentiment was directed primarily against the Chinese and South Americans, not against the European immigrant. Pomeroy, "California, 1846-1860," p. 297.

49. Richard M. Brown, "Pivot of American Vigilantism: The San Francisco Vigilance Committee of 1856," in John A. Carroll, ed., *Reflections of Western Historians* (Tucson, Ariz., 1969), pp. 111-112, 116.

50. See chaps. 3 and 4 for discussion of occupational mobility and property losses.

51. James D. Farwell, "Statement," ms. (BL, UC), p. 14.

52. William T. Coleman, "The San Francisco Vigilance Committees," *Century Magazine,* XLIII (November 1891), p. 144. Brown's study of 2,500 applications for membership in the committee found that the bulk of the members were from the Eastern Seaboard and from the Western European countries of France, Germany, England, and Scotland. "As to occupation, the vigilantes came largely from the ranks of the city's merchants, tradesmen, craftsmen or their young employees. Laborers were in a scant minority, and gamblers were forbidden to join." Richard M. Brown, "Pivot of American Vigilantism" p. 111. Other accounts confirm the propertied class bias of the 1856 Vigilance Committee. "The Vigilance Committee was composed of the most intelligent, best educated and property owning class of the city." Martin J. Burke, "Dictation," ms. (BL, UC), p. 4. In addition to Coleman, the most influential members of the Committee were said to be C. J. Dempster, J. W. Brittan, J. D. Farwell, M. J. Burke, and T. J. L. Smiley, all merchants except Burke. See C. V. Gillespie, "Statement," ms. (BL, UC); J. D. Farwell, "Statement," ms. (BL, UC); and James C. L. Woodworth, "Statement," ms. (BL, UC). Also Hubert H. Bancroft, *Popular Tribunals,* 2 vols. (San Francisco, 1887), II, 80-81, 86-87, 117-118, 121, 125-156, 418.

53. A few lawyers did join the committee, though probably the majority objected to the "mob rule" of the committee. One attorney, Isaac Wistar, noted that "many lawyers opposed the committee because they disliked the thought much less reality, of mob rule overhauling the carefully designed procedures of the law—no matter how corrupt or inefficient." See Isaac J. Wistar, *Autobiography* (New York, 1914), pp. 314-334. The executive committee membership list is from S. Colville's *San Francisco City Directory,* (San Fran-

cisco, 1856), pp. 226-227; and Dr. Henry Gray, *Judges and Criminals,* (San Francisco, 1858), pp. 99-110.

54. James N. Olney, "Dictation," ms. (BL, UC). The ethnic composition of the Vigilance Committee is difficult to determine. However there is no evidence to suggest that the foreign-born were any more numerous among the executive committee than they were among the ranks of the highly prestigious importer-wholesalers—those merchants who controlled the executive committee. Rudolf Glanz in *The Jews of California* (New York, 1960) states that of the 700 members of the 1851 Vilgilance Committee, 30 (4 percent) were Jews (p. 41). In 1856, Jesse Seligman, a German Jew, played a prominent role in the executive committee. William T. Coleman said that Frenchmen were numerous and performed with distinction due, he said, to their "superior military background"; Coleman, "Statement on Vigilance Committee," ms. (BL, UC).

55. Quotes from Scherer, *The Lion of the Vigilantes,* pp. 56, 58. Coleman's importing and commission business appears not to have prospered between 1850 and 1852. His financial success came after his marriage, in speculative real estate ventures. See William T. Coleman, "Papers," ms. (BL, UC). Coleman left San Francisco in late 1856 for New York where, for the next sixteen years, he conducted his successful shipping company. In 1863, Coleman was active in organizing middle-class opposition to the draft riots in New York. He later returned to San Francisco, lived atop Nob Hill and was seriously considered by the California Democrats as a nominee for the U. S. presidency.

56. Coleman, "Statement on Vigilance Committee," p. 35.

57. "I am instructed by the Executive Committee of the Committee of Vigilance to tender to you their thanks for the very liberal donation received from you by the hands of C. J. Dempster, Esq. [a merchant friend of Dibblee's] on the fifth instant," Signed "33 Secretary". Letter dated August 9, 1856, included in Harrison Dibblee's "Biography of Albert Dibblee," ms. (CHS). See also Aaron M. Burns, "Statement," ms. (BL, UC).

58. John Fay to his brother in New York City, August 20, 1856. Fay Family "Papers," ms. (BL, UC). T. J. L. Smiley, "Statement," ms. (BL, UC), p. 15. William T. Sherman, *Home Letters of William T. Sherman* (New York, 1909) p. 144. For similar reports see letters of San Francisco merchant Alex Grogan to F. D. Atherton in Valparaiso, Chile. Grogan served as Atherton's merchant agent in San Francisco for Chilean wheat shipments. Faxton D. Atherton, "Papers," ms. (CHS).

59. M. Morrison, "Letters," ms. (CHS).

60. James F. Curtis, a San Francisco merchant and officer of the First California Guard maintained his leadership position in his guard company after it reorganized as a "independent company" and served concurrently for a while as chief of police for the Vigilance Committee. Most members of the committee did not have military backgrounds, though a few, like Curtis and Isaac Bluxome (secretary of the committee and former member of the New York Seventh Regiment), had served in volunteer militia companies. See G. E.

Schenck, "Statement," ms. (BL, UC), p. 41. The Marion Rifles, San Francisco Blues, Washington Continental Guard, and National Lancers remained loyal to the city and the state. For further discussion on this point, see William T. Sherman's letter to Henry S. Turner of May 18, 1856, *Century Magazine,* XLIII (December 1891), p. 297.

61. Ibid., p. 298.

62. On this point see Alfred Tubbs, "Statement," ms. (BL, UC), p. 21, and Francis Pinto, "Diary," p. 197.

63. Washington may have been influenced in its decision not to support Governor Johnson because of reports from Milton Latham, San Francisco Collector of Customs and former merchant, who advised the Secretary of Treasury of the wide public support in San Francisco for the Vigilance Committee. See letter of Milton Latham to Secretary of Treasury James Guthrie, June 19, 1856, in U. S. National Archives *Correspondence* (microfilm copy, BL, UC). A lumber merchant observed: "Everybody was on our side. If we wanted a steamer, the Steam Navigation Company would furnish it." Tubbs, "Statement," p. 21.

64. Quoted by E. M. Tinneman, "Opposition to the San Francisco Vigilance Committee," M.A. Essay (University of California, Berkeley, 1941) p. 100. Of the 189 individuals identified as opponents to the Committee by Tinneman, only 17 (9 percent) were engaged in merchant occupations. See Appendix, pp. 158-162. Tubbs in his "Dictation" states that "most of the men in the Vigilance Committee were Northern men and those opposed to us were nearly all Southern men," p. 15; see also F. W. Macondray "Statement on the Vigilance Committee" in Macondray, "Papers," ms. (CHS).

65. Albert Dibblee to his brother William Dibblee in New York City (n.d.), included in Harrison Dibblee, "Biography of Albert Dibblee," ms. (CHS).

66. B. Brierly, *Thoughts for a Crisis,* 2nd ed. (San Francisco, 1856), pp. 6, 8, 16. The Rev. Francis E. Preveaux prophesied that "Good, great good . . . will be the result" of the committee's efforts. "We have long needed a revolution," claimed Preveaux, and "we are now in the midst of it." Moreover, "the Vigilance Committee is made up of our best men and the overwhelming part of our population is with them in sympathy. We rejoice in what is going on, though we regret that there should be cause for such measures." Francis E. Preveaux, "Papers," ms. (BL, UC).

67. Quoted from Rev. Scott's letter to the San Francisco *Pacific* dated August 4, 1856, in Conrad Wiegand, *Dr. Scott, the Vigilance Committee and the Church* (San Francisco, 1856), p. 13. See also William A. Scott, "Discourse for the Times," ms. (Huntington Library, San Marino, Calif., n.d.).

68. Dr. Henry Gray, *Judges and Criminals,* pp. 71, 75. H. H. Bancroft, *History of California*, vol. 6, p. 752; see also Bancroft's *Popular Tribunals,* vol. III, pp. 271-282, 348-353, 509, 528, 591-598.

69. Maxwell Brown, "Pivot of American Vigilantism," p. 114. One of the influential members of the Committee of 21 was Jesse Seligman, a German Jew and leading wholesale merchant in the city. Captain F. W. Macondray expressed in private what other members of the Vigilance Committee exclaimed

in public: that once the criminal element was eliminated, the work of the Vigilance Committee was complete. "The V. C. after cleaning the city from its moral filth and restoring the laws of their original purity quietly disbanded, and we earnestly hope that the time will never come when it shall be necessary to again call into action the V. C." Macondray, "Statement on the Vigilance Committee," in F. W. Macondray, "Papers."

70. The People's party agreed to support the fledging Republicans if, and only if, the Republican state candidates promised protection from the vigilantes and their "reforms." The Republicans quickly accepted the offer, and the "party of Free Soil, Free men and Freemont rode to victory on the coattails of urban reform." Roger Lotchin, *San Francisco, 1846-1856* (New York, 1974), pp. 234-235.

71. Crime statistics for the period 1851-1856 are sketchy and when available are not particularly reliable, reports Roger Lotchin in *San Francisco, 1846-1856.* Lotchin further states: "The reign of virtue was punctuated by frequent backsliding, yet all the while the press was claiming that perfect order prevailed. Even if the necessary statistics existed to prove the decline of lawlessness, such words as 'cleansed' and 'purified'—so frequently used by Vigilante defenders—would be wholly unjustified," p. 196. For the city's finances, see Edward Byrne, "Report on the City and County Finances Made Persuant to an Order of the Board of Supervisors" (San Francisco, 1856).

72. Richard M. Brown has suggested that the San Francisco vigilantes represented a typical frontier situation where men of "upper level backgrounds or aspirations" reacted to challenges to their authority from the lower classes to "re-establish the community structure in which they [the elite] were dominant." Further, according to Brown, the "Vigilantes of 1856 represented a struggle for power between two blocs of opposed religion, class and ethnic characteristics. Thus the vigilante leadership of upper and middle class, old American, Protestant merhants was aligned against a political faction based upon Irish-Catholics, lower class laborers." Brown's explanation fails to consider that the upper and middle classes never did control the city's political structure before 1856. Through the People's party, the merchants and their middle-class allies were not re-establishing themselves in politics but rather capturing the city's political machinery so as to preserve and regain what occupational status and financial resources remained to them after the economic debacles of the mid-1850s. Finally, Brown places too much emphasis on the anti-Irish bias of the 1856 Vigilance Committee. A few Irish merchants were members of the executive committee and many more were enrolled in the full committee. See Richard M. Brown, "The American Vigilante Tradition" in Hugh D. Graham and Ted R. Gurr, eds., *The History of Violence in America* (New York, 1969), pp. 156, 162, 168-169, 198; see also Brown's, *Strain of Violence* (New York, 1975), chaps. 4-5. For a discussion of the relative lack of discrimination faced by the Irish in California, see Patrick Blessing, "West Among Strangers: Irish Migration to California, 1850-1880," Ph.D. diss. (Univ. of California, Los Angeles, 1976).

73. The occupational prestige for members of the executive committee in-

creased from 54.5 in 1854 to 55.2 in 1860. This is in contrast to the occupational loss of 7.6 on the prestige scale experienced by all importer-merchants. See chap. 3, table 3.5.

74. Over 70 percent of the 1856 executive committee persisted in San Francisco through 1860. Of those members who resided in the city in 1852, over 80 percent persisted through 1860. This is an amazingly high persistence rate considering that only 24 percent of the general population and 62 percent of the city's high prestige merchants persisted through the 1850 decade. See chap. 3.

75. Albert Dibblee to his mother, August 4, 1859, in Harrison Dibblee, "Biography of Albert Dibblee."

76. Letter dated September 9, 1860. Harrison Dibblee, "Biography of Albert Dibblee."

77. *Alta California,* November 25, 1859; William Evitts in his *A Matter of Allegiances: Maryland from 1850 to 1861* (Baltimore, 1974), discusses the violence surrounding the 1856 municipal election in Baltimore.

78. The eternal benefits of the Vigilance Committee appear also to have permeated the historical profession. All the local histories of San Francisco written in the nineteenth century and well into the twentieth century defended the 1856 committee; see Bancroft, Young, Hittell, Byington, Kinnard, Soule, Cleland and Royce. Royce, who was the most critical, could still write, "The great committee was productive of more good than evil only because in the sequel it was not left to its natural tendencies [to remain in existence], but was constantly guided by cautious and conscientious men, whose acts were not always wise, but whose purposes were honest and rational." And finally, Royce concluded, the Vigilance Committee accomplished "not the direct destruction of a criminal class, but the conversion of honest men to a sensible and devout local patriotism. What it teaches us now, both in California and elsewhere, is the sacredness of a true spirit, and the great law that the people who forget the divine order of things have to learn thereof anew some day, in anxiety and in pain . . . the essentials of civilization had been fought for and gained." Josiah Royce, *California, from the Conquest: 1846 to the Second Vigilance Committee* (New York, 1948), pp. 357, 366. The exceptions to the generally sympathetic treatment of the committee are Roger Lotchin, *San Francisco, 1846-1856;* Bean, *California* (New York, 1968); and John W. Caughey, *California,* 2nd ed. (New York, 1953).

6. The Civil War, Railroads, and Manufacturing

1. *Alta California,* October 10, 1860.
2. For trade figures see Benjamin C. Wright, *The West is the Best, and California the Best of the West* (San Francisco, 1913), p. 143; see also *Merchants Magazine and Commercial Review,* vol. 45 (1861), pp. 41, 68; vol. 46 (1862), pp. 360, 362, and vol. 54 (1866), p. 213; see also Hubert H. Bancroft, *History of California,* 7 vols. (San Francisco, 1884-1890), VII, 115 n. 20, 119,

and Bancroft, "Scraps," ms. (BL, UC), vol. 12, part I, pp. 1-2. See also Benjamin Wright, *San Francisco Ocean Trade: Past and Future* (San Francisco, 1911), pp. 211-212.

3. John J. Earle, "Sentiments of the People of California With Respect to the Civil War," in American Historical Association, *Annual Report*, I (1907), 134.

4. "The Diary of A. L. Bancroft, 1861," *CHS Quarterly* (1950), p. 125.

5. Horace Davis, "The Home Guard of 1861," in Panama Pacific Historical Congress, *The Pacific Ocean in History* (1917), pp. 363-368. See also Harrison Dibblee's "Biography of Albert Dibblee," ms. (CHS), p. 104. Formed in 1861 by fourteen young men who were all members of the Congregational Church, the Summer Light Guard stated: "Believing that our duty to our God and our country is paramount to every other duty, and that our country's safeguard against the assaults of *foreign* and *domestic* foes, we, the undersigned, hereby form ourselves into a military corps." All members of the Summer Guard "ranked high in the social scale." B. E. Lloyd, *Lights and Shades in San Francisco* (San Francisco, 1876), pp. 127, 129. The city contributed $360,000 to the Sanitary Commission, additional evidence of San Francisco's support of the Union.

6. Albert L. Bancroft, "Compact Chronology" in A. L. Bancroft, "Papers," ms. (CHS). An employee of the U.S. Mint in San Francisco complained that by being paid in greenbacks he could only purchase goods worth forty-eight cents on the dollar. See Joseph A. Smith letter dated June 23, 1864, to his nephew, in J. A. Smith, "Letters," ms. (BL, UC). See also Caspar T. Hopkins, "The California Recollections of Caspar T. Hopkins," *CHS Quarterly*, vol. 26, p. 355; and RGD, "Calif." vol. II, p. 9.

7. Lee H. Wooley, *California, 1849-1913: The Rambling Sketches and Experiences . . . in That State* (Oakland, 1913) pp. 33-34.

8. Quoted by Ira Cross in *Financing an Empire,* 4 vols. (San Francisco, 1927), I, 324. Anyone who attempted to pay off his debts in greenbacks, without making due allowance for their depreciated values, would have "no credit or standing in the mercantile community." See Samuel Bowles, *Across the Continent* (Springfield, Mass., 1865), p. 342.

9. Quoted by Cross in *Financing an Empire*, I, pp. 356-357.

10. Bancroft, "Scraps," vol. 12, part I, pp. 64, 92.

11. Cross, *Financing an Empire*, I, p. 238; *Alta California*, October 29, 1863.

12. Mark Twain, *Roughing It* (Hartford, Conn., 1872), p. 420.

13. F. W. Macondray, "Letterbook," ms. (CHS). Macondray to James Otis of Boston, August 2, 1864.

14. San Francisco Chamber of Commerce, "Memorial to Congress," in *Merchants Magazine and Commercial Review*, vol. 46 (1862), pp. 152-154. Washington was also called upon to annex northern Mexico, an area which would serve as a new market for California's expanded wheat supply. *Alta California*, December 4, 1859.

15. Oscar Shuck, *The California Scrap Book* (San Francisco, 1869), pp. 586, 587, 589. The statement is that of Hall McAllister, a socially prominent San Francisco attorney, on the occasion of the opening of the steamship packets line to the Far East in 1866.

16. For an example of the disillusionment with the Far East trade see F. W. Macondray, "Papers," ms. (CHS): "Letter Copy Books, 1864-1874." Macondray and Co., whose chartered ships imported teas from China, found more lucrative markets in Australia which imported large quantities of California wheat in return for coal destined to power San Francisco's new industries in the 1860s and 1870s.

17. *Alta California*, February 14, April 18, and May 6, 1866, and September 28, 1867.

18. *The Marysville Appeal*, February 24, 1866, located in Bancroft, "Scraps," vol. 12, part I, p. 94.

19. Pacific and Colorado Steam Navigation Co., *The Colorado in its Relation to the Commerce of San Francisco* (San Francisco, 1865).

20. Pacific and Colorado Steam Navigation Co., *The Colorado . . .*

21. San Francisco Chamber of Commerce, *Report of the President* (1867), pp. 11-12.

22. For a good summary of the Colorado River trade scheme see Francis H. Leavitt, "Steam Navigation on the Colorado River," *CHS Quarterly*, vol. 22; for the part played by the San Francisco merchants, see also Hubert H. Bancroft, *Chronicles of the Builders of the Commonwealth,* 7 vols. (San Francisco, 1891-1892), V, p. 156, and Harrison Dibblee, "Biography of Albert Dibblee."

23. Statement of J. W. Stow, president of the San Francisco Commercial Association in its *Annual Report* (1868-69), p. 6.

24. *Alta California*, August 3, 1851. For the solicitation of state assistance by San Francisco, particularly the development of the city's port facilities, see Gerald Nash, "Government Enterprise in the West: The San Francisco Harbor, 1863-1963" in *University of Wyoming Publications in History,* vol. 33 (1966), pp. 77-93, 158-160.

25. *Alta California*, January 6, 1860; see also *Reese River Reveille*, February 23, 1866, included in Bancroft, "Scraps," vol. 12, no. 1, p. 33.

26. *Alta California*, August 9 and November 15, 1866; see also Bowles, *Across the Continent*, p. 332.

27. Henry George, "What the Railroad Will Bring Us," *Overland Monthly,* vol. I (October 1868), pp. 302-303, 305, 306.

28. Mel G. Scott, *The San Francisco Bay Area, a Metropolis in Perspective* (Berkeley, Calif., 1959), chap. 4.

29. San Francisco Chamber of Commerce, *Annual Report, (1869-70)*, p. 3. The recession began in 1867 and lasted until the middle of 1870. "Dry goods, clothing, etc. continue to be slaughtered at public auction. Stocks are heavy in the absence of any considerable demand." San Francisco *Commercial World*, September 10, 1867; see also San Francisco *Evening Bulletin*, May 8, 1969.

30. California Immigrant Union, "Letters," ms. (Cowan Collection,

UCLA). For officers and trustees of the Union, see C. T. Hopkins, "California Recollections," *CHS Quarterly*, vol. 27, pp. 168-170, and the San Francisco Commercial and Trade Association, "Papers," ms. (BL, UC).

31. Harris Newmark, *Sixty Years in California* (Los Angeles, 1970), p. 152. Los Angeles still preferred to bank in San Francisco, however, until well into the 1870s; p. 424.

32. Cross, *Financing an Empire*, p. 365.

33. San Francisco *Evening Bulletin*, August 6, 1870.

34. Bancroft, "Scraps," vol. 12, part I, p. 51.

35. F. W. Macondray to James Otis, July 28, 1869, in F. W. Macondray, "Papers," "Letter Copybook," p. 509.

36. Alfred F. Cohen, *Address on the Railroad Evil and Its Remedy . . .*, (pamphlet, San Francisco, 1879), pp. 14-15, 22. The Central Pacific Railroad also charged "much higher rates . . . for short than long distances, for small than for large quantities, and especially that discrimination was made between competitive and non-competitive points." Bancroft, *History of California*, VII, p. 628. See also pamphlet, San Francisco Chamber of Commerce, *Chamber of Commerce of San Francisco to Prepare Bills for Legislative Action on Subject of Fares and Freights* (San Francisco, 1874).

37. San Francisco Chamber of Commerce, *Annual Report* (1873-1874).

38. See the San Francisco Board of Trade, *Report of the Special Committee on Inter-Oceanic Travel* (San Francisco, 1880), p. 29; and the *Supplementary Report* (San Francisco, 1880), p. 14. Four of the five committee members were merchants, including Levi Strauss.

39. Allan Pred, *The Spatial Dynamics of U.S. Urban-Industrial Growth, 1800-1914* (Cambridge, Mass., 1966), pp. 51-52; and Stuart Daggett, *Chapters on the History of the Southern Pacific* (New York, 1922), pp. 281, 283; see also Julius Grodinsky, *Transcontinental Railway Strategy, 1869-1893* (Philadelphia, 1962).

40. Robert Elgie, "The Development of San Francisco Manufacturing, 1848-1880," M.A. thesis (Berkeley, Calif., 1966), pp. 9, 24, 54 n. 6, 124. By 1860 there were 36 cities that had more money invested in manufacturing than San Francisco and at least 50 cities that employed more men in manufacturing; Pred, *The Spatial Dynamics of Urban-Industrial Growth*, p. 73.

41. Allan Pred, "Manufacturing, 1800-1840," *Annals of the Association of American Geographers*, vol. 56 (1966), p. 337.

42. The interest rate in San Francisco reflected the shortage of capital in the city. The average annual interest rate for the pre-Civil War era was 24 percent. See Elgie, "The Development of San Francisco Manufacturing," p. 11 and Robert Trusk, "Sources of Capital of Early California Manufacturers, 1850-1880," Ph.D. diss. (University of Illinois, 1960), p. 29; see also Bancroft, "Scraps," vol. 48, section entitled "California Manufacturing Industries."

43. San Francisco *Evening Bulletin*, November 22, 1864; see also Cross, *Financing an Empire*, pp. 239-240, 255-256.

44. Bancroft, *History of California*, VII, p. 73; *Alta California,* July 6,

1866. Quote by A. S. Hallidie in "Manufacturing in San Francisco," *Overland Monthly*, XI (1888), p. 639.

45. H. Robinson, "Our Manufacturing Era," *Overland Monthly*, II (1869), p. 281.

46. Alfred L. Tubbs, "Dictation," ms. (BL, UC), p. 10.

47. John S. Hittell, *The Commerce and Industry of the Pacific Coast* (San Francisco, 1882), p. 117; for the Chinese in San Francisco, see Gunther Barth, *Bitter Strength*, (Cambridge, Mass., 1964).

48. Elgie, "The Development of San Francisco Manufacturing," pp. 28-34, 41, 44, and Hittell, *Commerce and Industry*, p. 100; see also A. S. Hallidie, "Manufacturing in San Francisco." Only the carriage and wagon industry appears to have been adversely affected by eastern (Michigan) competition. The railroad, says Elgie, actually forced San Francisco manufacturers to improve their efficiency.

49. By 1867 California had become a creditor rather than a debtor to the East; see *Merchants Magazine and Commercial Review*, vol. LVI (February 1867), p. 139; for capital formation of San Francisco manufacturers, see chap. 7 below.

50. Within the meat-packing industry itself, San Francisco ranked eighth behind Chicago, New York, Jersey City, Cincinnati, Indianapolis, Saint Louis and Brooklyn. A large portion of San Francisco's manufacturing grew out of the phenomenal boom of the state's agricultural production. California in 1880 ranked seventh in wheat production, second in wool (over 10 percent of the nation's wool came from California), and first in the production of barley. See Bancroft, *History of California*, VII, pp. 74-101; Hittell, *Commerce and Industry,* and City of San Francisco, "Assessor's Report," in *Annual Report* (1880-1881), pp. 3-14.

51. Tenth Census of the United States, *Statistics of Manufactures* (Washington, D.C., 1883), pp. 92, 435-437. In 1860 San Francisco ranked fourteenth in total population but failed to rank in the top 50 cities in manufacturing output ("value added"). By 1880 San Francisco ranked ninth in total population as well as in percent employed in manufacturing and manufacturing output. The urban ranking of San Francisco is identical when calculated on the basis of percent of the total occupational work force employed in manufacturing (35.3 percent). Employed in trade and transportation for 1880 were 28.8 percent of the total city work force.

52. Glenn Porter and Harold Livesay, *Merchants and Manufacturers,* (Baltimore, 1971), pp. 3, 10-11, 132, 196.

53. On this point see Allan Pred's discussion of the "initial multiplier effect" in his study, *The Spatial Dynamics of Urban Growth,* pp. 25-26, 179.

54. The Tenth U.S. Census (1880) for San Francisco lists 175 (2 percent) clerks and bookkeepers employed in manufacturing establishments, 798 (10 percent) who worked in professional and personal services, and 6,778 (88 percent) employed as clerks, salesmen, and accountants in stores.

7. A New Merchant Generation

1. Mark Twain, *Roughing It*, ed. by Henry Nash Smith (New York, 1959), part II, p. 132.

2. Approximately 20 percent of the first merchant generation had persisted in the city through 1880; about half of them remained in a merchant occupation.

3. One historian estimates that there were 16,000 Jews in San Francisco by 1880 or 7 percent of the city's population. See Robert E. Levison, "Jews in the California Gold Rush," Ph.D. diss. (University of Oregon, Eugene, 1968) p. 241. Another study found that 69 percent of San Francisco's largest Jewish congregation, Sherith Israel, were retail or wholesale merchants. See Jeffrey D. Saltzman, "Between Two Worlds: Jewish Merchants in a Changing City," Seminar Paper for Prof. Barth, Univ. of Calif., 1971, pp. 1-2, 14. See also B. E. Lloyd, *Lights and Shades in San Francisco* (San Francisco, 1876), p. 401, and Isaac M. Wise, "Rabbi Wise Sees San Francisco in 1877," *Pacific Historian*, II (1967), p. 13.

4. "The retail trade," reported the San Francisco *Bulletin* (September 22, 1871), "is chiefly in the hands of citizens of Irish birth." Edward Hutchinson, *Immigrants and Their Children* (New York, 1956), observed: "It was above all others the Germans who were the traders and dealers in 1880 and 1870. The commodities in which they were most prominent were, for males, clothing and men's furnishings, liquors and wines, gold and silverware and jewelry, cigars and tobacco . . . The Irish males had their greatest concentration among traders and dealers in junk, liquors and wines." (p. 109). The San Francisco experience of the Germans and Irish confirms Hutchinson's observation.

5. See Andrew Rolle, *Immigrants Upraised* (Norman, Okla., 1968), pp. 27-28; "Not many educated persons or merchants were among these Italian immigrants," p. 36. Probably the most famous first generation Italian immigrant to San Francisco was "A. P." Giannini, president of the local Bank of Italy, the forerunner of the largest bank in the world—the Bank of America.

6. The index may be derived by dividing the nativity distributions within a single occupational group by the total percentage of the foreign-born and native-born in the total labor force.

7. San Francisco *Bulletin*, September 22, 1871.

8. The recruitment pattern of the second merchant generation failed, however, to reflect accurately the *Bulletin's* observation that "the clerk and salesman of today is the merchant of tomorrow." A clerical and sales background appeared to be a more important training ground for the city's manufacturers, bankers, brokers, and corporate managers, than for the city's merchants. A member of the managerial class, for example, was two times more likely than a merchant to have worked in a clerical job. One-third of the managers in the sample drawn from the general employed population of the city in 1880 held as their first San Francisco job a clerical post, compared with only 14

percent of the merchants. Also the importance of clerical training seems to have declined among the merchant class. Of the first merchant generation, approximately 20 percent held a clerical or sales position immediately before their first merchant job in San Francisco.

9. The time spans between occupational "glimpses" in each sample are unequal and therefore the samples are not totally comparable. However, if in the 1880 sample there is less upward occupational mobility over a ten year span (1870-1880) than for the 1852 sample, where occupational mobility was measured between 1846 and 1852, then it seems reasonable to assume that the pace of occupational mobility for merchants had declined in San Francisco between 1852 and 1880.

10. The decline in occupational mobility for the second generation merchants reflected the general decline for all second generation males in San Francisco. Of the first generation of city residents, approximately half held jobs at the same occupational level in 1852 as they had prior to their geographical transfer to San Francisco (N = 55). Among the second generation, approximately three-quarters remained at the same occupational level between 1870 and 1880. (N = 197).

11. On the individual credit reports collected by RGD, the credit agency reported known business failure(s) and the cause(s). The credit rating for the individual suffered accordingly. From the 1880 sample, of those who were located in RGD, 21 percent had a history of business failure in the 1870s compared with 7 percent from the 1852 sample located in the credit agency reports for the 1860s.

12. See the San Francisco Commercial and Trade Association, "Folder," ms. (BL, UC); also the Dunbar "Brochure" in the same collection.

13. Merchants Protective Association, San Francisco Board of Trade, *Constitution and By-Laws* (San Francisco, 1877), and the M.P.A.'s *Annual Report* for 1878 and 1879.

14. Of the 252 business failures listed by RGD in a section entitled "Out of Business, 1869-71," 47 percent were merchants, 9 percent manufacturers, and the remainder mostly blue-collar skilled craftsmen (especially furniture and cabinet makers). Of the merchant failures, only 8 percent were importer-wholesalers, with the remainder equally divided between the general merchants (particularly hardware and dry goods) and the petty shopkeepers (clothing). The items traded by these out-of-business merchants were precisely the items produced and distributed in the 1870s by the city's new manufacturers. The out-of-business listing had a disproportionate number of Jewish or German surnames (particularly among the clothing and hardware store owners, who together composed almost 60 percent of the listed merchant failures). RGD Collection, ms. "California," vol. I.

15. Glenn Porter and Harold Livesay, *Merchants and Manufacturing* (Baltimore, 1971), p. 74. For a similar discussion of the connection between eastern merchants and the origins of manufacturing see George R. Taylor, "American Economic Growth Before 1840, An Exploratory Essay," *Journal*

of Economic History, vol. XXIV, no. 4 (December 1964), p. 436; the leading role played by the Boston merchants in the industrialization of their city is discussed in Frederic Jaher's essay "The Boston Brahmins in the Age of Industrial Capitalism," in *Industrialization in Nineteenth Century America,* Frederic Jaher, ed. (New York, 1960), pp. 188-262.

16. See V. D. Harrington, *The New York Merchant on the Eve of the Revolution* (New York, 1935), p. 145. Allen Pred in *The Spatial Dynamics of U. S. Urban-Industrial Growth, 1800-1914* (Cambridge, Mass., 1966), pp. 154-155, questions the predominant role of the eastern merchants in the development of industrial enterprises.

17. Caspar T. Hopkins's speech before the San Francisco Chamber of Commerce, reported in the *Alta California,* November 14, 1867.

18. San Francisco Board of Supervisors, *Valedictory of the Honorable Thos. H. Selby and Inaugural Address of Hon. Wm. Alvord* (San Francisco, 1871), pp. 7, 32.

19. San Francisco Chamber of Commerce, *Annual Reports,* 1867-1880. For the colonization proposal, see *Annual Report* of 1872.

20. Mean capital assets of merchants in 1870: petty shopkeepers, $4,900; general merchants, $25,200; importer-wholesalers, $56,200. From RGD sample (N = 144). For a discussion of how property figures were calculated, see appendix A.

21. "Moral character" as well as capital assets continued in the 1870s to be a prime consideration for RGD, and no doubt the city's lending institutions as well, in granting high credit rating. Anthony Trollope in a visit to San Francisco in 1875 observed: "If a young man [in San Francisco] can make friends and can establish a character of honesty to his friends and for smartness to the outside world, he can borrow almost any amount of money without security, for the purpose of establishing himself in business. The lender . . . is willing to run the risk of unsuccessful speculation." Anthony Trollope, "A Letter . . . Describing a Visit to California in 1875" (Colt Press, 1946), pp. 9-11.

22. Stephen Franklin, "Statement," in William Ralston, "Materials," ms. (BL, UC)

23. Wise, "Rabbi Wise Sees San Francisco: 1877."

24. Ira Cross, *Financing an Empire,* 4 vols. (San Francisco, 1927), I, 370-371. John S. Hittell, *The Resources of California* (San Francisco, 1879), p. 167.

25. The individuals were selected from the "Tax Assessment Appendix" in the San Francisco *Municipal Report* of 1880. Fifty from the sample of 84 were located in the *Municipal Report* of 1874, the first year the tax assessment appendix appeared, and by comparing assets (including stocks) in 1874 with those in 1880, profit and loss figures were generated. For this elite group, who were not representative of the general population, the average gain for the six-year period was approximately $32,000 or 93 percent. Profits for individuals who listed common stocks among their assets were 140 percent while profits for nonstockholders for the six-year period were approximately 29 percent.

There was a positive relationship between stock ownership and assets. For people owning total assets between $20,000 and $50,000, stocks composed approximately 15 percent of their total worth; the comparable figure for those with assets in excess of $50,000 was approximately 40 percent.

26. Oscar Lewis, *San Francisco's Mission to Metropolis* (Berkeley, Calif., 1966), p. 150. Robert L. Stevenson, *Works* (New York, 1906), II, 194; Rodman Paul, *Mining Frontiers of the Far West: 1848-1880* (New York, 1963), p. 57. Paul estimated that Virginia City and Gold Hill mines produced an estimated $300,000,000 in treasure between 1860 and 1880, and that much of this wealth filtered back to San Francisco.

27. Joseph L. King, *The History of the San Francisco Stock and Exchange Board* (San Francisco, 1910), p. 5.

28. Saltzman, "Between Two Worlds: Jewish Merchants in a Changing City," p. 14; Lewis Publishing Company, *The Bay of San Francisco*, 2 vols. (Chicago, 1892), I, 681.

29. See Albert Dibblee, "Papers," ms. (BL, UC); Henry Newhall, "Portfolio" and "Statements," ms. (BL, UC); Denis J. Oliver, "Biographical Sketch," ms. (BL, UC); and John H. Wise, "Interview," ms. (BL, UC).

30. Thomas Dibblee to his brother, Albert, February 13, 1873, and Albert to Thomas Dibblee, March 3, 1873, in Albert Dibblee "Papers," ms. (Private collection of Arthur Mejia, Jr., San Francisco, California). Albert Dibblee left an estate of approximately $500,000, 80 percent of which was invested in real estate. The estate of Isaac Friedlander, a commission merchant, also showed large investments in real estate in four separate counties. See the Friedlander Estate "Papers," ms. (CHS).

31. See Hittell, *Commerce and Industry,* pp. 49-50, 53; see also Earl Pomeroy, *The Pacific Slope*, (New York, 1965), p. 187.

32. Robert J. Trusk, "Sources of Capital of Early California Manufacturers 1850-1880," Ph.D. diss. (Univ. of Illinois, Urbana, 1960), pp. 28, 40, 166-168, 173, 176. Capital for expansion was more often than not derived from internal profits rather than outside sources.

33. B. E. Lloyd, *Lights and Shades*, p. 76. For Ralston's net worth, see the RGD Collection, "California," vol. 3, p. 339. Quote from Stephen Franklin "Statement," in William Ralston, "Materials," ms. (UC, BL).

34. See Andrew J. Ralston's "Statement" in the Ralston "Materials." Ralston formed the Bank of California in 1865 when his former banking partners (Donohoe, Ralston and Co.) believed that more of the firm's money should be invested in New York. For this and other biographical information on Ralston see Julian Dana, *The Man Who Built San Francisco* (New York, 1937).

35. Thomas Bell, "Statement," in Ralston, "Materials."

36. Eulogy printed in Ralston's biography included in Alonzo Phelps's *California's Representative Men* (San Francisco, 1882), p. 150.

37. Sample of 245 individuals from the U.S. Census of 1880 ("Schedule of Manufacturers" for San Francisco). Included within the blue-collar group

were those (10 percent) whose occupational background suggested blue-collar experience: cigar manufacturers who formerly operated cigar stands, merchant tailors, and former boot and shoe merchants. The percent of former blue-collar workers in manufacturing managerial and ownership posts would no doubt be higher if firms with assets below $50,000 had been included in the sample. Trusk in his study of 26 manufacturing firms ("Sources of Capital") found that half were organized by skilled craftsmen and eleven were started by merchants. Of the merchants, "nine made their profits dealing in the product they manufactured," p. 168.

38. The major industries in San Francisco, with the exception of mining equipment, were all connected to the traditional mercantile economy of the city or specialized in consumer goods—flour milling, sugar refining, tanning and leather processing, tobacco milling, shipbuilding, printing, cooperage, bag manufacturing, clothing, and liquor.

39. Domingo Ghirardelli, "Statement," ms. (BL, UC). David W. Ryder, *Men of Rope: History of the Tubbs Cordage Company* (San Francisco, 1954), p. 24. Most of the capital for the Tubbs Company appears to have come not from his ship chandlery business but from profitable real estate speculations; see also *Alta California,* July 15, 1866. A rather large number of retail clothing merchants in San Francisco, most of whom were German, had in their business partnership a relative who usually resided in New York and acted as buyer or manufacturer of the clothing goods. Levi Strauss and Co. and Weil and Woodleaf and Co. are but two of many examples which might be cited. See RGD, "California," vol. 1, pp. 190, 374.

40. See The Holbrook, Merrill and Stetson Co., "Papers," ms. (CHS).

41. See G. M. Josselyn and Co., *Catalogue* (San Francisco, 1880).

42. F. H. Hackett, ed., *The Industries of San Francisco* (San Francisco, 1884), pp. 55-56.

43. San Francisco *Commercial Herald and Market Review*, March 3, 1871; San Francisco *Call,* April 24, 1884.

44. E. R. Howe to his mother in Boston, dated July 9, 1871, in E. R. Howe, "Letters," ms. (BL, UC).

45. Based on the occupational tracings of 160 sons in the 1880 merchant sample (N = 958). The sons' slippage rate into the blue-collar ranks was directly related to fathers' occupational level. Sons slipping to blue collar: petty shopkeeper, 36 percent; general merchant, 21 percent; importer-wholesaler, 13 percent. Slippage of all 1880 sons, 25 percent; all 1850 sons, 10 percent. In both generations the sons of native-born merchants were less likely to slip to a blue-collar occupation than sons of foreign-born merchants. The San Francisco intergenerational mobility rate approximated eastern cities. Sons of white-collar workers in Poughkeepsie (c. 1880) and Boston (c. 1890) retained their fathers' white-collar affiliation at a rate of 70 percent (N = 149) and 80 percent (N = 97) respectively. The comparable San Francisco rate for 1880 was 75 percent (N = 160). Poughkeepsie and Boston figures included in Stephan Thernstrom's *The Other Bostonians* (Cambridge, Mass., 1973).

46. See San Francisco *Daily Examiner,* May 6, 1888, article entitled: "Coming Merchants: The Young Men Who Will Take the Places of the Old Ones."

47. RGD, "California," vol. 5, p. 450.

48. Of the first merchant generation (N = 643), the petty merchants persisted (1852-1860) at a rate of 37 percent; general merchants, 49 percent; and importer-wholesalers, 54 percent. Comparable rates (1880-1890) for the second generation (N = 958) were: petty shopkeepers, 28 percent; general merchants, 38 percent; and importer-wholesalers, 32 percent.

49. Community persistence rates in all occupations for employed males, 1880-1890: Boston, 64 percent; Waltham, 58 percent; Omaha, 44 percent; Los Angeles, 54 percent; San Francisco, 34 percent. Community persistence rates for "high white collar": Boston, 80 percent; Omaha, 59 percent; and San Francisco, 38 percent. For "low white collar" comparable rates were: Boston, 71 percent; Omaha, 48 percent; and San Francisco, 28 percent. For San Francisco, "high white collar" was calculated by combining importer-wholesalers and general merchants (N = 549); "low white collar" was based on persistence rate of petty shopkeepers (N = 409). For Boston and Omaha figures see Thernstrom, *The Other Bostonians,* p. 230.

50. In the 1880 decade the San Francisco growth rate for the first time fell below that of the state as a whole. Even in the 1870s Los Angeles' rate of growth had surpassed that of San Francisco. By the 1890s the southern California metropolis was growing at twice the rate of its northern competitor.

8. A Social Geography of the Urban Landscape

1. Robert E. Park, "The Urban Community as a Spatial Pattern of a Moral Order," in *The Urban Community*, ed. by E. W. Burgess (Chicago, 1926), p. 3. Park also noted: "It is because social relations are so frequently and so inevitably correlated with spatial relations; because physical distances so frequently are, or seem to be, the index of social distances, that statistics have any significance at all." (p. 18). For a thorough review of the historiography of urban geography, see Peter Goheen, *Victorian Toronto, 1850 to 1900: Pattern and Process of Growth* (Chicago, University of Chicago Department of Geography Research Paper No. 127, 1970), chaps. 1-2.

2. David Ward, "The Industrial Revolution and the Emergence of Boston's Central Business District," *Economic Geography*, vol. 42, no. 2 (April, 1966), pp. 152-171. For New York, see Allan Pred, *The Spatial Dynamics of Industrial Growth* (Cambridge, Mass., 1966), pp. 196-197.

3. Residential patterns and business locations for 1852 and 1860 were calculated from three separate samples: merchant sample (N = 641) and general sample (N = 652) taken from the 1852 San Francisco *City Directory,* and the 1851 *Monied Men of San Francisco* list (N = 127). All individual residence and business locations were then coded into a grid system of 87 districts, each district of approximately the same size (six city blocks). Residential and

business location patterns and distances between place of residence and place of business were then calculated from the respective locations in the grid system. The same process was followed for the 1870 and 1880 data utilizing a merchant random sample (N = 958) and a general random sample (N = 714) from the 1880 United States Census, and an elite random sample (N = 288) from the *Elite Directory* of 1879. Because the city directories of the early 1850s in San Francisco not only excluded over half the city's population but in addition often failed to note an individual's residence address, only 25 percent of merchant residences and 16 percent of the residences of the general population could be verified. However as the city directories extended their coverage over time, the percent of verifiable business and residential addresses increased.

4. Martyn J. Bowden, "The Dynamics of City Growth: An Historical Geography of the San Francisco Central Business District, 1850-1931," Ph.D. diss. (University of California, Berkeley, 1967), pp. 90-93.

5. Roger Lotchin, *San Francisco: From Hamlet to City, 1846-1856* (New York, 1973) chap. 1; see also H. Bancroft, *History of California,* 7 vols. (San Francisco, 1884-1890), VI, pp. 173-187.

6. Lotchin, *San Francisco,* chap. 1; see also Bowden, "The Dynamics of City Growth," pp. 125, 127, 129; James E. Vance, Jr., *Geography and Urban Evolution in the San Francisco Bay Region* (Berkeley, Calif., 1964), p. 18.

7. A few boarding houses apparently attracted former residents of a particular eastern city or catered to a specific ethnic group.

8. Mary S. D. Smith, "Letters," ms. (typed copy, c. 1854, CHS). Apparently, Edwin Smith never lived up to his promise to Mary and she returned to Massachusetts in July 1854—four months after she arrived in San Francisco.

9. The monied elite sample (N = 90) and those merchants for whom I could ascertain information on both property and residence (N = 25) were combined (N = 115). Goheen similarly located the commercial elite in the center of Toronto at a time (1860) when the process of suburbanization was already underway. *Victorian Toronto,* p. 126.

10. San Francisco *Daily Herald*, September 10, 1853.

11. Mary Prag, "Early Days," ms. (typed copy, Magnus Library, Berkeley, Calif., n.d.), p. 12.

12. Albert Shumate, *A Visit to Rincon Hill and South Park* (San Francisco, 1963), p. 3. The city prided itself on the residential community. The 1856 San Francisco *City Directory* (Colville and Co.) reported that the seventeen houses constructed in 1854 cost the builder $110,000. "The general situation of South Park is one of great beauty and salubrity. Omnibus lines run to it every ten minutes. The provisions give almost perfect security against fire. The remainder of the unimproved lots [51] are still in the hands of the original projector. When the design is carried out, the *tout ensemble* will be highly imposing and worthy of the oldest city in the Union." (p. 205.)

13. One early observer of San Francisco noted that "on Rincon Hill con-

gregated the New England people, families of sea captains and shipping merchants. A flavor of Nantucket and Martha's Vineyard." In the western residential section, "were many of the Southern families." Mary Prag, "Early Days," p. 2. Anson Blake, "San Francisco Boyhood," *CHS Quarterly* (1949), vol. 28, p. 215. When former residence was controlled, however, I discerned no distinct residential patterns or clusters.

14. For a description of various methods by which to calculate segregation indexes see Karl and Alma Taluber, *Negroes in the Cities* (New Haven, 1969), pp. 28-31, 195-245. See also Stanley Lieberson, *Ethnic Patterns in American Cities* (New York, 1963), chap. 2.

15. The difference in the segregation indexes between the native-born merchants and the foreign-born merchants was smaller than either the differences between the native-born merchants and the native-born general population or their foreign-born counterparts.

16. The early development of San Francisco's social space was similar to what Peter Goheen found in Toronto. It was significant, Goheen noted, that the "divisions of the social fabric [in 1860 Toronto] corresponded with those elements described by twentieth-century social science as characterizing the modern [industrial] city." Goheen, *Victorian Toronto*, p. 154.

17. Blue-collar workers in 1860 commuted an average distance of 540 yards (N = 295) while the comparable figure for all merchants was 980 (N = 200). Blue-collar figures computed from data in Robert Elgie, "The Development of Manufacturing in San Francisco, 1848-1880," MA thesis (Univ. of Calif., Berkeley, 1966).

18. Gertrude H. Atherton, *Adventures of a Novelist* (New York, 1932), pp. 24-25.

19. *Alta California*, February 4, 1851.

20. The percentage rates of wives in San Francisco were derived from the 1852 California State Census. The census did not specifically ask the marital status of an individual. However, it could be surmised that a female listed immediately after a male with the same last name was in most cases the wife. Caution was taken to exclude those male-female pairs where it appeared that it was in fact a sibling family rather than a marriage arrangement where children confirmed the relationship. Still some female siblings were no doubt counted as wives. This error may have been compensated for by those couples who separated after arriving in San Francisco between 1849-1852. Divorces were "readily obtainable" in California and were "growing very numerous" in San Francisco. See Frank Soule, John Gihon, and James Nisbet *Annals of San Francisco* (San Francisco, 1855), p. 504. The absolute percentages alone are less significant than the differences between the native-born and the foreign-born where the margin error would presumably be the same. It might be argued that the foreign-born brought their spouses to San Francisco at rates approximately the same as the native-born, but once in the city, were more likely to marry. However, given the fact that nine out of every ten foreign-born residents married foreign-born women and that the foreign-born

male to female ratio in San Francisco in 1852 was eight to one (compared to approximately five to one among the native-born adults), the explanation seems unlikely.

21. San Francisco, *City Directory* (San Francisco, Langley and Co., 1860). Cornelius Cole, *Memoirs* (New York, 1908), p. 82; female and male ratios calculated from U.S. Census Bureau, *Compendium of 1880 U.S. Census* (Washington, D. C., 1881). Female persistence rates are not known, so that in demographic terms we do not know the rates of female in- and out-migration through San Francisco. In San Francisco there was a large number of employed females, many of whom worked as prostitutes. There is some limited contemporary evidence to suggest that women too floated from city to city seeking employment just as men did. An interesting question is: what were the occupational opportunities for women in San Francisco considering the large population of prostitutes (which I estimate to be close to 2,000) in the city in 1870? Female demographic studies might give some important clues as to the degree of occupational opportunity available for women in nineteenth-century America.

22. An Irish male, regardless of occupation, was somewhat more likely to marry a female of the same ethnicity than a German male; for Jewish inter-marriage rates see Barry Supple, "A Business Elite: German-Jewish Financiers in 19th Century New York," *Business History Review* (1957), vol. 31, pp. 152-154, 163-174; and Mark Gerstle, *Lewis and Hannah Gerstle* (New York, 1953), pp. 116-126.

23. 1. New York: 1,206,299; 2. Philadelphia: 847,170; 3. Brooklyn: 566,663; 4. Chicago: 503,185; 5. Boston: 362,839; 6. St. Louis: 350,518; 7. Baltimore: 332,313; 8. Cincinnati: 255,139; 9. San Francisco: 233,959; 10. New Orleans: 216,090; 11. Cleveland: 160,145; 12. Pittsburgh: 156,389.

24. The average size of the household unit in San Francisco rose from 5.8 in 1870 to 6.9 in 1880. The average family size also increased from 4.9 in 1870 to 5.4 in 1880. Rankings in 1880 were: 1. St. Joseph, Mo., 5.76; 2. St. Paul, Minn., 5.74; 3. Omaha, Neb., 5.44; 4. Trenton, N. J., 5.42; 5. *San Francisco*, 5.38; 6. St. Louis, Mo., 5.38; 7. New York City, 4.96; from the U.S. Census, *Compendium of U.S. Census 1880.*

The foreign-born households and family units in San Francisco tended to be somewhat larger than those of the native-born for both the merchants and general population.

25. Quoted by Bion Arnold in *Report on the Improvement and Develop-ment of the Transportation Facilities of San Francisco* (San Francisco, 1913), pp. 411-417.

26. Goheen, *Victorian Toronto*, p. 11; Albert Shumate, *A Visit to Rincon Hill;* see also Edgar Kahn, *Cable Car Days* (San Francisco, 1936) and Samuel Bowles, *Across the Continent* (Springfield, Mass., 1865), p. 291. Appar-ently only the elite mourned the leveling of Rincon Hill. Most city resi-dents believed that the new fill area along the edge of the bay, designed to serve as the terminus of the railroad and the new area of expansion for

manufacturing industries, would usher in "a new golden era in San Francisco's economic development." See "The New City: A Dream of the Future," San Francisco *Newsletter and Commercial Advertiser,* August 7, 1869. The spread of industry into a residential section and the conversion of once fashionable residences into tenements was similar to what occurred in Boston during its industrial growth in the 1860s and 1870s. See Ward, "The Emergence of Boston's Central Business District," pp. 152-171.

27. David Ward, "The Emergence of Central Immigrant Ghettoes in American Cities, 1840-1920," *Annals of the Association of American Geographers,* vol. 58, no. 2 (June, 1960), p. 346.

28. Sample of 245 manufacturing establishments with listed assets of over $50,000 drawn from *Tenth U.S. Census* (1880), "Schedule of Manufacturers (San Francisco)." The percent of total blue-collar residences in these three districts is 73; petty shopkeepers, 57 percent; general merchants, 49 percent; importer-wholesaler, 29 percent; and elite 31 percent.

29. Amelia Neville, *Fantastic City* (Boston, 1932), pp. 180-86, 191; see also section entitled "San Francisco Society," in the *Elite Directory of San Francisco* (San Francisco, 1879), p. 233; "Belgravia of San Francisco" in the San Francisco *City Directory* (San Francisco, 1875), p. 12; also Neville, *Fantastic City,* pp. 178, 180; Julia Altrocchi, *Spectacular San Franciscans* (New York, 1949); and Gertrude Artherton, *My San Francisco: A Wayward Biography* (New York, 1946).

30. *Elite Directory of San Francisco* (1879), p. 234. The aristocratic European model evident in so many of the elite homes is illustrated in a superb photographic collection, accompanied by an informative text written by Roger Olmsted, and assembled by the San Francisco Junior League entitled, *Here Today: San Francisco's Architectural Heritage* (San Francisco, 1968); see also Carol G. Wilson, *Gump's Treasure Trade* (New York, 1965), p. 32; and James J. Ayero, *Gold and Sunshine* (Boston, 1922), p. 251.

31. Letter from the North Pacific Railroad to Albert Dibblee dated May 13, 1873, in Dibblee," Private Correspondence," ms. (collection of Arthur Mejia, Jr., San Francisco).

32. Quoted in Harrison Dibblee's "Biography of Albert Dibblee," ms. (CHS).

33. Harriet L. Levy, *920 O'Farrell Street* (Garden City, 1947), p. 16.

34. It was not possible to determine what percentage of business profits were used by Bancroft for personal or household expenses since business profits were hidden in his bookkeeping scheme. It would be interesting to know, for example, if the percentage of business profits utilized for personal and household expenses by Bancroft and others rose or declined as business profits increased. See Albert L. Bancroft, "Cash Account Books" in Bancroft Papers," ms. (CHS).

35. It was not uncommon in other cities that remnants of the wealthy class continued to reside in or near the central business district after most of their affluent colleagues had moved out. See H. W. Zorbaugh, *The Gold Coast and the Slum* (Chicago, University of Chicago Press, 1929), pp. 1-16; H. Hoyt,

The Structure and Growth of Residential Neighborhoods in American Cities (Washington, D.C., Government Printing Office, 1939); and David Ward, "The Emergence of Central Ghettoes in American Cities." Quote from Guillermo Prieto, *San Francisco in the Seventies,* ed. and tr. by Edwin Morby (San Francisco, 1938), p. 22.

36. ". . . every man's door-yard in the city is like an eastern conservatory . . . There is no aristocracy of flowers here, they greet you everywhere in greatest profusion." Samuel Bowles, *Across the Continent,* p. 291; see also Oscar Lewis, *This Was San Francisco* (New York, 1962), pp. 176-177.

37. Levy, *920 O'Farrell Street,* pp. 143-144.

38. Ibid,. p. 148.

39. Ibid., p. 196. As might be expected the merchants were more likely to have live-in servants than the general population of the city (18 percent vs. 7 percent). The affluent importer-wholesalers were five times more likely to have a live-in servant than the petty shopkeepers. The Irish were approximately one-third of the total servant class.

Ethnicity	Percent of Servant Class	Percent of Total San Francisco Population
Native-Born	21	55
Irish	34	13
German	14	9
Chinese	13	9
English-Scottish	4	4
French	4	2
Other	10	8
Totals	100	100
(N)	(287)	

Data from U.S. Tenth Census, San Francisco, 1880. The census listed 9,666 domestic servants (56 percent female) in the city in 1880 or 9 percent of the total employed population.

40. Distances were calculated only for the residents of the inner city (wards 1 through 10). Had the measurement scheme included people residing in wards 11 and 12 and outside the city limits, the differences between the blue-collar and white-collar classes (in the general merchant and elite sample) would no doubt have been far greater since the vast majority of white-collar workers commuted to the downtown central business distinct while the blue-collar workers (particularly in ward 11) commuted no farther than to the nearby factories. Robert Elgie in his "The Development of Manufacturing in San Francisco . . . 1848-1880" calculated the average commuting distance for the blue-collar worker (N = 2214 cases) to be 690 yards. (I have, for comparative purposes, converted his mileage calculations into yards.)

41. Commuting distances for merchants with assets under $25,000: 990

yards (N = 31); over \$25,000: 1,200 yards (N = 24). The business district had expanded in a southerly direction but had not changed its basic location. See also Bowden, "The Dynamics of City Growth," chap. 5.

42. Elgie, "The Development of Manufacturing in San Francisco." For a discussion of a similar relationship in Boston between commutation cost and commuting distance, see Sam B. Warner's *Streetcar Suburbs* (Cambridge, 1962).

43. In 1880 the average commuting distance for single employed males (N = 103) in San Francisco was 740 yards; married males, 880 yards. Comparable figures for the merchants (N = 203): single 730, married, 830.

44. Number of children and household size in San Francisco, 1880:

	Number of Children	(N)	Household Size	(N)
Native-Born				
Merchants	2.8	(105)	6.4	(224)
General				
Population	2.5	(70)	6.5	(298)
Foreign-Born				
Merchants	3.4	(430)	6.0	(724)
General				
Population	3.2	(190)	6.5	(426)

Data from U.S. Tenth Census, San Francisco, 1880.
Average commuting distance in yards in 1880 for merchants (N = 226): native-born, 1,070; foreign-born, 700. Within the general population (N = 104) the native-born commuted 970 yards and the foreign-born 750 yards.

45. See Lieberson, *Ethnic Patterns in American Cities,* p. 81. Both Lieberson and Oscar Handlin, in his *Boston Immigrants,* rev. ed. (Cambridge, Mass., 1959), discovered, however, that foreign-born populations became more integrated the longer they resided in a city.

46. See table 8.3. The indexes of segregation for each merchant occupational category is derived by subtracting the residential distribution of each merchant category from the general population mean distribution in each city district and dividing by two. Hence the segregation index for the merchants and elite vis-a-vis the general population (mean) is: petty shopkeepers, 10; general merchants, 15; importer-wholesalers, 36; and the elite, 33.

47. In both the merchant and general population samples there were wider disparities in the respective residential distributions when viewed from the perspective of occupation (table 8.3) than from the perspective of birth place (table 8.5). At all three merchant occupational levels, the difference in the residential distributions between the native-born and foreign-born merchants was smaller than either of the differences between the native-born merchants and the native-born general population or their foreign-born counterparts.

48. The *San Francisco Elite Directory of 1879,* p. 234.

49. Each of the 87 city districts was assigned an altitude (mean) derived from the U.S. Coast and Geodetic Survey of San Francisco Peninsula, 1869 [corrected to 1888.] See map collection, Bancroft Library, University of California. Altitude by class (in feet): blue collar, 74; general population, 83; property owners under $9,999, 89; petty shopkeepers, 95; property owners over $10,000, 126; elite, 126; wholesalers-importers, 136.

50. *A Social Manual for San Francisco and Oakland* (San Francisco, 1884), pp. 9, 17.

51. Julia C. Altrocchi, *The Spectacular San Franciscans,* p. 101; and Harold Kirker, *California's Architectural Frontier* (San Marino, 1960), p. 93.

9. A View toward the Nob

1. Kevin Starr, *Americans and the California Dream* (New York, 1973), p. 67.

2. E. Digby Baltzell, *The Protestant Establishment: Aristocracy and Caste in America* (New York, 1964), p. 7.

3. Argonaut Publishing Co., *Elite Directory for San Francisco and Oakland* (San Francisco, 1879), pp. 164, 193.

4. There is no elite list available for the early 1850s exactly similar to the 1879 *Elite Directory.* However the list of *Monied Men of San Francisco* published in 1851 does, I think, serve as a generally valid substitute.

5. Samuel Williams, *The City of the Golden Gate: A Description of San Francisco in 1875* (San Francisco, 1921), p. 33.

6. Ambrose Bierce, "The Ideal Bohemian, by One Who Does not Love Him," *The Wasp,* June 16, 1883.

7. See Edward R. Howe, "Letters and Papers," ms. (BL, UC).

8. Quotes from A. E. D. De Rupert, *Californians and Mormons* (New York, 1881), pp. 21-22, and B. E. Lloyd, *Lights and Shades in San Francisco* (San Francisco, 1876), p. 470.

9. Calculations for "length of residence" and for all subsequent elite tabulations are based on a 25 percent systematic sample of adult males from the *Elite Directory* list, both Christian and Jew. The variables of ethnicity and property for the elite, unfortunately, were not available for this study.

10. Rodman Paul, *Mining Frontiers of the Far West, 1848-1880* (New York, 1963).

11. Williams, The City of the Golden Gate, p. 33.

12. Theodore H. Hittell, *The Resources of California,* 7th ed. (San Francisco, 1879), pp. 21-22.

13. For examples of these "mug" books in San Francisco, see William H. Murray, *The Builders of a Great City: San Francisco's Representative Men, the City, Its History and Commerce* (San Francisco, 1891). Alonzo Phelps, *Contemporary Biography of California's Representative Men,* 2 vols. (San Francisco, 1881-1882). Martin A. Meyer, *Western Jewry: An Account of the*

Achievements of the Jews and Judaism in California (San Francisco, 1916). Oscar T. Shuck, *Sketches of Leading and Representative Men of San Francisco* (San Francisco, London, 1875). Lewis Publishing Co., *The Bay of San Francisco,* 2 vols. (Chicago, 1892); Lewis F. Byington, *The History of San Francisco,* 3 vols. (Chicago and San Francisco, 1931); Bailey Millard, *History of San Francisco,* 3 vols. (Chicago and San Francisco, 1924); S. J. Clarke Publishing Co., *San Francisco: Its Builders Past and Present,* 2 vols. (Chicago, San Francisco, 1913).

14. B. E. Lloyd in *Lights and Shades,* pp. 407-408, describing the modus operandi of Oscar T. Shuck, author of *Sketches of Leading and Representative Men of San Francisco.*

15. The ages of individual elite members could not be determined, and therefore age could not be controlled in the calculations.

16. For the use of prestige scores see discussion in chapter 3 based on Donald Treiman's "A Standard Occupational Prestige Scale for Use with Historical Data," *Journal of Interdisciplinary History* (Summer 1976).

17. The same pattern emerged when controlling for time—that is, looking at the 1870 decade for all three samples.

18. The lists are included with the *Elite Directory,* pp. 27-89; club membership lists are also included in the *Directory,* the city's first published elite listing. For a more inclusive list see *San Francisco Blue Book* (San Francisco, 1879).

19. Gertrude Atherton, *My San Francisco: A Wayward Biography* (New York, 1946), pp. 151-152.

20. Calculations for first generation of merchants based on occupational origins of the combined general merchants and importer-wholesalers (N = 108). See chapter 3 for further discussion of occupational mobility for the first merchant generation.

21. Williams, *The City of the Golden Gate,* pp. 28-29.

22. The all-male, WASP "P-U" Club, as it is affectionately referred to by members and nonmembers alike, allowed the author one very brief visit into its hallowed halls, after considerable correspondence. On that occasion, I was permitted (but with close supervision) to transcribe membership and trustees lists. I am indebted to Mr. Scott Martin of San Francisco for his assistance and persistence—which gained me access to these lists. See the Pacific-Union Club "Scrapbook" (ms.) which resides under the watchful but most friendly care of the club's librarian.

23. Of the nine First Unitarian Church trustees, only one listed himself as a merchant. Officer and trustee lists from Horace Davis, *50 Years of the First Unitarian Church* (San Francisco, 1891); Carol Green Wilson, *Calvary Through the Years* (San Francisco, 1930), pp. 102-104; and San Francisco Chamber of Commerce, "Papers," ms. (CHS).

24. Two-thirds of the Jews listed in the 1880 *Elite Directory* were employed in a merchant occupation compared to one-third of all elite members (including Jews). Officer lists from Jacob Voosanger, *The Chronicle of Emanu-El*

(San Francisco, 1900), and Pacific Orphan Asylum and Home Society, *Eighth Annual Report* (San Francisco, 1879).

25. Though I have made no systematic measurement of the number of leadership positions held by the 1850 elite compared with their 1880 counterpart, impressionist evidence from reading hundreds of "mug book" biographies suggests a higher division of labor among the 1880 elite group. A partial explanation may also be that as the San Francisco economy came to be more integrated into the national economy, an increasing number of local businessmen turned their attention from local to national concerns. This hypothesis is suggested by Sam B. Warner in *The Private City* (New York, 1964). In San Francisco, while the business leaders of 1880 may have directed more attention to the national marketplace than the merchants of the 1850s, I discovered no evidence to suggest that the 1880 business elite were any less involved in the city's civic affairs. They continued in the 1870s, as they had in the 1850s, to control the voluntary associations, and to a lesser degree the political machinery of San Francisco.

26. These rituals generally conformed to eastern upper-class standards in spite of the fact that "belonging to the best society in San Francisco cut no ice in New York." Gertrude Atherton, *Adventures of a Novelist* (New York, 1932), p. 142.

27. See San Francisco *Argonaut,* April 22, 1877 and February 9, 1878.

28. John S. Hittell, *Sources of California* (San Francisco, 1879), p. 21; *Elite Directory* (1879), p. 165.

29. *Elite Directory* (1879), pp. 163-165; for additional behavioral standards see pp. 223-255.

30. San Francisco Board of Supervisors, *Valedictory of the Honorable Wm. Alvord and Inaugural Address of the Honorable James Otis* (San Francisco, 1873). Ironically, but not surprisingly given his elite credentials and whom he represented, Otis in the same speech called for a large increase in the size of the city's police force.

31. San Francisco *Chronicle,* July 25 and 27, 1877.

32. San Francisco *Evening Bulletin*, July 25, 1877.

33. Gertrude Atherton, *California: An Intimate History* (New York, 1914), p. 292.

34. Hubert H. Bancroft, *Brief Account of the Safety Committee of 1877* (San Francisco, n.d.), p. 368. Bancroft noted that the committee made a thorough survey of the city's gunshops, and where they discovered large supplies, the committee posted a 24-hour guard "so as to secure of the arms and munitions from the access of the mob."

35. In 1877-78, San Francisco suffered a major economic depression. Farm production lagged due to a drought with the result that grain dealers shipped only one-half of the amount they exported in 1876. In 1877 the stock bonanza broke, business failed, banks closed, and factory production sagged. It was estimated that about 15 percent of the city's labor force was unemployed in 1878. For a further discussion of business conditions at this time, see chapter

6; see also Hubert Bancroft, *History of California,* 7 vols. (San Francisco, 1884-1890), VII, pp. 351-354.

36. See William Coleman, "Statement," ms. (BL, UC) on the 1877 Committee of Safety.

37. Martin J. Burke, "Dictation," ms. (BL, UC), p. 12; William Camp, *San Francisco: Port of Gold* (Garden City, New York, 1947), p. 271.

38. Henry H. Ellis, "Correspondence and Papers," ms. (BL, UC), folder 23. Ellis served as the chief of police during 1876-77. See also Coleman's "Statement" and Ellis's *From the Kennebec to California* (Los Angeles, 1959).

39. See Hubert Bancroft's biographical sketch of Coleman in William T. Coleman, "Statement," folder 1 for the arrangements with regard to the expansion of the police force. The elite's more active role in local politics in the late 1870s can be appreciated by the fact that just before 1877 and the Kearney agitation, no members of the elite sat on the board of supervisors. However in 1878, after the formation of the Committee of Safety, five of the twelve elected supervisors, in additon to Mayor Andrew J. Bryant, were elite members. The elite controlled the judiciary both before and after the 1877-78 disturbances.

40. Atherton, *California: An Intimate History,* p. 294.

41. Henry George, "The Kearney Agitation in California," *Popular Science Monthly,* XVII (August, 1880), pp. 434-435; *Progress and Poverty* (Modern Library Edition, Random House, New York, n.d.), p. 146.

42. Isaac M. Wise, "Rabbi Wise Sees San Francisco: 1877," *Pacific Historian,* XI (1967), p. 12.

10. Conclusion

1. B. E. Lloyd, *Lights and Shades in San Francisco* (San Francisco, 1876), p. 204.

2. Alexis de Tocqueville, *Democracy in America,* Philip Bradley, ed. (New York, 1945) I, 201.

3. Henry George, *Overland Monthly,* vol. I (1968), p. 301; Henry David Thoreau, *The Journal of Henry D. Thoreau,* 14 vols. (Boston, 1949), III, 266.

4. San Francisco's penchant for violence cannot be explained by either its relative youth or phenomenal growth rate. Other cities have matched or surpassed San Francisco in growth (such as Chicago) and there are too many examples of cities experiencing growing pains without resorting to violence. For a discussion of violence as "an urban rather than a frontier [western or rural] problem," see W. Eugene Holton, *Frontier Justice* (New York, 1974), chap. X; see also Richard Wade, *Violence in the Cities* (New York, 1969); Hugh D. Graham and Tedd R. Gurr, *Violence in America* (New York, 1969); and Irving Sloan, *Our Violent Past* (New York, 1970).

5. Earl Pomeroy, "Towards a Reconsideration of Western History," *Mississippi Valley Historical Review,* XLI (March, 1955), pp. 597, 593; see

also Benjamin F. Wright, "Political Institutions and the Frontier," in Dixon Ryan Fox, ed., *Sources of Culture in the Middle West* (New York and London, 1934), pp. 17, 22, 24.

6. Quoted by Kevin Starr in *Americans and the California Dream* (New York, 1973), pp. 363-364.

7. Walter Fisher, *The Californians* (London, 1876), p. 72-73.

8. Crocker quoted in Oscar Lewis, *The Big Four* (New York, 1959), p. 53.

Appendix A

1. For an instructive general history of the Dun and Bradstreet Company, see Roy A. Foulke, *The Sinews of American Commerce* (New York, 1941), Quotes from p. 348.

2. Ibid., p. 349.

3. For a discussion of this point see Edward Pessen, "The Egalitarian Myth and the American Social Reality," *American Historical Review,* vol. 76 (October 1971), pp. 995-997.

4. Harriet Levy, *920 O'Farrell Street* (Garden City, N.Y., 1947), pp. 5-7.

5. Property data could not be collected from tax assessment lists in San Francisco since almost all of the lists were destroyed in the 1906 earthquake. The few that survived the earthquake have since been disposed of by city officials.

INDEX

A. D. Remington Co., 78
Adams and Company, 37, 128
Age, and mobility, 80
Agriculture, 30, 33, 54, 147, 163
Alaskan fur trade, 84
Alcatraz (Bird Island), 5
Alert California (ship), 58
Alger, Horatio, 251
All about California (Immigrant Union), 159
Allen, Lucius, 148
Alsatian Jews, 115
Alta California (newspaper), 78, 147; citizen appeals of, 125, 126, 142; immigration of women reported in, 210; Jewish immigrants in, 115-116, 117; on mining, 151, 153; oversupply reported in, 38, 41; on transcontinental railroad, 157; vigilance committees in, 120
Alvord, William, 235
American Party, 128
American River, 9, 30
Anglo-California Bank, 77
Anti-Know Nothing Party, 128
Arbitration Board, 48
Arizona, 38, 154
Armor Co., 188
Army, 111, 156, 247
Aspinwall, William H., 19
Associations, voluntary, *see* Voluntary associations
Atherton, Gertrude, 238-239, 257
Atlanta, Georgia, 194
Auctions, 43-44, 87
Australia, 13, 26, 118, 188, 200

Babcock, William, 112
Baldwin Hotel, 243
Baltimore, 28, 68; export trade from, 33; joint-stock companies in, 13; manufacturing in, 164, 179, 187; migration from, 9, 11, 13, 16, 24, 25, 109-111; San Francisco compared with, 142-143
Baltzell, E. Digby, 232
Bancroft, Albert L., 187, 221
Bancroft, Hubert, 59, 91, 106, 187, 234
Bankers: departure rates for, 103; occupational mobility of, 73, 190, 237; residential patterns of, 202, 204, 205; social position of, 107, 175; wealth of, 88
Bank of California, 182, 185
Bankruptcy cases, 91-92, 193; Chamber

of Commerce petition on, 49; 1850s period, 37, 126; 1870s period, 177-178; municipal, 125
Banks: coin shortages and, 46; credit ratings and, 35, 36, 47, 181; failures of, 37, 91, 126; manufacturing investment by, 179; migration and, 17-18; specialization in commodities and, 52
Baptists, 114, 136
Bars, 38, 62
Battery Street, 26
Bavaria, 12, 115
Beacon Hill, Boston, 257
Beck, David, 112
Beef production, 147
Beekman family, 8
Bella Union, 77
Benicia, Calif., 6, 135
Berkeley Square, London, 203
Bierce, Ambrose, 234
Black immigrants, 118, 258
Blue-collar workers: business failures and, 96; departure rate for, 193; manufacturing and, 168, 186; occupational mobility of, 66-67, 69, 71-72, 76, 79, 176, 186, 190, 192, 194, 239, 250; out-migration by, 79; residential patterns 1850s and, 37, 38, 41; residential pat- 65-66; social mobility of, 254-255; wages for, 166; *see also* Working class
Boarding houses, 35, 202, 203
Board of Aldermen, 113
Board of Supervisors, 248
Board of Transportation Commissioners, 162
Bohemian Club, 243
Bohemians, 234
Bonestell, Louis, 77-78
Bonestell and Co., 78
Boot trade, 3, 118, 120, 167
Boston, 30; business connections with, 68, 93; communication with, 50; credit from, 35; foreign-born population of, 171; joint-stock companies in, 13; manufacturing in, 164, 179, 187; merchant network in, 61; migration from, 9, 11, 16, 17, 18, 23, 24, 109; occupational mobility in, 71-72, 79, 86, 193; out-migration in, 74; oversupply in 1850s and, 37, 38, 41; residential patterns in, 256-257; spatial ordering in, 196; trade and, 3-4, 31, 33, 57, 154; vol-